Monetary Stability through International Cooperation

Monetary Stability through International Cooperation

Essays in Honour of André Szász

Presented on 12 July 1994 on the occasion of his retirement from the Governing Board of De Nederlandsche Bank

Preface by Willem F. Duisenberg

Springer-Science+Business Media, B.V.

A CIP Catalogue record for this book is available from the Library of Congress.

ISBN 978-94-017-2360-2 ISBN 978-94-017-2358-9 (eBook)
DOI 10.1007/978-94-017-2358-9

Printed on acid-free paper.

Edited by A.F.P. Bakker et. al.
Edition: 1000

Acknowledgements

When we first advanced the idea to honour André Szász, upon his retirement from the Nederlandsche Bank, with the publication of a volume of essays, we had no inkling that so many would react with such great enthusiasm. In their letters of acceptance, many cited the important and inspiring contributions which André made to international meetings over a large number of years, as well as the friendship that had grown up between them and him. We can safely say that their feelings are evidenced by the quality of their essays. It much facilitated our jobs as editors.

Our aim has been to bring out the wide range of policy issues in which André has been involved over the years. The authors were asked to choose from a number of subjects relating to either European monetary integration or the international monetary system. The contributions date from January 1994 and were written by people with whom André has worked closely: fellow monetary diplomats from other European banks whom he regularly met at international gatherings, representatives from the International Monetary Fund, the Bank for International Settlements and the EC, Dutch colleagues from the Ministry of Finance and the Nederlandsche Bank. To all of them, we owe a debt of gratitude. Special thanks are due to our monetary court photographer Wolfgang Rieke. Finally, we want to express our appreciation to Martine Hijstek-Weeling for a perfect typescript, as well as to Marianne Jonker, Rob Wattimena, Katarzyna Hulsen-Plewko and Mireille Otten for the technical processing of this book.

The Editors

Contents

André Szász: fortiter in re, suaviter in modo

For over thirty years, André Szász has worked at the Nederlandsche Bank, where he started his career at the Research Department in 1960. Before long he gained his first experience of international cooperation when he became Alternate Member of the Managing Board of the European Monetary Agreement, the successor to the European Payments Union. Soon after that he became more deeply involved in the subject, when in 1970 he participated in the Ansiaux Group dealing with monetary matters on behalf of the Werner Committee; the discussions there on narrower margins eventually led to the establishment of the so-called snake. Upon his appointment as Executive Director of the Bank in 1973, he became a full member of the Monetary Committee of the EC and Alternate of the Committee of Governors of the Central Banks of the EC as well as G10-Deputy and member of WP3 of the OECD. In the course of time he has attended numerous IMF meetings. Most of the contributors to this volume of essays honouring André Szász serve, or have served, on these committees. Over the years he has gradually come to shift his attention from international to European monetary issues, and it was no coincidence that when in 1990 he was appointed part-time professor at the University of Amsterdam it was of European Studies.

André Szász' activities are inspired by his systemic vision. This is in line with long-standing Dutch views such as that contained in the final report of the Dutch delegation to the Bretton Woods conference in 1944, which stated 'that the Netherlands' interest in the IMF and the World Bank lay not so much in the comparatively minor direct advantages which these institutions had to offer the Netherlands as in the improvement in economic conditions and the expansion of world trade which they were trying to bring about'. The international monetary system envisaged by André Szász is, above all, a system aiming for stability. Here we see the influence of Dr M.W. Holtrop, President of the Nederlandsche Bank in the early years of André Szász' career. In the Bank's Annual Report for 1954, Holtrop stated that the Netherlands should strive for a system offering the best possible guarantees that each participating country has an interest in maintaining monetary

With Jean-François Pons(r), Director, EC Commision, at the meeting of the Monetary Committee in Berlin, 23 October 1992.

equilibrium at home. Szász favours a system based on external discipline and obligations for all, stimulating adjustment. In the never-ending debate on rules versus discretion, he is firmly on the side of those who give priority to rules, as a framework for the discretion that is indispensable to their application. A system cannot be created or operated without the continuing and constructive cooperation of all concerned, be it in an international or a European context. His own rules of behaviour are consequently governed by the twin objectives contained in the title of this book: stability and cooperation.

In Szász' opinion, the ideal system is one where the disciplinary effect of exchange rate obligations is reinforced by stringent stipulations on settlement and rules about permissible exchange rate adjustments. In his view, exchange rate stability is not an objective per se, but a way of attaining internal stability. He does not want an exchange rate system whose participants slide down the inflationary path in concert; his aim is a system which disciplines an inflationary country into putting its house in order. Why is he so attached to such a disciplinary system? Because an open economy like the Netherlands can only hope to attain stability if the rest of the world is stable, too. Furthermore, he knows from experience that stabilization measures, which are seldom popular in the short run, are easier to put in place when reference can be made to a manifest external need.

Anyone attaching such great importance to a system of stable exchange rates is bound to consider the question of how to maintain fixed exchange rates. André Szász' view of foreign exchange markets is characteristic. He sees them not so much as an irredeemable source of instability, but as a force, and a powerful one at that, propelled – because money is at stake – by highly rational calculations of estimated costs and potential gains, as well as close scrutiny of the authorities' behaviour as a clue to their future policies. That is why he considers it imperative for the authorities to pursue a consistent and credible exchange rate policy and to be seen to be unswerving in their determination.

André Szász has invested much time and energy in promulgating this view, both in the Netherlands and abroad. In 1979 he was instrumental in strengthening the hard-currency stance of Dutch exchange rate policy and played an active role in the domestic debates so as to gain political and public support for this policy at a time when the benefits for Dutch interest rates still had to be earned. Time and time again he argued, chart in hand, that lower interest rates are conditional upon a strong, not a weak, guilder. He was closely involved in the Bank's day-

In conversation with Karl-Otto Pöhl, Vice-President of the Deutsche Bundesbank, at the signing of the EMS Agreement, Basle, 13 March 1979.

to-day decisions on short-term interest rates, a series of small steps that together constitute a policy conveying a clear message to the markets: the Nederlandsche Bank has strong feelings about the strong guilder. In Europe, too, he has always been an avid proponent of an exchange rate policy entailing a two-way risk, and of an interest rate policy which gives high, and visible, priority to maintaining exchange rate stability. The aim has been to deter foreign exchange speculation by making it costly, risky and unprofitable. It is certainly satisfying to him that these considerations were incorporated, together with other elements, in the rules of behaviour drawn up at Basle/Nyborg in 1987. It is his view that the turbulent developments within the ERM over the past two years do not detract from the validity of these guidelines; on the contrary, they show what happens when these guidelines are not fully adhered to.

The great importance which Szász attaches to internal stability obviously also brings him to focus on those domestic factors which affect that stability. Two particular topics figure prominently in his

In good company... At the meeting of the Alternates of the EC Committee of Governors in Paris, 29 May 1990.

quest for stability: public finance and central bank independence. He has never let himself be persuaded by those monetarists who feel that the size of a budget deficit is irrelevant so long as it is not monetized and the central bank keeps the money supply in hand. Far from it. Szász is of the opinion that overly expansive policies and loss of control with regard to public finance place the central bank in an impossible position, undermining as they do the efficacy of monetary policy, threatening internal and external equilibrium and frustrating international policy coordination. It is worth noting that the axioms contained in his doctoral thesis include one which reads: the authorities cannot coordinate what they cannot control. André Szász sees central bank independence as a major contribution to price stability: the performance of the Bundesbank and his own experience at the Nederlandsche Bank have convinced him of that. He has learnt that such independence needs to be earned and nurtured, earned by means of a credible and consistent policy, nurtured by time and again warding off any threat of encroachment.

Just as central banking is his profession, so political analysis is his hobby, two subjects which merge in European integration. In recent years he has drawn attention to the political incentive to integration in Western Europe which originates from developments in Central and Eastern Europe, and their implications. In the trade-off of widening and deepening, he is seeking to square off the circle in variable geometry: extending stability to the East and the North, while at the same time strengthening the core in the West. Without being a politician himself, he is acutely aware of the political dimension of European integration. It is for that very reason that he belongs to the 'economists', who believe that economic convergence must precede monetary integration. He respects the political objective, but demands proof of the political will to accept the implications for national budgetary policies in particular. Central bank independence is another sine qua non, not just because of its contribution to price stability, but also as a precondition for effective monetary policy coordination between central banks participating on an equal footing. Time and again he brings these issues to the fore, and is on the look-out for opportunities to bring them up in the European discussion. He has consistently argued the necessity of agreement on the final objective of EMU, not because he wants to delay the process, but because he firmly believes that progress is conditional upon consensus about the substance of the final stage. Deeply convinced of the need for further European integration in these turbulent and uncertain times, he has been working tirelessly and constructively towards a united Europe.

Systemic vision and a sense of purpose are compatible with a pragmatic approach and a regard for practicalities, so long as it is in the interests of the ultimate goal. André Szász has a love-hate relationship with technicalities. He shows little interest in technicalities as such, convinced as he is that policy should dictate the technical aspects and not the other way round. But no sooner does he discern policy issues behind the technical discussions, than his attention is aroused. He loves to decode technical discussions into their policy implications. If proposed technical arrangements imply a threat to stability, his aim is to uncover this and to be in the front line fighting it. He gives careful thought to the timing and choice of the tactics to be used in negotiations, trying to think several steps ahead. If he has a message to divulge, he asks for the floor early. But if he has a compromise in mind, he will bide his time until everyone is sufficiently worn out to welcome a way out of the deadlock. In drafting sessions, he prefers to say nothing at all, apart from indispensible amendments of substance, hoping, in vain, that it will all be over soon.

'...a preference for private conversations and informal dinners...'
With Paul de Grauwe(l) and Lucas Papademos(r) at a conference in Athens, 1 September 1989.

When it comes to a choice of procedures, it is evident that he is inventive, to say the least. He knows the rules and he knows how to apply them to full advantage. He is interested not so much in the procedures themselves, as in their practical outcome, and in the opportunities they offer for attaining the objectives envisaged.

André Szász takes great care about the way he presents his views, making an effort to see things from the standpoint of the others so as to be as persuasive as possible. He makes allowance for political sensitivities, as he did, for instance, in his plea for central bank independence, which initially took the form of an argument for embedding monetary policy in checks and balances, only to be given more explicit shape at a later stage. He is on the look-out for persuasive arguments. When he picks up contradictions, it is not to score some debating-point, but to use the opportunity to bring out those elements which will support his own line of thinking. And last but not least, mention should be made of his sense of humour. During meetings, he generally uses his wit to underline some point in his argumentation. But privately, he likes to make jokes and relate anecdotes just for the fun of it. His colleagues know him to be a kind and determined man with a preference for private conversations and informal dinners, rather than official banquets and the like.

These are the ways of André Szász. As a central banker of a relatively small country, he is aware that his power is limited, and that he has to rely on his considerable analytic and persuasive talents. As a monetary diplomat, to allude to the title of his doctoral thesis, he believes in cooperation and constructive dialogue, where possible within the framework of a system making for stability and responsible behaviour for all. As a policy-maker, he sees the formulation of policy as a succession of decisions and he is therefore acutely aware of the need for consistency and continuity. The response of his colleagues at home and abroad, when invited to contribute to this book in his honour, was overwhelming. I am proud to be able to take part in this tribute to the distinguished career of a colleague with firm opinions of his own, and at the same time a genuine respect for the views of others, particularly when they coincide. In international meetings André Szász has consistently argued the benefits of credibility and stability for monetary policy. In the same vein, he has been an 'anchor of stability' in the Governing Board of the Nederlandsche Bank, where he will be missed as a colleague and a friend.

Wim Duisenberg

1 European monetary integration

The relationship between economic, monetary and political integration

Hans Tietmeyer

1 European Union and its main elements

The coming into force of the Treaty on European Union on 1 November 1993 opened up a new dimension for European integration. The term European Union conflates the three goals of economic union, monetary union and a certain degree of political union. These are closely related, but disparate aims which require considerable further clarification. The Treaty itself certainly provides no definitive and sufficient answer in the long run to this question.

The content and form of *monetary union* may be regarded as clear-cut. In economic terms it will be deemed to have been achieved once the exchange rates of the member currencies have been irrevocably fixed on the basis of free capital movements. The institutional requirement is the transfer of monetary sovereignty from the Member States to the Community, and hence the fusion of the various national monetary policies to form a common monetary policy under the exclusive responsibility of a European System of Central Banks. The Treaty has largely established the constituent elements of the envisaged monetary union.

The structural elements of an *economic union* cannot be defined as precisely. The completion of a common market with free movement of labour, goods, services and capital is imperative. By contrast, the extent to which the economic and financial policies of the Member States must be coordinated and subjected to joint rules, or even made a matter of common responsibility, cannot be stated with certainty. On this point the Treaty on European Union follows a decentralised concept based on the principle of subsidiarity.

Political union is, a priori, a largely imprecise concept that requires further definition. Conceived in terms of democratic and federal structures, it will not suffice for some hitherto national powers to be centralised in Community bodies. As far as possible, responsibilities must be clearly delineated and apportioned between the national and the Community levels in keeping with the principle of subsidiarity. In addition, appropriate checks and balances must guarantee that the responsibilities which are devolved to the various decision-making levels are exercised in a democratic manner. Judged by these criteria for a political union, the Maastricht Treaty still displays substantial shortcomings. Although some existing Community powers are strengthened and expanded, and the common foreign and security policy, as well as the justice and home affairs fields, are included in the Treaty in a very general way, the clauses on political union – in contrast to the provisions concerning EMU – do not adequately and definitively indicate what structure the envisaged political union is to have.

In the run-up to the intergovernmental negotiations on the Treaty on European Union, the Deutsche Bundesbank pointed to the close, mutual links which exist between Economic and Monetary Union on the one hand, and political union on the other hand. In its statement of September 1990, the Central Bank Council of the Bundesbank, in line with its function of advising the federal government, made it clear that, with the irrevocable fixing of exchange rates, the Member States would be giving up more than the right to decide their own national monetary policy. The statement pointed out that Economic and Monetary Union would also mean that 'the participating economies will be inextricably linked to one another in the monetary field, come what may', and that the implications – especially for the value of money – will 'depend crucially on economic and fiscal policy and on the stance of management and labour in all Member States'. The Central Bank Council concluded: 'In the final analysis, a monetary union is thus an irrevocable joint and several community which, in the light of past experience, requires a more far-reaching association, in the form of a comprehensive political union, if it is to prove durable[1].'

The Central Bank Council restated its reflections after the Maastricht Treaty had been negotiated and concluded. Within a positive overall assessment, above all of the Treaty's regulatory and institutional stipulations, it added the criticism that 'the Maastricht decisions do not yet reveal an agreement on the future structure of the envisaged political union and on the required parallelism with monetary union. Future developments in the field of the political union will be of key importance for the permanent success of the monetary union'.[2] The intention

1 Deutsche Bundesbank (October 1990), Statement by the Deutsche Bundesbank on the establishment of an Economic and Monetary Union in Europe, Monthly Report of the Deutsche Bundesbank.

2 Deutsche Bundesbank (February 1992), The Maastricht decisions on the European Economic and Monetary Union, Monthly Report of the Deutsche Bundesbank.

of the Central Bank Council in making this comment was especially to highlight the key significance of the follow-up conference, scheduled in the Maastricht Treaty for 1996, on the further development of the Community on the road to the completion of the European Union.

2 Economic and Monetary Union in the context of the Werner Report

The relationship between monetary union and political union was identified as a key topic well before the most recent debate on integration. It already featured in the disputes between the economists and the monetarists, as the press termed them, which marked the Community's first serious efforts in the direction of EMU at the end of the sixties. Whereas the economists took the view that enduring monetary integration, oriented towards stability, would be possible and assured only if the participating countries achieved beforehand a sufficient degree of convergence in their anti-inflation policy and its results, the monetarists tended to argue that the monetary ties and exchange rate constraints established in an early phase of the integration process would enforce the aspired convergence in terms of anti-inflation policy, or would at least make a crucial contribution towards achieving such convergence.

These basic positions, which naturally also allow for many intermediate positions and gradations, characterised at that time in particular the discussions in the so-called Werner Committee.[3] Inherent in them, right from the start, was the question of political union, i.e. how the process of monetary integration was to be incorporated into the broader political development of Europe. On this point especially the economists, who at that time included in particular the Dutch and German representatives, not only attached particular importance to convergence in anti-inflation policy at the moment of entering the final phase of monetary union; they have also always emphasised the importance of safeguarding the degree of convergence achieved in the course of monetary integration, and have pointed to the institutional safeguards needed for that purpose. They also made it clear that this objective not only requires permanent freedom of capital movements and a common monetary policy geared to stability, but that the achieve-

3 This group, chaired by the then Luxembourg prime minister, Pierre Werner, was commissioned at the end of 1969 by the Heads of State and Government of the states belonging at that time to the EC to write a report on the progressive implementation of Economic and Monetary Union. The author of this contribution was intensively involved, as a deputy German member, in the work of the group up to the final version of the Werner Report in October 1970.

ment and maintenance of stability also presuppose, as an absolute imperative, corresponding conduct in other economically relevant policy fields, and that monetary union geared to lasting stability thus needs to be embedded in a political union.

The basic position of the economists was clearly brought out in the Werner Report in a series of reflections. This manifested itself most distinctly in the reference to the need for a supranational body for economic policy and in the statement that the monetary union thus appeared as 'leaven' for the development of political union, 'which in the long run it will be unable to do without'.[4] Actually, these formulations, too, indicate a compromise between the two basic positions which, in the final analysis, are very difficult to reconcile. The compromise approach of the Werner Report is also evident in the originally disputed question of the sequence of the integration steps. In an attempt to bridge the conceptual opposites, the Report called for a parallel approach in the monetary, economic policy and general political spheres.

However, shortly after the Report had been presented it became apparent during the political consultations in the Council of Ministers that there was likewise no agreement between the governments of the, at that time, six Member States on the far-reaching economic and more general political links. The French government, in particular, at that time rejected agreements on supranational institutions and more far-reaching Community structures. They therefore opted initially to enter the first stage of the integration process only, and in doing so largely adopted the monetarist stance. The results of this first attempt to achieve Economic and Monetary Union at the beginning of the seventies are well-known. The lack of success of this first venture should not, however, be attributed solely to the economic divergences between the Member States and the deficiency of political agreement on how to proceed further. Another important factor was the extremely difficult world economic environment. Both the final collapse of the Bretton Woods system and the unparalleled oil price explosion led to diverse reactions in the Member States.

4 Werner Committee (1970), Report to the Council and the Commission on the realization by stages of Economic and Monetary Union in the Community ('Werner Report'), special supplement to Bulletin 11-1970 of the European Communities.

3 Revival of the EMU idea

The new thrust towards monetary integration undertaken in 1978 in the form of the European Monetary System likewise initially took the monetarist view as its principal starting point. It was, however, less ambitious than the Werner Report. With the creation of a parity grid, the system was, moreover, basically geared to the best performer in the anti-inflation stakes, and was hence given a credible economic orientation. However, by 1983 the new system had led to results similar to those of the currency snake in the early seventies. The stability of the system was ensured, above all, by the fact that the differences in fundamentals, which at first were very marked, were neutralised periodically through adjustments of the central rates.

France's adoption of a policy of the 'hard' franc in 1983 then initiated a process in which the hard-currency option became increasingly attractive and hence gained more and more support. From the German point of view this development was welcomed since it laid the foundations for the gradual emergence of a hard core of integration which, to an increasing extent, also allowed the economic conditions to arise for a credible development of a monetary union. The sustained advances made towards stability led to less frequent adjustments of central rates, and the system began to stabilise.

Towards the end of the eighties and at the start of the nineties this policy was regrettably overstretched. An important factor in this was the diminishing willingness to make the required central rate adjustments in good time. Despite the increasing liberalisation of money and capital transactions, however, it was possible to largely cover the existing and newly arising divergences by means of interest rate policy decisions.

During the revived discussions on Economic and Monetary Union and on the later Maastricht Treaty, the impression was moreover created that the central rates were not to be changed any more. The importance for the integration process of even such massive external shocks as German reunification was underestimated. Attempts were increasingly made instead to maintain nominal exchange rates which no longer accorded with the changed underlying conditions. The prolonged global economic upswing and the growth rates which accompanied it, for a time enabled a policy mix which made it appear risk-free to refrain from making exchange rate changes that were actually necessary.

The negotiations on the Maastricht Treaty, therefore, took place in an atmosphere characterised rather by optimism and faith in the feasibility of even monetarist approaches. Economic imperatives might have made a more marked impression on the Treaty if the most recent experiences of the EMS could have been reflected in it. As it was, the onset of the latest round of crises and tensions in the EMS did not occur until autumn 1992, i.e. after the Treaty had been signed.

4 Lack of an adequate political framework – a threat to EMU

What lessons can be drawn from the discussions and experiences described above in implementing the Maastricht Treaty? Irrespective of the circumstances in which it was drafted, the Maastricht Treaty cannot be described as a text which is unilaterally committed to monetarist ideas. On the contrary, it follows the positions of the so-called economists in important instances. This is especially apparent in the provision of the Treaty which lays down that the Union's economic system shall be that of an open market economy with free competition (Article 3a).

A clear economistic orientation is likewise displayed by the convergence criteria. Even if the economic rationale of certain criteria is debatable, overall they are nevertheless indisputably aimed at achieving convergence in terms of anti-inflation policy. The convergence criteria open up the possibility of keeping the convergence process free of tensions by requiring countries that are not yet ready for entry to improve their convergence by the time the decision on entry into the third stage is taken, and hence meet the conditions for membership of EMU.

The provision that neither the Community nor the Member States shall be liable for the public debts of an individual member state likewise corresponds to economic precepts. It ensures that no member can abuse the monetary union as an easy option for relieving its debt burden. The same tendency is evident in the Community surveillance of the budgetary policy of the individual states which, while in the second stage having a consultative character only, will, starting in the third stage, carry the power to impose certain sanctions and thus offer stronger protection against potentially dangerous misguided developments within the Union.

These provisions undoubtedly have an important protective function in respect of the enforceability of the uniform monetary policy required in EMU. Admittedly, this consideration does not answer the question of whether this economic protective measure is sufficient. After all, economic and fiscal policy remain fundamentally the province of the Member States. This raises the question, in particular, of whether the Treaty in its present form provides sufficient safeguards in the long run against imbalances between the centralised monetary policy and the decentralised decision-making powers in other policy areas. There is good reason to doubt this, at least as long as the process of clarifying the envisaged overall political structure has not been concluded. Without such clarification, the process of monetary integration faces dangers which could call into question the viability of EMU itself.

5 Dangers of disparate national policies

This perspective shows the great importance of the follow-up conference in 1996, as already envisaged in the Treaty, to decide on the further development of the Community towards completion of the European Union. The conference will have to ensure, in particular, that the monetary union will remain viable even if, despite the achievement of a high degree of anti-inflation convergence at the time of entering the third stage, centrifugal forces and divergences should manifest themselves at a later date.

One significant source of danger is differences among the individual European Union countries in terms of wage and income policies in the event of divergent productivity trends. Varied reactions to external shocks or radical changes in competitive conditions could likewise impair the viability of the monetary union, especially if such shocks affect parts of the Union only. For example, a process such as that of German unification would certainly have posed a challenge to the Union if it had already come into existence by then. The Union must, however, be able to master such challenges itself, since the forging of the monetary union is fundamentally conceived as an irreversible process.

Economic tensions may arise in the Union not only because of differences in economic and fiscal policy or sudden external shocks; in other fields, such as foreign and defence policy, too, scenarios are conceivable which would confront the monetary union with serious problems. Not only might the individual Member States be subjected to different fiscal burdens. Tensions could also easily arise on account of disparate national foreign policy stances in the conclusion of international monetary agreements and the determination of joint positions vis-à-vis the international monetary institutions.

Since it will no longer be possible to relieve tensions at the domestic level through exchange rate modifications, once the Member States have embarked on the third stage, contradictory national decisions in economically relevant policy areas will carry dangers for the monetary union. Such a situation could easily lead to pressure on the bearers of monetary responsibilities at Union level to adopt an accommodating monetary policy stance, aimed primarily at easing tensions, at the expense of monetary stability.

Of course, economic differences and frictions also exist in states which have an economic potential similar to that which the Union will one day have. One need only consider, for example, the United States and Canada. However, those two countries have a federal constitution which makes a political solution to such conflicts possible with the aid of wide-ranging federal powers and a series of overriding systems. Such allocations of powers and systems are not envisaged for the European Union at present. There are no relatively large central public budgets or Community-wide social security systems which, as in the two countries mentioned above, indirectly help to iron out regional disparities. What is more, a single foreign and security policy is self-evident for those two countries.

6 Lessons from history and the opportunity of 1996

It is true that, in certain circumstances, a monetary union can survive even without a federal environment, as is demonstrated by the Belgian-Luxembourg currency union, which has existed for many years. However, whether this is a model which could be transposed to Europe is a question open to doubt. For one thing, there is de facto a high measure of political linkage between the two states, which does not exist in this form between the other European countries. For another, Luxembourg has hitherto evidently been prepared to accept the implications of the stimuli imparted by Belgium as the economically and politically dominant partner. Whether this special relationship is transferable to that of the other Member States is highly dubious; in fact, it is scarcely conceivable that such a relationship between the member countries of a European monetary union could exist in the long term. It is most unlikely that lasting stability could be created in Europe in this way.

All the historic parallels likewise indicate that currency unions – above all between states of roughly equal size – can only survive in the long run if the participating countries not only have a sufficient level of convergence in economic and anti-inflation policy in the initial phase, but also possess the determination and strength to forge a more far-reaching and enduring political union. Whether the European Union, as defined so far in the Maastricht Treaty, which – apart from its unequivocally supranational structure for monetary policy – is basically aimed at securing interstate cooperation in the sense of a confederation, and not a federal state, will be able to achieve an enduring and sufficient measure of political solidarity among the participating countries appears to me to be at least doubtful in view of past experiences and the different traditions in Europe. The permanent renunciation of monetary sovereignty, the sole key area placed under Community sovereignty, could easily lead to a conflict in the envisaged monetary union with the insistence on sovereignty in other areas of importance for economic and financial questions, even if state action in this area is subjected to stringent coordination provisions.

Naturally, it is virtually impossible to abstractly define in advance the precise degree of permanent political linkage needed to ensure the success of the monetary union. Yet it is equally impossible to simply transpose the existing national structures and experiences to the monetary union's common level, even though some lessons can be derived from past experience of federal structures. In my opinion there is good reason to believe that, to ensure lasting success, a monetary union requires – over and above the joint central banking system – a more far-reaching political association than that defined in the Maastricht Treaty.

This does not mean that a centralised solution should be sought at Community level. On the contrary, the requisite political solidarity, on the one hand, and the necessary subsidiarity, on the other hand, can no doubt best be ensured in the longer term at Union level by way of a federal concept with a clear allocation of powers and responsibilities. By contrast, the mixed responsibilities, as have evolved in the EC over the past decades to the chagrin of many committed observers, run counter to such a concept.

It is quite apparent that, in some member countries, there are misgivings about any further expansion of the political component of the integration process. These are clearly motivated mainly by the fear that the national identity of the countries concerned could be jeopardised by a far-reaching union. The valid kernel of such reservations certainly needs to be taken into consideration in the process of expanding the Union's political component. On the other hand, the use of such arguments to block the path towards further development of political union could not only call into question the process of further integration but could also, in the final analysis and in view of the hazards outlined above, pose a threat to that which has been achieved so far.

It would be overstepping the bounds of a central banker's brief to map out suitable basic concepts of development towards political union. That is a task for the political bodies, the governments and parliaments. But the outcome of the intergovernmental conference scheduled for 1996 will no doubt be of great importance for the implementation of the monetary union and for ensuring its durability.

7 Concluding personal remarks

During the past decades, André Szász has not only contributed his great expertise and perceptive insights to the discussions on monetary integration in Europe; he has also been an efficient and skilful actor on the monetary stage itself. It is regrettable that he will shortly no longer be able to perform this role of active involvement, as he will step down from his current post at the Nederlandsche Bank in mid-1994.

Although this decision, coming after a very full career of public service in both the Netherlands and Europe as a whole, deserves our respect, I personally regret it, since it means that an important advocate of common positions will be leaving the monetary stage. I hope very much that, in the realm of academia, André Szász will pass on our common philosophy of stable money to future generations and will continue to participate in public discussions. For me his relinquishment of public office is coupled with the expectation, that, as a teacher, André Szász will expound his insights in the future in an even more forthright and challenging manner than he was able to do so in the past decades on account of the rigorous discipline associated with his function. His contributions to the public debate on matters of common interest will no doubt continue to be met with great interest. For that, as well as for his manifold personal interests, I wish him many more years of productive activity. Not only the Bundesbank, but also future generations will be grateful to this convinced European and advocate of stability.

Pros and cons of a two-speed monetary integration

Jean-Jacques Rey

1 Introduction

The concept of a two-speed Europe is a controversial and highly sensitive subject. Not unexpectedly, those who are inclined to favour such a concept usually see their country as one which should lead the way in the process of European integration and is eligible for progress along the faster speed. Others dislike the concept, arguing that it is inconsistent with the principles of equality and solidarity within the Community, that it tends to harm the political, economic or monetary credibility of the weaker countries and, therefore, that it further complicates their catching-up efforts.

An objective analysis can go a long way in removing the emotional content of the debate. An attempt in that direction is made hereafter. Section one goes back to the origins of the concept of a two-speed Europe. Section two is an overview of past experiences with various models or formulae of differentiation in the process of European monetary cooperation and integration. The third section explores the scope for differentiation in the pursuit of EMU aims such as defined in the Maastricht Treaty. The final section assesses the merits and drawbacks of moves and strategies based on differentiation.

2 Origins and significance of the concept of a two-speed integration

Although the fatherhood of the term 'two-speed Europe' is usually attributed to Willy Brandt, the official discussion on the acceptability of such a strategy has been triggered by the Tindemans Report on European Union, which was addressed to the European Council in December 1975. In this report, it was argued that, given the existing economic and monetary divergences, a simultaneous and significant progress of all Member States on the road towards further integration

The author wishes to express his deep gratitude to Dirk Michielsen, who graduated in Economics at the Institut d'Etudes Européennes of the University of Brussels, for the assistance received in preparing this essay.

appeared virtually impossible. In the absence of political and technical consensus on a common economic and monetary strategy, all possible avenues for moving out of the deadlock were to be considered. In this spirit, the following principles and approach were suggested to the European Council:

- those member countries which were able to make progress, on the basis of an action programme with respect to a particular area, should do so;
- those member countries which had valid reasons for abstaining, would be entitled to do so; they would receive the necessary assistance in order to be able to join the first group as soon as possible, and would take part, within the Community institutions, in the assessment of performances in the relevant area;
- the snake mechanism would be the starting point of this new strategy, provided economic and monetary policy coordination was strengthened and the snake was clearly made part of the Community undertaking.

Although the outlined approach involved the basic characteristics of a so-called two-speed approach, the report carefully avoided to use that wording explicitly. Moreover, the report stressed that the proposal had nothing to do with a Europe 'à la carte' as each member country was supposed to endorse and pursue the same goals. Only their implementation would take place at a different speed. It was also emphasised that the transitory acceptance of a more advanced degree of integration among some member countries was not an innovation in the Community: Article 233 of the Treaty of Rome had allowed for similar experiences in the case of the Benelux and the BLEU (Belgian-Luxembourg Economic Union).

The debate which was triggered by the Tindemans Report is typical of most of the subsequent discussions on the concept of a two-speed Europe. These express a high degree of political sensitivity and the arguments which are used are often somewhat overdone:

- at a time when the cohesion within the Community was completely lacking, Mr Tindemans had to defend himself against the view that he intended to divide Europe in a manner which would be devastating for the Community;
- the report was criticised on the grounds that Community law would only apply to those Member States which were unable to make progress; those invited to move forward were to do so on the basis of special arrangements, by analogy with Article 233 of the Treaty;
- on the other hand, the proposed mechanisms and measures were deemed insufficient in relation to the ambitious character of the new

approach; especially the proposed strengthening of the snake was deemed to be too technical and insufficient for revitalising economic and monetary cooperation.

Although this debate took place almost 20 years ago, it still carries useful lessons for those who care about promoting European integration, and yet appreciate the constraints which some countries face in the process:

- while the concept of a 'two-speed integration' may linger at the back of the minds, it seems both preferable and more accurate to refer to the more general proposition of differentiated moves towards integration; according to this broader definition, the factor 'time' continues to play a central role, but time differentiation is not restricted to a two-speed path, it also involves multi-speed scenarios;
- only those strategies which are consistent with the Treaty provisions and Community law should be taken into consideration; conversely, introducing some scope for differentiation has become a legitimate part of any breakthrough in the course of legislating for further European integration;
- irrespective of their characteristics and merits, monetary integration strategies cannot be considered in isolation because they must be supported by economic convergence and political determination.

It is precisely in the monetary field that a rich cocktail of differentiation formulae can be found. Broadly speaking, three different models can be identified:

- the precursor model, intended as such (Benelux) or not (BLEU); some countries set for themselves objectives which are accepted by others at a later stage; the enlargement of the Community is a case in point, as well as monetary association with third countries;
- the flexible model, whereby all accept a hierarchy of common objectives, but the move along this hierarchy remains basically – though perhaps not formally – within the decision of the countries themselves; this is the case, for instance, for the liberalisation of capital movements, or for the selection of margins within the snake and the EMS;
- the multi-speed model, which implies that a core group of countries is joined at a later stage by other countries, subject to a collective decision.

Some practical experiences with the first two models are reviewed in the next section. Section three reviews the scope for differentiation in the Maastricht Treaty, which, with regard to the EMU process, is very much in line with the third model.

3 Practical experiences of differentiated moves

3.1 *BLEU and Benelux*

3.1.1 BLEU

In 1921, long before the coming into existence of the EC, Belgium and Luxembourg decided to cooperate closely in the economic and monetary field by establishing the BLEU. The union aimed at linking both economies together, through a customs union and a monetary association.

Initially defined in rather loose terms, this monetary association has grown over time into an advanced form of monetary cooperation involving some aspects of a monetary union. The Belgian franc became legal tender in Luxembourg, but the latter country was to limit the volume of issue of its own currency. The responsibility for monetary policy, in particular external monetary policy, was entrusted to the National Bank of Belgium and a common exchange control system was managed by the Belgium-Luxembourg Exchange Institute.

This association is however not a fully fledged monetary union. The parity between both currencies is not irrevocably fixed; it was effectively modified in the 1930s and called into question at the occasion of the 1982 devaluation. The Luxembourg authorities operate their own banking supervision. More importantly, the cooperative arrangements in fiscal and economic policy are limited and fall short of any definition of an economic union.

The BLEU was obviously too small to serve as a model or locomotive for European monetary cooperation. Nevertheless, some useful lessons may be drawn from the experience. Although the rare tensions have been overcome and have sometimes led to a strengthening of cooperation, the coexistence of a quasi-monetary union, a loose form of economic linkage and a weak institutional structure created a fragile situation. In the case of the BLEU, the recognition of mutual interest and the absence of attractive alternative options have acted as the binding force in difficult times.

The BLEU has also helped both countries in preparing themselves for their insertion in the European Community and the European Union. Luxembourg had to abandon almost completely its monetary sovereignty, especially through the pooling of the major part of its official reserves. Belgium could not deviate from a policy stance of free capital movements and a strong currency, which has since evolved as a basic condition for taking part in the core group of European monetary co-operation.

3.1.2 Benelux

The Benelux Agreement, which reached its present form three years after the signature of the Treaty of Rome, was motivated by three basic goals: to consolidate the results already achieved, especially through the customs union of 1948 and the capital liberalisation agreement of 1954; to stimulate the progress towards the achievement of the Treaty objectives by acting as a precursor in some essential domains; to strengthen the position of the Benelux countries in the European decision-making process.

The Benelux countries thus aimed initially at becoming a positive pressure group in the European context. In the monetary field, the Benelux countries committed themselves to a common exchange rate policy vis-à-vis third countries and to the fixing and adjustment of their exchange rates by mutual agreement.

In practice, however, a specific common monetary policy at the Benelux level was neither feasible nor necessary. First, economic and monetary divergences between the Netherlands and Belgium were at times significant. Second, as the Benelux ambitions did not go beyond the EC objectives, they did not require specific institutional arrangements.

A major exception came about in the midst of the currency turmoil set off by the suspension of the gold convertibility of the US dollar. On 21 August 1971 the Benelux countries concluded an arrangement whereby the bilateral fluctuation margins were restricted to 1.5 per cent. Until the coming into existence of the snake in April 1972, this Benelux arrangement was the only adjustable peg mechanism in Europe and it played undoubtedly a crucial bridging role in European monetary co-operation at that difficult moment.

However, the smooth functioning of the Benelux 'worm', as it came to be known, was undermined by the different impact of the oil shocks on the economic situation and policy options of the Benelux countries. This divergence created tensions in the arrangement which led to the decision in 1976 to abandon the arrangement and to incorporate the Benelux countries into the snake without any special regime.

3.2 *Capital liberalisation*

The Treaty of Rome prescribed a removal of restrictions to capital movements to the extent necessary for the smooth functioning of the common market (Article 67). It allowed for a differentiated process of capital liberalisation. On the one hand, it provided for the possibility of an acceleration of the liberalisation process in line with the improvement of the economic situation (Article 71.2). On the other hand, the process could be slowed down e.g. by invoking the derogation clauses in case of disruptive capital movements (Article 73) or of severe balance-of-payments problems (Article 108 and 109). Several member countries have had recourse to these clauses at the end of the sixties and during the seventies as a consequence of unstable international economic and monetary relations and inappropriate national policies.

It should be added that, in application of the Treaty, secondary community legislation introduced a differentiation in the capital liberalisation process relying on distinctions between several kinds of capital movements rather than on different timetables for member countries in different economic situations. The approach was based on an attempt to distinguish between capital movements according to their presumed economic utility, with the liberalisation remaining optional for the lower rated items. This was apparent in the Council Directives of 1960 and 1962.

Prior to the Commission initiative in 1983-84, financial integration – in the dual meaning of removing capital controls and liberalising financial services – had hardly moved forward since the 1960s. After a tightening of the procedures for derogations in 1984, the Commission proposed, in May 1986, a timetable for the complete removal of capital controls; these proposals were adopted in only slightly modified form as a Council Directive in June 1988 with a view to being fully implemented in the Community by mid-1990.

Four countries were granted derogations until 1992 (Greece, Ireland, Portugal and Spain); a further extension was made possible for Greece and Portugal.

The acceleration of the liberalisation process may be attributed to three main factors: the growing recognition of the economic benefits from free capital movements and financial integration, the perceived inefficiency of controls and the positive impact of capital liberalisation on the credibility of monetary and exchange rate policies. In this respect, one may conclude that the maintenance of a regime of free capital movements in a number of countries has had a positive demonstration effect and has finally contributed to a removal of controls in the other member countries.

3.3 *Differentiation in the exchange rate regimes*

The snake arrangement did not provide in explicit terms for special regimes, with the exception of the recognition of the Benelux 'worm' and the conclusion of association agreements with third countries. The withdrawal of several countries from the arrangement, one after the other, was not foreseen and no provisions were available for imposing a limit on the exchange rate swings of non-participants or for ensuring cooperation with them. The so-called Duisenberg plan, submitted in July 1976, tried to fill this gap. The main purpose of the plan was to invite EC countries with a floating currency to declare a 'target zone' within which they would aim at containing their effective exchange rate. There would be no positive intervention obligations to defend this zone, but a negative obligation not to take action that would result in a move away from the zone. Such movements would trigger consultation on policy coordination. As the plan raised objections from Germany as well as from the floaters, it had to be shelved in March 1977.

Contrary to the snake, the EMS Agreement offered the possibility of wider fluctuation margins and non-participation in the Exchange Rate Mechanism, together with an invitation to join the normal regime of the 2.25 per cent fluctuation band as soon as economic conditions would permit to do so. Although it took ten years before Italy gave up the wide band and the United Kingdom felt that the time was ripe for participation, one might argue that these special regimes have been instrumental in moving the EMS towards more homogeneity. Moreover, the existence of the wide band has facilitated an early entry of newcomers such as the Spanish peseta and the Portuguese escudo.

In the light of the near-collapse of the system during the crises of 1992 and 1993, the question may arise whether the move towards a more homogeneous composition of the system had not been premature. However, this move was certainly not a major cause of the crises, as these were mainly triggered by misalignments of individual currencies as well as by the perceived lack of convergence between economic performances and policies.

4 The scope for differentiation in the Maastricht Treaty

The Treaty provisions on Economic and Monetary Union incorporate an unprecedented degree of potential differentiation between countries. For the first time since the origins of the European Community, it is recognised in the Treaty that all Member States may not share the same objectives in terms of economic integration. Two of them, namely the United Kingdom and Denmark, have not committed themselves to move to full monetary union. However, it may still be argued that a community of purpose remains, to the extent that these two countries have undertaken not to prevent the others from achieving the goal of monetary union, a statement which is embodied in a special protocol. Nor have these countries ruled out a change of mind at a later stage, leading them to join the monetary union. Nevertheless, the Treaty is consistent with the lasting coexistence of two categories of Member States, willing or not willing to take part in EMU. To that extent, differentiation goes beyond the original concept of a two-speed Europe.

Among those Member States which commit themselves to the final goal of monetary union, a further differentiation may occur to the extent that they may not all fulfil the criteria for access to EMU at the same time. In accordance with the Treaty provisions, the Council shall, not later than on 31 December 1996, decide whether a majority of the Member States fulfil the required conditions for the adoption of a single currency. If by the end of 1997, the date for the beginning of the third stage has not been set, the third stage is planned to start on 1 January 1999 between those Member States which fulfil the necessary conditions.

Those Member States which are not found to be eligible for the first move to monetary union are invited to keep their monetary identity until such time as they satisfy the requirements. In the meantime, they are referred to in the Treaty as 'Member States with a derogation'. At least once every two years, or at the request of a Member State with a derogation, the Commission and the European Central Bank shall report to the Council, which shall decide, as appropriate, on the termination of the derogations. In the meantime, Member States with a derogation shall treat their exchange rate policy as a matter of common interest. Although the derogations are not limited in time, it is assumed that Member States committed to EMU will in due course make the necessary policy adjustments allowing them to satisfy the criteria for access.

Leaving aside the special cases of the United Kingdom and Denmark, differentiation with respect to monetary union formally begins with the move to stage three and only by then. For instance, the central banks of all Member States, including in this case the United Kingdom and Denmark, will participate fully in the European Monetary Institute, regardless of their degree of commitment or preparation to EMU, and regardless of the constraints to which they may have subjected their exchange rate policy.

Of course, this is in line with the principle according to which monetary policy remains a national responsibility during stage two. It would be surprising, however, if the potential for differentiation which applies to the move to the final stage did not reverberate in some ways at an earlier stage.

One of the tasks of the European Monetary Institute will be to prepare for the instantaneous transfer of the responsibility for monetary policy to the ECB. Given the implications of this process for the adaptation of monetary policy instruments, of payments systems and of market practices in the countries concerned, and given the size of the implied investments in terms of time and money, it may be found awkward, at some stage, that monetary union would have to operate at short notice in a territory with hitherto undefined geographical boundaries. Ways should be sought in due time to reconcile the impeccable philosophy behind the convergence criteria with the sheer practicalities of getting ready to conduct a single monetary policy within a well defined area.

One of the convergence criteria laid down in the Treaty is explicitly rooted well within stage two, namely the requirement that the normal fluctuation margins of the EMS be observed for at least two years, without a devaluation of the currency against the currency of any other member. In this connection, the decision of 2 August 1993, to widen the bands temporarily, raises new issues with potential implications for differentiation. While it can easily be argued that the authors of the Treaty considered the 'normal' fluctuation margins as being the narrow band of 2.25 per cent on either side of central rates, it is doubtful that the narrow band could be re-established without submitting currencies to a demanding test of credibility, leading again to a process of differentiation. It can even be argued that the rationale behind this convergence criterion refers to the actual behaviour of the exchange rate for the currencies concerned, irrespective of any commitment for unlimited intervention, implying that the institutional restoration of the narrow band might not be a prerequisite for the monitoring of this convergence criterion. The scope for differentiation would then move further away from a collective political decision and lend more weight to market reactions in response to economic fundamentals and policy adjustments.

The upshot of these observations is the following. The Treaty introduces differentiation as a concept which essentially takes effect with the move to the final stage. However, as the dynamics of the move towards this point proceed, it may occur that the need to bring forward the prospective determination of the area eligible for monetary union emerges as a condition for the appropriate implementation of the Treaty. To that extent, the suggestion that a hard core of Member States may have to be identified with a view to lead the way into the final stage should not necessarily be regarded as inconsistent with the Treaty of Maastricht.

5 Concluding remarks

Past experiences and the provisions of the Maastricht Treaty indicate that time differentiation or multi-speed formulae are, at least in some circumstances, considered as an indispensable instrument in the integration process. They may indeed be needed to overcome a deadlock or a retreat in the integration process and may appear to be the only way to avoid political compromises which would detract the Community from its basic and essential objectives.

Against their merits, these strategies have however their limits and involve certain risks which have to be weighed carefully:

a Differentiation may be useful and even indispensable in the monetary field if and when internal and external monetary stability are to be pursued in an environment characterised by significant inflation differentials and insufficient economic convergence. This was fully recognised at the start of the EMS, especially in the light of the experience with the snake. As the snake did not provide for special regimes, there was no other alternative for members which could not comply with the provisions of the mechanism, including possible realignments, than to leave the arrangement. By contrast, the EMS Agreement itself allowed for some flexibility by means of a temporary wider band and non-participation in the exchange rate mechanism. These provisions have served a useful purpose to the extent that they have protected the system against a source of instability at a time when the beneficiaries were not ripe for full-fledged participation. Nevertheless, it should be recognised that the survival of the system during the early eighties was achieved much less by these special regimes than by the recourse to realignments and the accompanying adjustment measures.

The scope for differentiation may also have allowed the system to escape the danger of adopting the average performance as a yardstick for the pursuit of stabilisation policies or the symmetrical treatment of strong and weak currencies as the guideline for exchange rate management. This was not obvious at the start of the EMS which was seen by some as having been designed to promote symmetry. However, as experience was gained, a growing consensus emerged on the desirability of a disciplinary mechanism constraining participants to promote convergence towards a low level of price inflation. This objective has been enshrined in the Maastricht Treaty. The primary aim of monetary policy remains price stability. Access to stage three requires a rate of inflation which is close to that of, at most, the three best performing Member States in terms of price stability.

b Differentiation may act as an incentive for countries to take the necessary adjustment measures in order to join the best-performing group. A typical example has been the development of the EMS since the mid-eighties. Once the participating countries had unambiguously opted for a stabilisation policy, the system entered into – what French officials have called – a process of competitive disinflation. This process has also engineered a sequence of measures in the field of capital liberalisation as well as repeated moves to join the Exchange Rate Mechanism of the EMS, or to shift to the narrow band, as long as it acted as an attractive focus of stability. The succession of these measures and moves has undoubtedly favoured the revival of the idea of moving forward to EMU. Differentiation may thus become a factor of dynamic progress once the catching-up process has started and is gathering pace.

The desire by Member States to be regarded as serious candidates for entering stage three with the first group may have facilitated the acceptance of the need for severe adjustment measures in order to comply with the Maastricht criteria. However, as these measures were only required in the framework of a medium-term policy, the need remains to monitor the degree of political commitment to their implementation. This has been confirmed by the experience of the convergence programmes. These are statements of the medium-term economic policy strategies to be pursued by each Member State to reduce nominal divergences from the best-performing partners and to satisfy the nominal convergence criteria contained in the Maastricht Treaty. In most cases, they set out quantified objectives for the next few years focusing especially on the reduction of inflation and of imbalances in public finances.

The desire of countries to fight the suspicion that they might not be ready for entering stage three has obviously influenced the design of their programmes. In some cases, these have been based upon or developed from already existing national multi-annual fiscal adjustment strategies which were not successfully implemented in the past. Moreover, the underlying macro-economic assumptions have often proved too optimistic so that the targets in the programmes became obsolete very soon.

c The experience with the snake and the EMS demonstrates the difficulty to establish a satisfactory relationship between participating and non-participating countries. The latter are generally reluctant to accept binding procedures and to give up the flexibility and freedom they have acquired by opting-out or staying outside.

The Maastricht Treaty contains an attempt at providing a cooperative framework between union and non-union members. For example, in the monetary area, the ECB will include a special decision-making body, the General Council, which is entrusted with the task of promoting cooperation with the central banks of countries not taking fully part in the final stage of EMU. While this body has limited binding authority, it has an important advisory function, particularly in the preparation for the termination of the derogations. The practical importance of this organisational structure may depend on the number and size of the countries that do not participate in stage three.

d Differentiation does not justify excessive and lasting differences between the rights and obligations of Member States which would be inconsistent with the principles of liberalisation and non-discrimination. This applies in particular to the use of exchange rate flexibility and to capital controls.

Exchange rate stability is widely recognised as a necessary precondition for the good functioning of a single market. While there are different opinions on the degree of stability which is required for that purpose, the inconsistency of freely floating currencies with the implementation of a single market is broadly accepted. The major threat in this field is that countries could not resist the temptation to have recourse to competitive depreciation. This fear is also apparent in the calls for a reasonable use of the wider ERM-bands.

As the good functioning of the single market clearly imposes limits on intra-European exchange rate flexibility, appropriate surveillance in this area is called for. It will remain needed once the process of differentiation is extended to the point where Member States are divided between those which belong to the monetary union and those which do not.

e Finally, differentiation becomes meaningless if it boils down to twelve uncoordinated national policies. It thus implies the existence of at least a core group of countries which keep the momentum. Given its weight in the Community, especially in monetary matters, it is hard to imagine that Germany would not be part of any credible group of such countries. According to the Maastricht Treaty, the start of stage three in 1999 could take place even if less than a majority of Member States were found able to take part in the move. It would be difficult, however, to contemplate any credible and significant move to EMU unless a critical though unspecified mass of countries were involved.

Central bank and government

Jelle Zijlstra

1 Introduction

The institutions denoted as central banks perform different tasks in different countries. What they have almost invariably in common is their responsibility for servicing the banknote circulation, their oldest task. However, whereas in some countries they are entrusted with the supervision of the solidity of the private banking system, as reflected in its solvency and liquidity, in other countries this function is performed by different agencies.

The problem which will be addressed in this essay in honour of André Szász concerns yet another function of central banks, which may rightly be characterized as their primary task: monetary policy, that is, the deployment of an instrument of macro-economic policy which – together with other such instruments – may have a controlling effect on the course of the economic process. This being said, major questions arise. What is the essence of monetary policy? What are its limits and what is its relationship to other instruments of macro-economic policy? How may conflicts be prevented or resolved? All this has been the subject of so many publications that there would seem little point in attempting yet another exhaustive discussion of the numerous aspects involved. Nonetheless, some observations by an author able to draw on many years of experience as a cabinet minister (1952-1963) and as President of the Nederlandsche Bank (1967-1981) might shed some additional light on some of the issues.

2 The evolving framework of monetary policy

The problems with which we shall be concerned in this essay have not always faced central banks. More precisely, before 1914 the concept of instruments of macro-economic policy did not even exist for the simple reason that the concept of macro-economics had not yet been defined. National income is a term which dates from the 1930s, evolving in large measure from the work of J.M. Keynes. To the extent that central banks attempted anything like influencing macro-economic developments, they did so by maintaining the gold parity of the currency. The instrument they used to that end was discount policy, and that was practically all they had. The governments fixed the gold parity of the currency and the central banks were to maintain this parity for as long as they could with the aid of their discount instrument. In this well-defined area, they often enjoyed a high degree of independence. Phrased in simple terms, all that would later become known as monetary policy and the instruments of monetary policy, was limited to the pursuit of a single objective (maintaining the gold parity) and the use of a single instrument (discount policy). This is, of course, to some extent an oversimplification. Yet, this stylized simplicity provides an effective background to the complexities in this area which we shall consider later.

In the 1930s, this pattern underwent a dramatic change. The gold parities were abolished and fluctuating exchange rates required deliberate policies. Prices of the principal commodities collapsed, economic growth vanished, unemployment soared; in brief, drastic measures were called for. The central banks were relatively helpless in the face of these colossal problems. After 1945, however, matters were taken in hand with vigour. The value of the currency, both domestic (purchasing power) and external (the exchange rate) demanded deliberate policies. What was to be undertaken by the government and what responsibilities could be discharged by the central bank? In a large number of countries, new legislation was enacted defining the tasks and responsibilities of the central banks. From the chaos of practical problems, but also stimulated by major developments in economic theory, the contours emerged of the renewed post-war central banks. The key issue to be resolved was and is the existence of macro-economic problems which must be controlled with the aid of instruments of macro-economic policy. There are three areas where things may really run out of hand. Firstly, the government may fail to heed the demands of fiscal equilibrium, mainly by overspending. Secondly, the cost of labour – wages and related costs – may come to exceed the productivity of labour by a considerable margin. Thirdly, and this is by no means the least danger, the money stock may show excessive growth. These sources of disequilibrium are dangerous if they make themselves felt simultaneously, each of them reinforcing the effects of the others. Financial extravagances, if substantial and lasting, on the part of the government are not possible unless money creation is available as a source of finance. Overstrains in the labour market pushing up wage demands often arise from excessive spending by industry in the form of investment contingent upon additional money creation. One might truly say that here is a need for control and guidance. Or, phrased differently, one could say that ills must be prevented or, if they prove unavoidable, be cured in time.

Fiscal equilibrium is the outcome of the process of democratic decision-making. Spending and taxation are decided on by government and parliament. The cost of labour, with wages as its principal component, is determined in collective bargaining between employers and employees and cannot be influenced by the government except in an indirect fashion. But what about the third source of disturbance, money, the money supply, or in brief the monetary problem? What exactly is this problem and who has powers of decision in this area? In summary, developments just before and after the Second World War have given monetary policy a dimension which was simply non-existent in the hey-day of the gold standard. A set of policy instruments has evolved which can be used for good or for evil.

Traditionally, the value of money and the quantity of money have been viewed as the core of the monetary problem. In this traditional view, too little or too much money has identifiable consequences for the value of money and for the efficacy of the economic process. That is why it is important to know who can or ought to decide on the volume of the money stock: the government and parliament or an institution known as the central bank. However, if controlling the money stock is so crucial, it must first be sufficiently clear what exactly the money stock is, how it can be reliably defined. In a recent address (on the occasion of the conference 'A framework for monetary stability' held in Amsterdam on 21-22 October 1993), Benjamin Friedman came to devastating conclusions. We have seen all sorts of definitions of money - he said - from narrow money to broad credit, from M1 to MX, but none of them offers any real hold. This is due to the broad range of substitutes which have come to function as money in our modern times, a development which has attended financial innovation, deregulation and the emergence of an array of entirely new financial instruments. Within this chain of substitutes, the separations have almost disappeared. If, as a consequence, the concept of money cannot be defined with any degree of precision, regulating the money stock becomes, of course, highly problematic. Thus, Friedman concludes that the concept of the money stock must be relinquished as the essential element of monetary policy and be replaced by an entirely different entity which he refers to as information variables. The central bank must have at its disposal a vast amount of information in an extremely broad area if it is to operate effectively in the field of monetary policy. The doubts about the feasibility of using the concept of money as the basis for monetary policy, one might add, are not a new phenomenon. As early as in the pre-war years, Henry Simons discussed this problem in an article, which has become a classic since.[1] Without a precise definition of money there can be no effective monetary policy, so he concluded. And that still holds good today.

This essay does not seek to discuss these complications in more detail. However, some general consequences for the relationship between the government and the central bank do merit attention. The issues involved here are of major significance. The first concerns the objectives to be pursued. Are they defined in a broad or a narrow sense? Do they focus on price stability alone (maintaining the value of money) or do they also extend to such variables as employment, economic growth and balance-of-payments equilibrium? Secondly, the instruments to be deployed need to be considered. Here, too, either a broad or a more limited choice is conceivable. Should the instruments be employed for monetary policy alone or also for purposes of economic policy or wages and prices policy? Thirdly, a choice needs to be made as to the agents who will wield the instruments.

3 Objectives of monetary policy

As will be shown, the answers to these questions are interrelated. The argument in favour of an autonomous central bank, independent of government and parliament alike, must be underlain by a well-defined objective. For its achievement, the central bank must have an effective but limited range of instruments at its disposal. Other objectives in the financial and economic sphere require different instruments, to be wielded by the government, where necessary in cooperation with parliament. A few examples from existing central bank legislation may serve to demonstrate this point.

It is not surprising, for instance, that the Charter of the Bank of England, which has a highly dependent position vis-à-vis the government, does not provide for any specific objectives. A memorandum entitled 'On monetary policy', prepared by the Bank of England for the 1979-1980 session of the House of Commons, makes this abundantly clear. 'Economic policy is the responsibility of the government and is determined by ministers. Policy decisions are, however, the end product of the assimilation and discussion of studies, forecasts, advice and

1 Simons, Henry C. (1936), Rules versus authorities in monetary policy, Journal of Political Economy, vol. 44, no. 1, pp. 1-30.

proposals available to ministers from a wide range of sources, in which processes the Bank of England has a role to play which can be distinguished from that of government departments.' Consequently, in the United Kingdom, monetary policy is fully integrated into the economic policy pursued by the government. The central bank is no more than an – admittedly very important – adviser. The Statutes of the Deutsche Bundesbank, on the other hand, contain a brief but highly forceful formulation of the Bundesbank's primary objective. The Bank is to regulate the amount of money in circulation and of credit supplied to the economy, with the aim of safeguarding the currency. Although a subsequent section of the Statutes provide that the Bundesbank is to support the federal government's general economic policy, it is only required to do so if and to the extent that this is compatible with its primary objective. The Statutes go on to state, apparently in order to rule out any misunderstanding, that the Bundesbank is independent of instructions from the federal government. The Bank Act governing the Nederlandsche Bank provides for an intermediate form. Section 9 of the Bank Act formulates the task of the Bank as 'to regulate the value of the Netherlands monetary unit in such a manner as will be most conducive to the nation's prosperity and welfare, and in so doing seek to keep the value as stable as possible'. This is complemented by the government's power to give directions, which is, however, embedded in a range of stringent procedural safeguards.

These three examples warrant the conclusion that a well-defined, unique objective contributes to central bank independence or even autonomy. A broader set of objectives and, a fortiori, the absence of any objective cannot but bring the central bank within the purview of government policy.

In this context, it is interesting to note how views on these issues have evolved recently in the United Kingdom. On 16 December 1993, the All Party Treasury Committee of the House of Commons published a report advocating greater independence for the Bank of England, albeit in a somewhat complex manner. The primary objective would have to be price stability. But – the resemblance with the Nederlandsche Bank is striking – in the pursuit of that objective allowance would have to be made for what the report refers to as the spare capacity in the economy, in other words for fostering economic growth and employment. And – as the reader might have guessed – the government must have power 'to override the objective of price stability in exceptional circumstances'. This, and the fact that it would be attended by an inflation target to be set by parliament, effectively removes any expectations of a forthcoming revolutionary change in the relationship between the Bank of England and the Treasury.

The formulation of a well-defined objective – maintaining the value of the currency – has very real significance in another sense as well. It invests the task of the central bank with more than a merely economic dimension. Maintaining the value of the currency, price stability, avoiding inflation, these are all interchangeable formulations of an objective which, besides economic, has moral import. In this sense, one may rightly speak of maintaining the integrity of money. Debasement of the currency dislocates the economic system, causing the market economy to plot its course by a false compass and replacing an equitable distribution of sacrifices by the outcome of an obscure free-for-all between those who suffer and those who benefit from inflation. Thus, the smart use of the resulting opportunities is elevated into the most profitable economic activity. Inflation is economically inefficient, contrary to the essence of the market economy and, hence, of political democracy; above all that, it is wrong from an ethical point of view.

A central bank whose primary objective is the maintenance of monetary stability derives its powers from legislation but its authority in society to a large extent from the moral impact of this primary objective. It should, nay must, be able to keep the government at arm's length. The fact is that government and parliament are susceptible to inflationary temptations. Especially in periods around elections, the tensions between short-term considerations, which play such a major role in winning electoral favour, and the public good in the long run are particularly severe. Maintaining the integrity of money is an outstanding example of a long-term interest. In the face of the ever-changing political winds and tides, stable money is the indispensable and reliable compass for the ship of state. The central bank leadership must not merely act and explain its actions, it must also preach the true gospel.

All this has brought us somewhat afield from the more technical aspects of the performance of such a momentous task. Rather than discussing a multitude of technical details, we need to concentrate here on a few more fundamental aspects involved in central bank policy.

Even in cases where the central bank has one key objective – safeguarding the value of the currency – the manner in which it may pursue this objective is far from simple. In this connection, it is of major importance that one or more intermediate targets are employed. The most obvious is the volume of the money stock. (In a country which has pegged its currency to that of an anchor country, the exchange rate may be viewed as the nominal point of reference.) Central banks deploy a variety of policy instruments and techniques, such as discount policy, open-market policy and reserve requirements. In essence, however, two fundamental questions need to be answered. Is there a sufficiently strong, causal relationship between the money stock and the price level and can the money stock be defined with sufficient accuracy for use as an operational target? On each of these two questions, there is an abundance of economic literature. For the purposes of this brief essay, it need merely be noted that, in the absence of a satisfactory answer to each of them, a central bank, even if in principle independent, may be faced with major problems. If a workable definition of money and an operationally practicable causal relationship between the money stock and the price level disappear from view, monetary policy loses its unique character, becoming part and parcel of the overall set of instruments aimed at the ultimate objectives of economic policy. Under such conditions, it becomes highly problematic to draw any clear-cut dividing line between the scope of the central bank's operations and that of the government's general economic and financial policy, a situation which encroaches on and threatens central bank independence and autonomy.

An independent monetary policy of a central bank charged with the unique objective of price stability is not complete unless such a policy is firmly aimed at stability in the longer run. The confidence which the economic agents must be able to have in the currency cannot alternately be inspired and undermined. Hence, a central bank's independent monetary policy stands in need of rules dominating over discretion. Flexibility is, of course, required in day-to-day operations but always against a background of sufficiently stable rules seeking the achievement of longer-term objectives.

4 Wielding the instruments: the case of the Netherlands

As noted above, the Nederlandsche Bank has been assigned a clear objective which at the same time defines its relationship with the government. The objective – to keep the value of the currency as stable as possible in the interests of the nation's prosperity and welfare – is a typical product of the first few years after the Second World War. At the time, in reaction to events during the inter-war years, a managed currency was seen as the ideal option. Relieved of the bonds of a rigid gold standard, monetary policy, operated alongside other policy instruments, should contribute to effective macro-economic management. This view necessarily entails that the government should have the right to give the Nederlandsche Bank a direction if it considers this necessary for the effective coordination of its policies with those of the central bank. However, such a direction should be the exception rather than the rule. Lieftinck, the Minister of Finance who presented the relevant Banking Act to parliament, referred to a direction as a measure of last resort embedded in strict procedural safeguards. So far, the government has never exercised this power, a fact which the reader might find surprising. Has there never been any need for coordination? Or has there always been ex ante agreement between the government and the Nederlandsche Bank to such an extent that coordination has been spontaneous? There is even a third possibility in that, in the event of serious differences of opinion, the government may, behind the scenes, have threatened to give a direction, thus inducing the Nederlandsche Bank to adjust its policy in time. The most serene explanation is, of course, that potential conflicts have been prevented by means of effective consultations, thus doing away with the need for threats. In the period between 1952 and 1982, the author has been able to observe this hidden reality. As one who has sat on both sides of the table, he has closely witnessed the operation of the Bank Act in this regard. These observations lead him to conclude that the last explanation – the serene one – best approximates reality.

Before 1952, with Lieftinck as Finance Minister and Holtrop as President of the Nederlandsche Bank, policies had been fully geared towards reconstruction after the heavy devastation wrought by the war. Under such conditions, homogeneity of objectives is fairly simple to achieve. Moreover, there was consensus on the essential principles of monetary policy. Where the period is concerned during which he was one of the actors on the scene, the author remembers just one difference of opinion of some substance between the Minister of Finance (the author) and the President of the Nederlandsche Bank (Holtrop). In 1962 the Group of Ten was established in order to permit the mobilization of additional finance within the framework of the IMF: the General Arrangements to Borrow. In that context, the possibility was discussed that a number of major countries, including the United States, might simultaneously require balance-of-payments support, a situation in which the IMF's ordinary resources might prove insufficient. The difference of opinion centred on the question whether, in such an eventuality, the decision would lie with the Nederlandsche Bank or with the government. The Nederlandsche Bank held that the issue at stake concerned a genuine monetary operation, so that it was up to her to provide the funds, while the government might always intervene by exercising its power to give a direction. The Minister of Finance, however, held that such an event would only arise in conditions marked by such a disturbance of global monetary equilibrium that it was up to the government to take the lead. This has not, however, led to anything like a public conflict. The parties more or less agreed to disagree on the mutual understanding that, if the case would ever arise, prior agreement would be reached through consultation. In the event, the case never arose. When the US balance of payments had been so dislocated as to require substantial assistance from the IMF, with the attaching policy conditions, the United States ended the Bretton Woods system. This major country refused to allow the officials of the Fund (or, in a phrased coined by a US senator, the back-room boys of the IMF) to dictate their terms.

In the area of discount policy, no grave problems have ever arisen between the government and the Nederlandsche Bank. In practice, the central bank invariably decided on the magnitude and timing of changes in official rates, informing the Minister of Finance after having taken its decisions. There have, however, been some problems in regard of the introduction of credit restrictions. For a long time, the Nederlandsche Bank employed quantitative credit restrictions as its principal instrument of monetary policy, controlling the money stock by curbing credit expansion. To that end, ceilings were imposed on the growth of lending by each individual money-creating institution. This system of credit restrictions provided for a specific procedure which is, however, beyond the scope of this essay. Such measures were not, of course, without political implications, as a conflict was readily conceivable between the views of the Nederlandsche Bank, which might find a restriction of money growth desirable, and those of the government taking into account its overall aims for economic growth and employment. At times, tensions have indeed arisen in this area but they have on no occasion led to any public conflict. With the progressing internationalization of money and capital flows, the possibilities of controlling the money stock by means of such quantitative curbs on domestic lending have gradually disappeared, thus removing a potential source of conflict and tension between the government and the central bank.

How should one, with the benefit of hindsight, assess the system as it was laid down in the Bank Act just after the war? Great care has been invested in designing a statutory system for a very fundamental resolution of conflicts between the government and the central bank. In the area of monetary policy, the Nederlandsche Bank is allowed freedom of action unless, in a very momentous case, the government should intervene. In that event, the central bank must yield, though only after a stringent procedure which might bring the conflict before parliament. The procedure involves risks for both parties. The Minister of Finance cannot be sure that parliament will vindicate his action. Especially if the general public considers the central bank a better guardian of the currency than the government – which, like any government, may occasionally have a tendency towards laxer morals from a monetary point of view – the Finance Minister runs risks if he decides to confront the central bank in open battle. The central bank runs a grave risk as well. If it is given a direction by the government and, after having gone through all the required procedural steps, it is defeated, the consequences are far-reaching indeed. Not only should the President step down – and with him, in principle, the entire Governing Board – but a taboo has been shattered. Up to that time the government's power to give directions was a formidable weapon seemingly destined to remain unused. After all, as time went by after the introduction of the Bank Act and no direction was given, the awareness increasingly gained ground that the government was unlikely ever to use this power. A government which were yet to do so might create an impression that, after many years of careful and stable policies, more reckless views had come to prevail . However, had the government actually wielded its power, an entirely new situation might have been created. The fences would have been down, one might say, or to use a more striking metaphor, the Nederlandsche Bank can lose its (monetary) virginity only once. The result might have been a situation akin to that which the Bank of England has been in since the war. The Bank of England Act provides for the right of the Treasury to give directions, much in line with the system in the Netherlands. As became evident during the reading of the Bill in parliament, the Treasury's power to give directions was intended for use in 'exceptional and unusual cases' only. In practice, however, the original concept has deteriorated into such an extensive and effective involvement of the Treasury with the Bank of England that the use of formal directions has remained obscure theory. It is important to note that this continual involvement is also reflected in intensive contacts between the Treasury and the Bank at all levels of the organization. Such practices are unthinkable in the situation in the Netherlands, where the consultations between the Finance Minister and the central bank President largely take the form of weekly luncheon meetings, where the Minister is accompanied by a senior official. The results of the consultations are fed into the organization top-down, both at the ministry and at the central bank. If the reverse were to be the case, as it is at the Bank of England, the formal arrangement regarding the right to give directions would be eroded, becoming de facto unnecessary. The creativity of the ministerial opponent and of his staff in inventing ways to attain their aims by guile and cunning must not, incidentally, be underestimated. In the face of any such efforts, the central bank must stand firm. In respect of the manner in which the right to give directions may be exercised, yet another variant is conceivable. In order to avoid a conflict in the event of a serious difference of opinion, the central bank leadership could simply ask the government for a direction to remove any doubts as to where responsibility for a certain decision lies. This possibility must be rejected vigorously. It would greatly undermine the essential meaning of the right of direction and could bring the Nederlandsche Bank in British waters.

Meanwhile, all this has to a considerable extent become theory. The scope of national monetary policy has substantially narrowed as a result of the huge flows of money and capital which may move freely across national borders, owing not least to the existing and future European monetary integration.

5 Some other issues relating to central bank independence

To round off and complete the foregoing, a few additional observations need to be made.

Maintaining the value of the currency as reflected in its domestic purchasing power concerns merely one aspect of that value. The other is its value against foreign currencies. Here, too, the position of the central bank in relation to the powers of the government is of significance. Again, the problems involved are complex. Governments certainly have an important responsibility to this external value of the currency while central banks pursuing a policy aimed at domestic stability of the currency cannot afford to remain aloof in this area. This is unlikely to give rise to problems if the national currency forms part of a system of fixed parities. Under the former gold standard, under the Bretton Woods system or within the European Monetary System of fixed parities, the respective responsibilities of the government and the central bank are clearly defined. The government fixes the parity, with the central bank acting in an advisory capacity. However, in the absence of fixed parities, that is, under a system of floating exchange rates, the external value of the currency is determined in the exchange markets, thereby centring the problem on interventions in that market. A central bank enjoying an independent position in regard of the domestic value of the currency also needs a high degree of independence in respect of intervention policy. This is all the more true as, under present conditions, exchange rates, rather than reflecting purchasing power parities, must absorb vast capital flows, often generated by speculative expectations. A central bank which seeks to safeguard the value of the currency in a structural manner should, therefore, also be in charge of intervention policy in the exchange markets. In the Netherlands, this has been provided for in the Guilder Exchange Rate Act of 1978, which permits the Nederlandsche Bank to conduct its intervention policy independently, while allowing the Minister of Finance to communicate indication rates as a trigger for consultation.

In the context of the central bank's independence and autonomy vis-à-vis the government, another aspect also demands attention: the relationship with parliament. In the United Kingdom in particular, this is a highly sensitive matter. Whatever changes may be made to the Bank of England Act, parliamentary accountability needs to be maintained. Non-elected bodies whose parliamentary accountability remains hazy or obscure are anathema in British eyes. Yet, some reservations are in order here. Parliamentary accountability may easily degenerate into veiled dependence. The dealings which a central bank enjoying independence of the government may have with parliament should basically not extend beyond providing information, explaining the policy pursued and listening to the views of parliament. In the present situation in the Netherlands, such contacts with parliament would be inappropriate since the Minister's right to give directions clearly brings out where ultimate responsibility lies. The fact is that the Minister of Finance is also accountable to parliament if he decides not to give a direction. In the United States, the position is entirely different in that relations between government and Congress differ fundamentally from those in most other democratic countries. The relations between Congress and the Federal Reserve Board may, incidentally, be somewhat strained on occasion. The chairman of the Federal Reserve Board regularly makes an appearance in Congress to explain policies. At times, the US Congress is not averse from attempting to impose its will on the Board. One could say that the balance between Congress and the Board is somewhat unstable.

In any drive to invest the central bank with the highest possible degree of independence and autonomy, there are, apart from the question of a power to give directions – whether intended for actual use or not – a number of other issues which merit attention. Among the most important are the appointment and the security of tenure of directors. In the Netherlands, the President and the other members of the Governing Board are appointed by the King for periods of seven years. This makes for a well-balanced situation. After the seven years have elapsed, the government may decide on its own whether re-appointment is desirable. Appointments for an indefinite period of time are not a suitable option, implying as they do the possibility of dismissal at any time. Other aspects of the legal status of central bank directors also need to be reviewed. If the government were intent on undermining the position of the central bank, it could, quite apart from any other existing regulations, enforce an insufficient level of pay, thus reducing the central bank's authority to the point where the statutory independence of the central bank leadership becomes an empty shell. In the Netherlands, the arrangements in this regard are satisfactory. The government must admittedly approve directors' salaries as fixed by the central bank's Supervisory Board, but the pay of the central bank's staff, up to and including deputy directors, mirrors the development of pay levels within the private banking system. Thus, albeit indirectly, the level of directors' pay is also provided for. Finally, attention must be drawn in this context to the provisions of company law as they apply to the central bank. In the Netherlands, the Bank Act exempts the Nederlandsche Bank in a number of essential respects from general company law. Its balance and profit and loss account are adopted not by the general meeting of shareholders (which is the state, being sole shareholder) but by the Supervisory Board. This is of fundamental significance for the valuation of assets and the determination and the disbursement of profit. This independence in terms of company law helps to guard true central bank autonomy. If the government were to control this side of operations, the central bank would be confronted with the 'big boss' under its own roof.

6 Concluding remarks

In the foregoing, it has been argued time and again that a high degree of central bank independence is desirable. In conclusion, let us once more ask and answer the question why such independence is of overriding importance. The answer is essentially to be found in the objective of maintaining the value of the currency and in the acceptance of the need for this objective, not as one among other major objectives of economic and financial policy but as a condition for their achievement. The market economy requires this stability as a reliable compass for the acts of the economic agents. A democratic system of government requires this stability as a foundation for an equitable society. That is why, within the framework of parliamentary democracy, the central bank, as guardian of this stability, must not be allowed to be swayed by the shifting political issues of the day.

Traditionally, constitutional law has given great prominence to the trias politica, with the judiciary as one of its essential pillars. In this respect, special institutional safeguards have been incorporated into the law: judges are appointed for life and cannot be removed from office. Maintaining the value and the integrity of money is an issue on a comparable plane. Here, too, institutional safeguards are required to afford protection from encroachments by the political institutions.

Viewed thus, we have gone some way beyond the provisions of the Bank Act of 1948, which still refers to monetary policy as one of the instruments which can be used to foster the nation's prosperity and welfare, with the stability of money playing a role, though not one that needs to be safeguarded as the primary objective. If, in this wide-ranging area, the central bank were to find itself in conflict with the government, it may be brought to heel by a direction. Considering the views prevailing at the time, this was the best conceivable solution. At present, this is no longer so. In the light of the arguments advanced above, the German legislation presents a more appropriate solution, charging the central bank with one overriding objective – maintaining the stability of the currency – to which all other objectives are subordinated. The government has no powers to give directions and is unable to thwart the policy aimed at price stability.

It is gratifying, therefore, that the future central bank of the European Union will be based on the German rather than the Dutch model. If the European Central Bank, guarding the single European currency – even if its introduction will probably be some time after 1997 – truly appreciates its momentous task, it will need to be aware that, although it derives its authority from the provisions of the Treaty, it will have to earn this authority through its policy. Legislation can, after all, be changed and its application undermined. The ECB will have to establish the firm conviction among the European citizens, and strengthen and renew this conviction by its acts, that it is a faithful and trustworthy guardian of the value of the new European currency.

European exchange rate cooperation

Erik Hoffmeyer

1 Initiatives towards monetary union

European exchange rate cooperation during the 1972-93 period is unique in international monetary history. It has been and will undoubtedly continue to be subject of a vast number of studies and differing interpretations. I have attended the development at close range during the whole period, and have often had the advantage of discussing important issues with André Szász. We have, of course, not always agreed, but we often had similar appraisals of basic problems. The European exchange rate cooperation cannot be analysed solely as a regional fixed exchange rate system or a truncated Bretton Woods arrangement. It had obviously that aspect, too, in that it has been considered an advantage for the participants to have fixed exchange rates vis-à-vis their major trading partners. Within the EC, now the European Union, the driving force has, however, to a much larger extent been connected with the political aim of creating a monetary union among member countries. By strengthening monetary policy coordination and the scope for multilateral surveillance, a common exchange rate arrangement should, so to speak, become the spearhead of European economic and, eventually, political integration. It has been considered a dogma that a fixed exchange rate system was a necessary condition for the development towards a monetary union – but of course not a sufficient condition – that would include the more ambitious requirements, namely the political will to converge in various politically sensitive areas. All in all, however, fixed rates became the basis to build on.

Over time, four periods or waves of political initiatives can be distinguished as endeavours to move towards monetary union with a single monetary policy and irrevocably fixed exchange rates or a common currency. The first, that was interwoven with the second, was the German initiative under Karl Schiller, Minister of Economics and Finance, to create a European system of block floating against the dollar in 1971. In the end it was unsuccessful and had to yield to the attempt to re-establish the global fixed exchange rate system at the Smithsonian

Agreement in December 1971. The second was the blueprint based on the Werner Report of 1970. This blueprint was adopted in 1971 and – in 1972 – followed by the creation of the so-called snake exchange rate arrangement within the Smithsonian tunnel, and a political commitment to realize an economic and monetary union before 1980. The objectives of the first stage of the economic and monetary union were never fulfilled and an agreement on the premises to enter into the second stage could not be reached. However, the snake survived – although in a battered form. The third wave of initiatives came in 1978 with a German-French proposal to re-establish the European fixed rate system with participation of most EC member countries – the European Monetary System (EMS). The intention was to consolidate the arrangements and institutions no later than two years after the start of the scheme in a European Monetary Fund, which had several points of resemblance with a monetary union. Again, the wider objective – the second stage of EMS – was withdrawn, but the exchange rate system survived. The fourth round of political initiatives started with the Delors Committee in 1988 and was concluded with the Maastricht Treaty and the so-called Maastricht criteria. Now, at long last the precise criteria for entering an economic and monetary union ('the EMU') had been defined, and the road to EMU seemed to be cleared. However, markets soon reacted and put pressure on the exchange rate system, mainly because it was increasingly considered doubtful whether there was sufficient political will to move towards EMU. Following a year of unprecedented currency unrest and several attempts to keep the EMS intact, the authorities in Germany and France eventually gave in to market pressure and suspended the system.

2 Convergence and the defence of the exchange rate system

Over the years the debate about the exchange rate system and the conditions for realizing a monetary union has essentially focused on two groups of issues. One is the yardstick for economic convergence, and the other the measures to be taken in order to defend the exchange rate system on the road towards an economic and monetary union. On the first issue it can be said that differences of opinion were settled by agreeing on the Maastricht criteria regarding price stability, interest rate levels, public sector deficits and exchange rate behaviour. In essence, by agreeing on these criteria the stability-oriented model was adopted. Convergence should be aimed at the best performers – and not at some kind of average among members. Furthermore, the general philosophy implied by the Treaty was that fiscal policy should be used with great caution and that the problem of unemployment could not in a lasting way be solved by monetary and/or fiscal policy.

So much for the final criteria. Turning to the other issue – the defence of the exchange rate system – achievement of currency stability, of course, hinges on a number of instruments. Two of those instruments are of fundamental importance: the first is monetary policy adjustment; the second is the mutual commitment to unlimited short-term intervention. To this must be added that in case of serious – or 'fundamental' – disequilibrium, exchange rate adjustments must be undertaken promptly, but only as a last measure, when other instruments of adjustment fail. The two basic instruments – monetary policy adjustments and unlimited intervention – have had features of asymmetry, which have dominated attitudes and eventually became decisive among the forces that led to the suspension of the system in August 1993.

The asymmetry regarding monetary policy adjustment is connected with the role of the Deutsche mark as anchor currency of the system. Over the years, the Bundesbank has steadfastly pursued a counter-inflationary policy – with success. Pressure from other countries to modify this policy in a way that could potentially have an adverse impact on domestic price developments and, hence, on the anchor role of the Deutsche mark has persistenly been rejected. The successful performance of the German economy and the gradual shift to similar policies by partner countries led to growing monetary stability in Europe. However, in periods of major strains the asymmetric approach gave rise to difficulties for the decision-making process and thus the cooperative management of the system.

3 Limits to ex ante coordination

Until, in the final stage of EMU, a single monetary policy with a centralized decision-making process is established, the whole idea of central bank cooperation is that mutual consultation should take place before national decisions are taken. This appears clearly from the Council Decision of 1964 which established the Committee of Central Bank Governors. It is stated that consultations between central banks should take place 'so far as possible, before any decisions are taken by the central banks'. Equally, measures should be examined before they were adopted. The language was tightened further in the 1990 amendment, where it is specified that the Committee should 'normally be consulted before the national authorities take decisions on the course of monetary policy, such as the setting of annual money supply and credit targets'. It is important to note that it has not been possible to advance further than consultation. In practise, ex ante agreement on major policy issues is not possible at present. This was borne out by an investigation under the Delors Committee, where members were asked to reply to a questionnaire that was aimed at illustrating how far coordination could

Table Major instruments and policy measures to be applied in connection with the gradual realisation of Economic and Monetary Union

Country: Denmark

Instrument/policy measure	Who makes the decision ?[1]	Can under present provisions policies decisions be: communicated prior to implementation ?	taken after consultation ?	taken after coordination ?	Can the decision-making power be transferred to Community bodies without changes in national legislation ?
Monetary policy					
Change in central bank interest rates	CB	Yes	Yes	Yes	No
Credit policy	CB+ GOV	Yes	Yes	Yes	No
Reserve requirements	CB+ GOV	Yes	Yes	Yes	No
Open-market operations	CB	Yes	Yes	Yes	No
Financing of government deficits	GOV (CB)	Yes	Yes	Yes	No
Government debt management	GOV (CB)	Yes	Yes	Yes	No
Exchange rate policy					
Change in central rates	GOV (CB)	as a member of EMS these are common decisions			No
Change in intervention margins	GOV (CB)				No
Change in intervention credit mechanisms	CB (GOV)				No
Intervention policy	CB	Yes	Yes	Yes	No
Management of official reserves	CB	Yes	Yes	Yes	No
Fiscal policy					
Direct taxes	P	2	Yes	No	No
Taxation of interest and capital income	P	2	Yes	No	No
Indirect taxes	P	2	Yes	No	No
Budget balance targets	GOV	2	Yes	?	No
Other policy instruments and measures					
Incomes policy	GOV, P	2	Yes	No	No

1 CB= Governor, Central Bank Board; GOV= Minister, Cabinet; P= Parliament.

2 Government proposals can be notified when tabled.

be carried. The purpose was to identify how policy measures could be applied in such a way that a gradual realisation of Economic and Monetary Union could be achieved. The questionnaire had the following form, and by way of illustration, the Danish answers to the questionnaire are presented (see table).

Even though the concepts are admittedly unclear, some conclusions can be drawn from the answers. It seems evident that in no major policy area it would be possible to transfer decision-making power to community bodies. This would require changes in national legislation and that is not foreseen until the final stage of EMU. Furthermore, there are already under existing arrangements ample opportunities to consult and communicate between members. This is not surprising, given the whole idea of the Treaty of Rome. The basic problem is, consequently, whether it is possible to come closer to the border-line where decision-making is transferred to a common body. How far is it possible to advance on voluntary coordination? Even though it is not meaningful to try to define the word coordination, it must at least include members' willingness to adjust their policies mutually and that some clarification is reached through the machinery of examining national policy plans.

The answers were not precise, but they convey the impression that there are narrow limits to how far ex ante coordination can be carried on a voluntary basis. It applies in particular to the anchor currency country, Germany. This has also been borne out by the behaviour pattern during recent years. Short-term interest rates are consequently dominated by Germany and this asymmetry creates a problem because of differing national economic priorities among members. During the discussions in the Committee it has, however, generally been accepted that domestic economic pressure in Germany has justified the German monetary policy stance. Moreover, a loosening of German monetary policy with a view to easing tensions on partner countries' currency markets could erode the anchor role of the Deutsche mark to the detriment of all participants.

It seems hardly likely that coordination can be developed further until the final stage of Economic and Monetary Union is achieved, unless national legislations in the most important countries are amended. There is much talk about cooperation and coordination of monetary policy, but the hard fact is that it is unlikely that members will go further than exchange of information and analysis of what has happened and what may happen. In the Delors Report this question was summed up in the following way: '... under present national legislations no member country is able to transfer decision-making power to a Community body, nor is it possible for many countries to participate in arrangements for a binding ex ante coordination of policies'.[1]

4 Intervention commitments

The second basic instrument is the commitment to unlimited mutual intervention. The asymmetry in this respect is connected with the fact that interventions in support of weak currencies inflate the money stock in creditor countries. Normally, sales of Deutsche mark borrowed at the Bundesbank by other central banks have dominated the scene during periods of tension. Given the large amounts of intervention in the recent past, monetary policy in Germany has been affected. The Bundesbank has often stressed that German monetary policy must be aimed at preserving price stability within Germany and that money creation in connection with interventions would run counter to this aim. It must be recognized, however, that interventions over the last year – from the summer of 1992 to the fall of 1993 – do not appear to support this view (see figure).

The graph is based on Bundesbank information and shows that the heavy interventions in September 1992 had a substantial impact on German M3, but that this was offset during the following months. The influence of the June-August 1993 interventions on M3 shows the same picture, but much less dramatic. The increase in M3 is dominated by credit expansion from German banks and not by interventions in the exchange market. As the Bundesbank's own studies seem to suggest, monetary growth in Germany will only accelerate on a lasting basis if interest rates in Germany fall and/or if production and demand increase.[2] Thus, interventions do not seem to have a more lasting influence on monetary growth in Germany.

5 Conclusion

By way of conclusion, it can be said that the two asymmetries in the European Monetary System have been important in creating tensions and eventually have been decisive for the breakdown of the system. The first is the fact that a single anchor system with only limited possi-

1 Committee for the Study of Economic and Monetary Union (1989), Report on economic and monetary union in the European Community, (paragraph 61).
2 Deutsche Bundesbank, Monthly Report, January 1993, p. 31.

Figure Growth of M3 in Germany

Per cent of the previous month

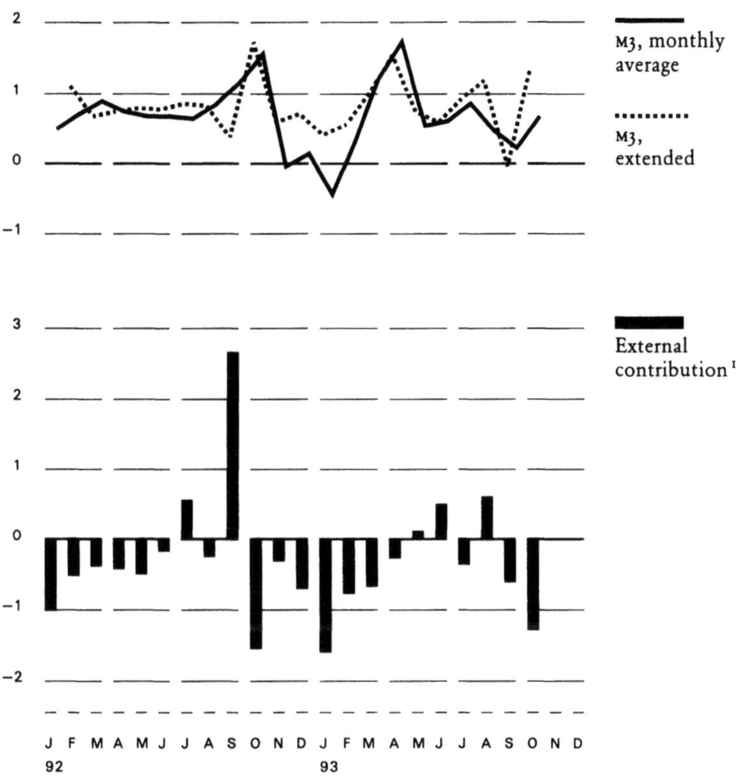

1 Contribution from changes in net external assets of credit institutions and the Bundesbank.

Source: Deutsche Bundesbank.

bility of negotiating a common monetary policy means that participants have to adjust their monetary policy to that of the anchor. Undeniably, this will from time to time create policy dilemmas. The second – the intervention asymmetry – is felt to impair German monetary policy, but is probably less burdensome than often believed. It is difficult to imagine that the first asymmetry can be solved, unless convergence reaches such a level that the singular anchor role of the Deutsche mark is substantially reduced. The second asymmetry seems to be less of a problem and could be mitigated by changing the settlement rules in such a way that creditor countries are reimbursed in their own currencies, if they wish so. Improved policies of convergence and amended settlement rules thus seem to be the key to re-establishing European exchange rate cooperation.

The economic and monetary relation between Germany and the Netherlands

Nout Wellink

'Of Germany's partners, the Dutch monetary authorities above all appreciate the importance of Germany's stability-oriented policy for the system. The role of the Deutsche mark as an anchor of stability. Maybe we realize more vividly than the other partners that, in the unlikely event that the Bundesbank could be persuaded to adopt another policy, the system would not be long-lived.'[1]

1 Introduction

Germany, Europe's monetary anchor: what could have been more inconceivable just after the Second World War, when the European countries, struggling with colossal overliquidity consequent on the forced financing of Germany's war efforts, the contraction of the real economic sector and the bilateral balance-of-payments surpluses vis-à-vis Germany, were compelled to undertake currency reforms? Yet Germany became Europe's monetary anchor, thanks to the vigour of its economic build-up during the 1950s and 1960s, and its monetary authorities' quest for stability. Thanks also to the collapse of the Bretton Woods system in the early 1970s, which created a need for a new anchor for the European exchange rates; the predominance of the German economy made the Deutsche mark the obvious choice.

Germany did not gain monetary supremacy without further ado. Other European countries with hegemonial currencies, such as France and the United Kingdom, put up a considerable fight. At the time of the snake arrangement, this eventually led to the delinking of their (and other) currencies from the Deutsche mark. Under its successor, the ERM, France at first balked at the idea, but then gradually came to accept the Deutsche mark as monetary anchor. However, France's importance and well-balanced policy, and the consequent gradual elimina-

A debt of gratitude is owed to Dr J.H. Garretsen, Ms R.M. Oort and Ms L.M.T. van Velden for their help in shaping this article.

1 Szász (1989).

tion of expectations of exchange rate adjustments, make for a new terminology. It may become more appropriate to speak of a German-French anchor or even, under certain circumstances, of a French anchor. But so far it has not come to that yet, notwithstanding the fact that the German economy is ailing three years after unification. The United Kingdom was long in bowing to the rules of the ERM (until 1990) and hence indirectly to German policy discipline, and dropped out again after about two years.

The currencies of the small, open European economies which have close ties with Germany have a totally different link with the Deutsche mark, both politically and economically, than the hegemonial currencies. This does not mean, however, that that link is maintained effortlessly, as we have seen from the turmoil in the foreign exchange markets in September 1992 and August 1993. This contribution will deal, briefly, with the relationship between the Deutsche mark and the guilder, a relationship which has grown stronger over the past decades, and which has ultimately led to what can be regarded as a de facto monetary union. It is therefore not surprising that since 2 August 1993 the guilder is the only currency which has continued to operate a 2.25 per cent fluctuation margin vis-à-vis the Deutsche mark.

2 Some facts

The Netherlands is renowned for its low inflation rate. In fact, prices rose so little in the years 1985-1990 that the Nederlandsche Bank spoke of a 'central bankers' paradise'[2] and fears arose that we would see a deflationary spiral such as that recorded in the 1930s. Yet in the 1960s and a large part of the 1970s, the Netherlands had been anything but a low-inflation country. Table 1 gives an impression of the relative performance of the Netherlands in the area of price movements since 1963. At first the Dutch inflation rate exceeded that in the OECD, and especially that in Germany (1963-1973). During this part of the Bretton Woods period, the Netherlands not only adopted the international inflationary climate, but added something of its own, notably in the form of a wage explosion in 1963. Later the Netherlands performance improved, the inflation rate falling below the average recorded within the OECD, though vis-à-vis Germany some further deterioration was in evidence. A new situation arose after the creation of the EMS in 1979 owing to the increasing success of our orientation towards Germany. The relatively

2 Wellink (1985).

Table 1 Inflation differentials

In percentage points

	Netherlands - OECD	Netherlands - Germany
1963 - 1973	+1.5	+2.4
1973 - 1979	-3.1	+2.7
1979 - 1989	-3.6	-0.5
1989 - 1994	-1.4	-1.1

Explantory note: Cost-of-living index (+ indicates a higher inflation rate in the Netherlands).

Source: Netherlands, CBS; Germany, BIS; OECD, Economic Outlook.

large inflationary differential vis-à-vis that country manifest since the end-1980s is due mostly to the unification and is presumably temporary in nature (see also table 4).

The gradual narrowing of inflationary differentials between Germany and the Netherlands has also had repercussions for the convergence of interest rates (smaller variability). As we can see from figure 1, long-term interest rate differentials have been minute since the early 1980s.

Short-term interest rate differentials decreased considerably only in the second half of that decade, and are presently even (temporarily) negative. This only goes to show that, in a monetary sense, the two countries grew increasingly closer, especially during the 1980s.

Figure 1 Interest rate differential Netherlands-Germany

Yearly averages

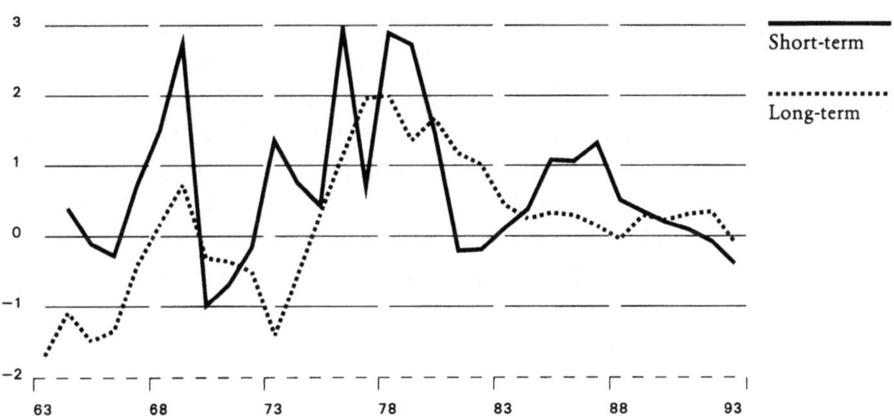

3 The policy pursued

3.1 *The more distant past*

It was the collapse of the Bretton Woods system which brought on the gradually increasing monetary orientation towards Germany, a new policy anchor being called for. However, the fundamental decision had been taken long before then, even though the consequences of such a move may not have been fully appreciated at the time. The German decision of 4 March 1961 to revalue the Deutsche mark by 5 per cent led Zijlstra, the then Minister of Finance who later became the Nederlandsche Bank's President, to remark: 'In that line of thinking, revaluation puts a brake on the import of inflation. Today, in the second half of the 1970s, that is something we all go for wholeheartedly. But in those days, it was novel. (.....) Germany, however, understood in time, though, and (the then Minister of Economic Affairs) De Pous and I realized after the German decision: either we follow the Germans or we knowingly import foreign inflation (.....). Late that Sunday evening, 6 March 1961, it was decided that we would follow the Germans'.[3] The argument for following Germany lay, according to Zijlstra, in the existence of a certain fundamental disequilibrium, as defined in the Articles of Agreement of the International Monetary Fund (almost continuous strain and even overstrain in the production process and in the labour market). In later years, this argument gradually lost clout, and the fight against inflation came to figure as the only argument. Take, for example, the following passage by the then Secretary-General of the Ministry of Economic Affairs, who wrote in connection with the exchange rate policy: '... that on this point policy should be led not so much by the uncertain effects on employment, as by the obvious consequences for prices'.[4]

However, it was some time before the fundamental decision to follow Germany and the Deutsche mark was consistently put into practice in everyday policy. Table 2 shows the bilateral devaluations and revaluations of the guilder against the Deutsche mark since the fundamental decision to follow that currency was taken in March 1961. Time and time again the guilder did not make the grade. Though the guilder could not follow the Deutsche mark it should be kept in mind that the post Bretton-Woods exchange rate system of the 1970s differed at least in one important respect form the EMS. As opposed to the EMS, unilateral decisions to re- or devalue were allowed. The events in 1973 illustrate

3 Puchinger (1978).
4 Rutten (1978).

Table 2 Devaluations and revaluations against the Deutsche mark

Percentages

27 October 1969	-9.3	18 October 1976	-2.0
21 December 1971	-2.0	16 October 1978	-2.0
19 March 1973	-3.3	24 September 1979	-2.0
29 June 1973	-5.5	21 March 1983	-2.0
17 September 1973	+5.0		

this feature. The unexpected German decision to revalue the Deutsche mark in June was countered by a revaluation of the guilder in September.

In all, the period after 1969 still saw a considerable cumulative devaluation of the guilder (central rate in 1969: Fl. 98.907; in 1994: Fl. 112.673); it may be noted that though considerable to the somewhat Calvinist Dutch mind, the devaluation was modest by comparison with major exchange rate fluctuations elsewhere. The picture emerging from table 2 speaks for itself. The policy-induced link of the guilder to the Deutsche mark grew increasingly stronger in the EMS period, i.e. after 1979; since 1983 it has been complete. The terminology used has meanwhile been adjusted. In the second half of the 1970s and the first half of the 1980s, the Nederlandsche Bank still spoke of the desirability of a close relationship between the guilder and the Deutsche mark, so as not to go against the grain too much but, as time went by, pegging the guilder to the Deutsche mark came to be unabashedly presented as a policy objective. It was always stressed, however, that this objective would remain in place only so long as German policy continued to be targeted at stability. As there has never been a real alternative, the Bank has always adhered to the principle (especially since the German unification in 1990) that Germany is catering not just to its own interests, but to those of Europe as well, when it continues to conduct a policy aimed at stability.

3.2 *The years 1979 and 1983*

Policy-wise, 1979 saw a turnaround in that since then day-to-day policy has also been increasingly aimed at a further strengthening of the link with the Deutsche mark. Here two factors played a role. First of all, there was the inception of the EMS on 13 March 1979, which, owing to its structure, in fact boiled down to 'European confirmation' of Germany's role as the anchor country. The second factor was the devaluation of the guilder against the Deutsche mark on 23 September 1979, a move seen by the Bank as a mistake, but providing valuable lessons for the future. With the Belgians loath to devalue their currency, especially against the guilder, and the Dutch desire to retain their link with the mark, even if it were to be revalued, the Netherlands and Belgium entered the negotiations on realignment with a common stance. This may have been a noble gesture of Benelux solidarity, but in the actual negotiations it proved a millstone around the Dutch neck because the other participants saw Belgium as weaker than the Netherlands and were not prepared to place the two countries on an equal footing. At the same time, the Dutch position was not strong enough, witness earlier devaluations, to prevent the guilder and the Belgian franc from receiving equal treatment, so that the Netherlands had no other option but to let the guilder be devalued against the Deutsche mark by the same percentage as the franc.

Deputy Director Henk Boot was the first to formulate the lesson to be learned (and in fact learnt) by the Bank from this experience: 'In my view, it is more essential to establish an irrefutable political fact, if possible: viz. to create an impregnable position in the market so that deviation from the Deutsche mark in the following round would be inconceivable'.[5] In terms of the policy actually pursued by the Bank, this meant that within the EMS band the guilder should stick closer to the Deutsche mark, and that any weakening would be tolerated only so long as it remained within limits narrower than those constituted by the maximum band width. Should these limits be exceeded, interest rates would have to be raised immediately. The consistent application of this policy has clearly contributed to the structural strengthening of the position of the guilder (see also figure 3).

Nevertheless, things again went wrong in 1983, and on 21 March of that year the guilder was once more devalued against the Deutsche mark. By contrast with 1979, when the negotiations were possibly not handled entirely adequately, the bilateral devaluation in 1983 was a decision taken voluntarily by the Dutch government against the advice of the Nederlandsche Bank. The government favoured a devaluation with a view to an improvement of the Dutch competitive position, whereas the Bank did not wish to put confidence in the guilder, which had taken years to build up, at risk. The Bank highly disapproved of the government decision to agree to a 2 per cent devaluation against the Deutsche mark. There can be no doubt that the admission in 1985 by the then Minister of Finance, Onno Ruding, that the 1983 devaluation had been a mistake was hailed with some satisfaction at the Bank. Ruding drew

5 Boot (1992).

the conclusion drawn earlier by the Bank: 'Whatever happens to the Deutsche mark: we follow suit'.

3.3 *Assessment of policy consequences*

Any assessment of the position of the guilder vis-à-vis the Deutsche mark centres on two factors: deviation from the central rate and the Dutch/German interest rate differential. A good indicator of the strength or weakness of the guilder, combining as it does both the above factors, is the forward rate. Figure 2 below shows the development of the forward index, i.e. the percentage by which the forward rate deviates from the central rate.

The 1970s were marked by diverging developments, with the guilder alternately weak and strong against the Deutsche mark. A much calmer picture is in evidence in the 1980s, the strength of the guilder in the early 1980s, as well as in 1992 and 1993, showing up clearly.

The unrest in the 1970s reflects, on the one hand, the external uncertainties ensuing from the oil shocks in 1973 and 1979, as well as the increased uncertainties in the foreign exchange markets consequent on the collapse of the Bretton Woods system. On the other hand, a role was undoubtedly also played by the unfavourable economic perfor-

Figure 2 Forward index guilder/Deutsche mark

Monthly averages

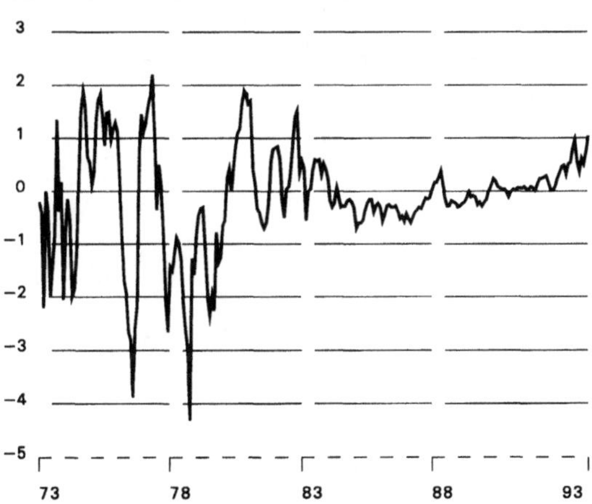

The forward index is the percentage deviation of the forward exchange rate from the central rate.

mance at home, as a result of which the 1980 labour income ratio was about 10 percentage points up on that on the eve of the first oil crisis, while the financial deficit was over 5 percentage points higher, and continued to expand further until a turnaround was effected in 1983. The 1980s saw a clearly discernible improvement in domestic economic conditions, brought on by considerable wage moderation and the start of the process of budget consolidation. In the period to 1990, the labour income ratio fell by over 10 percentage points (a drop later partly undone) while the budget deficit also decreased substantially. Monetary policy, increasingly aimed at pegging the guilder to the mark obviously also had a favourable effect on its position.

Figure 3 makes for greater insight into the development of the position of the guilder vis-à-vis the Deutsche mark. It compares the spot deviation (i.e. the difference between the central guilder/Deutsche mark rate and the spot guilder/Deutsche mark rate) and the forward deviation (i.e. the premium or discount of the guilder against the Deutsche

Figure 3 Development of the position of the guilder against the Deutsche mark

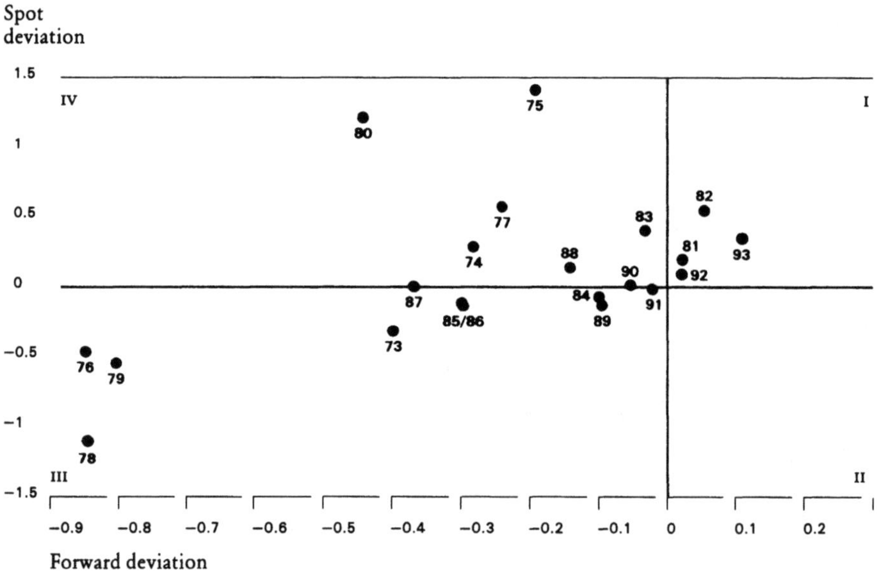

The spot deviation is the difference between the guilder/Deutsche mark central rate and the spot guilder/Deutsche mark exchange rate. A positive deviation signifies a strong position of the guilder against the Deutsche mark. The forward deviation is the premium or discount of the guilder against the Deutsche mark on the basis of the interest rate differential between the Dutch and the German three-month eurodeposit rate. When the Dutch interest rate is lower (higher) than the German rate, the guilder is at a premium (discount) versus the Deutsche mark

mark on the basis of the interest rate differential between three-month Euro-guilder and Euro-Deutsche mark rates). Figure 4 presents the changes in the foreign exchange reserves so as to permit assessment of the situation in respective years. It appears, among other things, that in 1981 the guilder was not as strong as figures 3 and 4 suggest.

Figure 3 contains four quadrants. Quadrant I implies a strong guilder against the Deutsche mark (positive spot deviation), while Dutch interest rates are lower than those in Germany (the guilder is standing at a premium). Quadrant II is empty. Quadrant III implies a weak and IV a strong guilder and Dutch interest rates exceeding those in Germany. Quadrant I is clearly the strongest and III the weakest from the viewpoint of the position of the guilder. In figure 3 the tendencies described earlier again show up markedly, especially the volatility recorded during the 1970s, the rapid shift at the end of that period towards the first, strongest quadrant and the movement to the left following the 1983 devaluation. Only in 1988-1989 does the damage done in 1983 seem to have been largely undone.

With hindsight, the Bank – so the somewhat cynical conclusion would seem to be – should be happy about the government's decision in 1983

Figure 4 Change in gold and foreign exchange reserves

Percentage of GNP

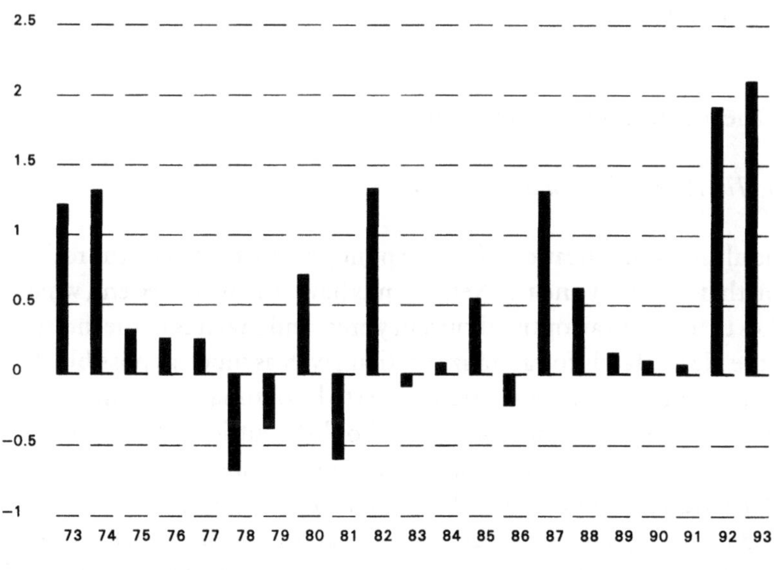

Change in gold and foreign exchange reserves excluding revaluation as percentage of GNP.

to devalue the guilder. Rarely has its exchange rate policy been so convincingly demonstrated to have been right. Thanks to this decision, as well as to the success later achieved in the field of inflation, the policy pursued by the Bank in the Netherlands has come to enjoy wide support, a factor which only adds to the strength of the guilder.

A question which could arise in connection with the events in 1979 and 1983 is to what extent the Bank has over time allowed sentiments with regard to the guilder to feed through to the exchange rate or to interest rates. Mr Boot's reflections on the 1979 devaluation indicate that from then on emphasis was to some extent shifted to the exchange rate. Yet this cannot be clearly concluded from the daily figures. If the percentage deviations of the Deutsche mark/guilder rate are plotted against the short-term interest rate differentials for the period 1979-1993, no clear picture emerges. (Owing to the abundance of observations, this graph is not shown here.) We do see, however, when looking at the period 1983-1993, that by comparison with the years 1979-1993, the interest rate differential and the deviation from the central rate have on average decreased. Compared with the period 1979-1993, the standard deviation of both the interest rate differential and the percentage deviation from the central rate were halved in the period 1983-1993. Some asymmetry is furthermore in evidence, as is also suggested by figure 3. The guilder is permitted to weaken up to a point, after which the (threat of a) further weakening prompts an interest rate rise. On the whole, a strengthening of the guilder is not, or to a lesser extent, followed by interest rate decreases.

4 The justification of Dutch policy

4.1 *The theory of optimal currency areas*

The ultimate justification of Dutch policy is constituted by the realization that Germany and the Netherlands have, to a major extent, what it takes to make up an optimal currency area, and that it is in the interests of the Netherlands to capitalize on that given as much as possible. We all know the theory. For a currency area to be optimal, economic developments in the countries concerned should be sufficiently similar. The less that is the case, which means that economic shocks are asymmetrical in nature, the more the real economic sector will have to be capable of adjustment (wage and price flexibility and/or mobility of the factors of production). The second requirement concerns the institutional characteristics of the labour market, in particular, and the openness of the economy. After all, the capability to adjust hinges on these institutional characteristics; moreover, the more open the economy, the more it stands to benefit from monetary union. The European countries had already concluded in the 1970s that the effectiveness of nominal exchange rate adjustments is rather small, real exchange rates undergoing only minor changes in the longer term.

The spate of literature generated by the plans to form a European monetary union has yielded new considerations. The pegging of the currency to the Deutsche mark could enhance the credibility of policy.[6] Phrased differently: this 'new' theory about optimal currency areas entails that the threshold to an optimal currency area such as EMU or a semi-optimal one such as the ERM could be reduced by the pegging as such. However, the turmoil in the ERM shows that this argument remains valid in the longer term only if the fixing of the exchange rate is underpinned by the actual economic developments.

However the theory of optimal currency areas works out in practice, there will be very few cases which meet all the required conditions for an optimal currency area. The 'safety net' is then constituted by the political will to bear the costs of a situation where not all conditions are fulfilled. Unfortunately, the formulation of that political will does not always make clear what those costs may be. They may take the form of income transfers to certain regions in the monetary union, but they could also entail relinquishing part of budgetary sovereignty. The experience gained after the German unification in 1990 shows, that if, on political grounds, too much is compromised on the fundamental economic conditions for an optimal currency area, the financial price may be very high.

4.2 *Germany and the Netherlands: an optimal currency area?*

The EC is not exactly what we would call an optimal currency area.[7] Only five countries fulfil the requirements for such an area to a reasonable degree, viz. the five which also figure in the scenario for a rapid establishment of a 'small' EMU (Germany, France, the Netherlands, Belgium and Denmark). This does not mean, however, that they meet all the requirements to a sufficient degree; labour market flexibility in particular still leaves much to be desired. This shortcoming can, however, be 'softened' by the political will to form Economic and Monetary Union, and to bear and share the ensuing costs.

6 E.g. Giavazzi and Pagano (1988).
7 Eichengreen (1990); Bayoumi and Eichengreen (1991).

Table 3 Measure of convergence with Germany (1983 - 1993)

	GDP		Inflation (CPI)		Unit wage costs		Short-term interest rates		Long-term interest rates	
	1	2	1	2	1	2	1	2	1	2
Germany	.	.	.	.	.	.	.	.	.	.
Netherlands	0.65	1	0.82	1	0.67	1	0.96	1	0.98	1
France	0.48	5	0.09	5	-0.06	5	0.01	6	0.45	5
Belgium	0.61	2	0.43	2	0.51	2	0.37	3	0.57	2
Denmark	0.17	6	-0.25	10	0.18	4	0.25	4	0.29	7
Italy	0.49	4	0.20	3	-0.39	9	-0.06	10	0.43	6
United Kingdom	0.22	7	0.03	7	-0.08	6	0.19	5	0.54	4
Spain	0.50	3	-0.03	8	-0.27	8	-0.05	9	0.56	3
Ireland	.	.	0.12	4	0.30	3	0.01	6	.	.
Portugal	.	.	0.04	6	-0.11	7	0.65	2	.	.
Greece	.	.	-0.22	9	-0.66	10	0.01	6	.	.

Column 1 gives the correlation coefficients; column 2 their ranking order.
Expanatory note: On the basis of quarterly data; for the interest rates, monthly data were used.

All variables in percentages: Short and long-term interest rates represent levels, the other variables changes on the previous corresponding period.

Table 3 shows, for the period 1983-1993, the convergence (on the basis of correlation coefficients) between a number of economic variables in Germany and their counterparts in the other EMS countries, as well as their ranking order.[8] Obviously much more sophisticated statistical calculations are conceivable, but in this context an impression of what place the Netherlands occupies on the list of European countries considered eligible for participation in a monetary union with Germany will suffice. In the first instance, the analysis focused on the years 1983-1993, because – as pointed out above – the guilder has been completely pegged to the mark only from 1983 onwards.

The objections which can be made to the simplicity of these calculations notwithstanding, the conclusion is warranted that as regards both the real economic sector, nominal developments and the financial markets, Germany and the Netherlands are very tightly linked. The Netherlands tops the list, and it is worth noting the difference between the correlation coefficients for the Netherlands and those for the other EC countries. A close second is Belgium, which is hardly surprising. If Greece and Portugal are left out of account, Italy, the UK and Spain lie at the other end of the spectrum. Small wonder that these three coun-

8 Calculations comparable to those underlying table 3 were made earlier by, among others, Van Paridon (1993).

Table 4 Measure of convergence with Germany (1989-1993)

Correlation coefficients

	GDP	Inflation (CPI)	Unit wage costs	Short-term interest rates	Long-term interest rates
Germany	.	.	.	.	.
Netherlands	0.74	0.55	0.75	0.96	0.99
France	0.56	-0.56	0.53	0.58	0.85
Belgium	0.71	-0.37	0.53	0.57	0.91
Denmark	0.61	-0.57	0.04	0.34	0.69

Explantory note: On the basis of quarterly data; for the interest rates, monthly data were used. See also the note to table 3.

tries were confronted with grave exchange rate problems in the autumn of 1992. Although caution needs to be exercised when using these correlation coefficients, the negative sign for the GDP relationship of the UK is worthy of note, indicating as it does that that country's cyclical pattern differs from that on the continent of Europe. It is not clear from table 3 where France and Denmark stand, two countries often cited as candidates for a core EMU. An assessment of the position of, for instance, France should make allowance for the fact that in the course of the 1980s, this country increasingly came to model its policy on Germany, a course leading to greater convergence with conditions there. Table 4 therefore repeats the calculations made earlier for the period 1989-1993.

On the whole, the outcomes are plausible, indicating that the correlation between the countries considered and Germany has strengthened considerably over the past decade. After all, practically all the correlation coefficients have gone up. The negative sign for the coefficients showing the inflation relationships with France, Belgium and Denmark reflects the inflationary consequences of German unification. By contrast with the Netherlands, inflation in these countries continued to decline after the unification, which had an upward impulse on prices in West Germany.

Tables 3 and 4 corroborate the impression that the Netherlands (one of the most open economies in Europe, together with Belgium and Ireland) and Germany have in fact been forming a currency union since 1983.

a First of all, the general economic developments in these countries are on average very similar. Earlier studies also showed that some 90 per cent of cyclical movements in German manufacturing output feed through (with only a very slight lag) to manufacturing output in the Netherlands. For a much broader aggregate such as GDP, the percentage is still about 75 per cent.[9]

b Secondly, there is a close similarity as far as nominal developments and conditions on the financial markets are concerned. Movements in German consumer prices are highly correlated with cyclical movements in Dutch consumer prices, the lag being no more than three months.[10]

c Thirdly, there are strong similarities between the German and Dutch labour markets where the nature of the process of wage determination is concerned.[11]

d In the fourth place, the Nederlandsche Bank has gained great credibility by pursuing a highly consistent policy. Any signs of the guilder weakening against the Deutsche mark, and short-term interest rates were raised, if necessary, considerably. This element of credibility made up for the initially still excessive public authority deficits. At the time of the last devaluation, in 1983, the financial deficit had, after all, been around 9 per cent of GDP, so that the Netherlands was still nowhere near to meeting the criteria for convergence later formulated in the Maastricht Treaty.

e Finally, the political and public will to keep the guilder pegged to the Deutsche mark strengthened in the course of the 1980s. Though the hard currency policy was at first regularly criticized, the criticisms died down as time went by and the policy proved successful. It has become clear to all that choosing Germany as the monetary anchor country was a logical step in the face of the reputation of the Bundesbank as one of the world's most independent central banks, with price stability as its overriding objective.

5 Conclusion

Conventional wisdom has it that the strength of the guilder lies in a reasonably sound fiscal policy, moderate nominal wage rises and a convincing monetary policy – objectives pursued not for a year or so, but over a series of years. The arguments are far from spectacular, but that does not make them less valid or topical. The Dutch performance in the field of public finance may not be outstanding, but over the past few years it has not been very bad either. In the course of the years, the

9 Berk (1992); Bikker (1993).
10 Bikker (1993).
11 Bruno and Sachs (1985).

public sector financial deficit has dropped (from a high of 9.4 per cent of GDP in 1982 to about 4 per cent in 1993) and the government is more or less managing to adhere to this policy, in spite of the unfavourable cyclical situation and adverse developments in other European countries: elsewhere deficits are going up (considerably), here the deficit is not decreasing any further. Secondly, nominal wage increases are comparatively modest in the Netherlands. This contributes to the required low rate of inflation and a reasonably healthy competitive position. In the third place, the Dutch monetary authorities have been highly successful in their unceasing efforts to persuade the markets that Dutch monetary policy assigns overriding priority to the exchange rate, not to interest rate levels. Interest rate decreases are politically popular, but may – if brought about at the wrong time – undermine the exchange rate.

As we have seen, the strength of the guilder does not come out of the blue, it is the result of significant policy efforts with regard to the budget, wages and monetary developments. Monetary policy alone cannot do the job; but without the highly consistent policy of the Nederlandsche Bank and the expected continuation of this policy in the future, the guilder would surely not be as strong as it has been for a number of years already, as evidenced by for example the problems confronting several countries with strong fundamentals in the summer of 1993. The cornerstone of Dutch monetary policy is its orientation towards the Deutsche mark. In the 1980s, the Netherlands achieved a hard currency through the pursuit of this policy, though not without effort and pain. In line with the exchange rate objective, nominal wages in the Netherlands were moderated very substantially in the first half of the 1980s and especially after 1982, though the advantages of a hard currency option (higher rates of growth and employment, and a decrease in the interest rate differentials vis-à-vis Germany) manifested themselves completely and very clearly only in the second half of the 1980s. In short, the benefits of the hard currency strategy accrued in the longer run only.

Even today, the hard currency policy modelled on Germany has a price. That is because the anchor country is itself now facing difficulties, generated by the German unification. Today we import not just the pros, but also the cons, of monetary union. To some extent, the Netherlands has, over the past few years, therefore had to contend with the same problems as Germany.

a Consumer price rises accelerated from 2.5 per cent in 1990 to 3.7 per cent in 1992 (comparable to the German figures of 2.7 per cent in 1990 and 4.0 per cent in 1992). In the EC as a whole, price rises decelerated during that period (from 5.5 per cent to 4.3 per cent).

b Profitability came under pressure. The labour income ratio went up from over 81 per cent in 1990 to nearly 86 per cent in 1992 (Germany 76 per cent in 1990; nearly 81 per cent in 1992), while in France and Italy it was wellnigh stabilized.

c Our economies being as integrated as they are, both in a monetary sense and in the real sphere, the Netherlands has imported not only German price and wage movements, but also German interest rate levels, even though we have succeeded in maintaining the slightly negative interest rate differentials vis-à-vis Germany.

Yet there is no reason to abandon the peg to the Deutsche mark; the short-term disadvantages felt by the Netherlands and the other EMS countries cannot outstrip the long-term advantages. There being as yet no alternative for the German anchor, Germany has to be supported in its efforts to regain monetary stability. In the meantime, the other European countries can limit the damage by conducting a sound policy at home. As noted earlier, the Netherlands may have experienced the same problems as Germany, but not to the same degree. That is only logical, as the Dutch policy mix (i.e. the relationship between monetary and fiscal policy) was much more in balance than that in Germany. The Netherlands' financial deficit has been going down whereas that in Germany has expanded considerably. A good overall policy pays off, witness the relatively mild recession in the Netherlands. On the other hand, the Dutch unemployment rate has been rising materially since mid-1992, owing, on the one hand, to the cyclical slowdown, and, on the other, to the continuing increase in the supply of labour. However, if we look at the development of the number of jobs (an expansion of over 1 per cent for 1992 and 1993 combined), the Netherlands still compares favourably (in spite of the too strong increase in real labour costs since the end-1980s) with the rest of Europe (where the number of jobs shrank by a total of around 2 per cent in 1992 and 1993 combined).

The recession, and the appreciation of the guilder following the crisis within the ERM, led to a complete turnaround in the development of inflation in the Netherlands in 1993. A similar weakening of inflation seems in the offing in Germany. Present expectations are that in 1994 labour costs in Germany will also develop favourably. If these developments persist, Germany will again be deserving of its position as monetary anchor of Europe and André Szász has every reason for contentment. It was, after all, he who always consistently propagated both the theory and practice of pegging the guilder to the Deutsche mark; time has proved him increasingly right.

References

Bayoumi, T. and B. Eichengreen (1991), Shocking aspects of European monetary integration, *NBER Working Paper*, no. 3949, Cambridge (Massachusetts).

Berk, J.M. (1992), Conjuncturele vervlechting Nederland-Duitsland, *De Nederlandsche Bank, Domestic Research Department Series*, no. 146.

Bikker, J.A. (1993), A leading indicator of inflation for the Netherlands, *De Nederlandsche Bank, Quarterly Bulletin* 93/3, pp. 43-57.

Boot, D.H. (1992), *Achter de coulissen van het beleid*, Amsterdam.

Bruno, M. and J. Sachs (1985), *The economics of world-wide stagflation*, Oxford.

Eichengreen, B. (1990), Is Europe an optimum currency area? *NBER Working Paper*, no. 3579, Cambridge (Massachusetts).

Giavazzi, F. and M. Pagano (1988), The advantage of tying one's hands: EMS discipline and central bank credibility, *European Economic Review*, vol. 32, no. 5, pp. 1055-1075.

Paridon, C.W.A.M. van (1993), *Persoonlijke relatie of knellende band? Over economische ontwikkelingen in Duitsland en de invloed op Nederland*, inaugural lecture on the occasion of assuming to the office of professor at the University of Amsterdam (VU).

Puchinger, G. (1978), *Dr Jelle Zijlstra, gesprekken en geschriften*, Naarden.

Rutten, F.W. (1987), Bijsturen van de economie, *Economisch Statistische Berichten*, no. 3136, pp. 4-7.

Szász, A. (1988), *Monetaire diplomatie: Nederlands internationale monetaire politiek* 1958-1987, Doctoral thesis, Leiden/Antwerpen.

Szász, A. (1989), Monetary policy in the European Community from the viewpoint of the Nederlandsche Bank, *De Nederladsche Bank, Quarterly Bulletin* 89/1, pp. 21-27.

Wellink, A.H.E.M. (1985), In praise of price movements, *De Nederlandsche Bank, Quarterley Bulletin* 1985/3, pp. 31-36.

The Exchange Rate Mechanism after the Basle/Nyborg Agreement

Henning Dalgaard

1 Introduction

The decision by the finance ministers of the European Union and central bank governors on 2 August 1993 to widen the margins in the European Exchange Rate Mechanism to 15 per cent was the culmination of a year, where one crisis succeeded the other. In reality this decision meant that the exchange rate cooperation as we have known it for more than 20 years ceased to exist, and was replaced by something much vaguer and less binding. I shall try here to present my personal view on three questions:

- Why did the system work well for so long?
- What went wrong in 1992?
- Would it be possible – and desirable – to re-establish the system?

I shall put some weight on the practical and technical aspects of the problems, since they are not normally given much attention, but are nevertheless of considerable importance.

2 The main features of the ERM

Exchange rate stability always depends on the credibility of the authorities involved. The credibility of the ERM depended on the credibility of the participating countries and the credibility of the system itself. The credibility of the exchange rate policy of a country depends on the economic situation and policies of the country. In the years prior to the summer of 1992 this credibility was strongly supported by a feeling in the market that the move towards Economic and Monetary Union was unstoppable, and that the risk of exchange rate changes therefore was minimal. The credibility of the system was a consequence of the existing rules and understandings. The EMS Agreement between the central banks containing the rules of the system is very detailed, but there are a few simple features, which are decisive for the system's credibility.

Firstly, there is the clear and unconditional obligation to maintain exchange rates within the published limits. Secondly, the ERM is a multilateral arrangement. Unilateral decisions on exchange rates are therefore, in principle, not possible. This limits of course the risk that any country would quickly decide to devalue its currency. This aspect of the arrangement was consciously enhanced by the procedure, which was decided for realignments. A realignment would take place only after a discussion in the Monetary Committee, and – more importantly – only after a meeting of all finance ministers and central bank governors had reached agreement on what to do. This procedure helped to convince the market that realignment decisions were not taken lightly, and that there was full agreement on decisions. Also the extensive procedure meant that, after a realignment another such decision was not likely to be taken in the near future because this would necessitate a new meeting of ministers and governors. Finally, credibility was reinforced by the unlimited credit facilities made available for interventions at the margin, ensuring that a central bank would not have to stop intervening due to a shortage of funds.

In 1987 these rules were supplemented by an understanding between central banks on how exchange rates should effectively be defended – the famous Basle/Nyborg Agreement. The main idea of this understanding was that central banks should defend their currencies in a flexible way by using all available instruments, in particular:
- intervention to neutralize temporary and limited flows;
- interest rate changes to influence the cost of taking positions in a currency; and
- exchange rate movements – within the fluctuation band – to increase the exchange rate risk (the closer a currency comes to its lower limit, the bigger the likelihood that its next move will be a strengthening, provided of course that there is confidence in its central rate).

In the following years the skilful use of these instruments proved sufficient to handle many situations where pressure was built up. It was recognized from the outset that these techniques had their limitations. If a situation developed where the market expected a substantial devaluation within a short period, it would be difficult to maintain stable rates, since even sizeable interest rate increases would weigh little compared to the expected gain. In such a situation a country would have to improve credibility by tightening economic policy in general, especially fiscal policy. In some cases these measures might also have to be supplemented with a depreciation of the central rate.

Starting in the early eighties a practice had been developed to limit disturbances from central rate changes. Realignments were normally kept so small that speculation in a realignment would be uninteresting. With margins of 2.25 per cent, adjustments of up to 4.5 per cent would be possible without profit to speculators, provided that the devaluing currency before the realignment was near the lower limit (which was typically the case) and that it moved close to the upper limit immediately after the realignment (which happened in many cases). Of course, exchange rate movements prior to and following realignments were not always so ideal. Nevertheless, on many occasions the modest size of realignments, combined with some shift in positions in the ERM band, gave rise to situations where speculators had little or no gain, even when they correctly foresaw a realignment. To prevent acute exchange crises it was understood that realignments had to be timely. This meant that they should be made before the market became convinced that they were imminent. Together, these rules and practices resulted in a situation, where realignment expectations were rare and speculations normally moderate, because the likely profit was small.

This does not mean, of course, that the system was perfect. In practice it was hardly ever possible to make a timely realignment, because the political resistance against devaluations was so strong that realignments normally took place only after severe pressure in the foreign exchange market. Also, the ERM central banks never succeeded in agreeing on a common policy against the US dollar. As all ERM currencies necessarily had to move in step against third currencies, the result was basically that the dollar level was decided by the Deutsche mark/dollar rate. Last but not least, a prerequisite for fixed exchange rates was coordinated decisions on monetary policy, in particular the level of interest rates. In practice, this problem was resolved by Germany deciding on German interest rates and other countries adjusting their policies to that of Germany.

3 Developments in the ERM until the spring of 1992

Although there were a number of realignments in the ERM before January 1987, the rules and an increasing convergence between ERM countries ensured that they did not occur too often, and were normally modest in size. Most importantly, realignments never went beyond a correction of a past deterioration of a country's competitive position. In fact, in most cases the competitive position was only partly restored as countries preferred to use a relatively strong exchange rate to dampen inflation. There was never any attempt to make competitive devaluations. From January 1987 to September 1992 – that is for more than 5 years – the ERM went without realignments. In this period the

Italian lira narrowed its margins from 6 per cent to 2.25 per cent, and the British pound, the Spanish peseta and the Portuguese escudo joined the system. Norway, Sweden and Finland demonstrated their interest in participating in the ERM by associating their currencies to the ECU. So on the surface the ERM did extremely well. More fundamentally, however, problems were building up.

Some of the participating currencies became increasingly less competitive. However, in the foreign exchange markets this was completely overshadowed by two factors. Firstly, the reunification of Germany weakened the German economy, relieving the pressure on the system. Secondly, confidence in the movement towards a monetary union led market participants to underestimate the exchange risk. International capital, therefore, moved to the weaker-currency countries, where interest rates were high. Without external pressure, no one wanted to take the initiative for a realignment. At the same time different attitudes to monetary policy began to be felt. It is ironic, that at a time at which there was more convergence on inflation and growth than perhaps at any time in the history of European exchange rate cooperation, the differences in the approach to monetary policy should give rise to problems. In all countries inflation was relatively low and growth very slow. But although German inflation was only moderately higher than elsewhere, the traditional German aversion against inflation meant that Germany felt it necessary to follow a relatively tight monetary policy whereas most other member countries wanted lower interest rates. The basic principles of the system were also undermined. The way the new members were taken into the system gave the impression that the central rates were decided by these countries alone, and that, therefore, the common commitment to these rates was smaller. As a result of these factors, the stability of the system became very dependent on continued progress towards a monetary union.

4 Mounting tensions in the ERM

The troubles began on 2 June 1992, when a Danish referendum on the Maastricht Treaty resulted in a majority of no votes. This invigorated opposition to the Maastricht Treaty in other countries, and gradually a feeling spread in the market that the establishment of EMU might not be so certain in the foreseeable future. This undermined the very high degree of credibility in the existing central rates, and the market started to look again at the fundamental economic situation in the different countries. The change of mood was reinforced by the fact that the Finnish markka had been devalued by more than 10 per cent in

November 1991, the first major devaluation of a European currency for many years. This had reminded the market that major exchange rate movements were still a possibility.

During the summer the doubts about the future of EMU rose, and as the date of the French referendum on the Maastricht Treaty (20 September 1992) came closer – with increasing doubt about the result – the market became nervous. This nervousness was first seen in the Italian market, where the lira came under pressure from early September. This looked like a traditional crisis, and Italy reacted in the traditional way by raising interest rates, by letting the exchange rate decline within the band, and by intervening. Towards the middle of the month these interventions rose to unprecedented amounts, and it was decided to devalue the lira by 7 per cent against the other currencies. Despite the fact that this was the most severe crisis in the ERM for many years, the decision was not taken according to the agreed procedure. No meeting was called for ministers and governors. Not even the Monetary Committee was called in. Instead the decision was taken after telephone concertation between the parties involved. The use of this procedure was taken by the market as a sign that authorities were not willing to confront the problems of the system. Never before had a realignment decision carried so little credibility.

Only three days later the crisis re-emerged, now concentrating on the British pound, but once again also hurting the Italian lira. The major reason for this crisis was a widespread feeling in the market that two major member countries, i.e. Germany and the United Kingdom, were in basic disagreement, and that they were not willing to defend the existing central rate. This time the reaction was fast, and very unusual. A meeting of the Monetary Committee was held, but again there was no meeting of ministers and governors. There was no attempt to seek a traditional solution with an adjustment of individual currencies. Instead the United Kingdom and Italy suspended their participation in the ERM. One of the reasons for this dramatic decision after only a few days of tension was that capital flows – and therefore interventions – rose to a level far beyond what had been seen before.

There are many reasons for the huge capital flows. During recent years exchange restrictions have been abolished and capital markets liberalised in most countries in the western world. As a consequence capital markets have been internationalised to an extent never seen before. Major investors like insurance companies, pension funds, investment funds, etc. have diversified their investments into a number of currencies. Technically this has been possible because many markets have improved in liquidity, and because new information technology ensures instant information all over the world on almost any market. With big outstanding positions, the consequences of a lack of confidence in a currency of course increase. There are much bigger positions to be unwound or hedged. And there is also a risk of much bigger speculative positions being built up in cases in which an exchange rate adjustment is expected. The quick and strong reactions of the market are partly the result of the fast flow of information, but even more they are a consequence of a move towards professional management of the enormous capital stock. Professional fund managers are ready to react immediately and forcefully to hedge risks or to exploit profit possibilities.

Big and sudden capital flows were always caused by mistrust in the authorities' will – or ability – to maintain stable exchange rates. During the last quarter of 1992 and the beginning of 1993 there were other cases of big capital flows. In these cases, however, the ordinary measures, sometimes combined with traditional adjustments of one or two currencies, were enough to quieten the situation. During the spring of 1993 the situation seemed to normalize, especially for the narrow band currencies. Tensions were decreasing in the currency markets and the exchange rates moved closer to the central rates. There was a considerable reflow of funds to countries which had been under pressure, and interest rates were declining in a number of countries to the same level as in Germany, or even lower.

5 The final break down of the ERM

However, in late June tensions reappeared once again. Interest rate differentials increased, and intervention became very substantial. When tensions became acute in late July, a realignment was discussed in the weekend 31 July – 1 August. For the first time since January 1987 the full procedure was used. The possible solutions were discussed in a meeting of the Monetary Committee and the final decision was taken in a full meeting of finance ministers and central bank governors. Unfortunately, it proved to be impossible to agree on a traditional solution, maintaining the rules of the system. After long and acrimonious discussions it was decided to maintain central rates unchanged, but to expand margins from 2.25 per cent (for Spain and Portugal 6 per cent) to 15 per cent. This was an enormous expansion of margins, allowing all countries to move much further than in any realignment since the beginning of the system in 1979. In reality it meant that the intervention limits were without relevance. There was no expectation that any of the currencies would reach the limits in the foreseeable future, and, consequently, the system of unlimited intervention credits was in practice abrogated. In connection with the official widening of the margins, Germany and the Netherlands declared that they would nevertheless continue to observe the old 2.25 per cent margins between their currencies. As the Dutch guilder had not been near the intervention limits for more than 10 years this decision was of little practical importance.

The break down of the system came at a moment at which there was in many respects better convergence of the economies of the remaining participating countries than before, particularly concerning inflation and growth. In Germany, France, the Benelux countries, Ireland, and Denmark inflation varied from below 2 per cent to below 4 per cent, and economic growth was also not far out of line, although regrettably at a very low level. It is true that there was some apparent disagreement on the best monetary policy to follow as Germany seemed to prefer a somewhat stricter monetary policy than the other participating countries. The difference was, however, not that big. Germany did lower interest rates and although there was some grumbling, the other countries basically accepted to let Germany decide the speed of interest rate reductions. At the same time it was generally recognized that the central rates between the remaining countries reflected the fundamental economic situation well. One can never tell what is the 'correct' central rate between two currencies, but the existing rates were certainly well within the margin of uncertainty.

Under these circumstances, one can wonder, what caused the pressure to start in June, and especially why it intensified so much towards the end of July. There were several reasons for this sudden turnabout in the mood of the market. The most important factor probably was that events gave the market the impression that there was a fundamental disagreement between Germany and France concerning the handling of the exchange markets. The level of activity in the German economy was seen to be improving. This of course lessened the pressure for lower interest rates in Germany, and it was feared that the Bundesbank would use this possibility for delaying further relaxation of its monetary policy. At the same time there was a widespread belief that Germany was not willing to continue to accept huge interventions, as they were seen as a threat to German monetary stability. On the other side the French economy was seen as weakening, and the French authorities were supposed to be very eager to reduce interest rates and, therefore, presumably not willing to wait and follow the movements of the Bundesbank. The mistrust of the market was reinforced as the market had just experienced a year, in which one government after another had made solemn statements that they would defend their currency forever, only to give in to pressure shortly after. Often these policy-reaffirmations were followed by depreciations of considerable size, giving rise to enormous profit to speculators. This led to a loss of credibility in public statements. In particular, authorities were unable to convince markets that they were willing and able to continue to maintain strict monetary policies despite their weak economies. The market therefore got the impression that the countries with weaker currencies might not be willing to fulfil the conditions for remaining in the system, while the country with the strong currency (Germany) was wavering in its support for the system. As a result capital flows surged in late July, leading to the decision to widen the margins.

6 Lessons from the crises

From the first days of the exchange rate cooperation there have been some critics, who have insisted that a system with fixed-but-adjustable exchange rates cannot survive for long, because tying exchange rates together requires more convergence and coordination than countries are willing to accept. After the break down of the system these critics must feel that their point has been proven. But is this really the lesson from this crisis? A number of factors are relevant in evaluating the events.

Firstly, the fact that five countries lived happily with exchange rate cooperation, from the beginning in 1972 until 1993, shows that the system had some ability to survive. Secondly, the system was not always handled well, and not always according to the agreed rules. A more convincing handling by the authorities – especially since the autumn of 1992 – might have made a difference. Thirdly, the huge capital flows that preceded the breakdown were caused by market expectations of aggressive interest rate reductions in a number of countries, with resulting declines in exchange rates. These soft interest-rate policies have not materialized, and exchange rates have in practice only briefly and to a very limited extent moved away from the old limits. So if authorities would have had sufficient credibility at the time when they declared that they would maintain a firm monetary policy, the pressure might not have come up. It should not be forgotten that the suspicion of the market was not pure imagination, but was based on conflicting signals sent out by ministers, central banks and politicians. Fourthly, the Deutsche Bundesbank was perhaps unnecessarily scared by the big interventions. If the central rates were reasonable – and all countries seemed to concur on this – and if the involved central banks were willing to make position-taking expensive, the flows should have been shortlived and, therefore, of little consequence for monetary conditions in Germany.

Perhaps the fundamental problem was that the system was too successful for a while – from 1987 to 1992 – and that therefore all – authorities, markets, etc. – came to expect too much from it. When the exchange rate cooperation was established no one had expected – or wanted – the system to ensure absolutely fixed exchange rates. It was acknowledged that as long as economic development differed from one country to another, exchange rate adjustments would be necessary from time to time. The benefits of the system were that it helped to concentrate the political will in the weaker countries on improving convergence with the strongest countries, and contributed to the avoidance of erratic fluctuations in exchange rates. In these two respects the system worked well. In the weaker countries it did help foster anti-inflationary policies, and exchange rates did move much more smoothly than one normally sees between floating currencies. The system also succeeded in preventing competitive devaluations. In fact, the development since 1992 has shown how wild fluctuations in the foreign exchange markets can be without a properly working system. The two currencies which left the system – the Italian lira and the British pound – depreciated by about 25 per cent and 15 per cent respectively, although the pound has recovered somewhat lately. And even currencies remaining in the system have moved excessively: the Spanish peseta has depreciated by almost 25 per cent. Even if such exchange rate movements cannot be called competitive devaluations as the countries had to give in to market pressure, they certainly are a sign of disorderly exchange markets.

From this perspective it is regrettable that the system has been discarded so lightly, and at a moment where the need for such drastic action was not really there. Developments after 2 August confirm this view. Even without the support of the system, exchange rates moved significantly away from the former limits for only a brief period. With full support from all participating countries it should have been possible to maintain the limits.

Nevertheless, now that the system is no longer operative, it may not be so easy to reinstate it. For the time being there seems to be very little support for the idea of returning to narrow margins any time soon. Indeed, there is some thought that one might move directly from the present situation to a monetary union. However, opinions may change again, and it may be worth giving a few thoughts to the way a system with narrow margins should work. Even if a few selected countries might be willing and able to establish a monetary union soon, a narrow margin system might be useful for those countries which could not join immediately. Also, one should not exclude the possibility that the way to the monetary union might take longer time than hoped for. In that case there would be a risk that countries with floating exchange rates will prove to be less rigid in their anti-inflationary policies. Not immediately, of course, but who can guarantee what will happen in a few years time after the next election?

There are still good reasons to try to seek stability in exchange rates – and in particular between the currencies of the European Union, and it is still likely that the existence of a framework for cooperation, such as the ERM, will promote such stability. It would indeed be surprising, if the result were to be that the last 20 year-long struggle to make the exchange rate cooperation work were to be discarded entirely. The importance of the ERM has extended far beyond the simple exchange rate cooperation. In fact, much of European economic policy cooperation has been centered around the ERM, and one should not underestimate the risk that this cooperation could degenerate if the ERM remains inoperative for any length of time.

7 Conditions for a return to ERM

It is, of course, possible to imagine different rules for an exchange rate system. Personally I see, however, no reason to discard the ERM. A lot of thought has gone into the creation of the snake system back in 1971, and the technical foundation was strong enough to survive the change into the EMS in 1979. It will not be easy to improve upon the basic rules as they are today, although naturally, there are details, which could be discussed. To make a return to the ERM with narrow margins a success requires, however, not so much changes of rules as a return to the original fundamentals of the system.

First and foremost, the central rates from the outset must be accepted by the market as being reasonable. This still leaves room for some choice, since the fixing of central rates is not an exact science, and since the acceptable level will depend on policy choices in the different countries. The primary condition for having the market accept the central rates is that all participating countries are seen to be fully endorsing them. There should, therefore, be no unilateral fixing of central rates. It should also be made clear to the market that all governments and central banks are in full agreement on the central rates, and that all central banks are ready to defend these rates to the extent necessary, using all available instruments. This implies that countries which see their currency weaken must be willing not only to intervene, but also to increase interest rates in order to make speculation more expensive. Countries with rising exchange rates should accept even very substantial intervention sales of their currency without complaint. These points are essential, because experience has shown that crises become dangerous if only there is doubt about the will of the authorities to defend the rates.

In the perfect world, necessary interest rate changes would be distributed among strong and weak countries according to mutual agreement. In real life the system could survive as it is at present, where Germany decides its own rates and all others adjust to that. The working of the system will, of course, be facilitated to the extent that Germany finds it possible to take the situation in the ERM into consideration in setting interest rates.

As regards the use of intervention, there may be good arguments in favour of intramarginal intervention to counteract moderate and short-lived pressures. But if tensions take on a substantial size, exchange rates should normally be allowed to move to the intervention margin. Provided that there is confidence in the central rates, this will increase the exchange risk for speculators. The Danish experience confirms this reasoning. For several years Danmarks Nationalbank consistently used the whole fluctuation band. When signs of pressure appeared, the rate of the krone was allowed to move to its lowest level, with the effect that domestic customers always supported the krone as they were confident that the central rate would be maintained and that the krone's weak position in the band was a good opportunity to sell foreign currency. Unfortunately, foreigners were not always equally convinced of the stability of the central rate. The main argument against letting the rate move to the limit, is that it is seen as a sign of weakness and that the exchange rate movement will tend to increase the problem. This attitude has developed, however, precisely because central banks have defended intramarginal rates, often at a high cost. If it was normal practice that rates were allowed to move to the margins when there was a surplus demand or supply in the market, then the drama of reaching the margin would disappear. This was by the way how the system was intended to work from the outset.

It should be important that central rates are credible, not only at the restart of the system, but also at any time in the future. It should therefore not be accepted that the credibility of exchange rates is undermined by a gradual deviation of cost developments and other macroeconomic variables. Necessary adjustments should be made in a timely manner, i.e. before sizeable speculation gets started. Great care would need to be taken to ensure that all changes are presented as agreed conclusions after careful deliberations at the highest level.

The conditions mentioned here basically mean unchanged rules, but stronger will to follow the rules. There may be other less important rules, which could be changed, for instance concerning the length and remuneration of intervention credits. Whereas the right to unlimited intervention credits is very important for the credibility of the system, the exact details matter less. With very liquid international capital markets, any ERM country is in a position where it can raise any amount of foreign currency in the international capital markets very quickly. Should potential creditor countries find quick repayment of intervention credits important to safeguard their monetary policy, official intervention credits need not run for more than a short period.

It is often said that the enormous amount of capital, which is floating around in the world, makes it impossible to defend fixed exchange rates. I do not think that this is true. Capital flows are decided by a big number of companies and persons. It seems unlikely that they would be able to gang up to bring down a currency. But if situations arise where it looks likely that the possible gain far outweighs the cost (in the form of an interest rate differential and a risk premium) many will – independently – try go get a share of the profit. So countries should take care to ensure that it never looks likely that they will have to accept a sizeable devaluation soon. This was the situation in the years from 1987 to 1992 where capital flows gave rise to few cases of serious pressure in the ERM.

So my conclusion would be that the break down of the ERM was not due to technical problems, but to a lack of political will to fulfil the conditions which would allow the system to work. It might even have been sufficient if public statements had been more supportive. It will be more difficult, but not impossible, to re-establish the system, provided that the political will is there. This may be unlikely for the time being, but the advantages of a system to promote exchange rate stability are big enough to make it worth-while hoping for a new political initiative. Perhaps an opportunity will arrive when the European economies start to expand again, hopefully in the not too distant future.

The importance of monetary targeting in the Economic and Monetary Union

Wolfgang Rieke

1 The Bundesbank's anchor role

When asked for his reaction to the plans for a European Central Bank a couple of years ago Alan Greenspan, chairman of the US Federal Reserve Board, is said to have replied: 'But Europe has the Bundesbank'.

The European Monetary System was still in good working order and some saw it already functioning as a 'quasi-monetary union'. Over the years the Deutsche mark had emerged as Europe's key currency to which other countries, inside and outside the Community, effectively pegged their exchange rate. Not the ECU, but the Deutsche mark was 'at the centre of the system'.[1] Central banks used the Deutsche mark for intervention purposes in the EMS and built up large Deutsche mark reserve holdings over time for this purpose. By implication or design, an increasing number of countries 'anchored' their monetary policy to that of the Bundesbank, hoping thereby to gain credibility for their efforts to reduce inflation to tolerable levels and build a solid foundation for durable monetary stability.

Adoption by the Bundesbank of annual targets for a key monetary aggregate – initially central bank money as a proxy for M3, and later M3 itself – effectively pre-determined the monetary policy stance not only for West Germany, but also for other countries. Some of them continued to announce their own monetary targets, using definitions and quantitative deductions of their own choosing, perhaps seeking to keep alive a semblance of monetary autonomy.

Acceptance of the Bundesbank's 'anchor' role did not mean that interest rates in other countries automatically, or even rapidly, converged to German levels. Rather, German interest rates were likely to mark the lower limit below which interest rates in Europe were unlikely to fall.

1 The Annex to the Conclusions of the Presidency of the European Council held in Bremen on 6 and 7 July 1978 stated: 'The European Currency Unit (ECU) will be at the centre of the system; in particular, it will be used as a means of settlement between EEC monetary authorities'.

Higher inflation rates in most if not all partner countries, and the implicit risk of exchange rate realignment from time to time to correct for a country's loss in cost and price competitiveness proved reason enough for higher short as well as long-term nominal interest rates, reflecting varying risk premiums. In some instances, high domestic inflation called for higher interest rates than necessary to stabilize the exchange rate within the band of the Exchange Rate Mechanism, causing large capital inflows that in turn made monetary control more difficult. Most affected were countries that had only recently liberalized cross-border capital movements or were in the process of doing so. Ironically, this experience contradicted concerns that removal of capital restrictions might cause large capital outflows, putting downward pressure on the exchange rate and forcing the central bank to resort to intervention supported by tighter monetary policy in the attempt to stabilize the exchange rate within the fluctuation band.

2 The inconsistent triangle

Full liberalization of capital movements within the Community and vis-à-vis third countries, finally agreed upon in 1988 as part of the Community's internal market program, was quickly seized upon in support of demands for a common monetary policy. An exchange rate system of the EMS type with fixed (though adjustable) rates and narrow bands, virtually free capital movements and national monetary policy autonomy was claimed to constitute an 'inconsistent triangle'. Hence the calls for a common monetary policy that would somehow spirit away the inconsistency. Some of the participants in the EMS had never left any doubt that acceptance of a fixed rate regime and of unrestricted capital flows had left them with little if any monetary policy autonomy, and they had acted accordingly. Other participants pushed strongly for a regime change aimed at common monetary decision-making in anticipation of the move to full monetary union.

Alongside, and going beyond the 'inconsistent triangle' logic, the implicit asymmetry of the system and its management increasingly came under attack along two lines: first, the Bundesbank's obvious unwillingness to apply intervention and monetary policy fully to the defence of agreed central rates in the ERM; second, the near-exclusive concentration of the Bundesbank's monetary policy on Germany's inflation problem and above target growth of M3 following unification, and its virtual neglect of broader European requirements.

German concerns about the expansionary effects of intervention on domestic bank liquidity or on the money supply (depending on the channels through which funds moved into Deutsche mark) and the Bundesbank's stubborn adherence to an annual money supply target had to be taken seriously, as events would show more than once, but they were not willingly accepted. For one thing, the Bundesbank was clearly felt to be capable of dealing with the monetary side-effects of intervention, and interest rate action to help stabilize exchange rates was seen to be a shared responsibility of both the creditor and the debtor central bank. For another, money supply targeting had gone somewhat out of fashion, as money demand functions proved less stable than originally foreseen in many countries. The Bundesbank's insistence on M3 as a fairly reliable monetary indicator and target variable was at best seen as old-fashioned and obstinate, at worst as a welcome pretext to pursue its own single-minded monetary policy.

From a German perspective – not only that of the Bundesbank – a common monetary policy had to wait until the start of the third stage of EMU. Only then would the required degree of convergence of economic and other policies of participating Member States and their actual performance, especially the trend of relative prices and costs, assure that 'the necessary conditions for the adoption of a single currency'[2] would be firmly in place. The criteria by which 'the achievement of a high degree of sustainable convergence' will have to be judged are set out in some detail in the Treaty.[3] The need for, and precise nature of these criteria were a subject of much debate in the preparation of the Treaty; so is the stringency with which they are to be applied, now that most Member States are considered unlikely to fulfil all or most of the criteria for some considerable time ahead, if ever.

The recent EMS crisis of 1992-93 should serve as a warning that lack of sustainable convergence in critical areas of economic policy and performance will at some point in time create severe problems for countries participating in a system of fixed exchange rates, and that it would also do so in a single currency area. 'Opting out' of the ERM and widening of the fluctuation margins were both excluded on political grounds, until they became inevitable to deal with dilemma situations which were recognized as politically even more unacceptable. A break-up of EMU – once it is in place – will by definition be ruled out as an available option to deal with problems arising from lack of economic convergence, or for other reasons. All the more reason to make sure

2 Article 109j of the Treaty on European Union.

3 Article 109j.1 and the Protocol on the Convergence Criteria referred to in Article 109j of the Treaty on European Union.

that the necessary conditions are in place that will exclude all risks of serious 'dilemma situations' arising at some later stage.

3 The single monetary policy in stage three

In the final stage of EMU, the newly established European System of Central Banks will have as its primary objective to maintain price stability. Without prejudice to this objective, the ESCB will also be expected 'to support the general economic policies in the Community'.[4] This cannot mean that the ESCB will be expected to accommodate developments and problems arising from lack of sustainable convergence in other policy areas, and their consequences for inflation in the conduct of the single monetary policy entrusted to it. Nor can it mean that the ESCB will be expected to be a party in efforts to maintain agreed fixed exchange rates with other member currencies in an EMS-type arrangement on the basis of 'symmetry of burden sharing' as far as intervention and interest rate action is concerned, or in such arrangements with major third currencies.

The extensive debates about the many issues relating to the role of a central bank – not only in the special EMU context – suggest that adoption of a money supply target would be an important help towards achieving the objectives of a single monetary policy in EMU. The Bundesbank's experience with a medium-term oriented monetary policy approach centred on a money supply target strongly supports the case for such an approach, notwithstanding the more recent difficulties arising in part from German unification. The arguments need not be repeated in great detail. Suffice it to say that the relatively short and thus operationally exploitable lags between instrument use and money supply effects provide strong support for a strategy focused on an intermediate target. Its ex ante discipline affects not only the central bank itself, but also government, employers' 'organizations' and trade unions, financial markets and the wider public. The formation of inflation expectations is likely to be positively influenced by the commitment to a monetary target that is seen to leave little or no room for the monetary financing of inflationary impulses in the economy or from outside.

For such an intermediate target approach to be feasible at the level of EMU, two essential conditions will however need to be in place:

4 Article 105 of the Treaty on European Union and Article 2 of the Protocol on the Statute of the European System of Central Banks and of the European Central Bank.

– a reasonably stable and predictable relationship between the target variable and the final objective;
– a sufficient degree of control over the target variable through the central bank's monetary control instruments.

The feasibility and effectiveness of the intermediate target approach to a single monetary policy in EMU will rest on an empirical assessment which takes into account the relevant features of the economic union, its degree of openness, its exchange rate regime vis-à-vis major third currencies, its financial structure, and the operational structure (degree of decentralization) of the ESCB, as well as the prospective changes in these conditions, some of them in turn likely to be a function of the move to EMU. It is not unreasonable to assume that money demand relationships in the Member States will still be found to differ initially and perhaps for some considerable time to come. Experience with inflation and reactions to it, including the recourse to flexible interest rate instruments, have differed widely and will only converge over time even within a single monetary area. Attempts to estimate a Union-wide money demand function raise a host of issues of a conceptual, technical and statistical nature, and great caution in drawing conclusions is likely to be indicated.

First empirical studies[5] point to a relatively stable money demand relationship at Union level as a basis for an intermediary monetary targeting strategy to be pursued by the ESCB in stage three. Factors of instability still in evidence at the national level would hopefully cancel out or diminish, as the need to employ interest rate policy to stabilize exchange rates no longer destabilizes domestic money demand and structural adjustments in national financial systems converge before entry into stage three.

Warnings against too much optimism must be taken seriously though. The ESCB will indeed be entering 'no-man's land' in more than one respect. But the experience gained so far with alternative strategies, including direct targeting of inflation, hardly provides convincing arguments in their favour, and is unlikely to do so. Inflation targeting is open to the obvious dangers of a strategy being replaced by mere tactics reacting to a moving target, whereas the well-known time-lags of monetary policy call for steadfastness in the pursuit of price stability as the final objective. Although the ESCB, and the European Central Bank as its central institution as well as the members of its Governing Council will be fully independent in their monetary policy responsibility, they

5 Monticelli, C. and M.-O. Strauss-Kahn (1992), European integration and the demand for broad money, BIS Working Paper, no. 18, Basle.

may well be exposed to temptations and even pressures of various kinds at the start, before having gained full authority and credibility for the ESCB's policy based on positive and widely recognized results. The temptations and pressures may be all the greater if, as cannot be ruled out, economic growth in the Union is deemed inadequate to reduce high levels of unemployment rapidly, while fiscal policy offers limited or no room for manoeuvre when measured against the entry criteria for stage three.

Targeting a broad monetary aggregate, incorporating a realistic estimate of growth potential and an ambitious normative inflation objective that builds and improves on the entry requirements on inflation (plus a 'velocity' factor), would provide additional insurance against such temptations and pressures. Credibility of the ESCB's policy would then not have to wait for final outcomes on inflation, but would right from the start find expression in, and rest on, the soundness of its strategy choice. The ESCB would also be on safer ground from which to deal with any 'surprises' that are bound to confront its single monetary policy in the environment of 'uncertainty', all preparations in stage two notwithstanding.

4 Further preparations

Time is surely not yet ripe to consider using the results of econometric studies undertaken so far to arrive at a Union-wide monetary aggregate for the purpose of monetary cooperation and coordination as early as in stage two. For one thing, this would be an attempt at a single monetary policy with full membership of all Member States regardless of their state of de facto convergence, whereas actual membership in a future single monetary policy is still highly uncertain. The outcome might well compromize the efforts to be made at a later stage, as the construction of a Union-wide money demand function based on national relationships would seem to be hazardous. The relationships arrived at will be biased, if only because observed national money demand relationships will have been influenced by the co-existence of a dominant M3-target-oriented monetary policy regime and several exchange-rate-determined regimes. Merely 'adding up' the various national money demand relationships could well produce a 'blunder', which if applied could equally disqualify the whole exercise once and for all.

Serious further work on the conceptual, technical and statistical requirements of an intermediate monetary target as a basis for the future conduct of monetary policy in stage three of EMU is required as part of the tasks of the European Monetary Institute, established on 1 January 1994. Though it is uncertain, and will remain so for some time, which countries will initially be able to move to stage three, and with what delays others will follow, analysis of the properties of Union-wide monetary relationships based on realistic assumptions about future developments may serve a useful preparatory purpose.

As part of the preparation for a single monetary policy in stage three, the EMI will also have to consider the choice of instruments and operational features necessary for that purpose. Although some of the instruments and operational features will find application irrespective of the preferred monetary policy concept, others will have to be judged in the light of the concept that is finally adopted. One consideration is likely to play a special role in the instrument debate, namely the insistence on as much decentralization as possible in the implementation of the single monetary policy. After lengthy debate agreement was reached on Treaty language which stipulates that: 'To the extent deemed possible and appropriate ... the ECB shall have recourse to the national central banks to carry out operations which form part of the tasks of the ESCB.'[6] Some Member States argued for an obligation on the part of the ECB only to act through the national central banks; this was recognized as too constraining and potentially a source of operational difficulties. The central bank's ability to satisfy the banking system's liquidity needs will depend greatly on the instruments at its disposal and the modus operandi agreed upon.

In this context, one question to be decided relates to the minimum reserve instrument preferred by some national central banks as a means to stabilize the demand for central bank liquidity and hence reduce the need for constant short-term fine-tuning, but also as a built-in brake to money creation over the longer term. Though there is still no agreement on the merits of minimum reserves as an additional instrument of monetary policy, a consensus appears to exist that the single monetary policy of the future ESCB will rely primarily on open-market-type policies conducted with the banking system, being the method answering most effectively to the requirements on both sides, those of a highly developed and open financial market and those of a central bank entrusted with the task of defending the value of the currency.

6 Article 12 of the Protocol on the Statute of the European System of Central Banks and of the European Central Bank.

European monetary policy coordination

Lucas Papademos

1 Introduction

During the second stage of EMU, monetary policy in the Member States of the European Union will face serious challenges. The transition to full monetary union, to be achieved by 1 January 1999 at the latest, presupposes the attainment of a sufficient degree of nominal convergence and the completion of the technical preparations and institutional changes required for the conduct of a single monetary policy. A central issue for monetary policy is how to achieve the internal and external stability objectives necessary for the transition to monetary union in an environment of increased capital mobility, financial integration and decentralized economic policy making by Member States. The Maastricht Treaty, which specifies the convergence criteria Member States must meet in order to participate in EMU, contains a number of provisions specifically aimed at facilitating the convergence process and at contributing towards the adoption of compatible monetary and fiscal policies. The establishment of the European Monetary Institute has as a primary objective to conduce to the attainment of nominal convergence through the strengthening of the coordination of stability-oriented monetary policies in the Union. In addition, the Treaty provisions which prohibit central bank financing of the public sector and its preferential financing by the banking system, with effect from the beginning of 1994, aim at enhancing the effectiveness of monetary policies and at achieving greater fiscal discipline in Member States. Finally, the implementation of the excessive deficit procedure within a new framework of multilateral surveillance intends to gear fiscal policies towards the fulfilment of the fiscal convergence criteria and the adoption of an appropriate policy mix. These Treaty provisions, however, cannot by themselves guarantee the necessary nominal convergence and the effective conduct of monetary policies.

Two key questions which need to be answered are: first, how monetary policy coordination can be strengthened within the new institutional framework of the European Monetary System, and second, how the coherence of monetary and economic policies can be ensured in

Member States and in the Union as a whole. The second question is crucial both for the fulfilment of the convergence criteria and for the efficient coordination of monetary policies aimed at price stability. André Szász has stressed in his work that fiscal consolidation and economic policy coordination are essential preconditions for monetary stability, sustained growth and for the viability of the European monetary integration process.[1]

Devising an effective scheme to strengthen monetary policy coordination and improve the policy mix in some countries during stage two would have been a difficult task, even before the recent turmoil in the EMS and the worsening of public finances experienced in most Union countries since 1990. One fundamental reason for the difficulties is that during stage two responsibility for monetary policy will remain with national monetary authorities. A second reason is that economic policies will also continue to be decentralized and not be subject to any common constraints other than those imposed by the new excessive deficit procedure. Developments over the last two years have complicated matters. The suspension from ERM membership of two important currencies in September 1992 and the widening of the ERM fluctuation margins on 2 August 1992 could pose new challenges to monetary policy coordination. Moreover, the substantial and widespread deterioration of fiscal positions, which is only partly due to cyclical factors, could hamper fiscal consolidation and the conduct of monetary policies.

This essay first focuses on some schemes which could contribute to a strengthening of monetary policy coordination and assesses their effectiveness in the new ERM framework. It then comments on the need for parallel progress towards monetary and economic stability and the implications for political cooperation in Europe.

2 Monetary policy coordination aimed at price stability

There is general agreement that a strengthening of monetary policy coordination is necessary for the efficient functioning of the EMS in stage two and the transition to full monetary union. This view is enshrined in the Treaty which states that a primary task of the EMI is to 'strengthen the coordination of the monetary policies of the Member States with the aim of ensuring price stability' (Article 109f of the Treaty and Article 4 of the Statute of the EMI). But the nature of this

1 For example, Szász (1988) and Szász (1990).

coordination has not been specified and the task seems more challenging in the aftermath of the ERM crisis and the widening of the ERM fluctuation margins on 2 August 1993. An effective monetary policy coordination framework calls for well defined common final objectives, an institutional setting and rules to guide the participating monetary authorities to conduct national policies so as to achieve these objectives. The Treaty states explicitly that the primary objective of monetary policy in the Union is price stability and that monetary policies in stage two should be coordinated so as to ensure the attainment of this objective. Given this common medium-term policy objective and current inflation falling within a range of 1 to 4 per cent in most Union countries, the coordination of monetary policies does not have to deal with potential problems arising from possible differences regarding final objectives, but rather it must address strategic and implementation issues on how to achieve them within the new financial, economic and institutional environment in the Union.

A central issue is whether an effective coordination of national monetary policies requires the adoption of explicit rules constraining the conduct of national monetary policies or can be based on more flexible cooperative arrangements among central banks. In the 1980s the EMS functioned well without the adoption of explicit rules, other than those implied by the Exchange Rate Mechanism, and within an institutional framework which involved cooperation among central banks but decentralized decision-making in the conduct of monetary policies. The EMS functioned remarkably well in the 1980s especially in view of differences in initial conditions among Member States, considerable fiscal imbalances in some countries, and sizeable disturbances in international financial markets. Although the findings of empirical studies are somewhat mixed, it is generally accepted that the EMS contributed to greater nominal convergence towards lower inflation. This convergence was not achieved by employing an explicit rule for the determination of the system's inflation, but by the adoption of an implicit rule. Since the early 1980s, Germany has provided the anchor for the system's price level by choosing its domestic inflation objective and setting an intermediate monetary target consistent with it, while other ERM members have adjusted their monetary policies so as to converge towards that inflation objective.

The considerable economic convergence achieved in the 1980s contributed to the maintenance of relative exchange rate stability in the EMS. Indeed, from 1987 to 1992 the ERM experienced a period of relative calm, without a general realignment. But the effectiveness of the ERM as a coordinating mechanism to lower inflation was subsequently tested.

The degree and pace of convergence towards low inflation was inadequate and resulted in significant losses in international competitiveness in some Member States, while fiscal consolidation efforts in many Union countries were insufficient and thus overburdened monetary policies. These developments, combined with a number of other factors, such as diverging cyclical positions and the effects of the policy mix in Germany, following the unification, on monetary conditions throughout the Union, created severe tensions. This culminated in the EMS crisis in the autumn of 1992, leading to the suspension of the pound sterling and the Italian lira from the ERM and several realignments. The system remained vulnerable in 1993 as markets concentrated on perceived policy conflicts between internal and external policy objectives and tested the viability of existing parities. Tensions re-emerged in the ERM in July 1993. Massive interventions and interest rate adjustments failed to stabilize markets and counter speculative capital movements, which were regarded as 'exceptional in amount as well as in nature'.[2] These developments led to the decision of 2 August to widen temporarily the ERM fluctuation margins to 15 per cent.

In the view of some economists, the 1992-1993 EMS crisis was not only a consequence of insufficient convergence but of the inherent instability of the system during the transition stage to full monetary union. The systemic problems faced by monetary policy in the Union are related to the 'inconsistency' of four elements of current economic and monetary arrangements: free trade, full capital mobility, fixed or managed exchange rates, and autonomy in the conduct of national monetary policies. The creation and efficient functioning of the single market imply that this inconsistency must be resolved by sacrificing the autonomy of national monetary policies and establishing a monetary union. But during the transition to the final stage and following the establishment of the single market which allows for high capital mobility, exchange rate stability and autonomous monetary policies may prove difficult to coexist. The scope for capital movements in highly integrated financial markets is such that it can generate tensions in the ERM, affecting the exchange rates even of currencies with sound economic fundamentals, if market participants were to perceive gains from potential monetary policy differentiation. The adoption of the wide fluctuation margins aimed at discouraging one-way speculative attacks, thus reducing the burden on interest rate policies and exchange market intervention. It has succeeded in doing that so far, while exchange rate stability has been maintained. It is not certain,

2 Communique of the European Community of 2 August 1993.

however, that this stability can be sustained and whether the system can foster convergence by exerting a disciplinary influence.

3 Frameworks for monetary policy coordination in stage two

This section reviews alternative frameworks for monetary policy coordination aimed at price stability, within the institutional setting envisaged in the Treaty: the responsibility for monetary policy decisions remains with the national authorities, while the EMI progressively plays an enhanced role in monitoring national monetary policies and in facilitating their coordination. Moreover, it is assumed that despite the widening of the ERM fluctuation margins, exchange rate stability remains a key policy objective both because of its implications for monetary stability and because of its importance for the efficient functioning of the single market.

3.1 *The status quo: exchange rate objectives*

A first scheme is the one that has effectively emerged since the widening of the ERM fluctuation margins. In this scheme, Germany continues to provide the main nominal anchor of the system, and monetary policies in most ERM member countries, especially those with relatively small and very open economies, are formulated and implemented by relying on the exchange rate as a nominal anchor and by trying to maintain the exchange rate close to the central parity. With the exchange rate as the intermediate target and 'coordinating link', interest rate policy must be subordinated to this external objective. In addition to the exchange rate, some other ERM countries employ as intermediate targets monetary aggregates which are chosen to be consistent with the domestic inflation objective and the external constraint. Finally, for non-ERM countries the coordination of their monetary policies towards lower inflation is based on either the adoption of consistent intermediate monetary targets or on a strategy aiming directly at a converging inflation target.

The present system, which involves a differentiated and flexible approach to monetary policy coordination, may be best suited to the different economic and financial structures of member countries and/or the prevailing economic conditions. Although it has functioned reasonably well so far, there is a risk that it may not ensure sufficiently effective monetary policy coordination under different circumstances, especially in the presence of sizeable asymmetric disturbances. In particular, the credibility of national monetary policies and of the EMS could be impaired if financial market participants do not have a clear view about the monetary policy strategy pursued at the national level and the likely policy responses in case of shocks or diverging economic developments which could create policy dilemmas.

3.2 *A Union-wide money supply target*

An alternative coordinating framework could rely on the setting of an aggregate money supply target for the Union as a whole (or at least for the ERM members) consistent with the medium-term objective of price stability, and a short-term inflation 'norm' which takes into account initial conditions and the temporary effects of special factors on inflation. The adoption of an aggregate money supply target is supported by the view put forward by McKinnon that in an area where currency substitutability is high between countries, each country's inflation depends more on the entire area's money supply rather than on the domestic money supply.[3]

The effective implementation of a coordination scheme based on a EU-wide monetary target hinges on the validity of the assumption that each country's inflation is determined by the Union's aggregate money supply rather than the national money stock, but it also depends on the fulfilment of other conditions: first, an agreement on a common short-term inflation target and on potential output growth for the EU area; second, a relatively stable and predictable velocity relationship between the EU-wide money growth and EU-inflation; and third, an operational framework enabling national central banks to control such an aggregate. The convergence of inflation between ERM countries and the shared commitment to price stability imply that an agreement on a short-term inflation target could be easier to reach than in the past. Moreover, empirical research suggests that EU-wide money can be meaningfully defined, the demand for it being at least as stable and predictable as the demand for national monetary aggregates[4], and thus that it could, in principle, be usefully employed as an intermediate target or indicator for monetary policy. These empirical findings should, of course, be interpreted with caution, as financial innovation, which could accelerate as a result of growing economic and financial integration in the Union, and behavioral changes may impair the stability of EU-wide money demand. The main difficulties, however, with employ-

3 McKinnon (1984).
4 For example, Monticelli and Strauss-Kahn (1992) and Van Riet (1993).

ing a EU-wide monetary aggregate for the coordination of European monetary policies relate to the operational problems that must be tackled in order to exercise effective control of this aggregate within the present institutional structure.

3.3 *Mutually consistent national monetary targets*

An alternative scheme for monetary policy coordination aimed at price stability could be based on a mutually consistent set of commonly agreed national monetary targets. Such a strategy, which was proposed in 1989 for the ex-ante coordination and ex-post surveillance of monetary policies in stage one, presupposes a set of commonly agreed final objectives, particularly annual normative inflation targets consistent with convergence to price stability. It also requires the adoption of conceptually compatible broad monetary aggregates, since the evidence in most Union countries suggests that the relationships of narrow measures of money to the final objective are less stable. In addition to the statistical and conceptual issues that must be resolved, the implementation of such a scheme faces difficulties relating to differences in the economic and financial structures in member countries, which imply that for some countries a strategy based on monetary aggregates may be inefficient, because of the variability of the relationship between monetary aggregates and inflation, and because of difficulties in achieving intermediate monetary targets. These considerations have led many Union countries, especially those with small and open economies, to pursue an anti-inflationary strategy relying primarily on the exchange rate as an intermediate target. The flexible approach to monetary policy coordination which has effectively emerged in the Union reflects, to a considerable extent, existing differences in financial structures and monetary transmission mechanisms. Although these differences are likely to diminish as the economic integration of the Union advances, they could still inhibit the adoption of a coordination framework based on a set of mutually consistent monetary targets in the immediate future.

Another approach to monetary policy coordination based on the setting of quantitative targets involving adherence to a specific operational rule by national central banks has been proposed by Russo and Tullio.[5] It requires that national central banks target the domestic component of the monetary base employing a certain rule and that they refrain from sterilising international reserve flows within the system.

5 Russo and Tullio (1988).

The operational rule is that each national central bank sets the growth rate of the domestic component of the monetary base equal to a multiple of the desired nominal income growth rate in the respective country. It is a procedure that can be consistent with exchange rate stability and allows for some flexibility in the choice of national nominal income objectives. This approach has certain merits in that it includes a specific procedure for the conduct of monetary policy compatible with exchange rate stability in a decentralised system of central banks. Its implementation, on the other hand, is not as straightforward as it might appear: a number of technical problems must be resolved, while the scheme's effectiveness in controlling inflation hinges on the stability of the relationship of the monetary base to nominal income and the degree of currency substitutability.

3.4 *Targeting of final policy objectives*

A monetary policy coordination framework need not rely on intermediate targets. In the wake of the ERM crisis and the damaged credibility of a coordinating mechanism requiring the targeting of exchange rates within narrow bands, and in the light of the difficulties encountered in some countries in finding reliable monetary targets, more emphasis has recently been placed on the advantages of frameworks focusing directly on final policy objectives. One possibility is the explicit targeting of inflation in a medium-term context; another is nominal income targeting consistent with the medium-term objective of price stability. Monetary policy coordination directly geared to price stability can be implemented more flexibly at the national level and this could be more effective in view of existing differences and expected changes in monetary transmission mechanisms, and in case of sizeable disturbances affecting the union asymmetrically. Increased flexibility, however, entails risks which may undermine the effectiveness and credibility of such an approach. The long time-lags and uncertainty in the effects of monetary policy instruments on inflation may impair the ability of central banks to act promptly and decisively when inflationary pressures build up. In addition, it can be argued that the higher degree of discretion inherent in this approach might make the conduct of monetary policies less transparent to the public and subject to political pressures with an adverse impact on policy credibility, especially when the fiscal-monetary policy mix is inappropriate. A blueprint for policy coordination which focuses directly on the control of nominal income and the management of a system of real effective exchange rates has been presented by Williamson and Miller.[6] This approach involves the management of interest rate differentials by central banks to maintain exchange rate stability, the adjustment of the system's average interest rate to stabilise the Union's aggregate demand, and an active fiscal policy at the national level geared to a domestic nominal income target. This blueprint provides for a general macro-economic strategy aimed at a broader set of final policy objectives and requires the coordinated use of both monetary and fiscal policy instruments. It is not, therefore, directly applicable to the policy issues considered here, especially in the light of the Union's present institutional set-up.

4 Conclusion

The foregoing review and assessment of possible frameworks for monetary policy coordination seems to lead to a rather discouraging conclusion. Each of the options considered has certain merits and demerits given the existing economic and institutional structure in the Union, thus making it exeedingly difficult to choose among them. Moreover, a return to the coordinating mechanism envisaged in the Treaty, namely the ERM with narrow fluctuation margins, would be premature if not counterproductive before certain conditions are established. The essential precondition is that, in all participating countries, the fundamentals determining exchange rate stability should be sound and be expected by markets to remain so in the foreseeable future. For this condition to be fulfilled, economic policies in these countries would have to be compatible with and supportive of monetary policies focusing on exchange rate stability.

The above considerations suggest that monetary policy coordination in the European Union can be strengthened by less formal means, which do not require new systemic arrangements constraining the conduct of national monetary policies. Indeed, within the new environment of highly interdependent and financially integrated economies, the increased flexibility in the operation of the EMS rules allowed by the wide ERM bands discourages speculative currency attacks and may prove that the present system is appropriate, provided that national central banks continue pursuing policies aimed at convergence towards price stability. The way to strengthen monetary policy coordination would be to implement compatible economic policies and adopt measures, of an institutional or technical nature, which can increase the credibility and efficiency of monetary policies. Establish-

6 Williamson and Miller (1987).

ing at an early stage the independence of all national central banks as required for EMU would enhance the credibility of stability-oriented policies and the consistency of policy responses to shocks. In addition, acceleration of the technical preparations necessary for transition to the final stage, including a prompt harmonisation of instruments and procedures, would increase market confidence in the determination of Member States to proceed as soon as economically feasible to a monetary union where price stability is the declared primary objective.[7] But the essential prerequisite for the coordinated pursuit of price stability by the central banks in the Union is the implementation of economic policies that can convince markets of the sustainability and mutual compatibility of national monetary policies.

7 A number of proposals have also been advanced with a view to improving the capacity of the ERM to resist speculative attacks by modifying the asset-settlement rules (See Collignon (1993), chapter VII.2). These proposals could be of interest in the context of an ERM with narrow bands provided they can be implemented without creating inflationary risks in the system.

References

Collignon, Stefan (ed.) (1993), *The EMS in transition, lessons learned from the experience of the EMS and the completion of the internal market; policy options to prepare stages two and three of EMU*, Paris.

McKinnon, Ronald (1984), *An International standard for monetary stabilisation*, Cambridge, Massachusetts.

Monticelli, C. and M-O. Strauss-Kahn (1992), Broad monetary aggregates and money demand in European countries: where do we stand?, *Economies et Sociétés*, no. 9, pp. 147-193.

Riet, A.G. van (1993), Studies of EC money demand: survey and assessment, *De Nederlandsche Bank, Quarterly Bulletin* 1992/4, March, pp. 61-73.

Russo, Massimo and Giuseppe Tullio (1988), *Monetary policy coordination within the European Monetary System: is there a rule? In: Francesco Giavazzi, Stefano Micossi and Marcus Miller (eds.)*, The European Monetary System, Cambridge, pp. 292-356.

Szász, André (1988), European monetary integration beyond 1992, *De Nederlandsche Bank, Quarterly Bulletin* 1988/3, December, pp. 51-59.

Szász, André (1990), *Rebuilding Europe* (inaugural lecture), Amsterdam.

Williamson, John and Marcus H. Miller (1987), Targets and indicators: a blueprint for the international coordination of economic policy, *Policy Analysis in International Economics*, no 22, Washington DC.

Economic policy coordination and the role of fiscal targets

Henk J. Brouwer and Bernard ter Haar

1 Introduction

The process of European integration towards Economic and Monetary Union is a unique experiment in history. It is a unification not by brute force, but by means of cooperation and coordination, governed by a treaty and other legislation. The Treaty of Maastricht gives a blueprint of the final goal of EMU and the path along which this is to be attained. The challenge will be to achieve the goals of the Treaty. The events of 1993 demonstrate that this is not a straightforward exercise. Almost immediately after confirmation of the goals of the Exchange Rate Mechanism of the European Monetary System, the mechanism barely survived severe turbulence stemming from a lack of adequate policies and policy coordination. It is clear that policy-makers, for better or worse, are more influential than a written text. Therefore, we know in advance that the path towards EMU will be an exercise in policy discipline, and not an exercise in reading a Treaty.

André Szász has witnessed the process of European integration and has participated in the art of policy-making over a long period. He has unrivalled experience in finding intelligent solutions to bridging the gap between European ambitions and practical difficulties. It is a great honour and challenge to contribute to this book, which is dedicated to him, with a topic he is deeply concerned with, that of fiscal coordination in Europe.

This essay focuses on the drive towards fiscal policy coordination in Europe in the context of monetary cooperation, which has reached a new height in the Treaty of Maastricht. The convergence criterion on public finances in this Treaty is especially noteworthy: definitive arrangements in an area that generally excels in vague and intangible intentions. But is it focusing on the right issue, and is it sufficient?

The authors are indebted to L.B.J. van Geest and P. Stek for their valuable comments and contributions to an earlier version of this essay.

2 Types if macro-economic policy coordination

2.1 *Introduction*

Two types of goals have held the attention of the European Community in the field of macro-economic policy coordination: exchange rate stability and the promotion of economic growth. However, whereas these goals have remained topical, both the motivation for coordination and the consequences for national policies have evolved over time. This holds in particular for the role of fiscal policy, whether to stimulate growth or to ensure stable exchange rates.

2.2 *Goals of exchange rate stability*

Since World War II, EC Member States have participated in mechanisms aiming for exchange rate stability: first, as part of the global framework of the International Monetary Fund; after the collapse of the Bretton Woods system, in a series of regional arrangements, leading up to the Exchange Rate Mechanism (ERM) of the European Monetary System by the end of the seventies.

In retrospect, it is hard to disentangle political motives and economic insights. While the Bretton Woods system meant to establish a new economic order to underpin political stability between the United States, Europe and the rest of the world, regional monetary arrangements in Europe were at least partly seen as important elements in the strong political drive to avoid another intra-European war by integrating Europe. Economically, international monetary cooperation originally intended to stimulate countries to put their own house in order and to prevent a recurrence of the competitive devaluations of the Great Depression. Therefore, the Bretton Woods system focused on permanent changes in the exchange rate. In the ERM the volatility of exchange rate movements became an important consideration as well; it was realized that uncertainty about future exchange rates could give rise to inefficient investment patterns and hamper international trade. Moreover, the overriding purpose of policy coordination shifted, especially in the ERM: price stability superseded a sustainable-balance-of-payments position as the purpose of the system. This can partly be explained by the increased freedom of capital flows; on the one hand, this simplified the financing of balance-of-payments deficits but, on the other, it complicated the setting of domestic money targets to attain price stability. Lastly, whereas the Bretton Woods system was set up as a protection against spill-overs of undisciplined behaviour of others, the ERM supports members in internal adjustment by letting them borrow credibility from the participating strong-currency countries.

2.3 *Consequences of exchange rate stability for fiscal policy*

Not only did the focus of exchange rate stability change over time, but so did the ideas about the consequences for national policies, especially fiscal policy. In times of less developed capital markets and less freedom of capital movements, the fiscal deficit was important for the monetary authorities for two reasons. It could contribute to a national savings deficit and hence a decrease of monetary reserves, and (depending on its way of financing) it was a potential domestic source of money creation.

In the seventies strict monetarists viewed fiscal deficits as irrelevant not only for the stimulation of economic activity, but also for monetary policy and thus for inflation and the exchange rate, as long as no recourse was had to monetary financing. Even the Nederlandsche Bank held the view that the deficit could be irrelevant for monetary policy, if the words of its illustrious late President, Marius Holtrop, are anything to go by: 'If it is properly financed, all right; if it is improperly financed, then it comes into the province of the central bank'.[1]

At present, the relevance of the budget deficit for monetary and exchange rate stability is internationally acknowledged, whether it is properly financed or not. A balanced mix of public deficit and monetary policy is required, if an overburdening of monetary policy is to be prevented. A stringent monetary policy in the face of a bloated deficit boils down to beating one's head against a brick wall. It is for this reason that the Monetary Committee of the EC concluded in its report on the recent turmoil in the EMS: 'The sound management of public finance is an essential element in the policy mix; the over-burdening of monetary policy in any country can have grave consequences for the system and all of its participants'.[2]

1 Evidence for the Radcliffe Committee, reprinted in: M.W. Holtrop (1972), Money in an open economy, Leiden, p. 125.

2 Monetary Committee (1993), Lessons to be drawn from the disturbances on the foreign exchange markets. The Committee of Governors drew a similar conclusion in its report on the recent exchange rate crisis: 'A successful management of the system depends on an appropriate policy mix. Monetary policy alone cannot bear the burden of ensuring both price stability and exchange rate stability in the EMS. It needs adequate support from fiscal policy and other policies'. Committee of Governors of the Central Banks (1993), The implications and lessons to be drawn from the recent exchange rate crisis, Basle.

2.4 *Fiscal policy coordination*

Before returning to the link between monetary and fiscal coordination, one might ask whether international fiscal policy coordination has an aim of its own, like the target of price stability and exchange rate stability in the field of monetary coordination. On the fiscal side, the situation is certainly more ambivalent. This is quite understandable, since fiscal policy covers a broad variety of issues each of which affects the economy in its own way. Fiscal policy is more than deficit policy. It covers the size and the structure of the government expenditures, tax policy and therefore also the policy of income distribution. Hence, while for monetary coordination the rule can be accepted that the objective of price stability in the long term is favourable for all, such simple rules are unachievable for fiscal policy coordination. National economies are not alike and domestic institutional arrangements display great variations. Therefore, economic policies have to be drafted carefully with an eye to domestic circumstances. Beyond this it should be realised that the power of approval of the budget is the cornerstone of national democracies, and cannot easily be combined with international agreements.

In the post-war period, most serious efforts to achieve fiscal coordination have been related to economic recessions. The rather disastrous experiences during the Great Depression brought home to governments that in the face of a severe cyclical downturn passiveness may not produce satisfactory results. The Keynesian revolution prescribed budgetary expansion as a reaction to an economic downturn. However, as international interdependence grew, the benefits of a national expansionary policy evaporated; national demand impulses had foreign spillovers through increased import demand and exchange rate pressures. Therefore, a coordinated budgetary impulse might bear fruit, where individual stimulation programmes would fall on barren ground.

A Keynesian solution to recession was applied in Europe in the seventies. Since the first oil shock had led to a synchronisation of the cycle in Europe, the impression of a consciously coordinated approach was easily established. In the eighties, a coordinated reaction to the recession was considered, but raised little enthusiasm in practice. The Keynesian approach had lost much of its appeal. Practical problems complicated an active anti-cyclical fiscal policy; due to substantial time-lags, anti-cyclical policies had a tendency to turn out to be pro-cyclical; temporary increases in the deficit proved to be tenacious, leading to considerable rises in the government debt-to-GDP ratio. Moreover, in the eighties it turned out that the Keynesian stimulative policy of the seventies had not solved the underlying supply-side imbalances which had been exacerbated by the effect of the oil shock. On the contrary, the surge in deficit, debt and inflation hindered structural recovery, undermined the credibility of economic policy and decreased the room for manoeuvre in the following years. Finally, economic theory turned towards the supply-side; under the assumption of rational expectations, an active anti-cyclical fiscal policy was held to render few positive effects.

However, present economic insights do not imply that governments should be lethargic; neither do the political dynamics. For better or worse, over the economic downturn in 1993 politically motivated action caused a substantial rise in the deficit in many European countries. In most cases only part of this rise was rooted in the cyclical developments. Hence, there was certainly no need for a coordinated fiscal stimulation approach on top of that. On the contrary, a strong coordination effort in the European Community resulted in a call for fiscal consolidation and a limitation of fiscal stimulation to the use of automatic stabilisers at most. Sound government finances would increase the medium-term credibility of economic policy, and so create more confidence in economic recovery. The recent coordination efforts rightly emphasized the need for structural adjustments to restore sustainable economic growth and to create substantially more employment. This exercise clearly underscored how large the common denominator in the macro-economic deficiencies was, indicating ample opportunities for coordination.

3 Economic and Monetary Union

3.1 *Introduction*

Returning to the relation between monetary and fiscal coordination, it is clear that the drive for fiscal coordination would be less strong if the monetary aspect were absent. In the discussion on monetary unification, the central question has invariably been whether monetary union would be sustainable, if specific arrangements for economic cooperation were missing. The more serious endeavours to achieve monetary union were always embedded in both an economic and a monetary union. On 1 and 2 December 1969, the European Council expressed the wish to see the Community develop into an economic as well as a monetary union through the implementation of a phased plan. Accordingly the Werner Committee was installed to elaborate this plan. On the basis of the interim report of the Werner Committee, the European

Council concluded on 22 March 1971 that: 'as regards budgetary policy proper, the margins within which essential elements of public budgets as a whole should lie, in particular the variation of their amount, and the size, mode of financing and use of balances, shall be determined at Community level'.[3]

This decision implies an effective centralisation of fiscal policy; public deficit, tax burden, the total of public expenditure and even the distribution over the various categories were to be decided at Community level. Today most of us will consider this phrase a complete anachronism, and we can note that at the time the European Council remained silent on a number of important issues, such as the overall purpose of fiscal policy, the decision-taking body (the Commission, the Council or perhaps even a new Community body) or the erosion of democratic control.

At the time, these issues remained unresolved, since the oil crisis pulled the process towards monetary union off track. It was not until the late eighties that the discussion on Economic and Monetary Union was resumed with the Delors Committee and the intergovernmental conferences. However, these were never as ambitious in terms of the level of fiscal coordination envisaged.

3.2 *Fiscal rules in the Treaty of Maastricht*

The necessity and the design of budgetary rules were extensively discussed during the negotiations on Economic and Monetary Union. There was the common notion that a balanced policy mix was to be ensured and an over-burdening of the centralised monetary policy of the European Central Bank to be prevented. Hence, sound budgetary policies were required. However, views differed widely on how these could be enforced.

First of all, it had to be ensured that financial markets could exert their disciplinary influence. In their endeavours to fulfil financing needs, public authorities should face the same regime as the private sector; monetary financing and privileged access should be prohibited, as well as a bail-out by the Community or individual Member States. Whereas the disciplinary effect of financial markets seemed useful, most Member States felt this would be insufficient to ensure sound budget-

3 Resolution of the Council and of the representatives of the governments of the Member States of 22 March 1971 on the attainment of Economic and Monetary Union in the Community, title I, section 3 (IV).

ary positions. Financial markets could disregard the no bail-out clause and continue financing for too long a time. Furthermore, experience indicates that financial markets exert their discipline rather erratically (e.g. the debt crisis in the eighties).

Discussion on additional measures centred on the question whether rules should be of a qualitative or quantitative nature. Qualitative rules leave more room to do justice to specific circumstances: institutional differences, changing economic circumstances or economic insights or differences in economic development. However, in the EC qualitative rules equal permissiveness. Experience shows that it is practically impossible at Community level to exact national policy adjustments, even if these are inevitable from an economic point of view. On this account, clear-cut quantitative rules are to be preferred, as they circumscribe the possibilities for unwarranted leniency. The Treaty on European Union has tried to get the best of both worlds. Article 104c on excessive deficits sets ceilings in quantitative terms. The government deficit may not exceed a reference value of 3 per cent of GDP; government debt may not exceed a reference value of 60 per cent of GDP or, if so, should approach this value at a steady pace. However, room for qualitative judgement has been created as well. A thorough examination, including all relevant factors, will take place before the existence of an excessive deficit is established.

The excessive deficit procedure plays a role from stage two onward. In stage two, Member States will endeavour to avoid excessive deficits (Article 109e, paragraph 4); the transition to stage three is impossible if the Council has decided that an excessive deficit exists (Article 109j, paragraphs 1 and 2); in stage three Member States shall avoid excessive deficits (Article 104c, paragraph 1). However, one should not interpret the excessive deficit procedure as an instrument of fiscal policy coordination as such. It is a kind of emergency procedure for exceptional instances to avoid that fiscal deficits exceed dangerous limits. The fiscal criteria are certainly not fiscal targets (but limits are often attractive targets). At least, this was the philosophy when the Treaty was drafted. Although it is difficult to follow this philosophy at a time when all Member States, except one, exceed the limits, it should be kept in mind that fiscal policy coordination is more than confining the deficit and the debt ratio. For the broader purpose of economic policy coordination, including the fiscal side, the Treaty establishes the multilateral surveillance procedure and the procedure for the submission of broad policy guidelines. The concern is, though, that these procedures do not entail commitment. Experience is limited so far, but it is clear that both procedures, in nature as well as in practice, are far from binding.

3.3 *Comparison with 1971*

In the field of fiscal coordination the Treaty of Maastricht is far less ambitious than the European Council was in 1971. This can be justified in several ways. One should start by realising that in 1991 no need was felt for an economic union in itself. In particular the idea that economic developments could – and should – be controlled by the size and composition of government expenditures had faded as the driving force behind the wish for coordination. In current thinking, economic policy should be made to measure. Given the differences in economic behaviour, structures, institutions and sizes, one could not expect an improvement in the quality of decision-making by centralisation. From the economic perspective, therefore, broad orientations on economic policy that take account of the spill-over effects and of the synergetic possibilities would be sufficient, leaving many degrees of freedom to the domestic level. Here the subsidiarity principle really holds. Certainly the notion of subsidiarity has strengthened during the integration process. But in reviewing this argument one should realise that the European Council in 1971 was monitoring a Community of six members, instead of the twelve that signed the Treaty of Maastricht. Anyway, given the very limited status of political integration so far, there would not be a central institution to which one could practically delegate power in respect of fiscal policy.

However, while it can easily be explained that the Treaty is different from the 1971 target, one could still question whether the present Treaty is sufficiently ambitious on the fiscal side. Possibly it is useful to distinguish between the second stage of the EMU and the third stage. Since it is good practice to start studying final goals and only after that how to achieve these, we start with the third stage.

3.4 *Economic policies in stage three*

In the third stage a unified monetary policy and irreversibly fixed exchange rates or a single currency for all participating countries will exist. In the ideal situation fiscal deficits in all these countries will be so far below the limits of 3 per cent of GDP that only in exceptional circumstances would this boundary be approached. So basically there would not be a policy mix issue to worry about, in the sense that a danger would arise that monetary policy could be overburdened by too lax a fiscal policy. That would not automatically imply, of course, the non-existence of any economic difficulty or economic pressures. There could be external shocks, different regions will face different life cycles of their industrial sectors, and excessive wage pressures may arise in certain areas or Member States. These types of difficulty require flexible economies but also adequate domestic policy responses to mitigate short-term difficulties. So in the ideal world it does not look as if a case for a strong centralisation of economic policy exists.

However, practice might be less ideal. In 1993 we have seen how rapidly fiscal deficits can increase to a far higher level than 3 per cent of GDP. If such a situation were to be repeated in the third stage, the policy mix might be under pressure indeed, and a conflict could arise between monetary and fiscal authorities. Also, we just assumed that economies were sufficiently flexible to overcome external shocks. If this were not the case, tensions could again arise between the monetary authority and (some of the) fiscal authorities.

This kind of problem has an economic and a political dimension. From an economic point of view, whether a deficit should be reduced or whether markets should be made to work, measures should be taken at the domestic level. At that level insight into the economic ills and into the practical possibilities to cure them is optimal. Furthermore, the country itself has to set priorities in government expenditures, choosing where to cut. The national government also has to face the social tensions that might arise because of the adjustment measures. However, at Community level and from the perspective of the other Member States, both in the political area and in the monetary area, one would like to be sure that measures are indeed taken. In the present Treaty such a guarantee is absent. The procedure on excessive deficits is the most far-reaching in this respect, but it stops at the possibility of fines, if a Member State fails to correct its deficit. Could one reach further in the present political status of the Community, while leaving the basic responsibility of choice at the domestic level? A practical possibility would be that the fiscal framework of a Member State with an excessive deficit has to be approved by the Community before the next budget can be enacted. We do not mention this to advocate such an approach here, but to illustrate the serious political consequences of a further strengthening of the procedure. A failure of voluntary coordination could finally have such a strengthening as its result.

Also in cases of insufficient economic adjustment one notices the imbalance between centralisation of the monetary area and the decentralised fiscal side. At first sight this imbalance seems to favour the monetary authority, the European Central Bank. Would a European authority not be more powerful than a national authority? However, one should realise that in practice a central bank cannot operate in a basically hostile environment. In countries with a successful central bank, monetary policy is founded on a tradition deeply rooted in societal values (and even those countries have experiences of prolonged excessive demand and high inflation). Especially central bankers feel uneasy about the fact that this tradition may not have spread broadly enough over Europe. However, it is certainly encouraging to notice the broad public acceptance of central bank independence in almost all Member States today. Furthermore, a serious selection of Member States that are really well prepared for the third stage might also increase the credibility of the institutional structure laid down in the Treaty.

3.5 *Economic policy in stage two*

The second stage is the preparatory stage which should create the circumstances under which a stable and sustainable third stage of EMU is possible. In this stage, and in the short time that is available, a tradition of monetary and fiscal discipline should be established. If one looks at the discussion about the second stage, attention focused on the convergence criteria, especially the deficit and debt criteria. One should realise, however, that the aim is convergence, not the fulfilment of the convergence criteria in itself. It is important to make this distinction, because one should not think that the fulfilment of the criteria at a certain date, irrespective of anything else, enables the economy to participate in a full monetary union; the true condition for participation is to have a stable and flexible economy. Stability is important, because one should avoid that the dynamics of the domestic economy could lead to a deterioration (shortly) after the transition to the third stage. Especially in the first years of the third stage, policy-makers will be less experienced than usual in handling difficult situations.

Flexibility means market flexibility and fiscal flexibility. Fortunately, attention for this subject is increasing. If one looks at the White Paper of the European Commission on growth, competitiveness and employment of December 1993, strong emphasis was given to the need to improve the functioning of the economy and the ability to adjust. Market flexibility will be a key issue for the coming years. It has been a goal of structural policy for a long time now, but results are slow to come, as long as, for understandable reasons, it is more popular among politicians to talk about reforms than to implement them. Difficult issues have to be addressed, like a restructuring of the social security system, a restructuring of labour market regulations, and severe cuts in government expenditure to enable a reduction of the tax burden. As one may notice, the importance of these measures is not related exclusively to EMU, but also to the economic difficulties in Europe in the first years of the nineties. The massive rise in unemployment because of insufficient lack of competitive power of Europe is a clear warning signal of what could happen on a domestic scale in the third stage, if a Member State does not adapt to the common policy stance.

Secondly, we mentioned fiscal flexibility. Governments need room for manoeuvre to react adequately to changing circumstances and economic challenges. The fiscal situation of a Member State should enable specific policies to keep the economy on its path of potential growth and to correct for disturbances that could not be corrected – in the short term – by the markets themselves. For the Netherlands as well as for several other Member States, fiscal flexibility can only be achieved after a release from the all-absorbing interest payments stemming from a very high government debt. So, flexibility goes hand in hand with fiscal stability. This demonstrates that the convergence criterion for the deficit extends beyond guaranteeing an adequate policy mix.

The structural conditions for stability and flexibility are not regulated in the Treaty of Maastricht. That would have been impossible, since most of these structural aspects cannot be described in measurable terms. What is clear from the above is the emphasis on domestic responsibility. It remains to be proved that the participants in the third stage can rely on that. But those who want to prove it, can do so in the second stage of EMU.

4 Conclusions

In this contribution we have tried to examine the scope for economic policy coordination, not only on its own merits, but in particular in the context of the economic and monetary integration in Europe. It is clear that centralisation of economic policy making cannot be the answer to all economic problems and imbalances, since most economies have their typically domestic features. Centralisation is, of course, an extreme form of coordination. Coordination of policies is useful indeed and will be even more so in the future, to the extent of establishing common priorities and broad guidelines on the necessary adjustment efforts. It is also clear that the basic drive behind economic and fiscal policy coordination in Europe stems from the intention to have a centralised monetary policy. The major concern here is that too lax economic and fiscal policies will overburden monetary policy, which in political terms could lead to the independent position of the European Central Bank being questioned. Rightly the Treaty of Maastricht focuses on the necessity of fiscal discipline. The fiscal limits that are included in the Treaty are not divine in themselves, but are an indispensable tool to achieve this discipline and to allow for judgement at Community level whether Member States adjust appropriately.

In the introduction we raised the question whether the rules of the Treaty would be sufficient. Those who seem to prefer further centralisation of economic power in stage three to guarantee that adequate measures in the economic field can and will be taken cannot, however, be sure that this central power would be used in accordance with their purposes. We have tried to indicate that in stage two of EMU the fulfilment of the set of criteria as laid down in the Treaty will not be sufficient in itself for countries to be ready to move to the third stage. The necessary stability and flexibility in the domestic economic structures and government finance could not be described in measurable terms in the Treaty, but these are certainly major challenges to be addressed in the second stage. A very important element of the Treaty is the examination to decide whether Member States can pass to stage three of EMU. By looking beyond the criteria themselves, and so by including the conditions on the status of the real economy, a very serious examination should result in a coherent group of countries which would have no difficulty in surviving a situation without a home-made monetary and exchange rate policy, and which, therefore, would be ready to reap the fruits of further economic and monetary integration.

The Monetary Committee as a promoter of European integration

Andreas Kees

1 European monetary fraternity

The Monetary Committee has many aspects. In the early years one of the chairmen described it as a 'club of like-minded personalities'. This was probably one of the most useful functions the Committee has served: 'to create short-cuts through the maze of official channels; to form a nucleus of high officials in every administration – treasuries and central banks – who know each other well enough to make instant communication possible on a personal basis and who trust one another sufficiently to put all their cards on the table. There have been many instances, when an agreement was reached only because members of the Committee got together on a confidential basis and explained the real reasons behind their national positions'.[1]

Throughout the 36 years of its history, the Committee has retained the character of a fraternity, moved beyond being a club of like-minded personalities and became a power centre within the institutional framework of the Community. New qualities have come to the foreground. Today, the Committee is one of the centres for preparing the consensus on macro-economic policy. As a promoter of convergence of economic policies towards best performance, its central task is to develop that consensus, which, once achieved, continuously requires new efforts to regain it in the face of rapidly changing conditions. In the field of economic policies it brings all issues of macro-economics and international finance to maturity before they pass to the table of ministers or of the Council. The Committee has been forged, above all, by the realignment decisions in the framework of the European Monetary System, in which it has defined for itself a unique style for developing political consensus; a style which it has extended to other economic and monetary decisions.

One of the internal sources of creative tension derives from the combi-

1 Quoted in: Conrad J. Oort (1978), At the twentieth anniversary of the Monetary Committee, in: Monetary Committee, Twenty years of the Monetary Committee, Brussels, p. 11.

nation of advisory and policy preparation functions. This imparts a vital driving force to the Committee as it proceeds on the analytical and operational fronts. Reducing the Committee to a purely advisory body – as some may wish – would kill its essence. On the other hand, going exclusively down the road of policy preparation would deprive it of a balancing factor making for its independence. It could also loose the minimum distance necessary for good policy advice. 'Thus it has the great advantage of being one step away from the often politically inspired compromises that are the inevitable building blocs of the Community. The Committee can afford to formulate its recommendations in the somewhat rarefied atmosphere of the independent expert.'[2]

The creation of the European Unit of Account and – subsequently – the ECU is an illustration of this, taken from policy preparation in the Committee's early history. Chairman Oort vividly described the meeting which took place in Paris in March 1975, 'when agreement was reached on the basket of currencies which was to make up the European Unit of Account. This was one of the occasions during my chairmanship when the tight-fisted financial controller in The Hague allowed me to give a dinner for the Committee. I shall never know why my friends at the Trésor, who were kind enough to organize the dinner, picked the Maison de l'Amérique Latine, unless they had a very fine feeling for the financial constraints imposed on a Treasury man. The food, I remember, was mediocre at best, but the ambience, the mutual understanding of our respective national positions, and some knocking of heads by the chairman all helped in reaching an agreement. I still possess the menu with on the back at least a dozen different columns of relative currency weights, all crossed out save one. The one was later duly accepted by the Council without discussion and is now the ECU'.

The Committee is not immune to disagreements and far from being a centre of perpetual harmony. On the contrary, contradictions are transformed so that they become sources of dynamism. Most important, since sovereignty in the core of economic policy rests in the hands of Member States, there is a tension between supranational and intergovernmental integration which has to be overcome. The Committee, leaning more towards the latter without loosing sight of the former, is the place where these tensions are resolved. This is one of the main tasks of this European monetary fraternity, whose members have strong and sometimes very differing ideas on the necessary advancement of European integration.

2 Quoted from the memory book of the Monetary Committee (internal document).

2 Facing external difficulties

Since its creation, the activities of the Committee have been more and more influenced by international difficulties. The shift of economic power in the international system and the disintegration of the Bretton Woods system inevitably had their strongest repercussion in Europe. Since, moreover, European countries have part of the responsibility for the good functioning of the world system, their first response was to do everything they could to re-establish a workable unitary system. Accordingly, a prolonged period of attempted reform was unavoidable and only gradually did an awareness grow that at least part of the reform had to be the creation of a European monetary identity which would promote stability in both Europe and in the wider world.

Members of the Committee generally bring with them some heavy international luggage. They have very often served previously in responsible positions in the IMF. In addition, in their national administration, they largely determine the instructions given to European directors of the IMF. Moreover, they are the deputies of their ministers in the Group of Ten. As regards G7, they are those who prepare the deliberations of Heads of State or of Government, some of them as sherpas. The conditions are thus ideal for striking a balance between the Community's external and internal interests. An example of an IMF-related activity was the proposal which the Committee made in November 1982 at the height of the international debt crisis: 'The Committee agreed on the outline of a possible package for the 8th Quota Increase, intended both to reflect views in the Community and to have a prospect of acceptance by other IMF members. The Committee foresaw four elements in such a package: a basic quota increase of at least 50 per cent; a new pre-arranged borrowing facility ... The Monetary Committee felt that a package on these lines would be very much in the interests of the Community ... and early agreement would make a contribution to confidence in the international monetary system at a time when such confidence was badly needed'.[3]

As regards assistance by the Community to the countries of Central and Eastern Europe, the crucial decision on burden-sharing within the Group of 24 was prepared in the Monetary Committee. In December 1990 it reported to the Council that 'in order to ensure adequate burden-sharing, one must be extremely cautious about naming an abso-

3 Outline of the Community position on current issues of international monetary policy on 15 November 1982.

lute amount of aid which one would be willing to mobilize. It was urged to ministers to negotiate first in terms of the percentage which the Community and the Member States would contribute to the total effort. A figure of 50 per cent was advanced as a starting position'. This figure determined the Community's strategy for a long period.

3 Steps towards a monetary identity for the Community

Within the Community, one of the Committee's strengths has been its continuous endeavour for capital liberalization; an activity confirmed in Article 109c of the new Treaty. The number one task, however, has been to reinforce the consensus for stability-oriented economic and monetary policies and the coordination of the economic policies of Member States within the Community. After the establishment of the European Monetary System it took some years before the new consensus became fully enshrined in the consciousness of all policy makers: the progress of the EMS does not hinge in the first place on the constraints deriving from mechanisms, but it depends rather, and above all, on the correct orientation of economic policy. Only after the March 1983 realignment did this conviction become strong enough to guide actions. In parallel with this, and partly contributing to it, the emphasis of the Committee's activities changed. Whereas at the beginning of the 1980s the emphasis was still on the strengthening of the EMS mechanisms, later debate moved more and more to the heart of economic policy concepts. The Committee became an important catalyst within the Community for the newly emerging economic policy consensus and for its transmission to the Member States. The frequency of realignments decreased and more stable exchange rates encouraged in their turn new efforts to improve convergence. This virtuous circle lasted until 1990. With the deliberations on Economic and Monetary Union, the tide turned. A perception of the EMS as a fixed rate system gained ground, with all the adverse consequences on convergence efforts and exchange rate stability. It is in this field of conceptual confrontation and conceptual integration that the future contribution of the Committee will be judged. It is also from here that its procedural activities find their justification.

As to procedures, everything started with country examinations, conducted in a Community of six members, twice a year per country. Nearly twenty years later the idea of multilateral surveillance exercises was developed and incorporated in the Basle/Nyborg Agreement of 1987. More recently, the Committee was putting the Community on the alert, long before the disturbances on the exchange markets of end

1992 and the temporary suspension of the normal fluctuation margins of the EMS of August 1993 led to a more realistic perception of the true requirements of convergence. In the spring of 1991, it suggested to the Council the establishment of crash programmes, designed to mobilize very far-reaching corrective forces in countries which were out of line and going beyond all that had so far been 'possible' and conceivable under coordination. However, the very necessary warning given at that time did not fully sink in. Some feared that crash programmes could degenerate into cash programmes with requests to the Community for money. Others were not ready to change policy to the extent needed. This led to a crisis in the Committee, but the idea survived in a weaker form in the convergence programmes related to Article 109e in the Treaty of Maastricht. Although less biting, convergence programmes have a certain potential to mobilize corrective forces if elements of the original idea can be put into practice and thus become an instrument for enforcing 'hard' coordination. At any rate, the Committee and in particular its chairman saw the writing on the wall in spring 1991. In his report to the Council he pointed out that 'in the matter of convergence, stage two cannot be seen as a mere extension of stage one. Stage two must be characterized by qualitatively different economic performance. Far-reaching changes will therefore be needed before it starts. We stand today at a cross-roads and some countries still have to take the fundamental decision about which way they want to go'.[4]

The operational expression of the Community's monetary identity really emerged predominantly from the activities of some individual Member States, starting with their decision to float as a block in the early 1970s. The Committee was not a mover in the first initiative for monetary union, prepared by the Werner Committee. Some of its activities related to the establishment of the European Monetary Cooperation Fund and the support mechanisms, but most of the decisions prepared in this period were taken by the Committee of Governors of the Central Banks of the EC.

By contrast, the Monetary Committee contributed actively to the preparation of the EMS, and in particular to the Resolution of the European Council of December 1978. The conclusions of the Presidency made it clear that 'the European Council agreed, on the basis of the preparatory work of the Council (Ecofin) and of the Monetary Committee and the Committee of the Governors of the Central Banks to set up a European

4 Statement of the chairman of the Monetary Committee to the informal Ecofin Council on 11 May 1991.

Monetary System...'. The political compromise resolving the previous conflict between the parity grid approach and the average-oriented basket approach was prepared in the Committee, largely on the basis of a contribution from the Belgian members.

4 Stronger efforts to meet the internal challenges

Some lessons can be drawn from this short historical overview. The Committee is well placed for the preparation of international monetary issues, where there are no competitors. This has been recognized and confirmed by Community legislation.[5] As to the centre of activity – the coordination of economic policies – the Committee has all the qualities to make it a key player: this has already been proved by its performance and by its impact on economic policy concepts. The composition and the confidential nature of the proceedings are also good assets. Most important, the force to develop 'hard' coordination[6] within the Community lies within its reach. However, there is no cause for complacency. More has to be done to give full effect to the mission which the Maastricht Treaty assigns to the Committee in the preparation of economic policies.

High flying projects for future integration are less to the taste of the Committee, but if challenged on this score it could show that it combines inspiration with a strong sense of responsibility. 'The Committee is particularly well qualified to promote monetary integration with a firm commitment to reality and a complete absence of illusionary speculations.'[7] Next time the European Council should remember these facts.

5 Upgrading the composition and new tasks with the start of EMS

To meet the greater need for monetary cooperation, the composition of the Committee was upgraded in 1979. The aim was to have members

5 Council Decision No. 64/301/EEC of 8 May 1964 says in legal words: 'Whereas there should be close coordination of the policies of the Member States in the field of international monetary relations and the most appropriate method of ensuring such coordination is for the necessary consultations to be held within the Monetary Committee'.

6 Hard coordination implies: to cut through the maze of political considerations; to confront possible 'danger scenarios' at an early stage; to develop discussion in a climate of confidentiality. It is not a matter of procedural tricks to by-pass national sovereignty. Without hard coordination there will be no proper fulfilment of the convergence criteria of the Maastricht Treaty.

7 Quoted from the memory book of the Monetary Committee.

from the highest level of officials, going up to that of Secretary of State. This move met with resistance at the time from within the administration of the Commission, since it strengthened the orientation of the Committee to policy formation.

At the same time, the Committee was asked by the Council to establish the common procedure for the adjustment by mutual agreement of central rates within the EMS (point 3.2 of the EMS Resolution). It is within this procedure that some of the most important activities of the Committee have developed since then. Political decisions on EMS matters moved out of the Council in both the physical and the legal sense: they are taken in the different institutional setting of the ministers and central bank governors, with the Commission also being involved. Starting with decisions on central rates, this procedure was extended to other EMS – and comparable – monetary decisions. The common procedure thus opened a distinctive kind of intergovernmental activity, creating a specific Community framework. The need to deploy convincing persuasion and the need to find a good consensus are the challenges which arise with this approach to monetary integration. Decision-making by consensus does not of itself lead to a weaker form of integration. It is not true that only majority voting allows advances to be made. In a Community of varying fundamentals and interests this can also be achieved by consensus, if pushed forward convincingly. The Committee has always made strong efforts to enhance the area of consensus by identifying elements of common interest.

At the beginning a struggle had to be waged against the threat of competitive devaluation. In the more recent past this danger was less substantial but it is significant that this threat has recently re-appeared. Moreover, in the early years of the EMS, countries sometimes tried to have an accrued deterioration of relative prices and costs fully reflected in a new exchange rate, but the Committee has always concluded that it should not propose this to the Council. Part of the differential was left unreflected in the exchange rate so as to exert pressure for measures of economic adjustment. All realignment proposals acceptable to the Committee went beyond the attitude of repairing a 'troubled situation'. The interests of the EMS and the interest in advancing in monetary integration were represented at the negotiating table and were reflected in the solutions which emerged. It is partly this which explains the length of the negotiations and which stands behind the dry words: negotiations continue until there is a solution acceptable to all.

6 Integration led by the EMS – different from the mainstream

Monetary integration has developed to a large extent separately from, but in parallel to, the classical framework of the Treaty of Rome. This mirrors the political and functional importance of the role of money, which is at the heart of national sovereignty and is the expression of national identity. As long as the responsibility for monetary policy remains unshared in the hands of the Member States alone, most activities on the level of the Community will follow the road of intergovernmental and inter central-bank integration. Until stage three of EMU this is, indeed, the road mapped out by the Treaty.

The distinct form of integration in the monetary field and the distinct institutional approach associated with it were already evident at the time of the foundation of the EMS. The EMS rests on a Resolution of the European Council, which was not truly an institution of the Treaty at the time.[8] Moreover, the operational structure of the EMS was created by an institutionally separate agreement among central banks. Only some ancillary elements were left to the Treaty of Rome (for example a Council Regulation modifying the Unit of Account used by the European Monetary Cooperation Fund).

Not surprisingly, there were efforts to bring the EMS closer to the Treaty of Rome and they came from the Commission. At the time of the revision of the Treaty by the Single European Act an attempt was made to endow the Community with a monetary capacity. The Committee examined a draft proposal by the Commission in detail and took the view 'that the incorporation of a monetary dimension should only take place in step with the setting of broader economic and political objectives. As an example of this the goal of Economic and Monetary Union was mentioned, which is already part of common resolutions made by the Member States' governments as well as of the Community's legal framework. By contrast the Commission's proposal in its present form would involve the danger of rooting a one-sided monetary approach in the Treaty'.[9]

Reflecting the proper logic of European monetary integration, the Monetary Committee has indirectly reinforced the intergovernmental

8 The European Council was anchored to the Treaty only at the time of the revision incorporating the Single European Act. Furthermore, even today, the European Council has no formal decision-making power with respect to EMU.

9 Report by the chairman of the Monetary Committee to the Ecofin Council on the possible inclusion of a monetary dimension in the Treaty of Rome, November 1985, p. 2.

orientation. Some may take the one-sided view that monetary integration has thus moved out of the Community. However, the Ecofin Council and the Committee are important and active parts of the Community. Given the unprecedentedly demanding requirements of monetary integration, the Community must be flexible enough to choose those forms and procedures which allow durable progress. This is not a matter for black-and-white decisions, quite apart from the fact that the tension between the two concepts of integration is a source of vigour within the Committee itself. If later judgements were to lead to the conclusion that the evolution has gone too far in one or the other direction, adaptations are always possible. The Maastricht Treaty itself reflects this tension since it incorporates some clear transpositions of intergovernmental tendencies, evidence of the finance ministers' hand in writing the Treaty. Nonetheless, the classical institutions of the Treaty of Rome have every opportunity to exercise their powers of persuasion.

The tension between supranational and intergovernmental integration not only affects the respective roles of institutions: it goes further and also influences the nature of the approach to coordination. Some of the actions of stage two may be characterized by such tension, which may turn out to be either helpful or harmful. Thus efforts to coordinate economic policy through broad guidelines as provided for in Article 103 seem to follow the classical line. They must however be freed from the heavy weight of the past if they are really to advance Economic and Monetary Union. Despite their upgrading and endorsement by the European Council, there is a danger of a reversion to a purely procedural exercise not unlike that of the Annual Report. By contrast the Article 104c procedure against excessive deficits – of different origin – could become an instrument of 'hard' coordination if pursued convincingly and with the vigorous involvement of the Monetary Committee. Since the Maastricht Treaty offers not so much an attribution of competences as encouragement to a more dynamic process, other approaches of this kind should be exploited.

7 No exclusive right of initiative in the field of monetary integration

Whereas in the classical area of the Treaty the Commission has a quasi-monopoly of putting proposals to the Council, such a proposal being necessary before the Council can act, things are different in the monetary field, which is an open area for competition among initiatives. Governments, the Council, the Monetary Committee and the European

Monetary Institute are now the main bodies having a right of initiative in this area.

It was not surprising that the Commission's initiative for the non-institutional strengthening of the EMS failed in the early eighties. The Committee stated, that 'it was recognized, that any set of proposals would have to strike a balance between the interests of potential creditor and debtor countries in the system. However, no general agreement proved possible in this group of proposals as the result of the Committee's discussion'. With these sentences the debate in the Council came to a quick end. By contrast, later Commission proposals for the liberalization of capital movements – 'primarily an obligation which flows from the EC Treaty and thus independent of the EMS' – were strongly supported.

There are numerous examples of proposals presented by the Committee to ministers and to the Council. Given their institutional status they do not generally bear the formal label of a proposal and it is difficult for an outsider to become aware of them. The Committee rarely comments on them; it is absolutely silent on realignment meetings. To aid a better understanding of the Committee's role and functions, some of its initiatives may be cited.

The Committee's suggestions presented in 1987 to ministers in Nyborg had the character of proposals. It was in Nyborg that the surveillance of economic policies was first introduced in the Community. 'This is to become an established procedure and the Committee will carry out surveillance ... on a regular basis ....'[10] Similarly the Council Decision of March 1990 on the attainment of progressive convergence of economic policies followed in substance a proposal from the Committee. To make its role clear, an obligation was inserted in Article 3 of the Decision that 'the Council's work on multilateral surveillance shall be prepared by the Monetary Committee'. This article served as a relevant precedent in the drafting of the Maastricht Treaty. A further example is given by the quinquennial reviews of the content of the ECU, which were negotiated in the Committee and adopted by the Council without debate. 'In view of its function and the particular legal situation of the EMS, the Committee had a special role to play in preparing the examination of the weights of the currencies in the ECU. At a special meeting at the beginning of September, the Committee put forward

10 Report by the chairman of the Monetary Committee to the informal Ecofin Council at Nyborg on 12 September 1987, p. 2.

proposals for revising the composition of the ECU.'[11] The initiating role of the Committee is seen in its purest form in realignments. When extended to other economic and monetary issues different institutional susceptibilities are respected and other appropriate forms are used.

8 Intergovernmental integration opened the way for the internal market

A growing consensus on the advantages of stability-oriented economic policies, supported by progress in economic policy coordination and the disciplinary effects of the EMS, prepared the ground for the Community's move to the single market. Without the earlier advances in monetary integration, the internal market initiative would probably not have found such a propitious political climate. However, the Committee never went so far as to conclude that the benefits of the single market could not be attained without full Economic and Monetary Union. 'In 1988, it reached the clear view that the single market can be established on the basis of present monetary arrangements: there is no operational reason to associate with it – as a prior, parallel or even subsequent condition – a completely unified monetary system.'[12] Projected into the future, this implies that what are required are, above all, strong efforts to solidify and to extend the zone of monetary stability in Europe. Furthermore, intergovernmental monetary integration should not be neglected.

9 A Committee with a distinctive position

Not all committees are the same kind of animal in the setting of the Community. Is the Monetary Committee a body which works in the shadow of the Commission and its controlled Comitology?[13] No, it is not. No more is it a body acting within and similar to the Council's General Secretariat. The Committee was the first to be created by the Treaty of Rome. Its tasks and its achievements have made it independent of both the Commission and the General Secretariat of the Council, with a position sui generis which has grown out of the particular

11 Monetary Committee (1985), Annual Report, Brussels, p. 8.
12 Report by the chairman of the Monetary Committee to the Ecofin Council in May 1988, p. 3.
13 In the European Community, Comitology signifies special rules and legally given deadlines, which advisory committees have to respect in producing their positions. The Monetary Committee is not subjected to any of these rules.

needs of monetary integration. From that distinctive position it serves the political masters of the Community, whoever they may be. If appropriate, it will present suggestions to the Commission, but its output is addressed predominantly to ministers and to the Council. The fact that the staff needed for its secretariat have to be supplied by the Commission does not affect its independence. The Commission provides two members of the Committee, as does every Member State. Any Community institution can ask the Committee for advice. It is not unusual for the European Council to mention the Committee.[14]

The principal reason for the sui generis position is the nature of economic and monetary integration as described above. Another explanation derives from the fact that half of the members come from central banks. As a general principle, the Committee takes advantage of the independent status of all members whenever necessary, but, more important, it has since the beginning been an unquestioned tradition that it respects the institutional independence of central banks, whatever their constitutional position in the national context. Members from central banks make invaluable conceptual and operational contributions to the Committee and the member from the Nederlandsche Bank has long been among those who have been most active in inspiring the work and in helping to develop proposals and bring them forward. Very often members from central banks are the necessary corrective force when others might be influenced too much by political considerations. This has happened from time to time in the context of the granting of a Community loan to a Member State. However, the interest plays in both directions, that is, also to the advantage of central banks. The low political visibility of the Committee puts central banks in the position of having an ear and – if wanted – a voice in the preparation of work for the ministerial level. Since stage three of EMU is not for tomorrow, this interest will remain for several years.

Members from ministries are equally in a unique position. Since they run departments in their national capitals, the Committee is a link as well as a catalyst from which European ideas emanate and where the feed-back can be received and digested. It acts, as it were, with two arms: the principal one operating on the level of the Community, the other – less pronounced – influencing thinking on European matters at the national level. A one-day meeting per month in Brussels, if supported by a strong substructure, allows the running of a competent

14 Conclusions of the Presidency of the European Council of Madrid (1989) and Birmingham (1992).

body. This would be destroyed if members were to behave like ambassadors, permanently present in Brussels.

Member States may also appoint two alternate members of the Committee and these are a substantial resource for its overall performance. Very often work is mandated to and prepared by the alternates, who then meet in special sessions under their own chairman. The strength of the alternates lies in the intersection of the technical and the political fields. Generally, their task is to offer technical solutions in operational form which make political sense. The preparation of the convergence criteria of the Maastricht Treaty was such a case. The Committee is also in the position to mobilize at any moment ad hoc groups to prepare specific issues (for example, legal aspects of the preparation of the EMS, and the technical conditions for the launching of Community loans). There remains scope to reinforce this substructure and to draw more on the capacity of national administrations.

The contributions of members are enhanced by the relatively independent position of the chairman, who is elected for two years on grounds of ability. The Committee has been forged by strong chairmen and by the astuteness of members in giving them that adequate room for manoeuvre which allows the whole Committee to act on the political level as a highly respected policy adviser. There is a fine balance of mutual respect in the interaction between members and their chairman. This is one of the nerves of the Committee, giving it its striking force. Developing forms of hard coordination of economic policies in the future may well require the Committee to build even more on that.

10 The working style of the Committee as a 'pre-policy maker'

Input to the Committee comes from several sources. The agenda and the orientation of work are the task of the chairman and the secretary. A great deal of the analytical groundwork is prepared by the staff of the Commission, who, for this purpose, are in a position similar to that of the economic unit of the (former) Committee of the Governors of the EC Central Banks. However, there is no exclusivity and all members contribute. Policy-oriented papers, with a request to report back, or an invitation to formulate alternative suggestions, are generally submitted to the Committee only by ministers and by Ecofin. The Commission hesitates to submit such papers because in the past amendments were made to formal proposals presented directly to the Council. It now prefers to ask the Committee for a preparatory debate of substance before ideas are couched in the terms of a formal proposal to the Council by the Commission. Such a discussion of substance can extend over many meetings including technical examination by the alternates' group. This allows a fairly large measure of agreement to develop before an official proposal is made and reaches the table of the Council. An example of this was the preparation of secondary legislation flowing out of the Maastricht Treaty.

The transformation of most of the input and of the Committee's discussion into policy-oriented papers of the Committee is the concluding task of the chairman, supported by the secretary. The Committee has developed its own forms of expressing the common interest over the years and they form today's tradition. The Community can achieve more than the sum of the performances of the Member States, but if the aim is to attain a higher quality of policy, proper centres of economic policy preparation are needed, having the courage to push things forward. If the Committee were not motivated by the ambition to meet this need, it would not serve the higher interest of the Community. It would loose its vital characteristics, its 'proprium', and move backward towards being a mere expert group.

The expression of the common interest is most strongly challenged when a realignment is prepared, at the end of which a new set of central rates has to stand. On these occasions the chairman has, at a certain point, to take the lead and formulate the common interest. It is he who in the end develops the proposal for new central rates. It is he who presents this at the ministerial meeting. There is no other Community body having the right of initiative in this core of monetary policy.

Consensus formation in this gradual way is the basic working style. The Committee shies away from being drawn down to the lowest common denominator. It likewise shuns the principle of equal distribution of dissatisfaction, and will not be a servant of the status quo. At the beginning of deliberations an attempt is first made to find out a sort of medium or common denominator, but every effort is then made to get beyond the average. The loadstar of the activity is best performance. It is for that reason that asymmetric solutions are favoured if they reinforce price stability. In presenting solutions to the Community at the political level, members indirectly commit themselves to advise their national authorities accordingly. Finally, there are many examples of occasions when the Committee did not hesitate to say no to unripe projects, since this served to shake things up and thus lead to better solutions.

11 The Committee's own external relations

'The EMS came into being at a time when the dollar's weakness was a main source of concern ... it developed during a period of extreme interest rate and exchange rate volatility at the very time our economies underwent a second oil shock.'[15] This quotation from a Committee report mirrors one of the Community's essential features, that of being a part of the wider world system. At the same time as creating the European monetary identity, Member States remain principal actors in the international system for which they shoulder up to a good quarter of the overall responsibility as expressed in IMF quotas. It is therefore somewhat artificial to distinguish between external and internal responsibilities. To the extent that the Community consolidates the zone of monetary stability and creates Economic and Monetary Union this also contributes to the stabilization of the overall system.

One set of external activities reaches to the international monetary institutions, including the EBRD. Other external links go right back to the Committee's original Statutes, approved in 1958. Article 14 of these Statutes invited it to 'establish close cooperation with the managing Board of the European Payments Union'. Today this seems outdated but it constitutes an opening for example towards EMI. The Committee has therefore never hesitated to engage in external activities in a formal way. Since the middle of the eighties it has gradually established consultation relations with several European countries: first with Norway, later with Austria, Sweden and, most recently, Finland. All are based on an exchange of letters between the monetary authorities of these countries and the Committee. This form of cooperation has proved to be very flexible, it can be extended according to the needs of the moment and it has been intensified at moments when issues of common interest made this necessary. New tasks are appearing for the Committee in Central and Eastern Europe, where the Community must go beyond balance-of-payments financing seek to exert – after some time – a stabilizing influence on exchange rate developments.

12 Contributing to the preparation of the work of the Council

Over the years, input to the ministerial level has become ever more intensive. For the Ecofin Council, the Committee is a key adviser in the field of monetary policy, international finance and macro-economic

15 Monetary Committee (1984), Assessment of five years of the EMS, Brussels (presented to the Ecofin Council on 12 March 1984).

policy. Preparation of Council meetings is conducted 'without prejudice' to Coreper[16] and without embarking on law-making. The Committee's impact at the political level is enhanced by the fact that a few members are Secretaries of State and represent their country in this capacity in the Council. Moreover, numerous other links exist. For example, the chairman is ex-officio invited to the Council's luncheons, where most mandates to the Committee originate, and which offer one of the few occasions for a frank exchange of views on economic policies at ministerial level.

The Committee does everything to reinforce the role of the Council meeting on economic and financial affairs (Ecofin). In its report of July 1990 on Economic and Monetary Union beyond stage one, presented as orientation for the preparation of the intergovernmental conference, point 55 proposes 'that, subject to the attribution of specific responsibilities to the European System of Central Banks by the Treaty, most central political and decision-taking powers in the running of the Union should be clearly attributed to the Council meeting on economic and financial affairs. This council should have the task of ensuring macro-economic and budgetary coordination, and should take the fundamental decisions on external monetary policy in consultation with the ESCB. It should also be required to coordinate those aspects of all Community policies which have an impact on the economic performance and cohesion of the Union'.

13 ... 'without prejudice' to Coreper

The Maastricht Treaty gives the Committee its 'charter' in Article 109c, which subsumes the relevant parts of the old Article 105 of the Treaty of Rome. The new article is a step forward in that it enshrines the policy preparation function, which has grown over the years. The third indent of the new article sets down as a task for the Committee 'to contribute, without prejudice to Article 151, to the preparation of the work of the Council...'. Behind the reference to Article 151 stands Coreper 'responsible for preparing the work of the Council and for carrying out the tasks assigned to it by the Council'. There may seem to be a danger of duplication of effort, but that danger does not come from the Monetary Committee which has for years directly prepared the work of the Council by virtue of its political and technical skills and the responsibilities of its members in the national administrations. Coreper is a

16 The Committee of the Permanent Representatives of the Member States, commonly referred to under the French label of Coreper. The functions and pretentions of this arm of the Council's machinery are high: Extra viam Coreper non nisi error.

generalist and the master of the Council's General Secretariat. By origin and vocation, ambassadors are an instrument of ministers of foreign affairs who, on their part, assist the European Council which brings together the Heads of State or Government and the president of the Commission.

Subordination of the Monetary Committee to Coreper would have far-reaching consequences: first, in terms of political influence and control of economic and monetary affairs within the Council and, secondly, on the future course of economic and monetary integration. There was at one moment a tendency to bring the Committee under the control of Coreper[17], motivated by the alleged interest of the unicity of the Council and the centralization of the centre. Economic and finance ministers have warded this off and will also continue to advance down the path of intergovernmental monetary integration. For this they will rely on an independent Monetary Committee. This is in the spirit of the Maastricht Treaty. After all, finance ministers were the masters of negotiations on the most important part of the Treaty, to which they gave their signature in both senses of the phrase. At a meeting in Oporto in 1991, the ministers and governors of central banks made it clear that no change is required in the Committee's position in virtue of which it prepares economic policy decisions directly.

14 Helping to draft the Maastricht Treaty

The Committee's most important single contribution to Economic and Monetary Union is to be seen in the convergence criteria of Article 109j. Roughly one year of intensive work and political pre-negotiations were needed to prepare this pillar of Economic and Monetary Union. Since progress towards EMU will depend on the observance of the convergence criteria, the Committee will be the appropriate institution to ensure their correct application.

A more visible contribution was the drafting of the Treaty itself. Here members played a key role at the level of personal representatives of ministers, where all decisions were prepared. The twelve heads of dele-

17 To demonstrate the position of Coreper it may be appropriate to quote a conclusion which was recently drawn by the Director-General of the Legal Service of the Commission and published in: The Maastricht Treaty on European Union (1993), Brussels, p. 65. In this conference the three pillars interpretation of the Treaty was criticized. Instead of this the metaphor of the Holy Trinity was suggested.
Mr Dewost, commenting on this debate, drew the conclusion: 'je voudrais en guise de conclusion poser une question irrévérencieuse. Puisqu'on parle de Trinité, qui est Dieu? Le Conseil européen ou le Coreper?'.

gations were members of the Committee. The Luxembourg Presidency made the secretary of the Committee his right-hand man. This was continued in the second half of the year 1991, when the chairman of the personal representatives happened to be chairman of the Monetary Committee at the same time. The efficiency and the spirit of the European monetary fraternity was working without impediment. The chairman of the conference of the representatives of the governments of the Member States wrote at the end of 1991: 'It is due to the quality, the dedication and the solidarity of the members of the Committee that the Treaty of Maastricht is written as it is'.[18] Nevertheless, the conference's activity was an example of the low political visibility of the Committee, following the principle 'that one can accomplish almost everything if someone else gets the credit'.

15 Respecting lines of demarcation while advancing

There is no aspiration to do more than political masters inspire and request. Coordination of the policies of Member States to the full extent needed for the functioning of the internal market and contributions to the preparation of the work of the Council open a wide enough field. Mr Delors once held a different view, expressed thus in a debate of the European Parliament: 'According to the present draft of the Presidency (of the intergovernmental conference), the Commission would not be able to play her part because the Monetary Committee would be turned into an Economic and Financial Committee, a sort of second Commission which, given its right of initiative and its place in the structure, would prevent the Commission doing its job and discharging its responsibilities. Consequently, if this Economic and Financial Committee is to be kept, consistency demands that Economic and Monetary Union be taken out of the Community and transferred to the intergovernmental sphere.'[19]

The Treaty did give an answer to this. As regards the European Parliament, the Committee has always responded to invitations from the Parliament to report to it. While fully respecting the particular institutional situation, the chairman has on several occasions set out the main lines of activity before the competent committee.

18 Quoted from the memory book of the Monetary Committee.

19 Official Journal of the European Communities no. 3-406, Debates of the European Parliament, 1991-92 sessions, p. 134.

16 Beyond 1994

With the passage to stage two in 1994, there was no formal change to the Monetary Committee itself. Some of its tasks became more demanding, but that has happened before. In particular (with an efficient introduction of the excessive deficit procedure), a stronger coordination of economic policies will be required. Hegel once expressed in his work on logic that: 'wenn alle Bedingungen einer Sache vorhanden sind, so tritt sie in die Existenz. Die Sache ist, ehe sie existiert'.

Encouraging the emergence of the conditions for Economic and Monetary Union will be the main challenge and the best contribution which the Committee can make. Monetary union through stability-oriented economic policies 'is already there but it does not yet exist'. In its field of activity the Committee is not the only promoter of integration, but in contrast to EMU, it is not only there, but it also fully exists, highly motivated and a source of dynamism. When all the conditions are fulfilled for stage three and for the establishment of a ESCB, the Committee will change in composition but not substantially in its tasks. Although there will be a change of name, today's activity will be subsumed into tomorrow's Committee just as tomorrow's name already influences today's behaviour. The future order which is being created will be crucially influenced by the spirit of the European monetary fraternity and by the vigour and drive of a unique centre of economic policy preparation.

The Committee of Governors as a forum for European central bank cooperation

Gunter D. Baer

1 Introduction

When at the end of 1993 the Committee of Governors of the Central Banks of the Member States of the European Community handed over its tasks and functions to the European Monetary Institute, it could look back at a history of nearly thirty years of monetary cooperation in Europe. Although press releases were occasionally issued and, since 1992, Annual Reports informed the public of the Committee's activities, the work was generally carried out discreetly behind closed doors in the context of the monthly meetings of the Bank for International Settlements. Nonetheless, without seeking a high public profile, the Committee evolved over years into the principal forum where Community central banks exchanged views on various issues of mutual concern, jointly analysed current and prospective economic and financial developments, formulated opinions and recommendations addressed to national and Community authorities, laid down principles and rules of common behaviour and, to the extent possible, coordinated their actions. It is probably no exaggeration to say that without the Committee's contributions, the conclusion of the Maastricht Treaty, the move into stages one and two of Economic and Monetary Union and the establishment of the EMI on 1 January 1994 would hardly have been possible.

André Szász joined the Committee as early as 1973 when he was appointed Executive Director of the Nederlandsche Bank. His balanced judgement and stringent reasoning earned him rapid recognition of his expertise in monetary policy questions and his contributions to discussions on the linkages between monetary and exchange rate policy, the importance of the policy mix and the need for central bank independence significantly influenced the Committee's evolving views on these issues. All these questions in fact played a decisive role in the process leading to the Treaty on European Union.

2 The main activities of the Committee

Although the focus of the Committee's work was on European monetary affairs, its agenda was determined as much by global developments as by the Community's strive for closer economic and monetary integration. The breakdown of the Bretton Woods system, the prolonged period of high inflation in the 1970s and the reverberations of oil price shocks and of the international debt crisis all affected deeply monetary relationships in Europe, sometimes impeding but frequently also stimulating efforts to promote monetary stability and to strengthen the framework for cooperation. As the interdependence of European economies increased, it became evident that no country could isolate itself from outside influence or disregard the spill-overs of its own action on the rest of the Community. Such interactions were felt most acutely in the interrelationships between interest rates, exchange rates and financial flows and their implications for price stability, and the work of the Committee naturally centred on these themes.

The Committee started in 1964 on a modest scale, in terms of both size and ambitions: it was composed of only five central bank governors[1] and its tasks were initially defined 'to hold consultations concerning the general principles and the broad lines of policies of the central banks, in particular as regards credit and money and foreign exchange markets, and to exchange information at regular intervals about the most important measures that fall within the competence of the central banks and to examine these measures'. In brief, the purpose of the Committee was to set in motion a process of mutual information. As strains began to surface more frequently in the Bretton Woods system in the second half of the 1960s, balance-of-payments and exchange rate questions increasingly came to the front of the Committee's discussions. Following an ad hoc arrangement for balance-of-payments financing in favour of France, the Committee decided in 1970 to set up the system of monetary support under which the Community central banks would provide short-term financing in the event of a temporary balance-of-payments deficit. Subsequently the adoption of the Werner Report for the attainment of a monetary union gave a strong impetus to the Committee's work. Firstly, in 1971 a new Council Decision invited the Committee to coordinate the central banks' monetary and credit policies and to study the harmonisation of monetary instru-

1 Luxembourg, one of the founding members of the Community, which forms a Monetary Association with Belgium and at the time had not yet established the Institut Monétaire Luxembourgeois (IML), was not represented on the Committee. The Director-General of the IML joined the Committee in 1974, first as an observer, and from 1990 as a full member.

ments. Secondly, one year later the system for narrowing the margins of fluctuation between the currencies of the Member States (the snake) was established. The Committee not only played an important part in the preparatory work, but provided also the forum for the Basle Agreement which laid down the rules and procedures for the very short-term financing of exchange market intervention. Thirdly, in 1973 the European Monetary Cooperation Fund was created – with a Board of Governors comprising all Committee members – to take over the administration of the very short-term financing and of the short-term monetary support, and to multilateralise the intra-Community settlement of positions resulting from interventions. These steps in fact defined the cornerstones of the Exchange Rate Mechanism which since 1979 has been in force in the Community.

For most part of the 1970s exchange rate issues remained the dominant theme in monetary cooperation, reflecting the varying fortunes of the snake and its dwindling membership in the wake of the first oil crisis and the widespread surge in inflation. In order to limit disruptive exchange rate effects and to cope with payments problems the short-term monetary support was activated on two occasions, efforts were made to develop a common policy vis-à-vis the US dollar and measures were taken to strengthen the snake. A strong political consensus about the desirability of greater monetary stability within Europe made it possible, towards the end of the decade, to rebuild a Community-wide exchange rate arrangement. Following the Committee's examination of the outline of the system, outlined in the Conclusions of the Presidency of the European Council in Bremen in July 1978, the establishment of the European Monetary System was politically agreed six months later, and after the Committee had defined the necessary operational procedures, the EMS became operative on 13 March 1979. The ECU was given a central role in the system, but the decisive operational features were broadly similar to those of the snake and the cohesion of the system depended essentially on policies pursued in the defence of bilateral parities. This became apparent in 1987 when the Basle/Nyborg Agreement was concluded which, in addition to some technical measures (such as an extension of the duration of financing obtained under the very short-term financing and the use of this credit mechanism under certain circumstances for the financing of intra-marginal interventions) developed a policy strategy of how to counter exchange rate tensions. Such measures comprised a more efficient use of exchange rate movements within the band, of interest rate changes and of exchange market intervention, but also confirmed the need for realignments if parities had come out of line.

Towards the end of the 1980s the Committee played increasingly a role in the planning and in the construction of Economic and Monetary Union. At the beginning the members of the Committee were involved in a personal capacity, serving on the Committee for the study of Economic and Montary Union (the Delors Committee), which upon invitation of the European Council studied and prepared concrete steps leading to a single currency in Europe. The Delors Report strongly influenced the political process which ultimately resulted in the conclusion of the Treaty of Maastricht. The Treaty's provisions, especially those governing the part on monetary union, mirrored closely the proposals and recommendations made by the Committee of Governors. The advice and active support of the Committee was also sought after the Treaty had been signed in February 1992 and preparatory work for the move to stages two and three of EMU, in fact, became next to cooperation of monetary policy the most important item on the Committee's agenda.

As the Community expanded over the years to twelve Member States, but more so because new demands were made on the Committee in the wake of progressive integration and the move towards EMU, the infrastructure supporting the Committee was built up steadily, especially after the entry into stage one in mid-1990. In addition to the Committee of Alternates, which had already been preparing the Committee's meetings for a number of years, several specialised Sub-Committees and Working Groups were set up and the Secretariat, including a research unit, increased to more than thirty persons.

The work of the Committee covered all monetary and financial aspects of concern to central banks and the Committee's advice and active participation in policy and institutional questions ranged from capital liberalisation issues to fiscal developments. However, in retrospect two distinct themes stand out prominently: how to enhance the prospects for stable monetary conditions in the Community and which practical and institutional steps need to be taken on the way to EMU. Both themes merit closer consideration.

3 Efforts towards more closely coordinated monetary policies

Cooperation with the aim of ensuring monetary stability was always at the heart of the Committee's activities. However, even if the medium-term benefits of consistent policies in closely intertwined economies were clearly recognised, putting the objective of coordinated policies into practice was a difficult and complex task. There existed no simple politically acceptable and easily practicable formula, not only because of the inherent conflict between national autonomy and a supranational policy stance, but also because economic policy-making is fraught with a high degree of uncertainty and, consequently, depends heavily on judgement. These difficulties are well known in the context of formulating and implementing policies at the national level, but they are compounded when the process is taken to the supranational level, as social preferences and relationships between policy instruments and final objectives may differ from country to country.

The basic issue in the coordination of policies is how to attain domestic goals without creating spill-over effects which would hinder the realisation of other countries' objectives. As the feedbacks of domestic monetary measures are most directly and quickly transmitted through the exchange rate, the question of how to enhance the consistency of monetary policy was, as the experience of the Committee has shown, always closely linked to the question of how to maintain exchange rate stability.

Initially monetary cooperation in the Committee consisted mainly of an exchange of views on current economic and financial developments. Efforts were made from time to time to improve the efficiency of the process of mutual information and consultation through a system of 'clignotants', i.e. warning signals to trigger policy responses whenever a country reached certain threshold values for some specific variables, such as inflation, budget and balance-of-payments deficits, official reserve levels, etc. However, while these attempts went some way in improving the analysis and led to a more systematic monitoring on the basis of more detailed statistics and studies, they had on balance little impact on national policy-making. However, this changed noticeably in the latter part of the 1970s when steps were taken to restore an exchange rate regime encompassing a larger number of Community currencies than those linked in the framework of the snake. Indeed, the view that flexible exchange rates would permit each country to choose its domestic policies in accordance with its own inflation-versus-employment preference and that under those circumstances Adam Smith's 'invisible hand' would avoid the emergence of disruptive imbalances among Europe's highly integrated economies, had never found much sympathy in a large majority of Community countries. The importance of stable exchange rates among the very open and highly interdependent continental European economies was always emphasised by André Szász who argued that 'it is therefore indispensable that within Europe exchange rates are managed'. This view was widely shared in the Community, even if at times a number of Community countries were not able to accept formal margins obligations.

The establishment of the EMS meant that the authorities had to keep a closer eye on the exchange rate, thus calling monetary policy into play as a means for cooperation. In an environment of progressive capital liberalisation, the adoption of fixed though adjustable parities in fact meant that the participating countries were taking a commitment to follow a common overall monetary stance which, in line with EMS objectives, was to lead to a zone of monetary stability. However, while the EMS Agreement laid down a set of rules and commitments to maintain exchange rate cohesion, to the extent possible, there was no clear prescription of how to achieve this zone of monetary stability, i.e. of how to decide on the appropriate thrust of the overall policy stance. In practice this did not matter much as long as there was an understanding on the division of responsibilities among countries participating in the Exchange Rate Mechanism. Germany, in pursuing a monetary policy geared towards price stability, provided the system's nominal anchor; and other participants, by pegging their exchange rate to the Deutsche mark, had a firm point of reference for their domestic monetary management. This assignment of roles not only promised the desired degree of exchange rate stability, it was also considered to be advantageous for all members: Germany benefited from stable exchange rates vis-à-vis its Community trade partners and other countries with higher rates of inflation were able to borrow credibility from a central bank with a recognised record of stability.

At the same time the exchange rate commitment helped them to reinforce discipline in other macro-economic policy areas and offered them a chance to lower inflationary expectations by enhancing over time the credibility of their own monetary policy stance. The rules implied, as André Szász recently recalled in a speech on 'The ERM seen from Amsterdam', that 'the main burden of the defence (of the exchange rate parity) is borne by the country whose currency is under attack and that the main weapon in the defence is interest rates, used not as a last resort but at an early stage'. However, in practice these ground rules were not always easy to apply, especially when monetary cooperation was rendered difficult as the causes of exchange rate tensions varied and national policy priorities differed.

Firstly, making the exchange rate the focal point of cooperation raised a number of complex analytical issues which could give rise to controversy about the 'correct' policies. For example, whenever exchange rate tensions occurred, a judgement had to be made whether they simply reflected market reactions to some sort of unsubstantiated 'news', were the result of emerging divergences in international competitiveness or had to be ascribed to actual or anticipated policy shifts which were prompting market participants to adjust portfolios. As each of these situations called for a different policy response – sterilised intervention to counter unwarranted pressures, a realignment of parities if it was impossible to restore competitiveness through other measures, or an adjustment in actual or intended domestic policies – the analysis of the source of exchange rate pressure was of key importance for deciding on the adequate cooperative policy response. However, since in reality it was frequently extremely difficult to disentangle with a sufficient degree of confidence the factors behind exchange rate tensions, it was not easy to agree on the appropriate counter measures. The second major issue was that even in the absence of acute exchange rate pressure the overall stance of monetary policy, reflecting the Deutsche mark's anchor role, was not necessarily seen to be appropriate with regard to the economic situation in individual countries or the Community's position vis-à-vis the rest of the world, thus giving rise to calls for an adjustment in German monetary policy or for a common policy vis-à-vis the US dollar. Especially in the early years of the EMS, monetary cooperation did not always succeed in reconciling national policies and performances with the requirements of a common policy stance at prevailing exchange rates, and parity realignments became unavoidable. Nonetheless, considerable progress was made over time and the commitment to EMS parities increasingly helped to promote stability-oriented policies and greater convergence in price performance, and produced, between 1987 and autumn 1992, an unprecedented long period of stable nominal exchange rates.

As a complementary step to monetary cooperation in the context of the EMS, the Committee introduced in early 1990 a common framework for monitoring monetary and economic trends in the Community. Its most significant feature was that, for the first time, the Committee began to carry out regular examinations of national monetary policies, comprising a forward-looking exercise and an ex-post surveillance to compare actual developments with earlier projections. It was in particular the ex-ante assessment, which, by aiming at a collective evaluation of the appropriateness of national monetary policies, sought to induce more closely coordinated and compatible policies without infringing on the prerogative of autonomous national decision-making. The basic idea was that in autumn, before firm conclusions would be reached on the course of monetary policy in the coming year, the national monetary policy intentions should be thoroughly analysed with regard to their implications for domestic price performance and their mutual compatibility. Following a joint assessment by the Committee, its views were expected to be taken into account by the national authorities in their final decision on next year's monetary policy stance.

While the approach was theoretically and intellectually well-founded, in practice it faced some serious technical difficulties which limited its usefulness for influencing national monetary policy decisions. Firstly, at the conceptual level it proved difficult to define sufficiently precise assessment criteria. Although price stability was the generally recognised final goal, allowance had to be made for the fact that inflation rates still diverged considerably among Community countries and that therefore price stability could not be realised within a one-year period. Neither would the necessary sharp tightening of monetary conditions have been desirable from a domestic point of view, nor would it have been possible without generating pressures in the Exchange Rate Mechanism. For this reason a medium-term view had to be adopted; national monetary policies were considered to be appropriate if they contributed to a lowering of inflation and were regarded as compatible if there was a reasonable assurance that they would not trigger exchange rate tensions.

Secondly, at the analytical level some significant technical improvements were introduced, but they did not eliminate the uncertainties inherent in monetary and exchange rate analysis. Projections of economic developments in each Community country were based on the same assumptions about external conditions, but the diversity of financial structures and differences in the transmission process and in the statistical coverage of monetary variables did not permit the use of only a few key intermediate variables in analysing the impact of an envisaged policy stance on the future price performance. Rather, the analysis had to be fairly eclectic and judgemental. This was even more the case when assessing whether national monetary policies – judged to be consistent with downward convergence in inflation rates – were compatible with stable exchange rate conditions. Given the tenuous relationship between interest rates, prices and exchange rates, no strong conclusions were possible and the examination could not go beyond a general assessment of potential risks to exchange rate stability.

Whether in retrospect the Committee's efforts to cooperate are seen more as a failure or a success, is a matter of perspective. For those who expect monetary cooperation to result in a strategic interaction in policy making, coming close to, or actually entailing, joint decisions by autonomous national authorities, the record of the Committee's achievements may be disappointing. Mechanisms such as the EMS or the Committee's monitoring framework with its regular, collective assessment exercises could not enforce a degree of policy harmonisation which might have possibly prevented the dramatic exchange market crises of autumn 1992 and July 1993. However, for those who accept that the uncertainties surrounding economic analysis and the different weights attached at national levels to specific policy objectives set limits to the coordination of policies, at least two remarkable accomplishments stand out from the Committee's work. Firstly, there can be little doubt that cooperation among central banks, even without achieving a systematic interaction in policy decisions, contributed significantly to an extended period of economic and financial stability, greater convergence in price performance and progressive economic and financial integration. Without this cooperation there is a great likelihood that national policies would have led to substantial disequilibria, requiring painful and costly adjustment measures in all Community countries. Secondly, the process of mutual information and consultation and the intensive discussions in the Committee certainly enhanced the understanding of, and promoted a convergence of views on, important questions of principle. Not only do all central banks nowadays agree firmly that the attainment of price stability is the primary objective of monetary policy but there is also a broad consensus that, in the longer run, the supply of money is the decisive determinant of price developments; that in the medium term there is no trade-off between inflation and employment and that the success of monetary policy depends crucially on its influence on market expectations and thus on the central bank's credibility. In fact, all these principles have been translated into the Statute of the future European System of Central Banks.

4 The Committee's contributions to the construction of EMU

Ever since the idea of creating an EMU was relaunched in the latter part of the 1980s, the Committee was closely involved in this process. Although the final decisions were the preserve of the political authorities negotiating the new EC Treaty, the Committee played an important advisory role and its proposals and recommendations have strongly influenced the plan for moving to EMU, not only in the realm of monetary questions but also in many other aspects of EMU. As mentioned earlier, the Committee's contributions were initially made 'ad personam' as members of the Delors Committee. However, as soon as the Heads of State or Government had decided to start stage one of EMU on 1 July 1990 and to convene an intergovernmental conference, issues relating to monetary union took a prominent place on the Committee's agenda. At first the work centred on the preparation of the Statutes for the ESCB and its predecessor, the EMI. After the Maastricht Treaty had been signed in February 1992, the Committee began considering issues relating to the setting-up of the EMI as well as various technical questions linked to the future single monetary policy.

Many of the Delors Report's recommendations on questions of principle and on measures to build a viable and successful EMU indicate the handwriting of central bank governors. Several of the 'core' messages are now fully accepted but were not necessarily conventional wisdom at the time of the Delors Committee's deliberations. This applies in particular to such fundamental points as: a monetary union requires a single monetary policy and thus implies the loss of national monetary policy autonomy; monetary policy decisions are indivisible and therefore do not permit a gradual handover of authority from the national to the Community level; price stability should be the pre-eminent objective of monetary policy and the decisions on such policies should be placed in the hands of an independent institution. But it also applies to some extent to a number of recommendations outside the narrow realm of monetary policy, such as the need for constraints on national fiscal policy and the emphasis on a market-oriented approach and adequate supply-side policies in the context of an EMU. These recommendations were all taken on board in the Maastricht Treaty.

The most important contribution of the Committee was, however, the preparation of a precise set of provisions which should govern the ESCB when it would be established at the time of entry into the final stage of EMU. The proposed model of a central bank for the Community, which many political authorities would have found difficult to accept only a few years ago, was adopted in the Maastricht Treaty virtually without any modification. This future ESCB is unequivocally committed to the attainment of price stability and in order to fulfil this objective it is given a degree of independence, practically unrivalled by any central bank in the world. Independence is ensured not only by shielding the ESCB's decision-making on monetary policy from interference by political authorities, but also by a number of organisational, operational and functional provisions, which, for example, include the prohibition of credit extension to the public sector and safeguards to avoid conflicts between monetary and exchange rate policies. As André Szász has pointed out, without acceptance of these fundamental provisions there would have been no agreement in Maastricht. And he added, 'one should be clear about its meaning': the Treaty does not assign priority to price stability over employment but it is based on the view that in the longer run price stability is a condition for sustainable growth. This, as André Szász notes, 'underscores the need for what can be regarded as the core provisions on EMU in the Treaty' – on the one hand an independent central bank committed to price stability and, on the other, measures to avoid excessive deficits in national budgets.

Obviously, the Statute for the ESCB as embodied in the Treaty can only set a framework and lay down principles. More precise operational features concerning the strategy, the choice of the instruments and the operating procedures of the single monetary policy as well as many related issues will still have to be worked out. This is one of the main tasks of the EMI which, however, can build on a solid basis of preparatory work carried out in these fields in the last one and a half years of the Committee's existence.

5 Concluding remarks

Over nearly thirty years the Committee of Governors has contributed as much to the process of economic and financial integration in Europe as it has responded to the requirements of the increasing interdependence between the Community economies. Monetary cooperation in the framework of the Committee covered practically any aspect of central banking but the overriding concern was invariably to help to create stable monetary conditions in the Community as a basis for sustained growth of output and high employment. At times efforts to maintain stable financial relationships between the closely-linked economies in the Community were thwarted by factors outside the control of the central banks, by changing policy objectives of individual countries or by difficulties in coming to a collective assessment which could have formed a basis for more consistent and more closely coordinated policies. However, the Committee has always endeavoured to find commonly acceptable solutions and, looking at these efforts as a continuing process, there can be no doubt that the Committee succeeded in promoting policies which were in the interest and for the benefit of all Community countries. This achievement was ultimately possible only because of the mutual trust and confidence which evolved in a closely-knit group of central bankers sharing the same beliefs and aims.

Techniques for stability

Henk Boot

1 Introduction

From its very beginning, European integration has included coordination of macro-economic policies. Under the Treaty of Rome, cyclical policy and exchange rate policy are to be considered matters of common concern by the Member States. The relevant provisions centre on each country's duty to ensure balance-of-payments equilibrium and confidence in its currency, in order to prevent exchange rate problems or curbs on external payments from impeding the development of trade within the common market. In this context, the Treaty established a group charged with promoting this coordination: the Monetary Committee, consisting of high-ranking officials of national treasuries and central banks. But, likewise from the very start, the question arose how to make coordination work in order to ensure that the consultations would be more than non-committal exchanges of views and information. That is the question with which we shall be concerned in this essay: what are the methods which have been developed to enhance the effectiveness of the European coordination exercises and what have been the incentives to give them more bite, particularly in the politically sensitive, but from the angle of policy coordination essential, area of public finance. A recurrent issue in this respect concerns the ultimate objective of these coordination exercises. In the spirit of the work of André Szász, this essay will take sides with the objective of stability in the sense of domestic price stability.

It is clear that, by its very nature, the process of coordination is unable to impose policies upon an sovereign state against its will. Both under the Treaty of Rome and under the Treaty of Maastricht, for as long as EMU has not been attained, competence for policy rests expressly with the national authorities. What the European consultations can do is to support those who, in their own country, advocate policies which the partner countries in Europe deem most desirable from a Community viewpoint. That is the approach which Van Lennep introduced within the Monetary Committee. In his memoirs[1], Van Lennep relates how, during the first working session of the Committee, when French policies were discussed, the French members were very much on the defensive while the others were far from critical. After having taken various members apart during the lunch break and impressing on them the need for greater candour in the interests both of France and of the Community, he was able to change attitudes permitting the Committee yet to formulate a useful recommendation.

2 A hopeful start

That was how the Monetary Committee started, looking for ways to come to ever-more effective coordination. At first, its work in this area consisted mainly of – initially semi-annual – country examinations in order to improve the partners' knowledge and understanding of each other's economic and financial structures. In addition, ad hoc recommendations were issued on specific situations and issues. Those who were active at the time in the research departments of central banks or finance ministries will no doubt remember that such an examination was a major event, especially if it focused on one's own country but also when other countries were up for review. In addition, the Committee conducted a study of the instruments of monetary policy, which was published later. One might say that the initial period was one in which the partners made each other's acquaintance, a necessary though not sufficient condition for effective policy consultations.

The Annual Reports of the Committee from these initial years convey the high expectations of these pioneering days. In 1961, for instance, the Annual Report noted that, as the range of policy instruments of the Member States improved, the future transition from coordination to centralization of decisions would be but a small step. And in 1964 the report raised the possibility that the consultative procedures which were not binding on the national authorities might at a later stage evolve into institutional procedures which could lead to Community action.

A major new development was in evidence when on 15 April 1964 the Council of Ministers accepted a recommendation to the effect that, in conducting economic policy, priority was to be assigned to stabilizing the levels of costs and prices. Among the targets to be used to that end was an upper limit of 5 per cent for the growth of public expenditure. In

1 Van Lennep (1991), pp. 92-93.

a number of respects, this was a significant step. It was the first recommendation to assign priorities for policy and introduce quantitative standards for public finance. Moreover, the Council was explicitly involved in the coordination process, a sine qua non since political issues were involved. Nonetheless, in 1965 the Committee had to conclude that fiscal policies in nearly all Member States had been below the mark, and interestingly enough Germany, the Netherlands and Belgium were singled out in this respect. Yet, the Council of Ministers confirmed the recommendation for 1965 and repeated it in a slightly modified form in 1966.

The second half of the 1960s saw more turbulent developments, with inflationary pressures intensifying and exchange rate uncertainties making themselves felt both within and outside of Europe. In 1966, the EC Commission presented recommendations for institutionalizing policy coordination at the level of the Council, providing for consultations twice a year and, where necessary, more frequently to discuss specific cases. Proposals were made to come to a set of indicators denoted as clignotants. These indicators were to relate to ultimate objectives in respect of economic growth and inflation as well as to intermediate targets in the monetary and fiscal sphere. However, the fiscal variable was merely described in qualitative terms rather than being formulated as an explicit threshold value. The initial notion that the indicators were to trigger special interim consultations within the Council has never been given practical effect. It proved difficult to agree on threshold values if they entailed operational consequences, in this particular case the obligation to consult the partner countries. Even though the consequences would not have extended beyond mere consultation, the nature of the indicator underlying the consultation would all too easily have forced the country concerned onto the defensive. Also, the considerable number of indicators would have given rise to fairly frequent ad hoc consultations. If a procedure is activated too often, the resulting consultations tend to degenerate into a routine matter, thus losing much of their effectiveness. Consequently, the indicators have never advanced beyond the stage of experimental application within the coordinating committees.

In the process of coordination, there is a considerable natural need to be informed in good time about measures envisaged by the partner countries in order to be able to make one's views heard before any final decisions are taken. The desire for prior consultation was already expressed in the 1962 Annual Report of the Monetary Committee. Towards the end of the 1960s, this matter became the subject of intensive discussion. No watertight legal obligations have ever been introduced; after all, countries must always retain scope to take urgent decisions at short notice, while it is not really feasible to draw up an exhaustive and detailed list of measures which require prior consultation. In terms of substance, too, problems are likely to arise: countries which fail to take necessary action are not subject to the obligation of prior consultation; in addition, there is a risk that increases in official interest rates, not invariably received with enthusiasm by the partner countries, might be delayed by such an obligation. For these reasons, preference is to be given to a form of consultation which, though not legally watertight, may produce quite satisfactory results if there is a sufficient degree of team spirit: the tour d'horizon, already noted in the Monetary Committee's 1960 Annual Report and presented in 1969 as a major new instrument. At that time, the Committee stated that henceforth it intended to start off its agenda with an exchange of views about the problems and prospects regarding economic and monetary policy. The tour d'horizon proved a useful instrument which, though falling into abeyance at times, was invariably resurrected later. Even today, it continues to play a significant role in the Committee's meetings. It permits members to provide information about recent domestic developments and, above all, to give prominence to the views and expectations prevailing in their home country, thus eliciting reactions from others, who may in turn stress their own priorities and preoccupations. In this way, the external interest may be incorporated into the national policy-making process. This exchange of views, which cannot by its very nature have any binding force, may prompt discussions fostering a measure of convergence of views.

In the envisaged set-up, practically all the clignotants concerned domestic variables, just one of them relating to an external aggregate. This shows that the system mainly sought to identify ill-balanced domestic developments rather than bring out any need for parity changes. This is typical of the EC approach towards policy coordination, which has invariably attached great significance to exchange rate stability since an integrating economic community with ever-growing trade among its members is most likely to thrive in an environment of exchange rate stability. When the Bretton Woods system was in its final stages and international discussions began to centre on possibilities for a more flexible system of parities, the EC tended in the opposite direction, looking for ways to maintain stability of intra-Community exchange rates. The best way of achieving this target is domestic adjustment but the Commission also advocated a different route – that of intra-Community lending. At the same time, attention was also given to the idea first mooted by Pfleiderer in 1964[2], to reduce and eventually eliminate the fluctuation margins surrounding the cross-parities of the Member States. By depressing the costs and reducing the processing times of intra-Community payments, this would be conducive to the development of trade within the Community. At the same time, it would constitute a precautionary measure in the event that wider fluctuation margins might be introduced in the international system. Both these elements – intra-EC exchange rate obligations and intra-EC lending – were developed in greater detail during the subsequent period.

Thus, from the very beginning, attempts have been made to strengthen the coordination process. Initially, the process sought to increase knowledge and mutual understanding, to identify incipient problems in good time and bring them up for discussion, with attention focusing largely on measures and instruments. In this manner, the necessary technical foundations were laid for the coordination discussions, but gradually it became ever-clearer that this would not be sufficient and that new routes would have to be taken. In its 1968 Annual Report, the Monetary Committee actually concluded that 'the degree to which price increases are now being tolerated in the Member States diverges considerably. Such differences must not be allowed to continue if we are to avoid that this will in time give rise to fundamental disequilibria in the relations among the Member States. In this connection, the Monetary Committee is aware that, considering the volume of their trade with the rest of the world, the countries of the common market could make a useful contribution to the world economy by pursuing policies seeking to make their group a centre of price stability. However, harmonizing the main objectives set by the governments of the Member States is not sufficient. The practical measures to achieve these objectives must also be coordinated'.[3] This statement aptly summarized the problems which would continue to face European policy coordination.

3 First attempt at EMU

The Memorandum of the Commission of 12 February 1969 on coordination of economic policy and monetary cooperation in the Community brought together the various elements discussed in the previous sec-

2 Pfleiderer (1964).
3 Translated from the Dutch-language version of the Werner Report.

tion. It contained proposals for more effective coordination, notably mandatory prior consultation for all important measures of policy and reconciliation of medium-term policy objectives; it also contained proposals for the creation of credit mechanisms. Together with the discussions in the Monetary Committee in this period, the Memorandum constituted a significant input for the Werner Report of 1970.[4] It can be argued that the prevailing exchange rate uncertainties, partly caused by shortcomings in domestic financial policies in the Member States but exacerbated by the staggering Bretton Woods system, provided one of the impulses for the first attempt at Economic and Monetary Union. It might be said that politics, dissatisfied with exchange rate performance, wanted to take over from the monetary authorities. In this process, there seemed to be more interest in the objective of avoiding exchange rate disturbance detrimental to Community trade and common agricultural policy than in the means to be used to this end, which appeared to be regarded as being of a technical rather than a political nature. The Commission, in particular, had taken a number of initiatives in previous years, culminating in the Memorandum of 1969.

The Werner Report noted that thus far the attempts at effective coordination or harmonization of economic policies within the Community had been unsuccessful. Among the shortcomings identified were the lack of adequately harmonized quantitative targets and the fact that recommendations were often couched in general terms. Hence, the Werner Report concluded that, in general, the consultative procedures had failed to produce the expected results, either because they were purely formal in nature or because Member States, relying on derogations, were able to evade their intended effects. Strengthening coordination was pinpointed as one of the principal tasks for the first stage. To that end, the coordination was to involve a measure of coercion, which was to be imposed gradually. Three times a year, a profound examination of the economic situation in the Community was to be conducted in order to establish common guidelines for policies. In this context, each country was to receive specified and detailed recommendations about the outlines of the economic policy to be pursued and was, without a single exception, to comply with the obligation of prior consultation. It was also advocated that the coordination should, once a year, lead to a more formal act in that an Annual Report on the economic situation in the Community was to be presented to the European Parliament and the national parliaments. This coordination exercise was to centre on the coordination and harmonization of fiscal policies,

4 Werner Committee (1970).

for which purpose each country was to be given quantitative guidelines.

The Werner Report provided a good analysis of the shortcomings of coordination as they had been in evidence so far: short on specifics and short on constraints. However, it did not go beyond procedures and powers, failing to come to grips with the substantive question as to the basis on which agreement on the medium-term objectives of economic policy could be achieved. It made no mention of any specific objective of stability which might be employed as a point of reference in policy coordination. In the Council Resolution of March 1971 its proposals for coordination during the first stage were largely adopted. It is worthy of note that the task of the Community organization of the central bank during the final stage was defined as assisting in achieving stability and growth, whereas the legal foundation and the measure of independence were allowed to remain vague. The introduction was delayed by the international monetary complications. It was not until the Council Resolution of March 1972 that the initiative was resumed; the Resolution provided for a consultative arrangement in the event that a Member State was to take or consider measures which departed from the agreed broad guidelines of economic policy. This was followed in February 1974 by the so-called Convergence Decision[5], which provided for three examinations of the economic situation in the Community every year; in addition, it formally introduced the obligation of prior consultation in the event of parity changes or similar exchange rate measures.

The new procedures, however, failed to improve efficacy. The recommendations continued to be non-committal in nature. A typical example is afforded by the fate of the Council Resolution of December 1972 about combating inflation, as described in the Nederlandsche Bank's Annual Report for 1973. In the Resolution, the Member States had declared that they would seek to reduce the rate of consumer price increase in the course of 1973 to 4 per cent; this had been attended by quantitative guidelines for curbing money growth and public expenditure. When, during 1973, it became ever-clearer that these targets would not in general be attained, the Council adopted a new Resolution in September in which the price target was no longer quantified. Finally, in December the Council adopted yet another Resolution which contained no quantitative guidelines at all.

5 Council Decision No. 74/120/EEC of
18 February 1974.

Of the laudable intentions of the Werner Report and the EMU Resolutions of 1971 and 1972, the only one to be achieved was the snake, leaving its tunnel after the dollar was floated. But the coordination was unable to prevent the snake from withering gradually, until in 1978 a Franco-German initiative led to its continuation in a new set-up.

4 Snake and EMS

When the snake had been reduced to just a small group of countries centring on Germany, but excluding France, 1978 saw the initiative to restore a European exchange rate system, the EMS. Generally, this initiative is considered to have been inspired by political rather than economic motives.[6] Indicative is the way in which the initiative was taken: a joint Franco-German initiative at the highest political level, following secret technical preparations outside the normal EC channels. The political motives derived notably from the uncertainties about the US administration then in office and the weakening of the dollar, calling for strengthening European cooperation and for broadening the European base so as to reduce dependence on the dollar's vicissitudes. The ultimate result was the Council Resolution of 5 December 1978 on the establishment of the European Monetary System. The Resolution was long on monetary detail, providing for ample financing and credit facilities, a settlement mechanism involving the ECU and some pooling of reserves on a temporary revolving basis, but weak on the economic side; apart from the divergence indicator, there were no new specific provisions regarding the coordination of economic policies. Nevertheless, the Resolution introduced an important innovation in that it contained an explicit stability objective: whereas the EMU Resolution of 1972 had merely mentioned the creation of its own monetary zone, the EMS Resolution referred to 'a scheme for the creation of closer monetary cooperation leading to a zone of monetary stability in Europe'.

It is generally recognized that the EMS has exercised a disciplinary action and has contributed to price stability within the EC. This action derives its efficacy primarily from the traditional preparedness within the EC to assign a high priority to intra-EC exchange rate stability. This is the very notion underlying the relevant provisions of the Treaty of Rome, which sought to counter situations where exchange rate movements would disturb intra-EC trade. This priority had also been a major motive for the first attempt at EMU, which had, incidentally, run aground by this time. The priority of exchange rate stability brings with it major

6 Gros and Thygesen (1992), ch. 2.

incentives for the participating countries to reconcile their domestic priorities. This is where the second contributory factor comes in: the determination of Germany to give high priority under all circumstances to the objective of domestic price stability, both in actual policies and in institutional arrangements. This enables the Bundesbank, with the strong support of German public opinion, to pursue steadfast stability-oriented policies. Although at times this is seen as a complication for European cooperation, there is more reason to view it as a salutary anchor of stability for the EMS. It might be said that, within such an exchange rate system, coordination of policies is ensured by the automatic pilot, with the German pursuit of stability as the gyroscope. Each country has committed itself to maintaining its exchange rate and, hence, must accept the consequences for domestic policy. In such a set-up, it is essential that the participants inform each other adequately about their domestic situation and policies and exchange views on a frequent basis. But the incentive for an adequate policy originates from the exchange rate commitment, as a devaluation is often seen as painful and is thus preferably avoided.

All this does not alter the fact that, from the very start, the technicalities of the exchange rate mechanism or, to continue the earlier metaphor, the settings of the controls of the automatic pilot, have been the subject of much discussion. The stability objective of the EMS involves some ambiguity, since dilemmas may arise and the relative priority of domestic price stability over exchange rate stability is not made entirely clear. For Germany, there is no doubt that domestic price stability comes first under all circumstances. But, as other countries sometimes find it difficult to be as strict, there have been discussions on technical modalities in the monetary field that should facilitate exchange rate stability per se. Much discussion has been devoted to the Community credit mechanisms, introduced in the early seventies and sharply increased when the EMS was established. To some extent, the argumentation was based on the stability objective: by making the credit subject to policy conditions, the recipient country would be given incentives to restore domestic equilibrium. But that would at best mean that the conditionality aims to redress the disequilibrium that coordination was supposed to prevent in the first place. Furthermore, this technique has not proved very effective in this respect, as too often the credit had already been agreed in principle on the political level before the detailed policy conditions were agreed with the authorities concerned. It must therefore be concluded that conditional EC credit constituted an attempt to remedy shortcomings in the coordination process, and not a very effective one at that, rather than to strengthen the process. Another argument that was advanced held that a large credit reservoir would be required to deter speculators by making clear that ample finance would be available. This argument is less concerned with stability since, as a rule, speculative outflows will not arise until doubts have taken root about the soundness of the policies pursued. Moreover, the availability of credit could detract from the disciplinary action of the Exchange Rate Mechanism.

Generally, the risk of a dilemma between domestic and external stability will be most pronounced in the event of external turbulence or asymmetrical shocks. A major country like France has proved itself prepared to conduct stringent disinflationary policies, and with success, but it has shown itself much more reluctant to undertake additional efforts if they are called for by external developments, such as the volatility of the dollar. Experience has shown that a weak dollar may create tensions within the EMS as some countries are much better able than others to accept the resulting deterioration of their competitive position. Hence, at regular intervals, attempts have been made to come to a common policy towards the dollar, signs of which were already evident in the initial plans to reduce the fluctuation margins; the EMS Resolution contains an explicit provision to the effect that the durability of the EMS and international cooperation require coordination of exchange rate policies vis-à-vis third countries and, as far as possible, a concertation with the monetary authorities of these countries. In practice, this has not led to tangible results. Such a common dollar policy could easily conflict with the pursuit of domestic price stability since support for the dollar would have to be provided by the countries with the strongest currencies, thus frustrating the monetary policies pursued by them. In Germany the joint float of the EMS vis-à-vis third currencies was actually seen as an opportunity to reduce the currency's vulnerability to the vagaries of the dollar. Moreover, for a long time the US authorities evinced a bare minimum of willingness to cooperate on the exchange rate front, and unilateral European support for the dollar, even if Europe were prepared to shoulder this burden, cannot be truly effective.

Finally, mention should be made in this connection of the divergence indicator included in the EMS Resolution as a trigger for consultation. The divergence indicator bears a closer resemblance to the reserve indicator as it was proposed at the time by the Americans in the Committee of Twenty discussions than to the clignotants introduced earlier within the EC. It reacts to exchange rate movements within the fluctuation band without heeding the underlying domestic causes, like the reserve indicator, whereas the clignotants had been designed to highlight the latter. Hence, it is unduly one-sided and cannot be seen as a distinct contribution to domestic price stability; it may even place the onus of adjustment on the most stable country if, in this respect, it stands out from the others. We need not, therefore, regret the fact that its significance has diminished markedly over the years.

Even after the start of the EMS there have been recurring discussions seeking to adjust the controls. Attempts have been made to increase credits, ease settlement rules and transfer reserve pooling and credit mechanisms to a fund so as to lessen creditors' influence. On the other hand, following a range of realignments in earlier years, 1987 witnessed the Basle/Nyborg Agreement, providing for rules of conduct, underlain by a more stability-oriented philosophy, to counter exchange rate unrest: not by means of credit-financed interventions but by rapid responses in terms of interest and exchange rate policy, warding off exchange rate unrest before it can assume major proportions and become uncontrollable.

Thus, a large number of attempts have been made, with varying degrees of success, to whittle down the stability-oriented set-up of the EMS in order to make it easier for some countries with less-than-perfect price stability to maintain exchange rate stability. As a result of political compromises, these attempts have not remained without consequences. Nonetheless, it is generally accepted that the EMS has made a major positive contribution to convergence towards price stability, even if more will be needed. The disciplinary action of the system is most direct in the area of monetary policy, where, as is also evident from the Dutch experience, currency depreciation within the band and, a fortiori, reserve losses provide a powerful signal for increases in interest rates. The effect is less direct, but definitely not non-existent, in regard of fiscal policy. France's decision in 1983 to continue its EMS membership and to accept the consequences for fiscal policy heralded the hey-day of the EMS. The exchange rate obligations imposed by the EMS may discourage the deterioration of public finance in individual countries. But they have been unable to prevent chronic deficits from being continued overly long or fiscal deficits of participating countries from mounting more or less in concert during the recent recession. The many years of exchange rate stability within the EMS contributed to a climate permitting a renewed attempt at EMU, though with a built-in time bomb which exploded when political resistance ultimately proved stronger than initially expected.

5 Second attempt at EMU

At the European Council in Hanover in 1988 the drive towards EMU was formally resumed when the Delors Committee was given its mandate. As argued by Szász[7], this renewed attempt was underlain by a strong political motivation deriving from the growing uncertainties in Central and Eastern Europe which were soon to be followed by the major upheavals in that region. These uncertainties underlined once more the need for close political cooperation within Western Europe. The drive towards EMU is to be seen in that context. It shares the political motivation with the EMS initiative of 1978, though at that time the uncertainties were to be found west of Europe across the Atlantic. Again, the move commenced with French and German political initiatives, encouraged at the highest political level. Contrary to the first attempt, dissatisfaction with exchange rate performance did not provide a motive. On the contrary, the exchange rate stability which had marked the EMS since 1987 had contributed to a climate of Europhoria in which EMU seemed a realistic and feasible objective. Some countries were, however, less than satisfied with the dominant position of German monetary policy, a situation which could only be altered if German conditions for EMU were accepted. This time, the political motivation was so strong that agreement was reached, permitting the objective of domestic price stability and the appurtenant institutional arrangements, notably the independence of the European Central Bank, to be embedded in the Maastricht Treaty. This contrasts sharply with the first attempt at EMU when lack of agreement had caused these two crucial questions to remain unresolved. The absence of a generally accepted stability objective and of a willingness to coordinate actual policies accordingly had been instrumental in the failure of the first attempt at EMU, which became apparent when the international monetary system was exposed to severe shocks and difficult choices had to be made.

The political constellation was thus propitious, permitting the Maastricht Treaty to lay a legal foundation for domestic stability in the final stage of EMU which may be rated as adequate in numerous respects. Yet it is equally important that the economic foundation for EMU – a high degree of domestic stability in the participating countries at the time of their accession – should be sufficiently strong. In this respect, a recurring problem is in evidence in that acceptance of price stability as the ultimate objective does not automatically ensure that policies in the short run will actually be aimed accordingly. Although the exchange

7 Szász (1993).

rate stability within the EMS at the time might suggest otherwise, the fundamental position in the early 1990s was not favourable. The Delors Report of 1989, echoing its precursor of some twenty years earlier, stated that especially in the area of fiscal policy the 1974 Council Decision on economic convergence had not succeeded in establishing an effective foundation for policy coordination. Even before agreement was reached in late 1991 about the provisions of the Maastricht Treaty, some changes had already been made in the coordination process. It was decided that stage one was to start in mid-1990; to that end, two coordination Council Decisions were altered. The role of the Committee of Central Bank Governors in the coordination of monetary policies was strengthened and the objective of this coordination defined more precisely: domestic price stability as a necessary condition for the proper operation of the EMS. The 1974 Council Decision was replaced in its entirety by a new arrangement for multilateral surveillance to a large extent based on learning by doing. In July 1991 the procedure for convergence programmes was introduced.

This pattern was continued in the Maastricht Treaty, which featured a number of innovations to foster stabilization. In order to be able to perform its task of strengthening monetary policy coordination, the EMI was assigned the unambiguous objective of price stability. Convergence criteria were specified for a number of variables, including inflation and public finance, which a country must meet if it is to qualify for the final stage of EMU. Moreover, it has been provided that the countries which still fail in this respect – at present most of them – will submit convergence programmes for discussion at the EC level, explaining how they envisage meeting the criteria in the years ahead. Furthermore, the countries have undertaken to avoid excessive fiscal deficits, defined in terms of the same threshold values as the convergence criteria; to this end, a procedure has been instituted which will take effect as early as in stage two, albeit without the possibilities of sanctions which will only be effective in the final stage.

All in all, policy coordination has been strengthened in a potentially significant manner. The criteria clearly quantify such strategic target variables as the fiscal deficit and the public debt ratio at 3 per cent and 60 per cent of GDP, respectively, while the convergence programmes constitute a technique of translating them into verifiable intentions for the coming years. Moreover, a strong incentive has been incorporated making for genuine coordination since a country which fails to meet the criteria will not qualify for the final stage. For as long as the political will to achieve EMU is strong, especially in the two major countries which again inspired the political initiative, it will constitute a powerful stimulus towards convergence for fear of being excluded from EMU.

This does not alter the fact that the arrangements for stage two bear the marks of political compromises which tend to weaken the orientation towards stability during this period. For instance, attenuating clauses have been added to the budgetary criteria to the effect that, in addition to levels, development over time will also be considered in the assessment of the results achieved. For the debt ratio criterion, this was unavoidable as some countries would otherwise have been a priori unable to qualify, but at a late stage of the negotiations a similarly subjective element has also been introduced for the deficit criterion. Moreover, it is to be regretted that a fixed date has been set for the start of stage two, without subjecting the transition to convergence conditions. Thus an opportunity has been missed to incorporate an incentive for fiscal consolidation or at least to prevent stage two from commencing under highly unfavourable fiscal conditions. The situation as it has now arisen will make extremely heavy demands on the excessive deficit procedure during stage two, as, measured by the criteria, practically all countries are running excessive deficits, detracting heavily from the efficacy of the procedure.

In principle, the technique of convergence programmes provides opportunities for effective coordination during the transitional stage. They are, after all, drawn up by the countries themselves, ensuring high levels of commitment, giving each country a feeling of 'owning' its programme. Each of the programmes is discussed individually within the EC consultations, enhancing the efficacy of the discussions by focusing attention on a single country and increasing the degree of specificity. Nonetheless, the discussions within the Monetary Committee have also revealed weaknesses. Often, the underlying macro-economic forecasts are unduly optimistic, veiling immediate needs for genuine adjustment. In this respect, we have come a long way since the 1950s and 1960s, a time when, as Van Lennep recalls[8], overly pessimistic growth forecasts were considered risky since they might give rise to calls for stimulating policies. Moreover, a number of programmes proved to be marked by a black-box approach, failing to specify clearly how the intended results were to be realized and complicating EC surveillance of compliance. It may be concluded that convergence programmes serve as a fillip to well-intentioned countries rather than as an instrument to exert pressure on countries where the pursuit of stability is less firmly embedded.

8 Van Lennep (1991), p. 181.

The Maastricht Treaty also provides that, as from the start of stage two, broad guidelines for economic policy will be drawn up annually. Experience with guidelines covering the whole of the Community has not, however, been favourable. In the past, such recommendations in specific situations have had little effect. Their routine application on an annual basis has left few marks on the coordination process.

This second attempt at EMU has thus introduced interesting innovations into the process of coordination. Yet, once again, giving practical effect to the agreed objectives has proved harder than had been anticipated or has been frustrated by grave setbacks. The two new procedures have had a difficult start and on 2 August 1993 new, very wide margins had to be set within the EMS. Once more, the question looms: will history repeat itself?

6 Back to the future

Looking back, it must be concluded that the history of European policy coordination has been a rather chequered one. After a hopeful start, setbacks occurred and what may be termed coordination fatigue set in. Attempts to restart the coordination process tended to encounter the same fate. The agreed coordination procedures all too easily degenerated into routine matters, with the participants tending to be guided by the non-intervention principle – the notion that if one is not too hard on others, they too will show leniency. Owing to considerations of sovereignty, large countries in particular are susceptible to this temptation, which may readily set a vicious circle in motion: large countries have the power to ensure effective coordination but are not always prepared to do so, whereas smaller countries are more prepared but are simply less influential. An added factor is that coordination is hardest when it is most needed, especially when convergence demands policy adjustment; under such conditions countries may be tempted to take part in the process for the sake of appearances but without giving it true substance. Hence, an essential condition for successful coordination is the existence of a powerful political incentive. Experience shows that a second, equally important, condition is a broad consensus about the ultimate objectives of economic and monetary policies, not merely on paper but in actual practice. These two conditions are closely interrelated: if the political will is strong, countries will more readily tend to conform to the stability objective without which no agreement is possible in European Union. Confidence in procedures as a panacea making for effective coordination has waned considerably. In the early 1970s, an elaborate set of new procedures was introduced, but in the second run-up to EMU the Council Resolutions in question have been withdrawn and superseded by multilateral surveillance which is to evolve through a process of learning by doing.

Nevertheless, in a process of trial and error, progress has yet been made over the years. In the first place, the knowledge of each other's economic and financial situation has been much improved, thus providing a necessary, though not sufficient, basis for effective coordination. The technique of regular tours d'horizon as well as frequent contacts of other types between the officials involved have contributed considerably to this situation. Also of importance in this respect is the much improved coverage by the financial press of economic and monetary developments. Furthermore, the political motivation has become very much stronger. The first attempt at EMU was motivated in part by the exchange rate turbulence of that time and that is also where it foundered. The EMS was established following an initiative at the highest political level and the present attempt at EMU, too, is strongly politically inspired. As a consequence, the ultimate objective of policy coordination has been defined more clearly over the years. The Werner Report was not based on any distinct objective of stability. The EMS was set up as a zone of monetary stability but even so left room for doubt as to the relative priorities of exchange rate and domestic price stability. In the present attempt at EMU, this doubt has been effectively removed: the primary objective of monetary policy is domestic price stability. Furthermore, there is at present more of a common economic philosophy, geared to a medium-term strategy aimed at stable, non-inflationary growth. Also, there is a broad consensus as to how the objective of price stability is to be interpreted in the progress towards EMU: an inflation rate of not more than 2 per cent per annum. In recent years, the ERM has brought the goal of convergence towards price stability much nearer, with inflation now averaging just over 3 per cent even if further progress is still necessary. But the ERM has been unable to prevent even countries in the core group from allowing their public finances to deteriorate to very serious deficit levels. In 1993, the average deficit in the EC was more than double the value still acceptable under the convergence criterion. Here, then, much remains to be done. Maastricht has introduced a number of potentially effective innovations in the coordination of economic policy. Initial experience with the convergence programmes has not, however, been very fortunate although it must be realized that cyclical conditions have been most unfavourable. The programmes contain too many elements of wishful thinking, concealing the need for immediate concrete action. It is to be hoped that the will to qualify in due course for EMU will be sufficiently strong to ensure that matters are firmly taken in hand in this respect.

Looking to the future, once EMU will have been established, the question again arises where the incentives will have to be found to come to grips with the issue of stability in the area of public finance. At that time, the Union will be able to operate a procedure with coercive elements, unprecedented within European policy coordination: the excessive deficit procedure. However, past experience shows that, in order to be actually and effectively used, procedures need to be backed by a strong political will. This requires that there should be a country or a political institution strong enough to enforce the procedure – either a major country with a strong tradition of stability or an institution representing the European interest and invested with sufficient political authority to be able to call non-compliant countries to account. For a true European, the choice between the two should not be difficult.

References

Committee for the Study of Economic and Monetary Union ('Delors Committee') (1989), *Report on Economic and Monetary Union in the European Community,* Brussels.

De Nederlandsche Bank, *Annual Reports* 1968-1979, Amsterdam.

Gretschmann, K. (ed.) (1993), *Economic and Monetary Union: implications for national policy-making,* Dordrecht/Boston.

Gros, D. and N. Thygesen (1992), *European Monetary Integration,* London.

Van Lennep, E. (1991), *Emile van Lennep in de wereldeconomie, herinneringen van een internationale Nederlander,* Leiden.

Monetary Committee of the European Community, *Annual Reports,* 1958 - 1969, Brussels.

Monetary Committee of the European Community (1979 and 1989), *Compendium of Community monetary texts,* Brussels.

Pfleiderer, O. (1964), *Währungsordnung und Europäische Integration,* Kiel.

Szász, A. (1993), *Towards a single European currency: ECU, Franc-Fort, Question-Mark, in: D.E. Fair and R.J. Raymond (eds.), The new Europe: evolving economic and financial systems in East and West,* Dordrecht, pp. 217-235.

Werner Committee (1970), *Report to the Council and the Commission on the realization by stages of Economic and Monetary Union in the Community* ('Werner Report'), special supplement to Bulletin 11-1970 of the European Communities.

Europe in flux

Tom de Vries

1 Introduction

The high hopes for Europe 1992 and for the Maastricht Treaty have been dashed by subsequent developments. Europe's foreign policy hopes have been disappointed by its dismal performance in the Balkans. Although dependent on trade, its members have been barely able to agree on a common negotiating position in the Gatt Round. And for the better part of two years, instead of moving towards monetary union, Europe has been in the throes of exchange rate crises.

In the economic field, circumstances such as the world recession and unforeseen consequences of German unification have played a role in these setbacks. But I will argue that some major policy mistakes have been made, and – worse – that some vital policies are still mistaken. European integration has always proceeded in fits and starts. Periods of hubris, like 1991 have been followed by periods of doom and gloom, like 1993, only for integration to move forward again later. Thus we should not be overly impressed by the current pessimism. Yet, it is my contention that Europe cannot move forward again without major changes in some basic policy choices. Europe will have to decide where it wants to go and how it wants to get there, given the new circumstances in which it finds itself and some old verities that reality has revealed once again but which had been forgotten. Without such a fundamental policy reappraisal the present stagnation might continue for a number of years.

2 Past mistakes

Economic and Monetary Union is the center piece of the Maastricht

When Tom de Vries died on 1 October 1993, he left a finished draft of the first parts of the article as well as a sketch and some notes with respect to the conclusions he wished to draw. On this basis editors have completed the article in memory of a teacher and long-term friend of André Szász. They hope to have done so in the spirit of Tom de Vries' intentions.

Treaty. It represents the Community's second attempt at creating a common currency. It is failing for reasons similar to those that brought about the failure of the first attempt prepared in the sixties. At the time, the requirements for monetary union were thoroughly analyzed. The conclusion, reinforced by recent analysis and, indeed experience, has been and remains that monetary union is possible, but requires the transfer of sensitive political powers to a common federal authority. These include not only decisions on monetary policy (interest rates), but also decisions determining the general shape of the budget, and affecting therefore the level of employment, inflation, and of taxation, and hence to some extent the role of government in society. It is thus not surprising that there exists no historical example of a monetary union without a political union, as the German officials keep pointing out.

Maastricht chose to largely ignore this analysis. It prescribed monetary union without progress on any meaningful European political authority. It did try to take at least some account of the earlier failure by adopting a few rules on budgetary policy, but these remain static and inadequate.

From the beginning a basic disagreement on how to proceed with European integration has manifested itself. It can be summarized by the words 'institution building versus real integration' or 'form versus substance'. The way EMU has been approached by the Community provides a good illustration. The next to last stage before the adoption of a common currency is a situation of irrevocably fixed exchange rates between national currencies. The Commission and some EC member governments appear to have operated on the assumption that by keeping exchange rates in the European Exchange Rate Mechanism unchanged, one would painlessly glide into monetary union. Producing the form appropriate for monetary union would somehow bring about the integration that is its prerequisite. In fact, of course, without substantive efforts to bring about European-wide agreement on policies affecting employment, inflation and taxation, exchange rates got further and further out of line, and any immediate cause could unleash an exchange rate crisis. When it came, the reaction of the Community was to change exchange rates as little as possible, and to salvage as much as possible of the existing system. The result has been continuing turmoil in the Exchange Rate Mechanism, which has prevented meeting the needs of member countries and in some cases may have imposed an unnecessary recession.

European integration has kept moving forward by creating disequilibria, e.g. a European Community for Steel and Coal that made no sense by itself and thus led to pressures for integration in other fields. This is the spill-over effect. But as Joseph Nye has pointed out, too much reliance on spill-overs risks to produce a spill-back, namely the collapse of your project and regression to an earlier stage. And while spill-overs might work in technical fields, even in coal and steel, when it comes to employment, inflation and taxation, spill-backs become the rule, as experience with monetary union shows once again.

3 Present policy failures

EMU is not a goal in itself, but part of a much wider, political objective, namely to enable Europe to play its role in the world. The alliance between France and Germany forms the political core of European unity. However, it is a major tactical policy mistake to identify that policy collaboration merely as the maintenance of a particular exchange rate between the Deutsche mark and the French franc.

Some countries blocked discussions on a realignment in 1990 in the mistaken belief that maintaining historical parities would promote Economic and Monetary Union. This bias for fixed rates was also inspired by the fear that others would devalue more. The most profitable course for currency speculators now would be a premature return to narrow bands, adhered to for some time, so that divergent inflation rates and economic policy make them irrealistic, but supported by governments. That is the situation the EC seems to want to get back to: narrow margins and inflexible parities which of necessity must get out of line. This is based on a serious misunderstanding.

More generally, it is a mistake to propagate that further movement to European unity needs a European currency in 1999 as laid down in the Maastricht Treaty. Laying down in 1991 what shall happen to currencies in 1999 never seemed realistic. That goal now appears to be unrealisable. This does not need to block further progress. But it does, in fact, as long as all attention is focused on the realization of the Treaty of Maastricht.

Politicians and civil servants have worked for years on the Treaty of Maastricht and they cannot give it up. In the process they have left their people far behind. They have created an institutional structure without sufficient political basis in their home countries. They have incurred considerable political cost in getting it ratified in countries like Denmark, the United Kingdom and France and are hung-up, having carried it there in adversity. And they ignore other problems that are more important and where some action would be possible.

Admittedly, European monetary union has the function of a symbol. Things are different from the situation in the United States with its huge domestic economy, where as a consequence interest rate policy is largely geared to domestic considerations and the exchange rate more or less left to fend for itself. The European economy is more segmented but rapidly integrating. It cannot afford to have fluctuating exchange rates among Member States. Convergence of economic and monetary policies is a precondition for stable exchange rates. Fixed, but adjustable exchange rates can create a positive interaction, the exchange rate commitment encouraging policies conducive to convergence.

That doesn't alter the fact that Economic and Monetary Union as laid down in the Maastricht Treaty will lead nowhere. Vital elements of real economic union and political union are lacking and it cannot confidently be expected that it will prove possible to remedy these shortcomings later on, once a start has been made on the basis of the arrangements agreed at present. A further transfer of sovereign powers is needed and there is no reason to expect that such a transfer could be imposed by invoking the argument that otherwise the progress already achieved would be lost. Recent experience does not support such an expectation at all.

4 The road to the future

The real objective of European integration has to be to ensure the role of Europe in world affairs. The world is changing rapidly and profoundly, and only a unified Europe can hope to influence the shape of things to come, instead of merely submitting passively to its consequences. East of Europe, fundamental changes are underway with an as yet most uncertain outcome. To the West, the influence of the United States, at present the sole remaining superpower, is on the wane.

Europe will have to concentrate on political integration and cannot afford to let itself be diverted from this effort by a futile quest for EMU. A choice will have to be made. Either EMU must be supplemented shortly with a political union and a real economic union, both vital if EMU is to be considered a realistic goal. Should the political will to agree on this be lacking, Europe will have to remain an area of sovereign states for the time being. EMU, which has shown itself to be prone to serious trouble, has no place in the latter situation. Whatever the choice, Europe has to clear the decks in order to tackle the real problems confronting it.

In the first place, enlargement needs to be taken seriously. There is not a chance Western Europe can escape Eastern Europe. Either it acts constructively, or it will be confronted with upheavals. Its inward looking, parochial vision of monetary union does not create a favourable impression on the rest of the world. And it will fail because its construction is unbalanced. Only by setting realistic goals for itself and by fostering stability in its internal relations, Western Europe can hope to be able to export stability to its Eastern neighbours.

Furthermore, it is crucial that France and Germany sort out their mutual relationship in present changed circumstances. Good cooperation between the two largest countries is indispensable for them to fulfil their traditional role in promoting integration in Europe. For a long time European integration was seen by France as a way to exert leadership, for which it was no longer strong enough on its own. Over the years, however, Germany has grown to be the most powerful state in the Union. Events on currency markets in 1992 and 1993 have demonstrated that, while Germany still is in the process of digesting the huge costs of reunification, its currency stands already stronger in foreign exchange markets than the French franc. For a while France could harbour the illusion to take over the hegemonic role, as French fundamentals rival at present Germany's. But France showed too much eagerness in using this opportunity for purely domestic goals – interest rate reductions – and consequently failed in its attempt to take over the anchor function.

In other fields, too, French priorities differ from those elsewhere in Europe, making it difficult for France to assume the leading role. The French attitude towards the security role of the United States in Europe differs from that of others, as evidenced by the expulsion in the sixties of NATO headquarters from Paris to Brussels. Another example is in the field of trade policy where in the final stages of the Uruguay Round negotiations France for a time was isolated from its European partners.

Europe has to realise that Germany is its most powerful national state. All will have to adjust to this fact of life, including Germany that will have to give content to this new role. In an end-of-20th-century democracy, short-term electoral interests of politicians too often come first. They face, however, institutions somewhat outside their reach, like the Supreme Court in the United States or the Bundesbank in Germany.

The people that are appointed to these institutions give naturally priority to their real mandate, even if they may get overburdened with this task. The Bundesbank, when faced with inadequate financing of the huge costs of reunification, did the right thing in giving priority to price stability in accordance with its mandate. Nevertheless, the resulting policy mix did have disrupting effects on the EMS. The experience of the United States shows that a country that cannot put its own house in order hurts its potential as a leader, and cannot be global banker, global police man, global moralist all at the same time. That same lesson applies to Europe and to its constituent countries.

It will take a long time, probably decades, before Europe can become a global power. For this it will need a genuine political union and a federal military force. It still is an open question whether all member countries have the stomach for that; Europe may need a professional army. Its military temerity and its political passivity in the case of the debacle in former Yugoslavia show how long a road still has to be travelled. If Europe wants to play its role in the world it has to restore order at home, establish close cooperation between its members large and small, and on that basis achieve a measure of common purpose. Then it can start to exert a stabilising influence in its part of the world.

Financial relations between the Netherlands and Belgium: 1943 to 1993

Jacques J. Polak

1 Introduction

Of the six countries that created the European Economic Community in 1957, the three smaller ones, Belgium, Luxembourg and the Netherlands, had for more than a decade made pioneering efforts at ever-widening financial and economic collaboration and integration. The three countries – the first two of which had been joined in the Belgo-Luxembourg Economic Union since 1921 – had concluded a monetary agreement dealing with exchange rates and mutual credits in 1943, had moved toward a customs union in the course of the 1940s and liberated capital movements substantially in 1954. They also entered upon an economic union in 1960, 33 years before the birth of the economic union of the Twelve. Although the passage of time and the creation of new institutions – the IMF, the European Payments Union (EPU) and above all the EC – have deprived the earlier endeavors at multilateral cooperation of much of their original significance, these pioneering efforts and their after-effects deserve more attention than they have so far received.[1]

A succession of political conflicts and, in the 1930s, the resurgence of protectionist tendencies, had prevented the Netherlands and Belgium from establishing close economic or financial relations in the inter-war period, in spite of many obvious parallel interests. But the proximity of the two governments in exile in London facilitated a determined attempt from both sides to strive for much closer cooperation in the post-war period. Personalities also helped: the two finance ministers, Van den Broek and Gutt, had become acquainted as the heads of the Dutch and Belgian colonial tin-mining companies (Billiton and Katanga) and had turned from competitors to collaborators and friends in the tin cartel of the 1930s.[2] The most important results of this cooperation were the pathbreaking monetary and trade agreements negotiated in London between the two countries. These agreements, and

1 For an early detailed discussion concentrating primarily on the trade, rather than the financial aspects of Benelux, see Meade (1957).

2 De Jong (1979), p. 682; Beyen (1949), p. 145; Beyen (1969), pp. 146-147.

the ensuing developments over the next fifty years, will be the subject of this essay. But first it is worth recalling another – virtually unknown – exercise in planned cooperation that did not materialize and that might have had some additional cooperative benefits had it come off.

2 Plans for coordinated representation in the IMF and World Bank

The two governments at all time considered their own steps towards closer bilateral financial relations as fully compatible with the ongoing discussions on a world-wide monetary structure as envisaged by the Keynes and White plans for an International Monetary Fund.[3] In these latter discussions they went far to coordinate their positions, looking ahead to acting jointly in the new organization once it became established after the war. This approach inspired them to give their delegations to the Bretton Woods conference one principal common guideline: to obtain for the two countries quotas in the Fund and the Bank large enough to ensure that, acting together, they would always be able to elect one Executive Director in each organization, which they planned to alternate between them. This objective – which involved the delegations in difficult negotiations in Bretton Woods, not only on quotas but also on the provisions for expanding the number of elected directors as the membership of the Fund increased – was achieved but, it appeared, with little room to spare. With the quotas set at Bretton Woods, it was expected that the five directors to be elected by 21 of the smaller members would have to compete for 25,500 votes, requiring a minimum of 5,100 votes to make sure of a seat.[4] The Dutch and Belgian quotas gave a total of 5,500 votes (5,850 including Luxembourg).[5]

At the inaugural meeting of Fund and Bank in Savannah (March 1946), however, the calculations made at Bretton Woods turned out to be no longer valid. First, the Soviet Union had not joined. This removed the votes of India (which replaced the USSR as one of the big five with an appointed director) from the competition. As Australia and New Zealand had not yet become members, their votes dropped out too. Thus the required minimum fell to 3,440. And, it appeared to general surprise, since some of the five directors would inevitably receive more than the minimum votes, it would be necessary to declare one or two other directors elected with fewer than the minimum.[6] After a series of

3 Quite explicitly on this, Gutt (1943).
4 The original Executive Board of the Fund consisted of 12 directors, of which five were appointed by the members with the largest quotas and two were reserved for the 18 Latin American members. This left five seats for the remaining 21 countries represented at Bretton Woods.
5 Broches (1945), pp. 11 and 58.
6 The comic confusion on this issue at Savannah is described in Horsefield (1969), pp. 127-129.

votes, the Netherlands (with the additional votes of Norway) and Belgium (still below the minimum with those of Luxembourg and Iceland) each got a seat on the Fund Board and on the World Bank Board.

Once established in 1946, this situation has continued to this day. To safeguard their separate seats, the two countries succeeded in gradually expanding their constituencies, sometimes in rather fierce competition. By the time of the 1992 biannual election, both constituencies had grown to nine countries, each with a voting power in excess of that of the Netherlands, Belgium and Luxembourg combined. Representing mixed constituencies that included industrial, developing and lately also 'transforming' economies no doubt added to the interest, and also to the importance, of the positions of the Benelux directors. But against this there has to be set the loss of the original objective of a structure ensuring close cooperation in Washington, and the coordination between Brussels and The Hague-Amsterdam that this would have required.

3 A monetary agreement and a customs union

The Netherlands-Belgian-Luxembourg monetary agreement of 1943 was the first of the network of bilateral European agreements designed to facilitate post-war trade by 'solving' up to an agreed point the problem of financing trade imbalances, or 'trade swings' as they were optimistically called at the time. All these agreements contained in addition understandings on the mutual exchange rate and provisions requiring consultation – in the Benelux case even agreement – before a change in that rate could be made. The initial rate between the guilder and the Belgian franc was set equal to their pre-war parity on the ground that the impact of the war on the two countries had been essentially comparable.[7] The drawback of the bilateral character of these agreements was recognized at the time, but it was hoped that this could be overcome by transferability within wider regional groupings. This finally materialized, for Europe and the related overseas territories in the European Payments Union, but not before 1950. As a further step to promote world-wide trade, a number of regional agreements might be connected through an international institution, in which the United States, as a large source of dollars, would take the position of the sun in the solar system. Dr J.W. Beyen, at the time a director at Unilever and financial advisor to the Netherlands government, one of the principal planners and negotiators during this period, believed that a gradual

7 Gutt (1943).

approach of this kind toward a world payments system was preferable to the immediate one-world approach of both the Keynes and the White plans.[8]

According to Beyen, who was one of its godfathers, the Benelux monetary agreement was 'baptized' in March 1943.[9] This, however, must have been a case of prenatal baptism: disagreements among the different ministries involved on the Dutch side – about which more will be said in the next section – held up the birth of the agreement until 21 October 1943. Even then, the Belgians seemed to have been more content with the baby than the Dutch. Minister Gutt gave an extensive account of the agreement on the radio for Belgian listeners. On the part of the Netherlands, on the other hand, the text of the agreement was not published in the 'Staatsblad' until nearly a year later.[10] Characteristic of the farsightedness of the Belgian-Dutch financial authorities was that they were the only ones in the 1940s who were prepared to proceed beyond a monetary agreement to the logical next step: the conclusion of a customs union. Started even before the monetary accord was fully settled, the far more difficult technical discussions on a common external tariff and a customs union took an additional year, but an agreement was signed in London on 5 September 1944. Ratification by the three parliaments did not take place until the second half of 1947 and the agreement did not become fully effective until April 1949.[11] Even then, numerous restrictions on the freedom of trade between the two countries remained, inspired first by Dutch concerns about payments deficits and then by Belgian employment concerns.[12]

4 Setting the invasion exchange rates

The monetary and trade agreements were major economic and political achievements – but they could have no practical impact on the conduct and financing of trade until both countries were liberated. But in

8 Beyen (1949), pp. 144-150. Beyen was the head of the Netherlands delegation at Bretton Woods and later, as Foreign Minister of the Netherlands delegation at the Messina conference establishing the EEC.

9 Beyen (1969), p. 147; De Jong (1979), p. 683.

10 *Staatsblad* E 76 of 26 September, 1944. The customs agreement discussed below was released on the same day. A joint press release in French by the three governments had been published in La Belgique Indépendante, 28 October 1943; if a text in Dutch was also released it did not survive in the files of the Dutch ministries concerned.

11 De Jong (1979), pp. 683-684; Volmuller (1981), p. 74. A common external tariff went into effect on 1 January 1948, but internal customs barriers remained in effect for an additional 15 months.

12 Boekestijn (1990), pp. 27-47. The original swing credit of BF 1 billion had proved inadequate long before. It was raised to more than BF 4 billion in June 1947 and other sources of credit, including the World Bank and the IMF, proved necessary to keep trade flowing before the EPU took over, Meade (1957), p. 21.

another context the monetary agreement became of immediate importance, and that was the process, which had already started before, of agreeing 'invasion exchange rates' with the British and American military authorities. To preserve the status of the national currencies of Belgium and the Netherlands, which had continued to function as the countries' legal tender under the German occupation, it was essential that the liberating armies and individual army personnel would use these currencies, rather than dollars, pounds or scrip for their purchases in liberated territories. That required the fixation of an exchange rate, even before the countries would be ready to engage again in international trade. The linkage of the guilder and the Belgian franc in Article 1 of the Benelux Agreement made it necessary for the two countries to come to compatible decisions on the respective exchange rates of their two currencies against the pound and the dollar.

4.1 *The Belgian position*

It proved far more difficult for the Dutch than for the Belgian government to come to a firm opinion on what the appropriate exchange rate should be. Belgium had, so to say, a natural choice, which at the same time appeared to provide an economically justifiable rate. An integral part of the Belgian Kingdom, the Congo, was free and economically prosperous. The Congo had had a currency of its own since 1908, the Congo franc, issued by the Banque du Congo Belge, which in peace time had always been at par with the metropolitan franc. After the complete occupation of Belgium and the evacuation of the Belgian government to Vichy (it moved to London a few months later), a decision was taken to devalue the Congo franc to parity with the French franc, a devaluation by almost one-third, from 3.37 to 2.28 dollar cents per Congo franc and to Congo franc 176.625 to the pound sterling. The economic reason for this decision is not clear; writing in 1943, the General Manager of the Banque du Congo Belge judged it as 'without any economic justification' and presumed it to have been taken for political reasons.[13] In any event, the Congo entered the sterling area at this rate, contributing its foreign exchange receipts (beyond its own needs and those of the Belgian government in exile) to the central reserves of the area. The Congo franc was a strong currency: in lending their foreign exchange surpluses to the Belgian government, the Congolese authorities opted to have their claims expressed in Congo francs rather than in sterling.[14]

13 Baseleer (1943), p. 124.
14 Ansiaux (1985), p. 14.

By 1943, the new rate for the Congo franc was a 'fait accompli' and from all signs the Congo prospered, exporting large quantities of copper, oil and oil-seeds, cotton, fibers, rubber, gums, coffee and industrial diamonds to Britain and the United States.[15] Not mentioned in war-time sources, the Congo was also the major source of uranium for the allied war effort. The question of a possible return of the Congo franc to the old rate simply did not arise. Rather, the obvious choice for the Belgian authorities was to resume parity between the metropole and the colony on the basis of the prevailing rate for the Congo franc. The devaluation of the metropolitan franc implicit in this choice was, after extensive studies[16], considered to be 'technically indispensable' by a government which could hardly be considered devaluation-prone. The Minister of Finance, Camille Gutt, had opposed devaluation of the Belgian franc when he held the same position in 1935 and, though a successor government had taken that measure (and thereby started the demise of the gold bloc), he still considered it to have been unnecessary 14 years later. He had also prided himself on having successfully opposed pressure for devaluation after he returned to the government in February 1939.[17]

In so far as there had been opposition in Belgian circles in London to the rate chosen, it came from those who wanted to devalue more; Paul van Zeeland, who had introduced the 1935 devaluation, again favoured a lower value for the franc than the government: 250 BF/$ rather than 176.[18] After its return, in its justification to parliament, the government defended itself implicitly against a possible charge of not having devalued enough by stating that the new rate had been selected so as to ensure that the post-liberation wage rate would have at least as much purchasing power as the pre-war rate. It further explained that while it had not chosen a rate based on the price level on the black market in Belgium, it could not either take its cue entirely from the level of 'controlled prices', which were often kept uneconomically low.[19] Whatever the government's precise line of reasoning, it is clear that by early 1943 (or perhaps even earlier) it had decided to set the rate for the Belgian franc at parity with the prevailing rate for the Congo franc.

15 Baseleer (1943), p. 125; Jennen (1943), p. 123.
16 Ansiaux (1990), p. 103.
17 Gutt (1949). Gutt, who had become the International Monetary Fund's first Managing Director in 1946, reported to the Executive Board of the Fund on 28 June 1949 on the discussions he had held, together with the Director of Research, E.M. Bernstein, in seven European countries on the question whether their initial par values as communicated to the Fund in late 1946 continued to be satisfactory.
18 Ansiaux (1990), p. 104.
19 Moniteur Belge, vol. 114, 7 October 1944, p. 380.

At the pre-war parity relationship between the guilder and the Belgian franc, the Belgian choice would imply a rate for the guilder against sterling of 10.69. But the Netherlands also had a colonial connection – and one that conflicted with that of Belgium. In February 1943, the Minister of Finance expressed the view that the exchange of foreign currencies for guilders by the liberating armies should take place 'at the same exchange rates as those which applied under the monetary agreement between the Netherlands Indies and the British empire, i.e. 7.60 (against the sterling) and 1.885 (against the dollar).'[20]

If this was indeed the Minister's view in February, it did not take him long to change his mind. He may well have been influenced by the contacts (already mentioned) with his Belgian colleague. From within the Dutch community in London he had received advice in the same direction: in a long letter with tables and graphs, August Kessler, a director of the Royal Dutch Shell, had argued that reintroduction of the pre-war rate of Fl. 7.60 per pound (which was then still in effect in the Netherlands Antilles) would be a 'serious mistake' that would create great difficulties to the reconstruction of the Netherlands economy. Kessler based his argument primarily on the much greater increase in the money supply since April 1940 in the Netherlands than in England – by a factor of 2.5 versus about 1.5, which he expected to manifest itself in larger price increases once the war-time controls were relaxed.[21] In any event, Van den Broek answered Kessler's letter at once, stating that as far as he could see at the time, he shared Kessler's view that the Fl. 7.60 rate should not and could not be maintained after the war.[22] A few months later, while on a visit to the United States, Van den Broek discussed the exchange rate question at the State Department and indicated that the Netherlands government wanted to set the guilder/sterling rate at 10.50, which would correspond approximately to the old gold parity of FL. 2.50 for the dollar.[23]

In fact, however, the exchange rate issue had by no means been settled within the bosom of the Netherlands government. One indication of this was the rather curious fact that the draft of the monetary accord with Belgium that the Minister of Finance submitted for approval to

20 Explanatory memorandum to the Royal Decree no. 2 of 4 February 1943 (authorizing the printing of new bank notes), *Staatsblad* D 67.
21 Letter from Kessler to Van den Broek, 24 March 1943.
22 Letter from Van den Broek to Kessler, 1 April 1943.
23 Letter from Van den Broek to Herbert Feis, adviser on international economic affairs, State Department, 30 July 1943, correcting Feis's minutes of the meeting of 26 July 1943 which referred to a rate of 12.50 Fl./£.

the cabinet on 14 April 1943 contained a blank for the most essential variable, the official rate between the two currencies, set in Article 1 (there were corresponding blanks for the Dutch commitments in guilders corresponding to the explicit Belgian swing credits of BF 500 million and BF 1 billion in Articles 5 and 6). The letter of transmission suggested that that rate could not be set pending a monetary agreement with the British that both the Dutch and the Belgians were hoping to achieve.[24] The Belgian view on this issue was that the guilder/franc rate should be set first, in the light of the situations in the two countries, after which the two parties should coordinate their positions on the rates for their respective currencies against third currencies.[25] This view in the end prevailed: the agreement was signed half a year before the final decisions on the invasion rates were taken and even longer before the countries signed bilateral agreements with the United Kingdom in March 1945.

A number of the critical views within the Dutch administration deserve to be recorded. Beyen, the person in London primarily in charge of post-war financial planning, had immediately taken issue with the gist of Kessler's advice to the Minister. He pointed out that the much smaller increase in the money supply in the United Kingdom than in the occupied Netherlands did not so much reflect a different degree of reliance on deficit financing as the fact that in the former country a large proportion of the deficit had been consolidated in war loans. The Dutch government had plans (about which his letter gave no details) to absorb much of this excess purchasing power after liberation and if these plans proved successful, the inflationary situation in the Netherlands would not be all that different from that in the United Kingdom. Thus while one could not predict the correct postwar exchange rate he suggested that a rate for sterling around Fl. 7.60 might well prove reasonable.[26] The response from others within the Netherlands establishment may have been delayed by the secrecy with which the Ministry of Finance treated the subject. Failing to recognize – or was it to admit? – the economic significance of the 'invasion rates', the Ministry consis-

24 Letter from the Minister of Finance to the other members of the cabinet, 14 April 1943. Van den Broek's letter made clear to his colleagues, however, that since he expected the Belgians to go for a rate of 176 BF/£, the adoption of the current Dutch-Belgian rate in the occupied territories would lead to a rate of about 10.56 Fl./£. (The difference of about 1 per cent from the correct cross rate of 10.69 Fl./£ was due to the fact that the letter used the rounded value of 6, instead of 6.053, Dutch cents to the franc.)

25 Gutt (1943). This view can also be read in minutes of a meeting between the interested ministers of the two countries held on 22 March 1943, that Van den Broek attached to his letter to the cabinet. The minute included the observation that 'this agreement could be signed independently from any other, as soon as the question of the parity between the two currencies is settled'.

26 Letter from Beyen to Van den Broek, April 1943.

tently took the line that these were merely unofficial accounting rates: 'the public in the Netherlands has no interest in this rate and does not even have to know it'. And it continued: 'The decision to pay with Netherlands money in the Netherlands has the great advantage that it is not necessary at once to fix an official exchange rate for the guilder, leaving the government entirely free to fix this rate later in consideration of all relevant factors'.[27] The Ministry continued to adhere to this narrow view even after the partial liberation of the country, when Van den Broek advised the Ministry of Foreign Affairs not to worry about any exchange rate for sterling: 'The only official rate that exists for the guilder is that against the Belgian franc... All that exists with respect to the pound sterling is that England has accepted for the settlement of the so-called invasion money, the rate declared by us to the English Treasury of 10.691 Fl./£. A monetary agreement with the United Kingdom that fixes this exchange rate is under consideration but has not yet come into effect'.[28]

As others in the government became aware of the exchange rate negotiations with the Allies and the Belgians – in which Kerstens, the Minister of Commerce, had initially not participated – objections began to be voiced against cheapening of the guilder and the attendant inflationary risks. Unfavorable press reports on financial developments in North Africa, Italy and France were cited in this connection. Kerstens expressed concern about foreign military authorities setting an exchange rate that might be prejudicial to the future economic and financial structure of the Netherlands.[29] Steenberghe, a previous Minister of Finance, warned from Washington, where he headed the government's Economic, Financial and Shipping Mission, against the

27 Letter from Van den Broek to Kerstens, 17 August 1943.
28 Letter from Van den Broek to Van Kleffens, 17 February 1945. As a matter of fact, reality had broken through as soon as the liberating armies entered the Netherlands. In view of the fact that the rapid advance of the allied troops might find them without an adequate supply of Netherlands bank notes, the Dutch authorities made a public appeal to the population to accept for the time being also French and Belgian bank notes, 'on the basis of the following rates of exchange....' (text of an undated public announcement).
29 Letters from Kerstens to Van den Broek, 11 August and 10 November 1943. However, before Van den Broek left for the United States, Kerstens had given his consent by telephone to the official rate for the Belgian franc of Fl. 0.06. But shortly thereafter (in a letter indicating only a limited understanding of the implications of the Dutch-Belgian agreement) Kerstens wanted to reopen this issue, and questioned the wisdom of 'making the determination of the rate for the guilder against world currencies dependent on a monetary agreement with a country whose currency had never had much importance for the monetary policy of the Netherlands'. (Letter from Kerstens to Van den Broek, 17 June 1943). An internal, unsigned, Ministry of Finance memorandum dated 4 August 1944, entitled 'Obstruction by Mr (sic) Kerstens to the conclusion of the monetary agreement with Belgium' expresses the lasting exasperation of that Ministry with the Minister of Commerce. The memorandum reports inter alia a threat by Van den Broek to resign if Kerstens refused to sign the agreement and it notes that in the end Kerstens had given up his resistance and signed.

impact on the domestic price level of the sterling rate mentioned by Van den Broek to the Americans.[30] Beyen also appears to have maintained his reservations with respect to that rate.[31]

4.3 *Convincing the Allies*

Whatever the sentiments within the government, it was clear that setting a rate for sterling and the dollar was not a unilateral Dutch, or a bilateral Dutch-Belgian, matter but also required Allied concurrence. The English did not prove difficult on this question, but when Gutt brought up the matter with the Americans in November 1943 he ran into a stone wall with Harry White.[32] Gutt's collaborator Hubert Ansiaux (later Governor of the Belgian National Bank) was asked to continue the negotiations with one of White's collaborators, (William H.) Taylor, whom Ansiaux describes as being 'd'une brutalité invraisemblable'. (This was the style practiced by many of White's assistants, not only vis-à-vis foreigners but also in dealings with officials from other US departments.) Taylor took the line that 176 francs per pound was out of the question but that he was willing to negotiate about a rate between 200 and 250. In the end, however, Ansiaux was able to satisfy White himself about the proposed rate by his answer to one question about the Belgian price level: 'What is the price paid in a cloak room?' 'One franc', Ansiaux pulled out of the air. White thought that over and concluded: 'Your rate is right'.[33] Shortly after that, there was at least one further, this time a multilateral, meeting at the Treasury, and the Dutch submitted a lengthy statistical and analytic note in support of the rate they had selected.[34] That note (of which I happen to have been the author) tried to demonstrate that a more depreciated rate would lead to unduly low real wages or needless inflation, and a more appre-

30 Telegram from Steenberghe to Van den Broek, 11 December 1943. Even after the decision on the rate had been taken and published (New York Times, 6 September 1944), Steenberghe continued to press for a change to a higher rate – which he understood to remain a possibility under the agreement with the Allies – in order to prevent excessive purchases by the military. (Letter from Steenberghe to Van den Broek 12 September 1944).

31 Cited from a somewhat cryptic remark in Gutt's 1949 report to the Fund Board cited above: 'Some here (the reference must be to Beyen, by that time the Netherlands Executive Director in the Fund) will remember the long discussions I had with some of our Dutch friends who did not first, at that time, want to do the same', Gutt (1949).

32 At the earlier discussion that Van den Broek had had with the State Department it had been made clear that exchange rates were a matter for the Treasury to decide.

33 Ansiaux (1990), pp. 104-106.

34 Letter from Crena de Iongh to White, 29 January 1944, transmitting a memorandum of the Netherlands government dealing with the 'rate of exchange for the Netherlands guilder after liberation'. The letter refers to a meeting at the Treasury two days earlier at which 'representatives of other governments' were present. These must have included the Belgians, but there is no record of the other government(s) that may have been represented.

ciated rate to undesirable deflation. But by that time the matter had presumably been settled to White's satisfaction by Ansiaux's exercise in purchasing power parity.

Even after the Americans had relented on the rate it took a few more months before the Allies were officially notified of the exchange rates chosen. Here again the Belgians took the lead. On 13 April 1944, Gutt wrote Van den Broek 'to confirm that at one of our last cabinet meetings the Belgian government decided to fix the exchange parity of the Belgian franc, from the day of the entry of the Allied troops into Belgium, at 1 £ = 176.625 francs or 1 $ = 43.827 francs (which) corresponds to 10.691 guilders to the £', and that he had advised the UK and US Treasuries accordingly.[35] Van den Broek then took the corresponding actions, invoking the same escape clause that Gutt had communicated in his letter.[36] In contrast to the pronouncements of the Ministry of Finance referred to earlier, minimizing the economic importance of the invasion rates, Van den Broek's letters followed the Belgian precedent and spoke of 'fixing the exchange parity of the Netherlands guilder'.

5 Exchange rates during the remainder of the 1940s

The development of the Dutch and Belgian economies in the early post-war years does not – to the extent that such a judgment can be made so long after the event – point to any clearly unsatisfactory results arising from setting the exchange rate for the Belgian franc on the basis of the rate for the Congo franc, or from setting the exchange rate for the Netherlands guilder on the basis of the Congo franc once removed. It deserves to be recorded, however, that when in mid-1945 Pieter Lieftinck took over as Minister of Finance in the Netherlands he was less than happy with the exchange rate decision that the government in London had taken, in part, he suggested, under pressure from the Allies. He judged that rate as 'too low rather than too high' but 'had not felt free, after considering all aspects, to try to change it'.[37] (His response to the devaluation of sterling three years later might suggest that his initial reservation on the rate had disappeared.) In any event, the drastic monetary purges introduced by the two finance ministers, Gutt

35 Letter from Gutt to Van den Broek (sic), 13 April 1944.
36 This clause read: 'It goes without saying that if a very long time elapsed between now and the landing of the Allied troops, or if the volume of quite unforeseen destructions wrought in Belgium (the Netherlands) before the landing were so much beyond expectations that it would have a marked detrimental effect on the economic situation of our country, my government would have to reconsider such a parity'.
37 Lieftinck (1946), pp. 2-3.

in Belgium and Lieftinck in the Netherlands, probably more than the precise exchange rates selected, were critical to the broadly satisfactory outcomes achieved in both countries.

By late 1946, therefore, the 'invasion rates' of 1944 still seemed appropriate to be communicated to the IMF as 'initial par values'. The Fund accepted the values communicated – as it did for all countries, having persuaded a few of them not to submit par values. But in the light of the events of 1949 it is interesting to note that the Fund, which at that time was paying more attention to price and wage movements than to balance-of-payments developments that might prove to be transitory, seemed more comfortable with the par value of the guilder, which was supported by strict wage and price controls, than with that of the Belgian franc, which reflected the more market-oriented approach of the Belgian government.[38] The submission of these par values was probably the last action in the area of exchange rates by the two countries fully in the spirit of their 1943 agreement. Curiously, the Netherlands did not ratify the agreement until November 1946 and Belgium never ratified it at all, so that it remained in effect on a provisional basis only under Article 17.[39]

Within two years of accepting the initial par values, the Fund began to reassess their lasting validity, in particular as concerns the European countries.[40] Among these countries, the balances of payments of the Netherlands and Belgium had developed quite diverging tendencies. Belgium had established itself as a persistent surplus country, the Netherlands as a persistent deficit country, and indeed much of the imbalances were between them: in 1949, the Netherlands' deficit with Belgium was one-third as large as that with the whole of the Western Hemisphere.[41] The differences in their economic and financial positions coloured the Dutch and Belgian attitudes in the process of widespread adjustment of par values that followed the United Kingdom's devaluation of sterling in September 1949. Essentially, on that occasion, the two countries went their separate ways, each focusing primarily on a new par value to the dollar and an appropriate competitive position against other European countries. There were frequent consultations over the crucial weekend, it being understood on both sides that devaluation by the same percentage would not be appropriate. But each country had considerable difficulties to come to its own decision.

38 Based on confidential Fund reports on the initial par values of the Netherlands and Belgium.
39 De Jong (1960), p. 328, note 1.
40 International Monetary Fund (1948), Annual Report, pp. 22-24, discusses the relevant considerations quite openly in a section entitled 'Adjustment of par values'.
41 International Monetary Fund (1949), Proposed change in the guilder, (files of the Netherlands Bank), p. 2.

To the Fund, the proposal of the Netherlands to devalue by the same percentage as sterling, and much more than Belgium, seemed entirely natural. Months before, Bernstein (the Fund's Director of Research) had been told in the Netherlands that that country 'would devalue the guilder at the same time and to the same extent as sterling'.[42] But, probably because sterling was devalued more sharply than anyone had anticipated[43], this was no longer the agreed Dutch view on 18 September 1949. From Washington, where he still was after the Fund's annual meeting, Holtrop (supported by Beyen, the Netherlands Executive Director) urged Lieftinck and the cabinet to limit devaluation to some 24 per cent. They argued that this would mitigate the inflationary impact, reduce the pressure for wage compensation and keep competitive pressure on the export industries.[44] But Lieftinck was able to persuade the cabinet to go as far as the British, primarily on account of agricultural and shipping interests.[45] One should not overlook the fact, of course, that the economic arguments put forth reflect to some extent different personal attitudes towards the exchange rate. Holtrop and Beyen, who would nowadays be considered as belonging to the 'hard currency' school, attached considerable weight to the exchange rate as a disciplinary factor, while others (among them Lieftinck) would put primary emphasis on the competitive benefits of a relatively low rate. This also became evident on a later occasion. When in March 1961 first Germany and immediately afterwards the Netherlands proposed a 5 per cent revaluation to the Fund, Lieftinck, then the Netherlands Executive Director in the Fund, told me, in a telephone conversation 'in code': 'I did not like the mother and I like the daughter even less'.

Belgium found it even more difficult than the Netherlands to formulate a response to the British challenge. It first proposed to abandon the defense of its par value and allow the franc to fluctuate; it even managed to get the Fund's hesitant blessing for this step. But two days later Belgium had become sufficiently concerned about the dangers of a fluctuating rate to declare a new par value 12.4 per cent below the old one.[46]

42 Bernstein (1991), p. 59. A similar observation is recorded in Black (1991), p. 66.
43 De Nederlandsche Bank (1949).
44 De Nederlandsche Bank (1949). Two lengthy telegrams sent to the Prime Minister through the Netherlands embassy in Washington DC on 18 September 1949 stated a common position in favour of a devaluation of 24.2 per cent on the part of Stikker, Holtrop, Hirschfeld (previously Secretary General of the Ministry of Economic Affairs), Beyen and Van der Valk (respectively Netherlands Executive Director and Alternate of the Fund).
45 De Nederlandsche Bank (1949). A further argument for a Dutch devaluation somewhat larger than that of some other countries on the continent was the desire to leave some margin for cost and price increases resulting from further internal liberalization and from the removal of price controls and subsidies (Lieftinck (1973), p. 32). For a description of the confused seesaw debate in the cabinet sessions of 18 and 19 September 1949, see Maas (1991), pp. 219-222.
46 Horsefield (1969), pp. 240-1.

Although, as mentioned, the two countries consulted about their evolving changing exchange rate plans in the hectic days of September 1949, that experience was also the end of a common, or commonly agreed, exchange rate policy. After having overcome its post-war balance-of-payments weakness by the early 1950s, the Netherlands generally tended to follow the 'hard-currency' policy of Germany. Except for a recent period in the late 1980s and early 1990s, Belgium's policies were not as closely associated with those of Germany and were, in almost all instances, less 'hard'. In 1961, Belgium did not follow the German and Dutch revaluations. In May 1971, when Germany and the Netherlands allowed their currencies to float, Belgium maintained the official rate for current transactions while relying on the free market for capital transactions to absorb the impact of the inflow of dollars.[47] At the Smithsonian, for once, the guilder and the Belgian franc were appreciated by the same percentage against the US dollar (11.57 per cent), 2 percentage points less than the Deutsche mark.[48] But within two years, in September 1973, the guilder was revalued by 5 per cent in the snake, following a 5.5 per cent revaluation of the Deutsche mark in June.[49] The Netherlands and Belgium thus entered the European Monetary System in March 1979 with a BF/Fl. rate of 14.5. This rate survived the first realignment in the EMS, in September 1979, but only after long negotiations that left the Dutch outmanoeuvered and thoroughly unhappy with the outcome: a 2 per cent depreciation against the Deutsche mark in the company of the Belgian franc, the French franc, the Italian lira and the Irish punt.[50] Over the next decade, the Belgian franc lost value against the guilder in six realignments (October 1981, February 1982, June 1982, March 1983, April 1986 and January 1987), ending with a central rate of about 18.3 BF/Fl.[51] And in August 1993 the guilder was the only currency to maintain the narrow margin against the Deutsche mark while Belgium, together with all other countries then still in the EMS, chose the new 15 per cent margin.

In part, the practical demise of the 1943 provisions to agree on parity changes reflected the fact that other approval mechanisms had taken the place of these provisions. Membership in the Fund put the parities of both currencies, not only their common parity but also those against third currencies, under the authority of the Fund. Later, the European Monetary System instituted a rule of unanimity for any change in cen-

47 De Vries (1976), p. 522.
48 De Vries, (1976), p. 555.
49 De Nederlandsche Bank (1973), Annual Report, p. 93.
50 A full account on the negotiations of 23 September 1979 in Brussels is found in Boot (1992), pp. 155-164.
51 Ungerer, et al. (1990), p. 55.

tral rates within the group. But if maintaining a common exchange rate policy, or even a common currency, had suited the interests of the two countries, nothing in their membership of wider groupings would have stood in the way of doing so. The Belgium-Luxembourg monetary union – helped, no doubt, by the dominance of one of the two partners – has remained intact through seventy years of institutional change in the world and in Europe.

7 Concluding observations

Considering the 1943 agreement from the perspective of 1993, the conclusion we must come to is that the role of the Belgo-Netherlands monetary agreement was essential at the time and yet of transitory importance. To give the impetus to a customs union between the two countries it was necessary, in view of the expected shortage of foreign exchange in the post-war years, to line up mutual financing (which soon had to be enlarged) and this in turn was facilitated by a common approach toward post-war exchange rates. In addition, the bold initiative taken by the two countries at an early date gave encouragement to a broad network of similar arrangements among the countries in Europe. The Benelux customs union prospered and became the nucleus of the European Economic Community in 1957; it can fairly be said that the demonstration effect worked. But as early as September 1949, as we have seen, the original exchange rate approach started to crumble.

The need for swing financing, believed essential for trade liberalization fifty years ago, has of course long since disappeared; for Belgium, it never existed. What is perhaps more interesting to observe is that the history of the two countries' progress toward economic integration over the past fifty years does not provide evidence of a compelling need for a common currency, a fixed exchange rate, or even closely agreed exchange rate policies. Exchange rate changes of modest size since 1949, generally in the direction offsetting previous changes in real exchange rates, have not proven harmful, and have probably been helpful, to continued integration. Which should give one hope that even if European Economic Monetary Union does not become a reality in accordance with the Maastricht timetable but wide swings in real echange rates continue to be avoided, the single market that took effect at the beginning of 1993 may nevertheless develop into a major source of expanding welfare for the continent.

References

Ansiaux, Hubert J.N. (1985), Eté 1940: les vagabondages de l'or et du gouvernement belges (II), *Revue générale*, no. 3, pp. 3-15.

Ansiaux, Hubert J. N. (1990), *Souvenirs 1908-1987* (privately printed), Brussels.

Baseleer, R. (1943), Finances of Belgian Congo in relation to war economics, *The Banker*, pp. 123-126.

Bernstein, Edward M. (1991), The early years of the International Monetary Fund in: *Frenkel, Jacob A. and Morris Goldstein (eds.), International financial policy: essays in honor of Jacques J. Polak*, International Monetary Fund, Washington DC, pp. 58-63.

Beyen, J. W. (1949), *Money in a maelstrom*, New York.

Beyen, J. W. (1969), *Het spel en de knikkers: een kroniek van vijftig jaren*, Rotterdam.

Black, Stanley W. (1991), *A levite among the priests: Edward M. Bernstein and the origin of the Bretton Woods system*, Boulder.

Boekestijn, Arend Jan (1990), The formulation of Dutch Benelux policy in: *Griffiths, Richard T. (ed.), The Netherlands and the integration of Europe 1945-1957*, Amsterdam, pp. 27-47.

Boot, D.H. (1992), *Achter de coulissen van het beleid*, Amsterdam.

Broches, A. (1945), *Report of the Bretton Woods conference* (in Dutch, mimeo), New York.

De Jong, A.M. (1960), *De wetgeving nopens de Nederlandsche Bank 1814-1958: een historische studie*, 's-Gravenhage.

De Jong, Louis (1979), *Het Koninkrijk der Nederlanden in de Tweede Wereldoorlog*, vol. 9, 's-Gravenhage, pp. 681-684.

De Nederlandsche Bank (1949), Minutes of the 306th joint meeting of management and Governing Board (4 October 1949), Amsterdam.

De Vries, Margaret G. (1976), *The International Monetary Fund 1966-1971*, Washington DC.

Gutt, Camille, *La portée de la convention monétaire belgo – luxembourgeoise – néerlandaise: un exposé de Monsieur Gutt à la radio* (published in: La Belgique Indépendante on 4 November 1943).

Gutt, Camille (1949), Report to the Board (of the IMF) by the Managing Director, June 28 (from files of the Bank of England).

Horsefield, J. Keith (1969), *The International Monetary Fund 1945-1965*, Washington DC.

International Monetary Fund (1948), *Annual Report*, Washington DC.

Jennen, J. (1943), The Belgian Congo in wartime, *The Banker*, February, pp. 121-123.

Lieftinck, Pieter (1946), *Note to the second chamber of parliament on 21 January 1946* (Bijlage II, Handelingen van de Tweede Kamer der Staten-Generaal, 1945 – 1946, no. 2).

Lieftinck, Pieter (1973), *The post-war rehabilitation of the Netherlands*, 's-Gravenhage.

Maas, P.F. (ed.) (1991), *Parlementaire geschiedenis van Nederland na 1945*, Nijmegen.

Meade, James E. (1957), Negotiations for Benelux: an annotated chronicle 1943-1956, *Princeton Studies in International Finance*, no. 6, Princeton University, Princeton (New Jersey).

Ungerer, Horst, et al. (1990), The European Monetary System: developments and perspectives, *IMF, Occasional Paper,* no. 73, Washington DC.

Volmuller, H.W.J. (ed.) (1981), *Nijhoffs geschiedenis lexicon, Nederland en België,* 's-Gravenhage/ Antwerpen.

The integration of former Eastern Bloc countries into Europe

Leonhard Gleske

1 General remarks

The collapse of the communist regimes has created a great opportunity for ending once and for all the political and economic division of Europe of the past decades. The countries of Central and Eastern Europe have the possibility to be integrated into the system, imbued with the values of political democracy and a free market economy, which has been so characteristic for the development of Western Europe since the last war. We are still very much at the outset of this process, which will make heavy demands above all on the former Eastern Bloc countries, but will present no less of a challenge to the countries of Western Europe as well.

In many, though not all respects, the experiences of the countries of Western Europe in rebuilding their economies after the destruction and dislocation of the last war hold valuable lessons for the countries of Central and Eastern Europe, as they struggle to build up their national economies and open up their borders. On their part, the countries of Western Europe, however, would do well to remember how heavily they were able to rely on the generosity of the United States in the difficult task of rebuilding their own economies in those post-war years. American support was not only reflected in high levels of financial aid but also in a readiness to keep the American market open to imports from Western Europe at a time when most of the Western European countries themselves maintained import restrictions. Although these restrictions were gradually reduced, they nevertheless remained in force for a very considerable time. Acceptance of relatively low wage levels and undervalued Western European currencies were also essential elements of this picture.

Naturally, this attitude on the part of the United States also had the country's own interests at heart – not only its interest in political stability in Western Europe, in view of the confrontation with the communist regime in the East, but also its interest in economically stable markets for American business. This orientation towards long-term objectives has proved beneficial to the United States in every respect. In its relationship with the countries of Central and Eastern Europe, Western Europe today has similar long-term interests: political stability in these countries, against the background of the difficult process of transformation, not least in terms of the social aspect involved, and the creation of potential markets for the future.

If the process of transforming the economies in Central and Eastern Europe does not meet with success, or even if this success is merely a long-time coming, the political goodwill enjoyed by the first generation of reformers could rapidly be exhausted. The election results in certain countries, such as Poland and Russia, highlight this risk. Apart from destabilising political conflicts, which would not leave Western Europe unscathed, there would be a threat of a growing migratory pressure. This threat would be felt by Germany in particular, but also by the other countries of the EC. In such a situation, there would be a risk that, in the debate about the problems of Eastern Europe and how to respond to them, the EC countries could become increasingly divided, thus weakening the Community. If, on the other hand, the countries of Central and Eastern Europe manage to achieve satisfactory economic growth through an export-oriented economic policy, comprehensive privatisation of the remaining state enterprises and through well-aimed efforts to encourage new businesses, the Western European economy will benefit too. Central and Eastern Europe has the potential to develop into an important long-term export region for the EC. Despite relatively high rates of growth, the share of Eastern Europe in exports from the individual EC Member States currently only tops 3 per cent in the case of a few countries. For most of them it is generally less than this already low figure. This highlights the future potential for EC exports to Central and Eastern Europe.

There is another aspect, too, which deserves consideration. The countries of Central and Eastern Europe potentially form an important source of cheap imports and low-cost semi-manufactures. This would be of value in maintaining the competitiveness of EC industry vis-à-vis the United States and Japan, a potential which also holds out new opportunities for direct investment in these countries by Western European business.

All this presupposes, however, that the EC opens its markets permanently and without restrictions to imports from Central and Eastern Europe. There is hardly a more important contribution that the West could make towards improving the opportunities for growth in the reforming countries. The industrialised countries will be failing in their duty unless they open their borders to those products with which Central and Eastern Europe has a particularly good chance of being competitive. Imports of 'sensitive goods' – agricultural produce, textiles and metal products – will not be without problems for the economies of Western Europe. Opening the borders to the East will intensify the enormous structural pressure for change with which the Western European countries have to cope. In an environment of free competition and free trade, low-tech and labour-intensive industries in Western Europe will no longer be able to compete with suppliers from the East. Integration of the economies of Central and Eastern Europe will intensify the pressure to develop new areas of growth and employment in the EC Member States. This process must be such as to embed the countries of Central and Eastern Europe firmly in the international division of labour. The EC countries will be compelled anyway to accelerate the process of structural change. They have to remove the obstacles to growth and also to implement a more marked differentiation in wage levels, both between industries and within individual industries, in the interests of full employment. A protectionist industrial policy would be the wrong road to take, also from the viewpoint of the developed industrialised countries themselves. For the countries of Central and Eastern Europe, it would be fatal. In particular, it would prohibit the realisation of long-term opportunities for both sides and confirm the division of Europe that we thought had been overcome.

In this process of integrating the countries, which for many decades have been organised as planned economies, into the Western world based on the principles of the market economy, the main burden of adjustment lies with the countries of Central and Eastern Europe themselves. Likewise, it is their responsibility to pursue economic, monetary and fiscal policies which are decisively geared to fundamental reform. Western countries and organisations can give assistance as providers of capital, as suppliers of know-how in the various fields of economic policy, business management and marketing, and not least as free-trade partners. However important and decisive that assistance may be in so many respects, it remains nevertheless supplementary compared with the gigantic tasks which the countries of Central and Eastern Europe can only accomplish by their own efforts.

2 The transformation process

For several years now, the economies of Central and Eastern Europe have been going through a multi-faceted, complex and lengthy process of change. They are making the transition from a command economy based on central planning and rooted in state ownership of the means of production, towards a market economy based on private ownership and prices which are determined by market forces. Obviously, this process is being pursued with very different levels of enthusiasm and zeal in the individual countries. Experience to date with this process of reform and transformation has taught us several lessons and revealed certain facts.

The process of reform must be comprehensive. There can be no half-way house between central planning and a free market. Solutions of this kind, as they were attempted in Hungary and Poland even in the communist era, have yielded unsatisfactory results. Certain countries, like Ukraine, are about to discover this for themselves all over again.

3 The importance of a stable framework

The process of reform and transformation needs to be carried out within a stable framework. Prices can only perform their coordinating and allocating function in a market economy if they reflect the relative scarcity of the factors of production and of goods in the markets as accurately as possible. Inflationary processes, however, distort price relationships. They lead to misallocation and impede the smooth functioning of a market economy. From the outset, therefore, the process of reform must be marked by a determination to prevent the inflationary processes which may arise from freeing prices and dismantling subsidies or, in cases where they are inherited from the past, to contain them. Stability-oriented monetary, exchange rate and fiscal policies are a major condition for the success of the restructuring process. In view of the rigidities of the real economy, such policies can run into considerable difficulties, and every attempt at stabilisation may initially meet with only limited success. This makes it all the more important that the market players and the population at large should be convinced that the monetary and exchange rate policies conducted are consistently aimed at stability, even if inflation rates initially remain high by Western standards. As long as the monetary and exchange rate policies pursued succeed in establishing this conviction and the high inflation rates are steadily, albeit slowly, being reduced, a great deal will already have been achieved. Despite all the unsatisfactory results, Poland so far provides a good example of the value of a confidence-building policy of this kind in combating inflation. Examples of failure on this front are countries like Russia and Ukraine. There, unrestrained central bank financing of government deficits and corporate losses has led to hyperinflation which not only causes social problems but also hampers the necessary process of restructuring in the real economy.

4 The reform in the organisation of production

All efforts to achieve financial stability risk being jeopardised and risk producing an extended period of recession with serious political and social tensions if they are not forcefully accompanied by basic reform in the organisation of production. As long as there is no competition, the former mega-producers and state-owned monopolies, which are often still headed by civil servants and managers who have never learnt to fight their corner in a competitive world, continue to control the market. They do so with their cost-based pricing methods and, in collaboration with their workforces, they fight every attempt at rationalisation and cost cutting. As long as these corporate structures are not dismantled, whether by the pressure of market forces or otherwise, the war against inflation will meet with limited success. Combating inflation must therefore not be restricted to monetary measures alone. It must go hand in hand with structural measures, on which particular emphasis needs to be placed. The consistent aim of structural policy must be to improve supply. The introduction of competition is particularly important in this context, and privatisation is the most promising route towards the achievement of this objective. In this sense, structural policy is therefore also anti-inflationary in effect and takes some of the pressure off the monetary stabilisation policy.

Given the monopolistic structures which continue to exist and the very slow progress towards the introduction of competitive structures by means of privatisation, the quickest way to introduce competition is by external competition, i.e. by the liberalisation of foreign trade and the consequent opening-up of markets. The opening of borders in the East, however, as already explained, must be matched by opening the borders in the West, how difficult this may seem in certain areas.

5 The exchange rate

In this context, the decision as to what is the 'right' exchange rate, i.e. an exchange rate reflecting competitive relationships, plays an important role for the countries of Central and Eastern Europe. There are no clear-cut criteria on which to select an exchange rate regime. The decision may come down in favour of fixed or floating exchange rates, depending on the degree of economic interdependence with other countries and the capacity of the economy to cope with adjustment. In the context of a stabilisation policy, however, the exchange rate plays a significant part.

If the exchange rate is pegged to the currency of a major trading partner, the decision to defend this exchange rate parity implies a commitment to pursue economic, monetary and fiscal policies aimed at stability. The monetary and budgetary discipline imposed by pegging the exchange rate pays dividends if the national monetary and fiscal policy continues to be credible in the eyes of the markets and the general public. However, governments and central banks must take care to ensure that the exchange rate truly reflects economic reality. If the inflation rate is higher than that in the reference country, as has so far usually been the case – or in the event that a currency basket has been chosen as the anchor for national policy, higher than the average inflation rate in the countries whose currencies make up the basket – the problem has to be addressed of maintaining confidence in the national monetary, exchange rate and fiscal policies, despite the unavoidable depreciation in order to prevent appreciation in real terms. This is best achieved if the inflationary effects of currency depreciation are prevented from being translated into higher prices by a stringent monetary and fiscal policy. Poland has so far managed to pursue this kind of policy with a fair amount of success. Despite gradual depreciation within the framework of a permanent crawling peg and the need for more substantial devaluations from time to time, Poland has so far succeeded in bringing down the rate of inflation, even though an outside observer would rate this success at best as relative and, by Western standards, one would like to see greater signs of success.

A country commits itself even more strongly if it opts for a currency board system. In addition to pegging the exchange rate, such a system involves the obligation to back the national currency in full with foreign exchange reserves. In other words, the central bank can only create money if this is matched by a corresponding inflow of foreign exchange. That in turn depends on capital inflows, which will only be forthcoming if the policy of the country concerned enjoys sufficient confidence abroad, or on export surpluses, which likewise necessitate domestic economic, monetary and fiscal policies to foster international competitiveness. Estonia has so far pursued this kind of policy with a surprising amount of success, subjecting its domestic policies to the constraints of the currency board system.

The alternative to a fixed exchange rate is basically a floating exchange rate. In a system of floating exchange rates, however, the exchange rate can no longer play the part of the nominal anchor. Monetary policy must then be geared directly to domestic price stability. The central bank must itself exercise the discipline necessary to maintain this stability. As an indicator of the success of such a policy, however, even a floating exchange rate plays an important role. In other words, even a floating exchange rate does not obviate the need for domestic monetary, fiscal and economic policies which, geared to domestic stability, at the same time guarantee external stability. The stability of the exchange rate – whatever the exchange rate regime – is ultimately the result of domestic economic, fiscal and monetary policies. A stable exchange rate is in any case an important element in the confidence of the business community and the general public. It can of itself have a beneficial effect on the economy.

6 Convertibility

Like the exchange rate, the convertibility of the currency is ultimately the result of domestic monetary, fiscal and economic policies. Full convertibility for the currencies of Central and Eastern European countries can only be achieved when there is a prospect of stable balances of payments, underlain by policies which are primarily domestically oriented. That does not rule out partial convertibility, e.g. for residents on a 'free market' segregated from the official one. But such measures should only be transitional. Moreover, domestic policies must be such as to ensure that the free market exchange rates do not differ unduly from the official rate. This, too, will help to build confidence.

Stable balances of payments, which are a precondition for convertibility, do not exclude the possibility of trade deficits, provided that the offsetting spontaneous capital imports, on which the countries of Central and Eastern Europe depend, are generated. In this respect, too, the necessary conditions must be created. One such condition provides for a policy which also creates confidence abroad. In addition, foreign investors need to be sure that they can repatriate profits and capital without restrictions. In other words, there is a need for 'non-resident convertibility' for all payments associated with capital movements. The risks to the balance of payments represented by such convertibility will be limited, once the condition of economic, fiscal and monetary policies which create confidence abroad is fulfilled.

7 The establishment of efficient financial markets

In the multi-faceted, complex and long drawn-out process of restructuring the economies of the Central and Eastern European countries, the establishment of efficient financial markets and banking systems is of particular importance. They constitute the transmission mechanisms which are necessary if a monetary policy geared to restoring and maintaining price stability is to be effective. The formation of savings and capital needed for the development of these economies requires an adequate degree of domestic stability to get off the ground and grow. Despite their important function as a catalyst, inflows of foreign capital, which likewise require stable conditions, can at most supplement local savings and capital; they can never replace them. Finally, the market-oriented allocation of capital as one of the factors of production – whose efficient use is crucial for sustained and smooth growth – demands a differentiated banking system and efficient money and capital markets.

With regard to the allocation function of the banks and the financial markets, the former president of the Federal Reserve Bank of New York, E. Gerald Corrigan, has even stated that, of all the elements of structural reform essential to the transition from a centrally-planned and controlled economy to a market economy, none was of greater significance than the reform of the banking and financial system.

An important step early in the process of reform in all of the countries of Central and Eastern Europe was and is the transformation of the previously all-embracing state banks. They served a function both in the implementation and the control of the economic plan and have been transformed into a two-tier banking system. This system consists of a central bank, on the one hand, which concentrates exclusively on central bank functions and is equipped with the powers and instruments necessary to conduct an effective monetary policy, and credit institutions, on the other. The latter, if possible, are put into private ownership; in any case they need to have independent management. While in competition with each other, they are linked through a well-functioning money market, which constitutes the actual field of operation for the market-oriented instruments of the central bank's monetary policy.

Within the foreseeable future, the formation of savings and capital in the Central and Eastern European countries will largely take the form of deposits and savings with the commercial banks, savings banks and cooperative institutions. The efficient utilisation of this capital for the provision of credit will therefore be an essential task of the banking system. This would also correspond to the experiences of the Western European countries during the phase of post-war reconstruction. Bond and share markets can only gain real significance and stock exchanges are only able to perform their important market function when, with rising living standards, the financial assets of private households have reached such proportions that increased diversification of investment – whether directly or indirectly through insurance companies, pension funds, investment funds, etc. – will also benefit the bond and share markets. For some time to come, therefore, the credit institutions in the countries of Central and Eastern Europe will continue to play a decisive role in the allocation of capital. This makes it all the more important for these institutions to operate in an efficient manner. In this respect, they still have a long way to go, however. In this slow process of reform, the inherited mentality of the past tends to impede progress.

In the past few years, two-tier banking systems have been created in all the Central European states as an initial step towards reforming the system. The various functions of the previous all-embracing state banks have been divided up by transferring the quasi-commercial activities of the state banks to newly established, but still state-owned commercial banks, which now serve certain regions or sectors of the economy. Responsibility for monetary and lending policy has been retained by the state banks, which are now also in charge of the supervision of the banking industry that has become necessary. As central banks, they have de jure a wide variety of instruments at their disposal for implementing monetary policy. However, where these instruments are market-oriented rather than dirigiste in nature, their application and effectiveness is limited by the shortcomings of the interbank money markets which still have to be successfully addressed.

In the states which were part of the former Soviet Union, including the Baltic states, the formation of two-tier banking systems is still very much in its early stages. Their attempts to create national currencies and break free from the rouble will have to be attended by a clear separation between central bank and commercial bank functions. Apart from Yugoslavia, which introduced a two-tier banking system back in 1965, the formation of banking systems structured on the principles of a market economy with a clear separation between central bank and commercial bank functions in the Central European countries of the former Eastern Bloc is a development which only began with the process of political liberalisation, i.e. since 1987. A few countries like Hungary and Poland permitted the establishment of new private banks at a relatively early stage, partially involving foreign banks or at least foreign interests. These banks are not burdened with the sometimes very low-quality lending portfolios of the former state banks and their activities are not restricted to certain sectors or regions. On the other hand, events in some countries have also shown how the new climate, marked as it is by still inadequate banking supervision, has permitted unsound lending operations. Such a situation might all too easily cause the system of the market economy to become discredited.

Another problem inherited from the past is the de facto segmentation of the banking system and the associated low level of risk spreading. The lending portfolios of the former state banks were transferred to the newly founded banks, either by sector or by region. Despite the relaxation of former restrictions on lending, the loans granted by the commercial banks have remained very much concentrated on one particular region or sector. Moreover, although most of the commercial banks are able to compete for deposits, the bulk of private savings has remained in the hands of the savings banks, which are still partially centralized. To fund their lending, the banks are thus forced to rely very heavily on the central bank.

A particularly difficult problem facing the banks is the poor quality of their lending portfolios. In many cases, considerable credit risk had already arisen under the old central planning system. This did not, however, give the state banks undue cause for concern, since all credit was granted in accordance with the state planning directives. With the transition to a market economy, however, these risks were clearly brought to light, especially since many of the investments financed by credit under the old planning system proved to be unprofitable misinvestments in the new economic order. Moreover, several factors have contributed to a deterioration in the profitability of many companies: the phasing-out of subsidies and the creation of new price structures after the deregulation of the pricing system; the recession which has hit all the former command economies of Central Europe since 1990; the opening-up of markets to international competition and the collapse of trade among the countries of the former Eastern Bloc, especially with the former Soviet Union and its successor states.

The result of all these factors has been an accumulation of considerable credit risks for the banks. In the absence of even crude valuation criteria, it is almost impossible to estimate the order of magnitude involved. In all of the countries of Central and Eastern Europe, however, it must be extraordinarily high. In view of the large number of bad debts and the risk they represent to the entire banking system, it may ultimately be necessary to share this burden between the banks and the state. This holds true despite the fact that most of these countries are already running large public debts and need to control their budget deficits. Sooner or later, the governments of these countries will have to recognise the inevitable consequences of this situation, which represents another inheritance of the past, however painful this may be for the national economy. The banking system holds a key position in the process of transformation and its proper functioning is of crucial importance to the ultimate success of the transition to a market economy.

8 Concluding remarks

In conclusion, some general remarks on the degree of integration of the economies of Central and Eastern Europe are in order. For many years, Western Europe has been going through a process of far-reaching economic integration. At the heart of this process is the European Union, with twelve European states as its members. The European Union faces two problems: its enlargement to include the countries of the European Free Trade Association in the north and the centre of Europe, and its deepening in the form of its evolution into a full-fledged Economic and Monetary Union. This is not merely an economic process. It also demands a very considerable willingness to accept political union if the monetary union is to be viable. These are still highly controversial problems. Progress towards integration in Western Europe is, therefore, still hesitant. It appears very likely, not least because of the far-reaching political implications of the integration process, that different groups of countries will proceed at a different pace.

What are the chances of including the former socialist countries of Central and Eastern Europe in this integration process? Some of these countries have already clearly expressed their desire to join in the process. Where Poland, the Czech Republic and Hungary are concerned, these are countries which, because of their cultural and historical ties, have always felt to be part of the West. For these countries the forced inclusion in the communist Eastern Bloc was accordingly difficult to accept historically. It is probably, therefore, not entirely coincidental that the disintegration of the Eastern Bloc began with efforts to introduce reforms and gain independence in some of these countries. To this extent, the efforts of these countries ultimately to become members of the European Union are backed by arguments rooted in history. Even the Baltic states could advance such arguments. On the other hand, it is realistic to expect that it will be a long time before these countries, by pursuing a convincing economic policy, are able to satisfy the economic conditions for membership of the European Union. And as they make this journey, they will need all the political and economic support they can get from the West.

11 The international monetary system

The merits of stable exchange rates

Hervé Hannoun

1 Introduction

The highly negative consequences of the collapse of the Bretton Woods system, i.e. monetary instability, gave rise to an accrued appreciation of the benefits of stability. Monetary stability is now widely considered to be a common good, a prerequisite to sound, lasting growth. At the international level, this realization led to the inception of a monetary system that has become somewhat more orderly since 1985, although much remains to be done. At the European level, monetary stability became an objective much earlier, and the advent of the EMS was a momentous step forward. The need for monetary stability has only increased in the past years. At the level of individual nations, France and the Netherlands provide two examples of monetary policies that, for the past ten to fifteen years, have resolutely targeted internal and external monetary stability. A comparison of their experiences may be enlightening.

2 A more stable international monetary system: a difficult, yet essential objective

Exchange rate stability is not easy to achieve in the current international financial environment. The importance of financial market transactions in determining exchange rates is now equal to that of transactions on goods and services, if not greater. In the early 1980s, a high deficit in a country's trade or current account balance immediately affected its currency and could even generate an exchange rate crisis. At present, markets still take these factors into account, but their impact has decreased considerably. This is because current transactions on goods or services now represent only a fraction of the flows recorded in the total balance of payments. The link between capital movements and flows of goods and services has weakened. In both Germany and France, current transactions, which represented 75 per cent of total inflows and outflows in the balance of payments fifteen years ago, now account for only 30 per cent or 40 per cent.

Therefore, exchange rates are a function of two factors: the current account balance, determined by competitiveness and the soundness of the economic fundamentals, and the balance of capital movements, determined by a combination of the same economic fundamentals and a key element, usually called credibility or confidence. This change in the pattern of balances of payments, which stems from the development of capital movements not related to transactions on goods and services, has led to greater exchange rate instability throughout the world.

There are three reasons for the massive expansion of financial transactions. The 1973 collapse of the Bretton Woods fixed exchange rate system and the ensuing flotation of currencies led to exchange and interest rate instability. In this volatile context, market operators turned to hedging transactions and to arbitrage and speculation to protect their positions or to generate profits. Secondly, financial markets have become increasingly integrated and global, and there are no restraints on the free flow of capital. Furthermore, substitutable financial securities portfolios have grown rapidly, due to the rise in the public debt of most industrialized countries and the financing of the balance-of-payments deficits of certain countries. Thus, exchange rate stability is essential, but it may be difficult to achieve in the new financial environment that has emerged in the last twenty years.

3 Exchange rate stability and smooth functioning of the world economy

A certain degree of exchange rate stability is essential to the smooth functioning of the world economy. The past twenty years have demonstrated that floating exchange rates have many drawbacks for the world economy. The various attempts to restore order since 1985 to help alleviate them have improved the situation somewhat, but they are as yet insufficient. The proponents of the floating exchange rate system vaunted its advantages. They claimed that it:

- discouraged speculation by increasing uncertainty;
- provided for the automatic adjustment of balances of payments;
- made domestic monetary policies more autonomous.

In fact, the consequences of international exchange rate instability have been very serious for economic agents, governments and monetary authorities. For economic agents, in particular businesses, the resulting volatility and uncertainty have made forward planning much more difficult. If exchange rates fluctuate wildly, as they did in the early

1980s, they no longer can be used as reliable indicators for economic decision-making. When exchange rates vary by 30 per cent within a twelve-month period, with a subsequent complete trend reversal, as was the case for the dollar in 1984-85, economic operators are left guessing where to invest best their long-term funds. Ensuring optimal international resource allocation therefore becomes impossible. One of the consequences of exchange rate instability was the need to devote substantial technical, financial and human resources to foreign exchange risk management. Even when exchange rates were roughly consistent with the economic fundamentals over a long period of time, their short-term variations remained a source of uncertainty in international financial and commercial relations. This uncertainty inevitably constitutes an obstacle to the balanced development of trade.

For governments, exchange rate instability induces permissiveness, a misleading sense of autonomy and a lack of cooperation. Firstly, the idea that flexible exchange rates increase each country's autonomy, allowing it to choose its own rate of inflation and growth, has diminished the willingness of the major industrialized nations to coordinate their economic policies. Secondly, because they believed in this illusory autonomy, certain countries implemented unbalanced fiscal policies for lengthy periods. This was the case in the United States during the 1980s. American budget deficits were associated with an exchange rate appreciation, which mitigated the domestic inflation resulting from the budgetary laxity. The drain on worldwide savings caused by these semi-permanent deficits largely contributed to keeping real interest rates high, affecting global growth. In general, a floating exchange rate system may induce governments to postpone the inevitable real adjustments and to defer remedial action aimed at reducing trade imbalances, on the pretence that spontaneous exchange rate adjustments will automatically redress their external accounts. As a result, floating exchange rates tend to encourage permissive policies or benign neglect.

For monetary authorities, there is a risk of discrepancy between exchange rates and economic fundamentals. A floating exchange rate system may result in gross misalignments of exchange rates. The dollar, for example, swung from FF 10.60 in March 1985 to FF 5.35 in March 1987! The volatility of currencies and interest rates following the collapse of the Bretton Woods system has also fuelled the rapid growth of derivatives. Finally, floating exchange rates are supposed to discourage speculation by increasing the degree of uncertainty. However, the flexibility of systems like the ERM with fluctuation margins of 2.25 per cent and even, temporarily, 15 per cent also make it possible to introduce a significant degree of two-way risk.

As trade barriers fall, exchange rate stability has become increasingly important. The progress made towards free international trade, particularly with the successful outcome of the Uruguay Round at the end of 1993, could still be jeopardised by wild exchange rate fluctuations. It would be contradictory to seek the elimination or reduction of all physical and administrative barriers if, at the same time, wildly fluctuating exchange rates continue to create invisible barriers. In the early 1980s, events demonstrated the vulnerability of free trade in the absence of exchange rate stability. In the United States, an overvalued dollar in 1984-85 generated a strong demand for protectionist policies. This threat to free trade caused the American administration to become more receptive to a certain degree of international stabilization of exchange rates. The North American Free Trade Agreement has also demonstrated that sound exchange rate management and free trade go hand in hand. The Central Bank of Mexico determines a target range for the exchange rate vis-à-vis the dollar, within the official limits unilaterally defined and defended.

The increasing financial integration of industrialized economies has also contributed to making exchange rate stability even more essential than in the past. When a significant portion of the government debt of a large country is held by non-residents (approximately 40 per cent in Germany and 30 per cent in France), the authorities have a vested interest in ensuring that its monetary policy protects the external value of its currency.

4 Attempts to restore order in the international monetary system

The various attempts to restore order in the international monetary system since 1985 have helped alleviate international exchange rate misalignments. Even during the periods of extreme exchange rate instability in the 1970s and early 1980s, the monetary authorities never really neglected exchange rate movements. Since 1973, the international monetary system has, in fact, experienced a managed floating of currencies. Central banks increased their interventions rather than let rates be determined by the markets alone. It is clear that the monetary authorities cannot allow a strategically important price such as the exchange rate to be totally exempt of all guidance. In economic literature, the concept of a 'target zone' by John Williamson corresponds to this approach.

1985 was a watershed year for the international monetary system. By then, the American authorities had modified their stance, opening the way to exchange rate agreements between the major industrialized countries. These agreements were designed to ensure that the parities between the principal currencies did not diverge for any length of time from their long-term equilibrium level. Joint statements were made concerning the developments deemed desirable for specific currencies, and central banks took concerted action on foreign exchange markets. This period was marked by three events.

The Plaza Agreement (22 September 1985) signed between the five major industrialized countries represented a key step forward, as it signalled a willingness to resort to a coordinated management of floating exchange rates. The G5 countries thereby acknowledged that the exchange rates were not consistent with the situation of the American economy on the one hand, and that of the European and Japanese economies on the other. In particular, they declared that 'exchange rates should better reflect fundamental economic conditions'. They also admitted that concerted action might be required in certain circumstances, and affirmed their willingness to work together 'for some further, orderly appreciation of the main non-dollar currencies against the dollar'. The new stance had very concrete effects on the market. The American authorities, which until then had taken little, if any, part in the joint central bank interventions, took resolute action. The results were spectacular: the dollar fell by 14 per cent against the French franc, 14.5 per cent against the Deutsche mark and 17 per cent against the yen between 20 September and 30 December 1985. More remarkable still was the fact that the dollar's retreat was orderly and did not lead to the 'crash landing' many had anticipated.

The Louvre Agreement (22 February 1987) between the seven most industrialized nations was another landmark event, as it explicitly acknowledged the need for a certain degree of long-term exchange rate stability. While the Plaza Agreement was a reaction to an emergency situation, the Louvre Agreement reflected a joint determination to stabilize exchange rates. The finance ministers and central bank governors of the G7 countries agreed that the substantial changes in exchange rates since the Plaza Agreement had 'brought their currencies within ranges broadly consistent with underlying economic fundamentals'. They stated that 'further substantial exchange rate shifts could damage growth and adjustment prospects in their countries' and they undertook to 'cooperate closely to foster stability of exchange rates around current levels'.

The agreement functioned well for nine months and helped stabilize the dollar until October 1987. Difficulties arose following the stock market crash, when the American authorities reacted by reversing the rising trend on domestic interest rates. The market then considered the dollar's fall to be inevitable. The second Louvre Agreement on 22 December 1987 was designed to shore up the first and to counter these expectations by preventing any further decline in the dollar. It contained provisions that were never published on the reference bands to be defended and the means to be implemented. The agreement proved very effective: speculative pressures against the dollar abated in January 1988 and the currency subsequently remained fairly stable for over a year.

The Bercy Agreement (7 April 1990) between the G7 countries was the first relating to a currency other than the dollar. Until then, while the G7 had tried to regulate the dollar's fluctuations against the currencies of the other G7 countries, the fluctuations of the latter currencies against each other were not checked. The meeting on 7 April 1990 reinforced the arrangement by proclaiming that the yen's decline against the other G7 currencies 'had undesirable consequences for the global adjustment process'. From then on, joint exchange rate management applied to the yen versus the EMS currencies, as well as to the dollar versus the yen and the EMS currencies. The agreement on 7 April 1990 also proved successful, halting the yen's decline against the other currencies. The yen subsequently showed a steady tendency to appreciate and to return to a level more compatible with the fundamentals of the Japanese economy.

An assessment of the world economy during this period shows that whenever exchange rates were stable, there was also greater prosperity. Like all other protectionist measures, devaluations that are not based on economic fundamentals and are not carried out in agreement with the country's trade partners only worsen the overall situation. These agreements would not have been as successful without closely coordinated economic policies. The past two or three years have demonstrated that the impact of the G7 communiqués diminishes when markets sense a weakening in international coordination. The main limitation of the agreements is their dependence on the cooperation of the major countries. A sound and balanced international monetary system can only be achieved by substantial improvements in international monetary and economic cooperation. By accepting to work towards closer cooperation, the major countries would be merely conforming to the obligations of every IMF member state. Article IV of the Statutes of the Fund states that 'each member undertakes to collaborate with the Fund and other members to assure orderly exchange arrangements and to promote a stable system of exchange rates'.

5 The influence of central banks

Central banks exert an effective influence on exchange rate fluctuations. A frequent question is whether the balance of power between central banks and foreign exchange markets has not shifted to the benefit of the latter. Any reply must first consider the diversity of the players in exchange markets. The monetary crises of 1992 and 1993 pushed new players to the fore. Together with the large international commercial banks and a few multinational companies, investment banks from English-speaking countries and hedge funds have gradually come to play a major role. The recent emergence of non-banking institutional investors (pension funds, insurance companies, mutual funds, trust funds, hedge funds) has been one of the major changes in foreign exchange markets.

The players on foreign exchange markets are therefore increasingly diverse. There are many types of operators and operations, ranging from interbank trading, carried out by the large commercial banks, and foreign exchange transactions related to the global management of securities portfolios by investment banks or institutional investors, to leads and lags in international trade payments. As a result, there is no clear distinction between central banks on the one hand, and a homogeneous group of market players on the other. The central banks are not the only players following a strategy based on the economic fundamentals. A large section of the market realizes that the fundamentals always prevail in the medium term, and applies the same approach. They are called 'fundamentalists' as opposed to 'chartists'. This is why a comparison of the central banks' foreign exchange reserves ($ 556 billion at end-1992 according to the BIS) with the much higher amounts traded daily on the markets ($ 880 billion per day) is not significant and does not imply that the shift in the balance of power has been detrimental to central banks.

Cooperation between central banks has a multiplier effect, proving that central banks still have powerful means at their disposal. In particular, the management of the European Exchange Rate Mechanism with widened bands since August 1993 has demonstrated the capacity of central banks to prevent exchange rate instability.

6 Exchange rate stability in Europe

In Europe, exchange rate stability is a promising concept destined to lead to a fixed parity system and a single currency before the end of the century. From the outset, the Member States of the Community realized that open trade barriers and monetary stability were closely related. The founding fathers of the Treaty of Rome did not have to consider setting up an orderly exchange rate system for Europe, since such a system already existed for all industrialized nations within the Bretton Woods Agreement. Nevertheless, paragraph 1 of Article 107 of the Treaty of Rome stipulates that 'each Member State shall treat its policy with regard to rates of exchange as a matter of common concern'. From this point of view, the EMS and EMU represent successive stages in Europe's joint determination to complete the common and then the single market. The decision made on 2 August 1993 to widen the margins temporarily is consistent with this standpoint.

The exchange rate stability provided by the EMS since 1979 has contributed substantially to the considerable growth of trade within Europe. In France, for example, trade with the eleven European partners accounted for 51 per cent of total foreign trade in 1980, and 62 per cent in 1992. The increasing economic integration of European Community states has heightened the need for exchange rate stability. In addition, the effectiveness of devaluations has decreased as economic integration progresses. Exchange rate stability is therefore fully consistent with the logic of the single market. The single market provides for total freedom of cross-border flows and far-reaching legal, regulatory and fiscal harmonization to reduce or eliminate invisible barriers. Exchange rates are a vital element in price formation, and if they are not managed, the monetary barriers Europe worked so hard to dismantle in the past ten years might reappear.

But in a world where capital moves freely, the need for exchange rate stability implies that monetary policies have to be more closely coordinated and economies have to converge more and more. As a result, economic integration both increases the need for exchange rate stability and forces economic policies to converge. This is why the completion of Economic and Monetary Union in the near future has become so important for Europe. A common monetary policy will then replace those of individual nations. Moreover, a single currency will unleash the full beneficial effects of the single market in terms of growth and business activity. European companies need a single currency in their domestic markets to enjoy an equal footing with their foreign, and particularly North American, competitors. Therefore Europe has agreed to complete the single market by introducing a single currency. Such are the stakes in Europe's endeavour to achieve stable exchange rates. They constitute the true reason for the recent contrast between the stability-oriented approach, which is widely preferred throughout Europe, and the floating system approach.

The widening of fluctuation bands does not jeopardise the objective of exchange rate stability in Europe. The decision of the ministers of finance and the central bank governors of the EC on 2 August 1993 comprised two essential aspects:
- Central rates remain unchanged: by declaring that 'having regard to the fundamental economic situation of the Member States participating in the system, the current parity grid is fully justified', the ministers and governors reaffirmed their support of exchange rate stability. Despite what certain market operators may have initially expected, the decision of 2 August 1993 was not intended to install 'de facto floating', allowing the Member States sufficient room to carry out aggressive interest rate cuts.
- A temporary widening of the fluctuation margins: this was the monetary authorities' technical response to exceptionally large capital movements. It is a tool to discourage speculation by introducing a 'two-way risk'. André Szász has probably been the best theorist and practitioner of this concept.

Since last August, the ERM has demonstrated the priority given to exchange rate stability in Europe. The members of the ERM have endeavoured to preserve the external stability of their currencies. All refrained from competitive devaluations and none tried to profit from the 15 per cent fluctuation band by drastic interest rates cuts, which could have endangered the stability of their currency. This proves that the ERM is much stronger than expected.

7 A comparison of the French and Dutch pursuit of stable exchange rates

Netherlands and France have long recognized the importance of exchange rate stability for open and highly integrated economies. The Netherlands has been more successful in the pursuit of this objective than its ERM partners, and the guilder was the only currency to escape speculative pressures in July 1993. As a result, the Netherlands was the only country to maintain the 2.25 per cent fluctuation band with the Deutsche mark, in keeping with a specific bilateral agreement. For the past twelve years, France and the Netherlands have pursued the same objective – stability – reaping considerable benefits for their economies.

March 1983 was a turning point for the two countries' economic and monetary policies. It was a watershed in the monetary history of France and the Netherlands. When the Bretton Woods system collapsed in 1973, the Dutch authorities decided to maintain their currency's stability vis-à-vis the Deutsche mark because of the openness of the Dutch economy (foreign trade currently accounts for 41 per cent of GDP) and its relatively modest size. However, in the 1970s, the guilder was devalued several times in the European monetary snake. By the 1980s, there was an accrued need for monetary stability, but the key date was 21 March 1983, when the guilder was devalued 'for the last time' against the Deutsche mark. In the course of the general realignment in March 1983, the Dutch government decided to devalue its currency by 2 per cent, against the advice of monetary authorities. This move, which ran counter to the commitment to maintain the guilder's parity against the Deutsche mark, made by the monetary authorities at the beginning of the 1980s, was not well received by the markets.

The Dutch government drew two lessons from this unfortunate experience. Firstly, markets react badly to political interference in monetary policy. It follows that central bank independence must be guaranteed. Secondly, 'credibility is hard to achieve and easy to lose', to quote André Szász. The Dutch experience is exemplary: not until the beginning of the 1990s did the Netherlands' monetary policy regain the credibility it had damaged in 1983, although the Dutch authorities steadfastly gave absolute priority to their currency's parity stability. It is well known that André Szász contributed greatly to this effort.

Exchange rate stability has always been one of the guidelines of France's monetary policy. However, until the beginning of the 1980s, the fact that the French economy was not as open as the Dutch economy led the authorities to believe that there were certain advantages to devaluing. Devaluations were frequent in France on the grounds that they would boost growth and make up for the insufficient competitiveness of the business sector. But the ensuing spurt of growth was quickly cancelled out by the 'stop-and-go' policies that were necessary to avoid economic overheating. The most blatant result was an inflation rate higher than that of our partners. All economic agents, employers and employees alike, became accustomed to devaluations and planned for more monetary depreciations and inflation. This led to a self-generated cycle of depreciation-inflation-depreciation. The vicious circle was not halted until 1982. In March 1983 France reaffirmed its anchoring in the EMS and embarked on a policy aimed at maintaining the French franc's external value. This was supported by a prudent domestic monetary policy and an overall macro-economic stance designed to durably rebalance the country's external accounts; increases in nominal income were kept down and wage indexation was phased out.

The exchange rate gradually stabilized while the magnitude and frequency of the currency's realignments diminished, ceasing entirely after January 1987. Since then, the French franc/Deutsche mark parity has remained remarkably steady. The recent reform of the Banque de France's Statutes to guarantee its independence testifies to our long-term commitment to monetary stability. During the past decade, France's economy has opened up increasingly and foreign trade on goods now represents 22.5 per cent of GDP. This has only served to fortify the determination of the authorities to preserve the franc's internal and external value.

The monetary policies of France and the Netherlands have set an auspicious framework for their economies. The monetary stability policies pursued by France and the Netherlands for at least twelve years have improved their competitiveness and ensured favourable financing terms, giving them the means to benefit fully from a global recovery. In both countries, competitive gains were obtained in the best possible way through cost control, particularly of labour costs, and improved product quality. Exchange rate stability meant an end to the use of devaluations as an escape route, and forced businesses to control their costs. Domestic industries were forced to achieve sound structural price competitiveness and good 'non-price' competitiveness. The latter is an increasingly important asset in international trade. In the current context of global competition, the older industrial nations must prevent their producers from slipping downmarket. This risk arises when currencies are devalued. Currency depreciations, the easy solution applied by certain countries, can only bring temporary, illusory gains in competitiveness. They tend to lead to slack cost management, which in turn rapidly erodes the competitive edge obtained by devaluing. The result is a vicious circle of inflation and devaluation. The BIS analysis of real exchange rates, whether defined on the basis of consumer prices, unit wage costs or producer prices, shows that France and the Netherlands have achieved competitive gains vis-à-vis the rest of the OECD area since 1986.

The steady pursuit of stability has also given the monetary authorities of both countries the credibility needed to obtain favourable conditions on the credit markets, particularly at the long end. In the Netherlands, this credibility has been well established for several years. By 1990, Dutch interest rates were closely aligned with those of Germany, and in 1992 they fell even lower. At the end of December 1993, the 10-year interest rate on Dutch bonds was 5.51 per cent, compared to 5.53 per cent on German bonds. Thanks to its strong monetary strategy, the Netherlands boasts one of the best yield curves for 1-month to 10-year maturities in Europe, excluding Switzerland. France's monetary policy credibility has also improved considerably in the past few years. A key factor has been the authorities' insistence on maintaining the franc's internal and external value since the widening of the ERM fluctuation margins. This has been reflected in the spectacular fall in long-term rates, which, at the end of December 1993 were, almost on par with those of Germany. In both countries, the current level of long-term interest rates will help boost investments.

8 Concluding remarks

Europe is prepared for the advent of a more orderly international monetary system. At present, however, no European currency, regardless of the policy followed by its monetary authorities, is able to supplant the dollar. The European money area is still too fragmented. The dollar's dominance and the potentially disruptive effects of its erratic fluctuations on the world economy remain, despite the undeniable achievements of the G7. Considerable progress will be made with the completion of EMU and the introduction of a single currency. By the end of the century the single European currency, like the dollar, will enjoy widespread use in international markets. The anti-inflationary focus of monetary policy should also contribute to the strength of the single European currency. The existence of a new currency traded on vast markets will open up a whole new range of possibilities for raising capital and managing financial assets. A united Europe will bring far more weight and influence to bear in negotiations with its partners, notably the United States and Japan. It will be in a better position to promote coordinated economic policies, more balanced strategies and a more stable international monetary system.

Turbulence in the foreign exchange markets: old and new lessons

Lamberto Dini

'It had become abundantly clear (by 1971) that when markets think an exchange rate is untenable, enormous flows of speculative funds can move from one currency to another'.[1]

1 Introduction

For many years, I have had the privilege of exchanging views on monetary and exchange rate matters with André Szász at least twice a month in various fora, notably in Basle and Brussels. His contributions to the discussion are a model of synthesis and combine wisdom with authority. In recent years, he has been the most consistent advocate of the three Dutch precepts for exchange rate stability: do not pretend that your monetary policy is autonomous with respect to that of the anchor country; maximize the central bank's independence of political authorities and make full use of interest rates to prevent speculation by enhancing the market's perception that risks are two-way. André's wisdom is based on his long involvement in international monetary affairs; he often supports his arguments with examples from the Bretton Woods period, which he knows from direct experience and which he has studied carefully, particularly between 1972 and 1974, when he was a member of the Committee for the reform of the international monetary system (the Committee of Twenty). To pay tribute to his long career, I shall also turn back to the Bretton Woods system in an attempt to assess the extent to which the 'lessons' that can be drawn from the recent turbulence are really new.

2 From adjustable to fixed exchange rates

The fact that no realignments were made after 1987 is widely seen as one of the main causes of the crisis that broke out in the European Monetary System in the summer of 1992. From its inception, the system had

1 Solomon (1977).

worked as a fixed-but-adjustable parity regime, but from 1987 onwards it increasingly came to be seen by both authorities and markets as a fixed parity regime. The 'adjustable' part of the original design, which had been confirmed in the Basle/Nyborg Agreement of 1987, was progressively forgotten. Thus, when tensions arose, realignments were fiercely resisted and finally decided under very strong market pressure and on a piecemeal basis. The two documents prepared in May 1993 by the Committee of Governors of the Central Banks of the EC and by the Monetary Committee gave considerable emphasis to this point and recommended a more frequent (or less infrequent) use of exchange rate adjustments. The authorities' ability to prevent market pressures through timely realignments was seen as the key to restoring the credibility of the system. In the light of what happened to the Italian lira, the pound sterling and the Spanish peseta (three currencies which had come to be widely perceived as overvalued), this proposal appeared unobjectionable. While it is agreed that exchange rates should not be allowed to move too far out of line with economic fundamentals, the jury has not yet returned a verdict on whether frequently adjusting parities is actually a feasible option in all circumstances.

We know all too well why the authorities resisted realignments in the EMS. André Szász himself has often reminded us that it took his country several years to recover from the loss of credibility caused by the guilder's devaluation against the Deutsche mark in 1983.[2] In spite of very sound domestic policies and developments, Dutch interest rates jumped above Germany's and remained higher until 1990. The point is that the authorities are nearly always faced with the problem of what the literature calls 'time inconsistency'. They must take markets by surprise if they are to avoid speculation, but this is hardly possible more than once. Moreover, in order to persuade markets that there will not be another 'surprise', the authorities not only have to reaffirm their commitment to exchange rate stability in even stronger terms, which aggravates the credibility problem in the following round, but must also take radical action to change domestic policies requiring political consensus. Since this is something that cannot be done 'frequently', the system is likely to degenerate into a crawling peg (as in the early 1980s) or turn into a quasi-monetary union (until the next crisis).

This dilemma was clear to the authorities under the Bretton Woods regime and was always resolved by fiercely resisting realignments. Indeed, these occurred almost only when market pressure became overwhelmingly strong. The authorities were frightened by the

2 Szász (1993).

memory of the consequences of earlier realignments, such as the sharp devaluation of sterling in 1949, which was followed by the realignment of thirty other currencies, and the revaluation of the Deutsche mark in March 1961.[3] This realignment, which the German authorities had repeatedly excluded, changed market psychology because it led speculators not to trust official denials. Especially after the return to current account convertibility, governments were inhibited from even considering a change in their dollar par values for fear of provoking large anticipatory capital flows.[4]

In 1964, soon after becoming Prime Minister, Harold Wilson decided 'irrevocably' not to devalue. He apparently feared that such a course would not only fail to resolve the basically structural problems of the British economy but would also be politically disastrous for his party and unwelcome to the Americans; devaluation thus became 'the unmentionable' in government circles.[5] As Wilson put it: 'The financial world at home and abroad was aware that the post-war decision to devalue in 1949 had been taken by the Labour government. There would have been many who would conclude that the Labour government, facing difficulties, always took the easy way out by devaluing the pound. Speculation would be aroused every time that Britain ran even into minor economic difficulties – or even without them'.[6] One may disagree with the British Prime Minister, but it is hard to deny that his arguments carry considerable weight.

When credibility and time inconsistency issues enter the domain of high politics (as has almost always been the case with major decisions about parities), they inevitably become subject to broader political considerations. In November 1968, De Gaulle decided not to devalue the franc; 'a franc devaluation would be a blow both to French prestige and to President De Gaulle's prestige ... Devaluation would, in particular, weaken French leadership in Europe vis-à-vis Germany'.[7] Political factors are also important in explaining why Germany did not revalue the Deutsche mark in the spring of 1969, when capital inflows from the United States and several European countries reached historically high levels. Elections were due in the autumn, opinion polls showed the public to be against revaluation and exporters' reaction to the small one made in 1961 had virtually ruled out a repetition.[8] In the end the Deutsche mark was revalued in October, by the new government.

One of the obstacles to efficient decisions on parities is the question of

3 Yeager (1976).
4 Eichengreen (1993); McKinnon (1993).
5 Yeager (1976).
6 Obstfeld (1993).
7 Solomon (1977).
8 Yeager (1976).

which country should bear the burden of adjustment, and in what form. During the 1960s and early 1970s, the United States authorities considered a Deutsche mark revaluation, or an easier monetary policy in Germany, as the right cure for their balance-of-payments problems, since a devaluation of the dollar against gold would have undermined the credibility of the dollar as a store of value entailing possible broad systemic consequences. For the German authorities, instead, the expansionary US monetary policy was the main cause of the disequilibrium. Divergent views on who should adjust and how have also arisen recently within the EMS.

Finally, devaluations were resisted because it was feared that they would cause a large deterioration in the terms of trade with only a small improvement in the trade balance.[9] The old elasticity pessimism played a minor role in the recent history of the EMS, but was replaced by what can be called 'inflation pessimism', i.e. the fear that devaluation would mainly affect domestic prices rather than the real exchange rate.[10] This pessimism was widespread and soundly rooted in the analysis of events in the 1970s and 1980s. Indeed, most economists were wrong-footed by the good inflation performances of the United Kingdom, Italy and Spain in 1993.

3 Asymmetry

A pegged exchange rate system requires a high degree of mutual consistency of national monetary policies. In principle, this objective can be achieved through coordination or an asymmetric arrangement whereby only one country (the 'nth country' in Bretton Woods language, the anchor country in EMS language) can exercise monetary independence. While the Bretton Woods system and, more clearly, the EMS were designed to be symmetric, both proved to be highly asymmetric in practice. I regard this as a major weakness: if the 'nth country' – for whatever reason – is unwilling to cooperate, it may be very difficult for other countries to reconcile domestic and external objectives and avoid major exchange market strains.

In 1944 it was not intended that any national money should become the dominant currency in the system as a whole.[11] Currencies were treated as equal in the IMF Articles of Agreement because, in principle, each country was required to maintain its par value by intervening in

9 Laffer (1977); Miles (1979); Salant (1977).
10 Ciampi (1992).
11 McKinnon (1993).

the currencies of all the others.[12] A small bias toward asymmetry was implicitly introduced in the Articles of Agreement by the provision that 'the par value of the currency of each member country ... be expressed in terms of gold as a common denominator or in terms of the United States dollar'. In practice, the United States was the only country to peg its currency to gold, while all the others fixed their parities in terms of the dollar. The dollar thus became the 'nth currency', allowing the United States to ignore exchange rate and other balance-of-payments constraints; other countries could either follow US monetary policy or, if they were unable or unwilling to do so, realign their dollar parities.

The EMS was designed as an even more symmetric and cooperative system than the Bretton Woods system. In particular, the agreement established that, when two currencies reached their bilateral margin of fluctuation, intervention would be compulsory and carried out by both the central banks involved, with unlimited finance provided through the very short-term credit facility. Intra-marginal interventions were also to be officially financed, up to a certain amount. An ECU-based indicator would show which currency was diverging from the mean and hence identify the country that should bear the burden of adjustment, and realignments were to be decided collectively. The actual working of the EMS was quite different, however: the divergence indicator was virtually never used; until 1992 interventions were almost always intra-marginal and carried out by the weak-currency countries using their own reserves. During the recent crisis strong-currency countries did intervene at the margin, but the burden of interest rate adjustment fell almost exclusively on the weak-currency countries.

In both systems, non-anchor countries gained in terms of financial and price stability, at least initially. In addition, the choice of the dollar as an anchor in the Bretton Woods system was obviously related to the dominant size of the US economy and the role of US aid in European reconstruction. Non-anchor countries nonetheless incurred a cost in terms of a loss of monetary autonomy that was exacerbated by the rigid interpretation of exchange rate adjustments in the actual working of the systems, both suffering major strains when these costs became too large.

The history of the two systems suggests that it is difficult not only to replace asymmetry with coordination, but also to replace one leading country with another in a pegged exchange rate regime. The role of Ger-

12 Obstfeld (1993)

many as the EMS anchor country was not seriously questioned, even when German fundamentals became less sound than those of other EMS countries. Specifically, in 1992-93 the inflation differential between Germany and France was more than two percentage points, but the French authorities were unable to bring short-term interest rates below the German level without triggering unsustainable market pressure on the franc. Despite France's recently acquired virtuousness, developments in the markets did not allow it to replace Germany as the anchor country. In the Bretton Woods system, the situation was different as in the 1960s financial markets rated Germany more highly than the United States. After 1967, Deutsche mark rates in the Euromarkets were almost always below those of the dollar, although Germany generally succeeded in keeping its domestic rates above those of the United States through controls on capital inflows. Nonetheless, Germany did not become the 'nth country'. The inconsistency was not resolved, and in the end the system collapsed.

4 The intensity of market pressures

It is difficult to determine the extent to which market pressures have increased compared with the Bretton Woods period. However, 20 or 30 years ago they were already powerful enough on several occasions to overcome the authorities' resistance to exchange rate adjustment, since almost every major realignment was instigated by a reserve crisis. In spite of controls and in relation to some scale variable, the capital flows that occurred during some of these crises were not much smaller than today. In the sixties and early seventies, when holdings of foreign exchange reserves and nominal GNP were ten to twenty times smaller, flows out of and into individual currencies during episodes of market pressure reached several billions of dollars in just a few weeks, or even days. In several cases market pressure led to the 'temporary' floating of a currency and the subsequent setting of a new parity.[13] On 17 November 1967, the day before sterling was devalued, the Bank of England supported the pound's parity with more than $ 1 billion of reserves, or about 1 per cent of GNP. This compares with a loss of reserves on 16 September 1992 corresponding to just over 2 per cent of GNP. In addition, in June 1972, a few months after the United Kingdom's official reserves had reached an all time high of $ 7 billion, there was an outflow of $ 2.5 billion in just six working days. Strong currencies also came under very heavy pressure. In May 1969 the reserves of the Bundesbank

13 Solomon (1977) and Yeager (1976) provide a detailed chronicle of many instances in which the authorities' ability to resist market forces was seriously undermined.

grew by over $ 4 billion in seven business days, which, in relation to the stock of German central bank money or GNP is very close to the rise that occurred in September 1992. In 1971, capital outflows from the United States led to a staggering $ 31 billion increase in the reserves of the other G10 countries. This can be set against net sales of Deutsche mark by ERM central banks in the order of $ 100 billion between June and December 1992.

The Report of the Group of Ten noted the 'suddenness with which selling pressures gained momentum' in the summer of 1992.[14] Again, this was not entirely a novelty. In the Bretton Woods system, moments of strength and weakness alternated rapidly, particularly in sterling's case: '... the weakness that brought devaluation in 1949 gave way to strength and rumors of upward revaluation in 1950-51 and then in turn to the crisis of 1951-52. Only weeks before the downward float of 1972 the British balance of payments had been healthy; the pound had been quoted well above its central rate against the dollar'.[15] 'Speculative movements against the pound... could make any weakness in the balance of current payments into a serious crisis within a few weeks.'[16] France also underwent a sudden reversal of fortune in 1968. French international reserves had been growing for several years, but then in May social and political turmoil erupted and the franc 'almost overnight lost its place among the stable currencies of the world'.[17]

Despite these similarities, international capital markets have hanged significantly since the Bretton Woods days. Financial innovation, technological progress and the removal of capital controls have affected the structure of financial markets. Conceptual and technical difficulties[18] make it hard to establish the extent to which integration has increased relative to the Bretton Woods years, but it undoubtedly has, and the changes since then have 'increased the scale of the pressure that can be exerted against an exchange rate when market sentiment shifts'.[19]

5 Determinants of exchange rate pressure

Capital mobility and more sophisticated investment techniques have complicated the task of managing a fixed-but-adjustable exchange rate system as they increased the importance of both short-run factors, such as cyclical divergences, and expectations. The perception that cyclical

14 Group of Ten (1993).
15 Yeager (1976).
16 Katz (1955).
17 Yeager (1976).
18 Goldstein and Mussa (1993).
19 Yeager (1976).

considerations might lead to changes in monetary policy played a key role in the crisis of some European currencies in 1992-93. This mechanism was present, but not so powerful in the Bretton Woods system, in which exchange rate crises were mainly due to 'classic' balance-of-payments disequilibria, caused by losses of competitiveness or inappropriate, expansionary macro-economic policies. The time markets took to react to the prospect of, say, a cyclical downturn was probably long enough for the cycle itself to reverse. In today's world, instead, the anticipation of a downturn is likely to produce a rapid and powerful reaction. The same may hold for other events, such as a temporary terms-of-trade shock.

As I mentioned earlier, market forces in the Bretton Woods system were actually strong enough to force exchange rate devaluations. The novelty is that markets now react much more frequently and in response to a wider range of motivations. This is probably the key distinction between today's financial environment and the earlier one, characterized by low capital mobility. Since it takes less time for markets to react, the problem of time consistency facing the authorities is now more acute. To be sure, cyclical divergences also played a role in the Bretton Woods system. Indeed, it can be argued that its collapse in 1971 was partly due to monetary policies having diverged in response to the very slow growth of the US economy in 1969-71, while most European countries and Japan were still expanding rapidly. However, other factors were also at work, such as the acceleration of inflation and the deterioration of the current account in the United States. More importantly, the massive outflows of capital from the US, mostly in the direction of Germany, did not so much precede as accompany the exceptional rise in German short-term interest rates, from below 4 per cent at the beginning of 1969 to almost 10 per cent in the first half of the following year. US interest rates also rose, but by much less, and only briefly touched a peak of 8 per cent in January 1970. As the pressure became unsustainable, the Deutsche mark was floated and then revalued. The difference compared with recent events in the EMS is quite clear. Unlike the United States in 1969-71, France kept its short-term interest rates above Germany's for most of 1992-93; markets thus acted on the expectation that this policy would not be sustainable rather than on actual divergences in monetary policies. In addition, France did not have the inflation or current account problems that plagued America towards the end of the Bretton Woods system.

Classic conditions of external disequilibrium were at the root of most of the exchange rate crises in the Bretton Woods system. For instance, the recurrent problems of the pound sterling in the 1960s can be attributed to high relative inflation, low competitiveness and persistent current account deficits, aggravated by repeated attempts to stimulate growth through expansionary macro-economic policies. The strength of the Deutsche mark was attributable, instead, to low inflation and persistent current account surpluses. By contrast, booming demand, rising inflation and current account deficits contributed to both the crisis of the lira in 1963, which was successfully overcome through a tight monetary policy, and of the French franc in 1969, which had to be devalued by 11 per cent.

Another important difference between now and then, which is probably obvious but should not go unnoticed, concerns public finances. Fiscal imbalances were not a major cause of exchange rate tensions during the Bretton Woods system years. The low stock of public debt meant that monetary policy was not constrained by interest rate increases being unsustainable in the medium term, whereas several European countries recently saw the 'credibility' of their monetary policies undermined because of the large debt burden. At the same time, since the authorities did not have to correct fiscal imbalances, the countries in the Bretton Woods era were able to use fiscal policy more actively to achieve external objectives, in both surplus and deficit countries.[20]

6 Conclusions

In this short essay I have described the common features of the Bretton Woods system and the EMS, as well as some of the differences. In both cases the conclusion is the same: managing a system of fixed-but-adjustable exchange rates is extremely difficult today. The similarities suggest that certain problems are inherent in such systems. Resistance to realignments was not a special feature of the EMS, strengthened perhaps by expectations in the late 1980s of a smooth advance to EMU. At the very least, this indicates that it may be very difficult to avoid the 'mistake' of excessively resisting realignments. Asymmetry is another important common feature. Both systems underwent a serious crisis when the role of the pivot country was called into question. The 'moral' is that it is very hard, though – I trust – not impossible, to coordinate monetary policies so as to minimize conflicts between the domestic and external objectives of all the countries participating in an exchange rate agreement. This difficulty clearly weakens the system, since strains develop whenever the policy priorities of the core country differ from

20 McKinnon (1993).

those of the others. The third shared feature is that, even with the tight capital controls which were in place during the Bretton Woods years, market forces were powerful enough to force exchange rate adjustments. This lends support to the view that controls are not the answer to the problems of the EMS today.

As to the differences, I have drawn attention to the larger size and greater integration of today's financial markets and their ability to exert strong pressure, in response not only to classic disequilibria in fundamentals but also to actual or expected short-run cyclical developments. The dollar crisis of 1970-71 was primarily due to large actual divergences between interest rate policies in America and Europe, coupled with the rapidly growing US current account deficit. By contrast, in July 1993 markets acted massively on the perception that domestic conditions would result in French interest rates not being sustainable. The larger role of expectations and short-run developments in determining market behaviour makes the task of managing the system much more complicated than it was in the Bretton Woods years. Finally, I underscored the importance of the fiscal imbalances in Europe today. Contrary to 20 or 30 years ago, budgetary policy can hardly be used for cyclical purposes, so that adjustment through exchange rates is even more necessary. In addition, large public debts tend to undermine the credibility of interest rate hikes as a means of defending established parities.

Summing up, I would suggest that the real inconsistency is not so much between fixed exchange rates, independent monetary policies and capital mobility, but between internal and external objectives. A country may decide to accept the constraints on monetary policy that an exchange rate agreement imply, but the key question is whether it has the 'political ability ... to maintain macro-economic stability without monetary policy autonomy'.[21] The EMS and the Bretton Woods system both functioned smoothly while countries had a strong and widely recognized interest in following the policies of the pivot country, but serious strains developed when policy requirements diverged or were perceived by markets to be divergent.

Since last August, the ERM countries have succeeded in maintaining a very high degree of exchange rate stability without the coercion of formal rules. As is well known, intervention only becomes obligatory at the 15 per cent margin, but all the countries involved are trying to avoid using such a wide band. According to some observers, this arrangement may continue to work, while others think that a return to narrower mar-

21 Group of Ten (1993); Bordo (1993).

gins will eventually be necessary to maintain the desired degree of exchange rate stability. The key argument in support of the first view is that the essential ingredient for exchange rate stability is the commitment to coordinate monetary policy, possibly by accepting the leading role of the pivot country, while narrow intervention margins are not essential and may even be destabilizing. Wide bands are preferable because they enhance the market's perception of a two-way risk, a condition that, as Szász constantly emphasized, is an essential antidote to speculation. More generally, a flexible commitment, allowing temporary deviations from the target (through the use of wider bands) may be more credible than a rigid one.

It is too early to judge the merits of this view. One point is clear, however: the received wisdom of the founding fathers of both the Bretton Woods system and the EMS is turned upside down. In short, the implicit suggestion is that a quasi-flexible exchange rate regime is needed to stabilize currencies and, perhaps paradoxically, that a regime of fixed (but adjustable) exchange rates ends up by being destabilizing. In the coming months it will be necessary to watch two crucial aspects. First, convergence: the increased flexibility of the exchange rate system should not weaken the drive to adjust domestic policies. Secondly, credibility: markets will have to be convinced that the authorities are willing to pursue stable exchange rates, irrespective of formal rules and announcements. Over the longer run, it will be essential to show that such an arrangement can withstand the asymmetric shocks that will inevitably arise. Undoubtedly, André's precepts for stable exchange rates will be put to the test.

References

Bordo, M.D. (1993), The Bretton Woods international monetary system: a historical overview, in: *M.D. Bordo and B. Eichengreen (eds.), A retrospective on the Bretton Woods system,* Chicago/London.

Ciampi, C.A. (1992), *Audizione del Governatore della Banca d'Italia per l'esame delle conseguenze dei recenti avvenimenti sui mercati monetari e finanziari,* Banca d'Italia, Rome.

Committee of Governors of the Central Banks of the Member States of the EC (1993), *The implications ans lessons to be drawn from the recent exchange crisis,* Basle.

Eichengreen, B. (1993), Epilogue: three perspectives on the Bretton Woods system, in *M.D. Bordo and B. Eichengreen (eds.), Retrospective on the Bretton Woods system,* Chicago/London.

Goldstein, M. and M. Mussa (1993), *The integration of world capital markets,* paper presented at the Conference on changing capital markets: implications for monetary policy, Federal, Reserve Bank of Kansas, Jackson Hole, 19 - 21 August.

Group of Ten (1993), *International capital movements and foreign exchange markets,* a report to the ministers and governors by the Group of Deputies.

Katz, S (1955), Sterling's recurring post-war payments crises, *Journal of Political Economy,* June.

Laffer, A.B. (1977), Exchanges rates, the terms of trade, and the trade balance, in: *P.B. Clark et al., (eds.), The effects of exchange rate adjustment,* Washington DC.

McKinnon, R. (1993), The rules of the game: international money in historical perspective, *Journal of Economic Literature,* vol. 31, March.

Miles, M.A. (1979), The effects of devaluation on the trade balance and the balance of payments: some new results, *Journal of Poitical Economy,* June.

Monetary Committee of the European Community (1993), *Lessons to be drawn from the disturbances on the foreign exchange markets,* Brussels.

Obstfeld, M. (1993), The adjustment mechanism, in: *M.D. Bordo and B. Eichengreen (eds.), A retrospective on the Bretton Woods system,* Chicago/London.

Salant, M. (1977), Devaluations improve the balance of payments even if not the trade balance, in: *P.B. Clarck et al. (eds.), The effects of exchange rate adjustments,* Washington DC.

Solomon, R. (1977), *The international monetary system,* 1945-1976, New York.

Szász, A. (1993), *Towards a single European currency: ECU, Franc-fort, Question-Mark, in: D.E. Fair and R.J. Raymond (eds.), The new Europe: evolving economic and financial systems in East and West,* Dordrecht, pp. 217-235.

Yeager, L.B. (1976), *International monetary relations: theory, history, and policy,* New York.

Macro-economic performance and the international monetary system

Alexandre Lamfalussy

1 Introduction

The above title, which was suggested to me by the editors of the present volume would at any time have presented me with a broad and complex task, not least because the result will no doubt be scrutinised closely by André Szász, whose contributions to thought and policy-making in this field over many years have been of immense value to the international community. But, in present circumstances – by which I mean in the aftermath of the 1992-93 exchange rate turbulence in Europe, and the move to a 15 per cent fluctuation band for most currencies remaining in the Exchange Rate Mechanism – my task is even more difficult than it might have been. In particular, it seems well nigh impossible to define clearly and precisely just what the 'international monetary system' now is, let alone how long the present arrangements in the European Union will persist. At the same time, it is clear from the original Articles of Agreement of the IMF that the Bretton Woods negotiators believed that there is considerable scope for international monetary arrangements to affect global macro-economic performance. Indeed, the Bretton Woods conference itself was largely the result of a widely-held belief that such arrangements (or the lack of them) had been one of the important factors contributing to the highly unsatisfactory economic performance of the inter-war years.

In what follows, I shall therefore not concentrate especially on the particular international monetary arrangements which happen to be in place during the winter of 1993-94. Instead, I will try to discuss in more general terms some of the ways in which, in today's world, the international monetary system might influence national or global macro-economic performance, whether for good or for ill. And in doing so, I shall have particularly in mind the revolution which has occurred in international financial relations in the combined wake of deregulation, liberalisation, the explosion of financial business made possible by electronic technology, and, connected with the latter, financial innovation. Against such a background, my main theme will therefore be to ask to what extent international monetary arrangements might, for example, assist or hinder the effective control of inflation, promote sustainable growth and employment, and facilitate the smooth adjustment of international payments imbalances. And, given that the system seems likely to continue to comprise elements of both fixed and floating exchange rate arrangements, it will be convenient to discuss my theme under these two headings.

Before doing so, however, we might consider whether, under either heading, there exists any common analytical framework which could be used. For example is there a relevant analogy between the quantity of international liquidity (the means of settling all kinds of international transactions) and the domestic money supply? Unfortunately, any analogy is not exact, nor – more importantly – is it by any means the whole story. Apart from a relatively small amount of internationally created means of settlement, in the form of the IMF's Special Drawing Rights and reserve positions in the Fund, the bulk of such means consists of national currencies in countries' foreign exchange reserves. In this context, the role of central banks' gold reserves is now much reduced. On top of this, there is now a serious measurement problem, given that additional reserves can in effect be borrowed easily in today's globalised and liberalised financial markets. But unless and until such borrowing is attempted, it is of course not possible to get an idea of its potential size. In addition, its size is likely to be inversely related to a country's need for it. It is also of course likely to be only temporarily available, as are also the borrowing arrangements within the European Monetary System. Thus, at least in a quantitative sense, the use of the analogy with domestic money supply does not seem likely to be a promising approach. Qualitatively, though, the concept can be of some use (see below). In any event, the term 'the international monetary system', as customarily used, is a much wider concept than that of international liquidity alone. It usually refers to those institutional arrangements, policy rules, adjustment responsibilities and customary practices and procedures which govern the international monetary relations and, more broadly, the economic interactions between national economies. Hence, other important features of the international monetary order which might have links with macro-economic performance are: (a) the exchange rate system and the process by which exchange rates are determined; (b) the degree of international capital mobility, which, as I have already noted, has increased dramatically since the 1960s and early 1970s; and, following from the first two features, (c) a growing, if intermittent, stress on some international coordination of economic policies in general, something which is now partially formalised in the surveillance duties given to the IMF, and, perhaps, increasingly in the future for Europe, those of the European

Monetary Institute. However, in the wake of the 1992-93 European exchange rate crises, it is not yet possible to foresee to what extent the status quo ante will be restored: that is, some combination of fixed rate arrangements in Europe and some degree of floating between the major currencies.

2 Fixed exchange rate regimes

Returning for a moment to the amount of international liquidity in the global system, there is one obvious and traditional mechanism, especially under a system of fixed exchange rates, by which an excessive provision of liquidity (however defined) may at least exacerbate, if not set off, inflationary and unsustainable macro-economic developments. Access to excessive liquidity can relax the balance-of-payments constraints faced by countries. A country pursuing an excessive and inflationary demand policy might thus be able to finance the resulting current, and possibly also capital account deficits at an unchanged exchange rate and for an overly long period, rather than rein in demand to deal with both the balance-of-payments deficit and inflation. Inflationary pressures can also threaten in other countries if, conversely, capital inflows are attracted by sounder economic policies and performance than the average, and have to be countered by overly-lax monetary policies in the interest of holding down the exchange rate. This was already a concern for Germany long before the 1992-93 turbulence in the ERM brought it to prominence again. Especially towards the end of the Bretton Woods fixed exchange rate system, at the beginning of the 1970s, there was a veritable explosion of international reserves as central banks sought in vain to tackle the growing loss of confidence in the dollar. The alarming bout of inflation which followed seemed uncannily linked to this, though, even with hindsight, there is room for disagreement about the role of other factors such as the oil price shock, and deficiencies in the international coordination of macro-economic policies in general. Such a development seems, however, much less likely today: the major currencies are floating, with only limited and sporadic official exchange market intervention; SDRs are not going to be issued in inflationary volume; and, finally, the recent events in the European Monetary System were not allowed to result in an inflationary issue of that system's main reserve currency.

Turning to other aspects of macro-economic performance under a fixed rate system, there have also been occasions when some commentators have criticised international monetary arrangements as hindering growth and exacerbating unemployment. For example, it was often said, that the Bretton Woods fixed exchange rate system imposed asymmetric balance-of-payments adjustment responsibilities on deficit countries. As a result, it was alleged, such countries were sometimes obliged to implement overly restrictive macro-economic policies. My own view, however, is that the bulk of the adjustment burden often fell – rightly – on the deficit countries, simply because their domestic policies had become inappropriate. Indeed, it seems to me a more general truth that it is usually to the soundness of domestic policies that one should first look for balance-of-payments adjustment, rather than trying to deal only with the secondary consequences of inappropriate national macro-policies.

A topical and historically rather unusual example concerns the present very high level of unemployment in Europe, and its apparent relationship to the attempt to hold to fixed exchange rates in the ERM. The essence of the argument is that the current policy mix prevailing in Germany, coupled with the policy choice of a number of European countries to continue to peg their exchange rates to the Deutsche mark, has kept real interest rates in these countries at levels that are inappropriate in the light of the unemployment situation. I find this argument unconvincing for several reasons. The first is that a large part, perhaps a very large part, of their unemployment is unconnected with the level of global demand. The rate of unemployment has been on a rising trend across successive business cycles in most European countries. Something is wrong with the working of the labour markets. Secondly, after years of growth, a cyclical downturn was unavoidable, irrespective of the level of real interest rates. Thirdly, and perhaps most importantly, it is by no means certain that the depreciation of these currencies would have allowed a substantial decline in interest rates – or, to put it more precisely, a decline in long-term interest rates which would have been more pronounced than that achieved with the current monetary policy stance. The comparison between French and UK long-term interest rates is quite revealing in this respect. The explanation lies in the fact that the stability of the exchange rate relationship with the Deutsche mark has played a major role in defusing inflationary expectations, and therefore its abandonment would in all probability have had the effect of re-igniting such expectations. In short, neither the structural problems of European labour markets, nor the problems created by Germany's policy mix can be handled by changing the exchange rate regime.

3 Floating exchange rate regimes

Another topical feature already referred to, is the ability which many countries now have to go into the liberalised and globalised financial markets and borrow international liquidity – sometimes in advance of need. One powerful argument used here is that private markets would be unlikely to lend to countries pursuing unsound policies. Far from fuelling inflation or inflationary policies, such considerations suggest that the markets would be likely to provide an important degree of discipline on national policies – perhaps especially in cases where exchange rates are floating and where the discipline exercised by a fixed rate commitment is therefore absent. In practice, it has not been clear that such discipline has always been exercised consistently, or even in the appropriate direction. For example, the international banking system committed funds to the developing world on a scale and in a manner which led in 1982 to a major and costly crisis, not only for the countries concerned, but for the lenders themselves as well.

A little later, between 1982 and 1985, international capital flowed into the United States in large amounts, despite the opening-up of a large and chronic budget deficit. Indeed, the scale of this inflow was such that it drove up the international value of the dollar to a level which exacerbated the current account deficit, and which, eventually, according to nearly all observers, represented a massive overvaluation. This event was perhaps the most spectacular example in a world of greatly increased capital mobility of the tendency for exchange markets, under floating, to move real exchange rates in medium-term cycles of over- and undervaluation. This phenomenon might well have adverse effects not just on balance of payments and the international allocation of resources, but also on inflation and, possibly, even unemployment.

Taking first inflation, it may well be that the response of domestic costs and prices to changes in import costs is asymmetric. That is, the price and cost-raising effects of a medium-term downswing in the exchange rate may be greater than the opposite influences when the exchange rate begins to rise again. If so, the net effect of a medium-term swing in exchange rates may well be adverse for inflation. The more open the economy, the more likely this is. In particular, it helps to explain the desire of the smaller EMS countries to commit themselves to a fixed exchange rate regime. Such a regime can of course not just protect such countries from the inflationary effects of swings in floating exchange rates; it can also in partner countries, so long as the 'anchor' country remains a low inflation one, assist in lowering inflation, and keeping it down. The example of France in recent years is one of the most striking ones. The case of the United States between 1985 and 1987 may at first sight seem to be a refutation of the asymmetry argument. The dollar declined by something like 50 per cent from its early 1985 peak, but US domestic inflation remained under control. By chance, however, the dollar's decline coincided with a fall in international oil prices, while exporters to the United States apparently adjusted their prices to some degree with a view to maintaining their share in the American market. Clearly it would be unwise to rely on such offsetting factors in all countries and under all circumstances.

As to other aspects of macro-economic performance, it seems fairly obvious that large medium-term cycles in real exchange rates are likely to cause unnecessary and unsustainable movements in current account balances of which the correction can often prove to be costly. A corollary of this is that investible international capital resources are likely to be misallocated, thus reducing the productive potential of the world economy below what it might otherwise be. And, when the inevitable adjustment phase comes and real exchange rates return towards their equilibrium levels, activities – in both surplus and deficit countries – which had earlier been profitable, will no longer be so. As a result there is likely to be a degree of, at least temporary, unemployment of labour as well as of a new but uneconomic capital stock. Further, there may also be 'knock-on' effects on business and consumer confidence more generally, and thus on domestic growth and employment. Something of this kind may just have been seen in Japan, especially given the speed of the rise in the real exchange rate of the yen in 1993, although the direction of the movement seems to be right from the point of view of balance-of-payments adjustment.

4 Implications and conclusion

In the most general terms, the primary conclusion to be drawn from all this, is precisely the same as the view held by the Bretton Woods negotiators fifty years ago. But it is a conclusion which is now drawn in entirely different circumstances and for very different reasons. In a nutshell, the present international 'system' still has the capacity to impose macro-economic costs as well as providing benefits, unless policy-makers handle it in an appropriate way. The main underlying reason for this stems from the revolution in private international financial markets which has taken place over the past fifteen to twenty years. Liberalisation, globalisation and technological progress in those markets caused a high degree of international financial integration and capital mobility adding to the greater integration of real economies which took place earlier as trade flows were liberalised. In other words, economies' real openness is now matched by their financial openness, and is perhaps even exceeded by it.

In theory, both of these developments should be beneficial to the production capacity of the world economy. However, as was learnt more than twenty years ago in the case of real economic integration, greater openness to trade implies that a greater degree of international macroeconomic policy coordination is necessary, whether under floating or fixed exchange rate arrangements. One of the disadvantages of insufficient policy coordination was well illustrated during the inflationary explosion of 1972-74. It is fairly widely acknowledged now that in attempting individually to nudge their economies out of recession, the industrial countries paid insufficient attention to the fact that trading-partner countries were doing the same thing. Consequently, in setting their demand management stances, countries tended to underestimate the strength of demand in their export markets. The scale of this unrecognised international multiplier effect was such that global aggregate demand exceeded forecast levels by a significant amount. Thus, whatever other factors of a cost-push nature were at work, unintentional excess demand was also a contributor to the resulting upsurge in inflation.

The question now is whether the wholly new extent of international capital mobility requires additional policy attention in order to reap in full the benefits of free and open markets, while minimising their potential costs. Whether such costs exist is of course a contentious matter. Nevertheless, I would submit that in several asset markets over the last few years, we have had examples of at least temporary, but damaging, mispricing. In the exchange markets, this has been seen in the way in which, under floating, the markets do not necessarily push exchange rates to something like their equilibrium levels and then leave them there. I have already cited the example of the dollar in the early 1980s. In the fixed rate ERM we have also recently seen examples of huge pressures being brought up to bear indiscriminately on various currencies. Consider, for example, that only some months ago the French franc and other currencies came under such intense attack that the ERM very nearly had to be abandoned altogether. And yet already by late December 1993, the French currency, for example, had returned to within 2 per cent of its (unchanged) central rate against the Deutsche mark. If the risks and costs of speculative foreign exchange transactions were borne only by those participating in them, then such phenomena would be of no more concern to public authorities than the activities of a casino. But if, as I have tried to illustrate, foreign exchange market developments can have wider effects – i.e. there are externalities – then public policy classically comes into the picture.

But what should public policy do, in particular, to provide some kind of realistic anchor for exchange rates? In my view, and notwithstanding the events of 1992-93, official exchange market intervention still has a role to play, particularly as a device for signalling the views, and perhaps policy intentions, of the authorities. But given the potential scale of capital flows now, it is clear that intervention can not be the sole instrument for delivering exchange rate stability without seriously compromising other important policy goals, particularly that of price stability. Nevertheless, in my judgement, serious consideration should be given to the possibility of increasing the scale of intervention at times of unreasonable exchange market tensions. But this should not go so far as to risk any serious boost to inflation. Indeed, for this as well as for other well-accepted reasons, any increased willingness to resort to greater intervention should be accompanied by an even greater stress on stability-oriented macro-economic policies over the medium term. In fact, it is probably not going too far to say that the key to a sound international monetary system now is increasingly to be found in sound domestic policies. If such policies prevailed universally, it could well be that little more would be required in terms of international policy coordination. In practice, however, it seems likely that explicit coordination would still be required, or at least advisable. For example, as has been seen, within any given overall stance of macro-economic policies, the mix of monetary, fiscal and other policies may still differ. In addition, there is always the possibility of exogenous shocks suddenly occurring, either asymmetric ones, or symmetric ones to which different countries might initially react in non-symmetric ways.

Beyond this admittedly discretionary set of guidelines defined in only a rather general way, it seems that little more could, or should, be done. In particular, there is no way back via the resuscitation of stringent controls on international capital movements. Not only are they undesirable and costly per se, it is also not clear that they could be made effective nowadays without considerable difficulty, if at all. It really is only the redoubling of efforts for sound coordinated national policies which makes that the international monetary 'system' of today is likely to facilitate the world economy's taking full advantage of the potential benefits of a more liberal, market-oriented world order.

National financial liberalisation and international economic cooperation

Andrew D. Crockett

1 Introduction

The years during which André Szász has been an active participant in international monetary affairs have seen enormous changes in world financial markets. The development of new financial instruments and the abolition of barriers to competition have combined with the removal of exchange controls to create a capital market that is truly global in scope. This has brought large benefits to the users of capital markets, savers and investors alike. At the same time it has added to the problems of policy makers, in two dimensions. It has increased the dangers of systemic risk, by making it easier for financial failure to spread from one market to another. And it has made it harder to exert macro-economic control through influencing credit market conditions in a single capital market.

In this essay, I will try to examine both the nature of the changes that have taken place (and still continue) in the world's major financial markets, and the implications of these changes for official policy. I will interpret the term 'liberalisation' broadly, to include not just changes in official regulations, but the whole range of financial innovations. The paper begins by considering briefly the underlying forces that have made for liberalisation and innovation. It goes on to describe in more detail the main features of the changes that have taken place in financial structure. Next, it considers some of the principal implications of these changes. This serves as a background for a concluding section addressing the policy issues that arise in an international context.

This paper was prepared while the author was Executive Director at the Bank of England. Neither the BIS nor the Bank of England is responsible for the views expressed.

2 Sources of change

The forces of innovation and deregulation are closely linked. Deregulation can be a spontaneous act, but it can also be forced on the authorities when market innovations make existing regulations impossible to apply. Similarly, innovation can be an independent force for change, and also a response to opportunities offered by deregulation. The past thirty years have seen a confluence of forces that have combined to bring about the most far-reaching changes in the financial services industry since the development of modern banking. At the risk of oversimplifying, four underlying forces have provided the impetus behind the changes that have occurred.

First, the revolution in the communications industry has transformed the ability of economic agents to process information quickly and cheaply. The computer revolution had its origins outside the financial sector, but has had major implications for financial structures. It has brought about a dramatic reduction in the cost of storing and processing the information that is at the core of financial services. It has permitted the development of new financial instruments that would previously have been too complicated (and therefore too costly) to find a ready market. And it has given rise to a large increase in the volume of transactions relative to the underlying asset stocks.

A second force making for deregulation and innovation has been the growing acceptance of the open market economy as the basis of economic organisation. This has led to a questioning of restrictive practices in all fields. The process of deregulation has been slower in the financial sector, because of a widespread feeling that it is 'different' from other activities. Still, the financial sector could not remain immune to the general philosophy that transactions freely entered into should not be restricted unless there were identifiable social costs associated with them.

The third underlying force for change in the financial system has been the growth of international trade and investment. Throughout the post-war period, international trade has grown twice as fast as world output. International investment has grown even faster (although precise figures are hard to come by). This has meant that the demand for international financial services has grown, as has the need for investment vehicles to permit economic agents to manage international portfolios of assets and liabilities.

Fourth, the upsurge of inflation in the 1970s, and its slow decline in the 1980s has made savers and investors increasingly aware of the risks involved in future contracts. This has led to growing efforts to provide protection against such risks through the development of new instruments to enable economic agents to match better payment flows and receipts.

3 Features of financial change

A key feature of the financial changes that have occurred over the past twenty years has been deregulation. Deregulation has taken place, both as a deliberate response to the desire to extend the principle of open markets, and out of recognition that financial innovation was making existing restrictions ineffective. Many of the most prominent restrictions in the early 1970s applied to banks. At that time, banks in most countries were subject to ceilings on the interest they could pay on deposits and sometimes also on the rate they could charge on loans. These ceilings were part of a comprehensive network of formal and informal arrangements that set banks apart from other institutions. Banks were seen as 'special' both because of their central role in the payments system, and because they were the most important institutions for mobilising and allocating savings. Their stability was therefore important for the stability of the financial system more widely. That stability could, it was believed, be undermined by excessive competition. Hence arrangements grew up that both prevented banks from competing aggressively and compensated them for this lack of freedom by giving them a large slice of endowment income.

Since banks were prevented from competing on price, other forms of competition emerged: a proliferation of branches and ancillary services, cross-subsidised by the rents derived from the excess profitability of basic banking services. Not surprisingly, when other institutions (such as money market mutual funds) found ways of providing basic banking without costly additional services, they began to eat into the banking franchise. The result was an intensification of the pressure to remove restrictions on banks. In most OECD countries, there is now no effective barrier to the payment of interest on checkable accounts. Banks are also free to set their own lending rates. In order to compete with other institutions, banks have also reduced costs by eliminating overheads associated with branch networks and 'prestige' services. Other restrictions have also come under scrutiny. In the immediate post-war years, national stock markets were often quasi-cartels, with restrictive provisions on membership, on listing of stocks and on commissions charged for transactions. There were also barriers to the listing of stocks on foreign exchanges. Most of these restrictions have now been abolished, with the exception of those deemed necessary for protection of investors and good business practice. This has greatly increased the scope for markets (such as stock exchanges) to compete with institutions (such as banks) in the intermediation of funds between final savers and final investors.

The growing importance of markets has been associated with two other major trends of the past thirty years: the increased role of institutional investors and the securitisation of assets. Pension funds and unit trusts (or mutual funds) have steadily increased their share of financial intermediation over the past thirty years. The bulk of household sector savings is devoted to provision for retirement, and it is natural that savers should seek vehicles that are tax-efficient and geared to long-term capital growth rather than short-term stability of nominal value. In most countries, there are substantial tax advantages to formally designated pension schemes. This, together with the professional fund management expertise offered by pension funds, has underpinned the growth of this form of investment. Even in the absence of tax advantages, the perceived benefits of professional management have resulted in an increasing shift of savings toward institutional investors. Unit trusts and mutual funds generally do not enjoy special tax advantages, but have seen their share of household financial assets grow rapidly over time. The figure below shows how managed funds in the United States have increased their role over the period 1960-1990.

Securitisation is a trend that is newer, but will almost certainly gather (figure) pace and spread over coming years. There is both a general and specific meaning to securitisation. In its general sense, securitisation can be understood to mean the mobilisation of funds through the issue of marketable instruments rather than through non-marketable debt. The fact that large corporations now fund themselves largely in their own name (through the issue of commercial paper and longer-term bonds) is an example of securitisation in the general sense. It reflects the fact that institutional lenders (such as banks) have diminishing information advantages in assessing the creditworthiness of major borrowers. This is another manifestation of the communications revolution in improving access to information. If institutional lenders do not possess information advantages that permit them to lend at lower rates than the generality of investors, then borrowers will see advantages in offering securitised debt. The liquidity of such instruments is itself an attraction to holders. Moreover, if institutions such as banks have to make capital provisions against such lending, this will constitute an additi-

Figure Growth of institutional investment in the United States

Percentage of financial assets

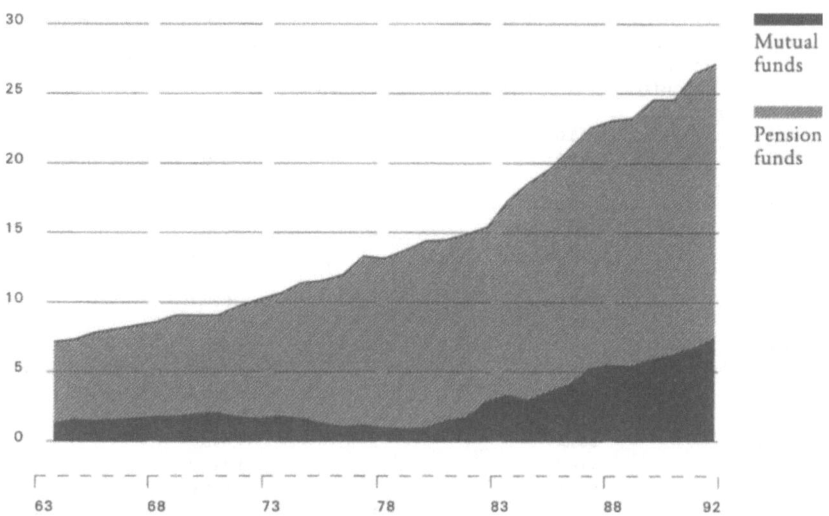

Source: Balance sheets for the US economy.

onal cost not incurred in market borrowing. Securitisation in the specific sense is usually taken to mean the combining of individual loans into a package that can be offered as a marketable security. The attraction to banks is obvious: they can use the activity in which they have a comparative advantage – loan origination – to generate fees, while avoiding the need to hold the resultant assets on their own books, thus tying up capital. The attraction to ultimate investors is the acquisition of a relatively high yield asset. The higher yield is purchased at the expense of some additional uncertainty as compared with claims held through banks. However, if the risk-pooling characteristics of the marketed security are well-designed, the increase in risk to the ultimate holder need not be large. For example, consumer debt instruments such as household mortgages and credit card receivables have traditionally had low and/or stable default ratios. A security comprising a large number of mortgages or receivables has a market value that is actually relatively simple to predict. Table 1 shows that, in the United States, mortgage and consumer credit-backed securities are now three-quarters as large in value as conventional lending by banks. The process of securitisation has gone less far in other countries, but seems likely to gather pace in the years ahead.

Table 1 The increase of securitisation in the US (1973 - 1993)

Billions of dollars

	A Mortgage debt outstanding (mortgage pools or trusts)	B Consumer installment credit (pools of securitised assets	C Total loans and leases (all commercial banks)	Securitisation as a percentage of bank lending (i.e. A+ B/C)
1973	18.0	.	449.0	4.0
1974	23.8	.	500.2	4.8
1975	34.1	.	496.9	6.9
1976	49.8	.	538.9	9.2
1977	70.3	.	638.3	11.0
1978	88.6	.	754.2	11.8
1979	119.3	.	857.4	13.9
1980	142.3	.	922.1	15.4
1981	163.0	.	981.8	16.6
1982	216.6	.	1,050.3	20.6
1983	285.1	.	1,141.7	24.9
1984	332.1	.	1,327.4	25.0
1985	415.0	.	1,464.8	28.3
1986	565.4	.	1,598.7	35.4
1987	718.3	.	1,717.3	41.8
1988	811.8	.	1,865.0	43.5
1989	917.8	48.8	2,013.8	48.0
1990	1,079.1	79.0	2,102.7	55.1
1991	1,250.7	103.6	2,106.1	64.3
1992	1,425.4	120.4	2,115.4	73.1

Source: Federal Reserve Bulletins.

The securitisation of assets previously held in banks' balance sheets is an example of the 'unbundling' of separate activities previously undertaken in a single institution. In a non-securitised world, banks would raise funds from investors, make loans to borrowers and manage the resultant portfolio of assets. With securitisation, it may be a pension fund that taps the initial savings and holds the asset, a bank that originates and sells the loan, and a financial service company that undertakes the task of administering the loan service. Since the three functions are quite different, there is no economic reason requiring that they should always be performed within one institution.

Another major feature of recent decades has been the globalisation of capital markets. The increased importance of institutional investors has contributed to this. In their search for higher yields and risk spreading, institutional investors have sought to offer savers portfolios of assets with an increasing share of foreign investment. They have been aided in this by the removal of most remaining exchange controls. The internationalisation of investments is still at a relatively early stage, measured by the share of private sector savings assets represented by foreign assets. It is, however a share that is growing rapidly (see table 2).

The growth of international investment can also be seen in the rising volume of cross-border securities transactions (see table 3). In the United States, for example, cross-border transactions in securities were the equivalent of only 2.8 per cent of GNP as recently as 1970. They were some 9.3 per cent by 1980 and almost 100 per cent by 1990. There is nevertheless scope for the process to go further, as can be seen from the data for the United Kingdom. In that country cross-border securities transactions were the equivalent of 7 times GNP in 1990. These figures

Table 2 Institutional investor's holdings of foreign securities

As a percentage of their total securities holdings

	1980	1985	1986	1987	1988	1989	1990	1991
United States								
Private pension funds[1]	1.0	3.0	4.0	4.0	4.0	4.1	4.2	5.2
Japan								
Life insurance companies	9.0	26.4	28.9	31.4	31.1	33.9	30.0	28.4
Non-life insurance companies	7.4	19.4	21.5	21.5	22.3	26.1	29.1	28.5
Trust accounts of banks	2.2	14.0	17.1	16.7	15.3	17.0	19.4	22.1
Postal Life Insurance	0.0	6.7	9.2	11.2	11.3	11.2	11.6	12.1
Norinchukin Bank	4.3	10.3	14.8	15.0	18.3	20.7	22.7	32.6
Canada								
Life insurance companies	2.1	2.2	2.8	3.4	2.4[3]	2.7	2.3	2.7
Pension funds	6.1	6.6	7.0	6.6	6.8	6.8	6.0	7.6
Italy								
Insurance companies	11.7	10.1	8.1	8.4	10.4	.	11.6	9.7
United Kingdom[2]								
Insurance companies	6.9	17.3	19.7	15.7	17.7	22.3	20.7	.
Pension funds	10.3	17.8	19.5	15.8	20.9	25.4	23.6	.
Belgium								
Insurance companies and pension funds	1.7	3.3	3.8	3.3	2.8	3.9	3.3	.
Netherlands								
Insurance companies	5.2[4]	10.3	11.0	11.0	11.4	10.1	9.3	10.3
Private pension funds	10.6[4]	13.8	17.6	18.0	19.3	21.3	21.1	23.5
Public pension funds	1.7[4]	2.8	3.0	3.3	3.7	4.2	5.2	5.7
Sweden								
Insurance companies	.	.	.	1.5	1.6	4.0	10.4	12.5

1 Tax-exempt funded schemes (excluding IRAS).
2 Pension funds exclude central goverment sector but include other public sector. Unit trust investment allocated as follows: 50 per cent domestic at end-1989 (on the basis of partial survey results); other years calculated in proportion to changes in the measured share of foreign assets.
3 Break in series from 1988 Q1.
4 1983.

Sources: Bank of Italy; Bank of Japan, Economic Statistics Annual and Economic Statistics Monthly; Sveriges Riksbank, Quarterly Review; De Nederlandsche Bank, Annual Report and Quarterly bulletins; InterSec Research Corporation; National Bank of Belgium; Statistics Canada; UK Central Statistical Office, Annual Abstract of Statistics and Financial Statistics.

Table 3 Cross-border transactions in bonds and equities

As a percentage of GDP

	1970	1975	1980	1985	1990	1992
United States	2.8	4.2	9.3	36.4	92.5	.
Japan	.	1.5	7.0	60.5	118.6	69.9
Germany	3.3	5.1	7.5	33.9	57.5	87.2
France	.	.	8.4[1]	21.4	53.3	118.1
Italy	.	0.9	1.1	4.0	26.7	.
United Kingdom	.	.	.	367.5	690.1	.
Canada	5.7	3.3	9.6	26.7	63.8	113.3

Explanatory note: Gross purchases and sales of securities between residents and non-residents.
1 1982.
Source: National balance-of-payments statistics.

reveal another important trend in recent years: the growth of the gross volume of transactions relative to net flows. This growth in transactions volume reflects both demand side and supply side factors. On the demand side, portfolio managers seek to reallocate their holdings of assets and liabilities in response to a mass of new information about financial instruments that is constantly becoming available. On the supply side, reductions in information costs have made transactions much cheaper, and in some cases reduced the costs of portfolio reallocation to negligible proportions.

There are no fully consistent statistics on the volume of financial flows. Some idea of turnover relative to underlying stocks can be gained from the figures for individual markets. In the US government bond market, for example, notified daily transactions amount to about a quarter of total bonds outstanding. In other words, the entire stock of US Treasury bonds turn over on average once every four days![1] In other markets turnover is less, but the upward trend in turnover is clear (see tables 4 and 5).

The growth of financial market turnover, together with the integration of markets and the increased professionalism of investors has led to a demand for new products to permit position taking and hedging. Financial intermediaries have devoted considerable ingenuity to devising new types of financial instruments with characteristics designed to

1 This figure includes repurchase operations. But even if these are excluded, the entire stock turns over on average every 15 days.

Table 4 Size/turnover of government bond markets

Items	1970	1980	1992
United States			
Nominal total marketable government debt (in billions of US dollars)	248	595	2,754
Approximate average daily turnover (in billions of US dollars)	2.6	17.6	180.1
Turnover as a percentage of debt	1	3	7
Number of days to turn over total stock of debt	95	34	15
United Kingdom			
Nominal total marketable government debt (in billions of pounds sterling)	20	82	144
Approximate average daily turnover (in billions of pounds sterling)	0.1	0.6	4.9
Turnover as a percentage of debt	0.5	0.7	3
Number of days to turn over total stock of debt	200	137	29

Explanatory note: Figures do not include repo transactions.
Sources: Federal Reserve Bulletins and Bank of England, CSO.

appeal to the particular requirements of different market segments. In particular, the past ten years have seen explosive growth in derivative markets. A derivative product is a contract whose characteristics depend on the prior existence of primary financial instruments and whose value derives from changes in their prices. Among the most common derivatives are futures and options. These constitute contracts to purchase or sell primary financial assets at some future date (futures) or under certain conditions (options). Futures and options enable portfo-

Table 5 Net foreign exchange market turnover

Billions of US dollars a day

	March 1986	April 1989	April 1992
United Kingdom	90	187	300
United States	59	129	192
Japan	48	115	128
Singapore	.	55	74
Switzerland	.	57	68
Hong Kong	.	49	61
Germany	.	.	57
France	.	26	35
Australia	.	30	30
Canada	9	15	22

Source: Goldstein et al. (1993), p.24.

lio managers to protect themselves against price changes in the period between the date when the contract is written and the date it comes into effect.

But derivative markets have wider uses. They enable the various yield characteristics of an asset to be 'unbundled' into their constituent parts. An American purchaser of a Japanese bond is buying a long-term yield in yen terms that can be considered as the weighted sum of an infinite number of short period holding yields. He is also buying an exchange rate risk (assuming he wishes to translate his yen return into dollars) and, if it is a corporate bond, a credit risk. He may also acquire additional features attached to the bond, such as a warrant to acquire equity in the company at some future date at a fixed price.

It is unlikely that an investor would wish to hold precisely the combination of features represented by a particular asset. In the absence of derivative markets, however, he had little choice in the matter. Primary financial instruments came as a package. Now, however, an investor can, in effect, strip out those aspects of the package he does not wish to hold. Alternatively, he can buy a derivative instrument that contains the features he wishes to add to his portfolio. One consequence of this is to arbitrage away differences in yield for similar components of a security in different markets. If the pure interest return on an asset begins to vary in any market, funds can flow in or out without having to acquire the exchange related risk that would accompany the holding of primary assets. Derivative markets therefore help unify markets both geographically, sectorally and across currencies. It is not easy to measure the size of derivative markets. The notional value of a contract can be very high. However, if the circumstances under which the contract is likely to enter into effect are remote (e.g. an option with a strike price that is high relative to the current price of the underlying asset) the market value of the contract may be quite small. Nevertheless, the growth of derivative markets has clearly been substantial. Table 6 shows the recorded notional value of futures and option contracts reported in the main international markets. The amounts outstanding grew almost ten-fold in the six years 1986-1992.

4 Policy implications

What are the policy implications of the changes described above? First, it should be noted that financial innovation has led to substantial improvements in the services offered by financial markets to end users, regardless of their geographical location or economic sector. Investors

Table 6 Market for selected derivative instruments

Notionol principal amounts outstanding at end-year billions of US dollars equivalent

Items	1986	1989	1990	1991	1992
Exchange-traded instruments[1]	589	1,768	2,291	3,520	4,783
Interest rate futures	370	1,201	1,454	2,157	3,048
Interest rates options[2]	147	388	600	1,073	1,385
Currency futures	10	16	16	18	25
Currency options[2]	39	50	56	60	80
Stock market index futures	15	42	70	77	81
Options on stock market indices[2]	8	72	95	136	164
Over-the-counter instruments[3]	500[7]	2,425	3,450	4,449	5,346
Interest rate swaps[4]	400[7]	1,526	2,312	3,065	3,851
Currency/cross-currency interest rate swaps[4,5]	100[7]	449	578	807	860
Other derivative instruments[4,6]	.	450	561	577	635
Memorandum item					
Cross-border plus local foreign-currency claims of BIS reporting bank	4,031	6,498	7,578	7,442	7,365

Sources: BIS, International Banking and financial market developments report; Futures Industry Association (BIS); various futures and options exchanges world-wide; International Swap Dealers Association (ISBA); BIS calculations.

1 Excludes options on individual shares and derivatives involving commodity contracts.

2 Calls plus puts.

3 Only data collected by ISDA. Excludes contracts such as FRAS, otc foreign exchange options, forward foreign exchange, equity and commodity swaps and options, and warrants on equity.

4 Contracts between ISDA members reported only once.

5 Adjusted for reporting of both currencies.

6 Caps, collars, floors and swaptions.

7 Estimated figures.

have an incomparably wider choice of instruments in which to hold their wealth. The markets in which they deal are deeper and more liquid than in the past. Borrowers are able to tailor the instruments in which they borrow to better fit the time path of their cash flow, and the uncertainties which surround it. And the greater international mobility of capital has contributed to a distribution of funds that better reflects the international pattern of savings propensities and investment opportunities.

The benefits of liberal and innovative capital markets deserve to be stressed, because proposals are often put forward to curtail some of the freedoms that have grown up. It is true that capital flows can sometimes undermine official objectives, such as fixing exchange rates, or damping down excessively rapid economic expansion. In fact, however, proposals to control capital markets can often reflect an attempt to reconcile inconsistencies in other policies. A common example is the wish to combine low domestic interest rates and a high external value of a currency. It would be unfortunate if resolving these inconsistencies in such a way as to minimise short-term political costs led to longer term interference with the efficient allocation of resources that a free capital market provides.

Increased efficiency and competitiveness in the financial sector has led to a second policy implication. This is that financial institutions are more vulnerable to losses and, at the limit, to being forced out of business. Because of the nature of the financial sector, and the role played by confidence, the disruptive failure of an individual institution can have consequences for systemic stability. Financial innovation has therefore called for new approaches to supervision and regulation. The aim of supervision is multi-faceted: to see that financial intermediaries are generally speaking, well-run; to ensure that they are adequately capitalised to withstand losses (or at least can be wound up in an orderly manner); to create safeguards against contagious loss of confidence; and to provide a measure of competitive equality among financial intermediaries from different sectors and different countries. This is a tall order. One of the effects of the changes that have taken place over the past two decades has been to transform financial activity from a 'relationship basis' to a 'transactions basis'. When banks were the preeminent financial institutions, and operated in a protected environment, things were quite different. Banks knew their customers, and provided them with a wide range of services that were not always carefully costed or appropriately charged for. There was a large element of cross-subsidisation. This was not particularly noticeable, however, since there were no competing institutions offering lower priced services. Moreover, banks had a large 'endowment' income, arising from the large share of resources that were placed with them free of interest.

The position of banks has considerably diminished, however, and with it the role of 'relationships' between financial intermediaries and their customers. Banks have become highly competitive institutions. They have lost their earlier role as privileged intermediaries between depositors who were relatively insensitive to interest rate considerations and borrowers who were, in the main, of high creditworthiness. They have to compete in the marketplace for both assets and liabilities. A feature of competition in any industry is that less efficient providers make losses and are forced out of business. But, as noted above, bank failures are not quite the same as failures in other sectors of the economy. There is a much greater risk of contagion which, because of the central role of banks in the payments system, could have serious consequences for the economy as a whole. An official response has therefore been needed to deal with the increased potential for damage from bank failures in an innovative and deregulated environment. Given the international nature of financial activity, regulatory policies need to be effectively coordinated if they are to produce competitive equality along with systemic stability. The response of the international community to this challenge will be described below.

A third implication of capital market integration is that true monetary policy independence is a thing of the past. It is clear from what has been said above about derivative markets that 'pure' interest return tends to be harmonised in all markets and at all maturities. Any changes in nominal yield in different currencies are, in effect, the exact counterpart of discounted future changes in exchange rates. This does not (or not yet) mean that monetary policy is impotent. If countries allow their exchange rates to be flexible, the authorities can still change short-term interest rates in domestic currency. The equality of total yields across currencies is then maintained by corresponding changes in exchange rates (and hence in the expected future appreciation or depreciation of the currency). For a variety of reasons, economic agents are not indifferent to whether financial returns come in the form of interest yield or change in currency value. Moreover, since currency values are more flexible than the prices of goods and factors of production, exchange rate changes can have real effects on international competitiveness. The basic fact remains, however. The more open an economy, and the greater the degree of capital mobility, the harder it is for monetary authorities to exert the control over monetary conditions that is described in text books. Moreover, such monetary policy independence as remains becomes entirely dependent on the willingness to allow the exchange rate to move flexibly.

5 International cooperation

The above discussion suggests an important agenda for the international community in coming to terms with the changes in financial markets that have characterised the period since the breakdown of the Bretton Woods system. There are two major aspects to this agenda:

a how to adapt the regulation of the financial system so as to pursue at the same time the goals of efficiency, competitive equality and systemic stability;

b how to cooperate in the implementation of macro-economic policy so as to counteract the economic cycle without generating excessive fluctuations in exchange rates.

Ensuring systemic stability in the financial system in turn encompasses two tasks: first, supervising the major financial institutions; and second, ensuring that the payments system itself is resilient to disturbances if and when they occur.

Dealing first with the question of institutional supervision, this has traditionally focused on banks. This is because banks have been thought to have the greatest capacity for causing systemic damage. Their balance sheets are large, their liabilities are liquid, they are at the centre of the payments system, and it is among banks that the danger of 'contagion', whereby the failure of one institution leads to fears for the safety of others, is greatest. The principal protections against bank failure are adequate oversight and adequate capital. Here, however, an inherent conflict arises between the need to underpin the security of the banking system and the desire to permit banks to engage in legitimate competition with institutions offering similar services. If banks in one jurisdiction are subject to highly restrictive regulatory constraints, they may become 'safer', but will lose business to non-bank competitors, or banking institutions in other jurisdictions. But if regulations are relaxed to help banks to compete more effectively, the danger of a failure becomes greater.

This conflict between safety and prudence, on the one hand, and competitive equality, on the other, would be even more acute in the absence of international regulatory collaboration. Banking has become an international activity. Bank customers, too, are international. If different national jurisdictions applied different regulations and capital standards, banking activity would quickly migrate to the centre with the lowest regulatory costs. There would be, in effect, 'competition in laxity'. It is quite evident, therefore, that the regulation of financial intermediation in a world of global markets has to be based on close coordination of regulatory standards. The most important step so far in this process has been the July 1988 agreement among the G10 countries to require minimum capital standards against credit risk. In brief, these standards require the holding of a minimum of 8 per cent capital against credit risk. Broadly speaking, at least half of the capital requirement must be held in the form of equity and retained reserves, with the remainder being subordinated debt and various other near-capital instruments. Credit risk is measured by reference to 'risk assets' which are arrived at by applying a risk weighting to asset items. Ordinary commercial lending is weighted at unity with, for example, inter-bank lending weighted at 20 per cent and lending to governments and government agencies of OECD countries (plus Saudi Arabia), which is deemed to be risk-free, at zero. Certain off-balance sheet items, such as guarantees, are also included in the measure.

The 'Basle Accord', as it is called, includes other provisions, such as the permissible degree of concentration of lending to a single borrower. The accord has, by common consent, led to a marked increase in the resilience of the international banking system. Nevertheless, the attempt to quantify capital standards can lead to changes in bank behaviour that call in question the appropriateness of the original rules. The 8 per cent capital requirement was selected as a figure that was broadly appropriate to an average portfolio consisting of loans to borrowers of varying creditworthiness. Over time, however, it is possible that the more creditworthy borrowers would find it cheaper to borrow in capital markets in their own name. The higher the cost to banks of providing the capital required to support their loan portfolios the more likely this is to happen. Banks' portfolios could then become increasingly concentrated in loans to less creditworthy borrowers. If portfolios thereby become more risky, it might then appear appropriate to require a further increase in capital ratios, and so on. One way of dealing with this problem would be for supervisors to differentiate among loans in calculating capital charges. Loans to blue chip companies might require less capital to be set aside then lending to more doubtful borrowing categories. This idea has attractions, but also a number of obvious drawbacks. How would supervisors judge the quality of individual loans without themselves duplicating, and eventually taking over, the task of credit assessment that properly belongs to banks' managements? For this reason, supervisors remain rightly reluctant to depart from the simplicity of a straightforward rule.

Another problem with fixed capital ratios is that they create a bias in favour of using off-balance sheet derivative products to hedge risks rather than claims in the interbank market that have to be held on the balance sheet. Derivative transactions, as well as trading positions in primary financial instruments, involve risks relating to changes in interest rates, exchange rates or market values. The G10 countries have recognised that these risks also need to be brought into the supervisory net. A discussion paper was published in mid-1993 and it is hoped that agreement on capital charges for market risk can be reached before the end of 1995.

Even if a broader basis of capital requirements can be agreed upon for banks this would still not remove all risk of financial failure. Nor should it, since the possibility of failure is a necessary part of the incentive structure in a competitive market place. Accidents can always happen in which a rapid erosion of a bank's standing leads to a loss of liquidity and failure. Moreover, institutions that are not subject to the rules applied to banks are increasingly important players in financial markets. These include investment banks, non-financial corporations, and the financial arms of non-financial corporations. Internationally agreed capital requirements can always be extended to these other institutions, but that is a time-consuming process and will still not be sufficient to eliminate all risk of institutions failing (one risk that is almost impossible to guard against completely is that of a fraud such as occurred at BCCI).

In the absence of further action, it cannot be excluded that the failure of a major institution with large liabilities would have major consequences for the financial system. This brings us to the second of the two supervisory tasks mentioned above: to ensure that the payments system itself is sufficiently resilient to prevent the failure of a major institution from having knock-on effects for the stability of the financial system at large. The pursuit of this objective is the main reason for the current impetus to upgrade and strengthen payments systems. Payments and settlements systems are the veins and arteries of the financial body. If they are interrupted, for whatever reason, the consequences can be severe. When a business fails, all of its payments due are frozen until it has either been restructured or placed into bankruptcy administration. If the business concerned is a financial institution that is active in the capital and money markets, its daily payments and receipts could well be a substantial multiple of its capital. And if payments are settled only at the end of the business day, all of them could be frozen as a result of a failure during the day.

Two approaches to limiting this source of payments system risk are possible. One is to find some way of offsetting payments and receipts during the day so that an institution is liable only for the net amount. The other is to move to 'real-time gross-settlement', whereby each payment is executed at the moment the underlying transaction is made, and not at the end of the business day. It is this second approach that has been chosen by most central banks as the best way to improve the resilience of payments and settlements systems in the longer term. It means that institutions making payments can only do so when their account at the settlement agent (usually the central bank) is in credit, or if they have adequate collateral to finance an overdraft. This in turn will require more precise scheduling of payments and receipts during the day. Modern data-processing systems, however, can generally manage the 'queuing' of payments orders, and appropriate financial incentives can help in discouraging troublesome payment delays.

The development of appropriate payments system standards also involves international cooperation because of the integration of the global financial system. The existence of different time zones, with different ends of the business day, and the need to settle cross-border payments raise questions that can only be addressed adequately in an international context.

5.2 *Macro-economic policy coordination*

Quite apart from the supervisory issues just discussed, the liberalisation and globalisation of financial systems present important questions of macro-economic policy coordination. It has been recognised for some time that it is not possible to continuously achieve the three objectives of:

a fixed exchange rates;
b independent monetary policy; and,
c free capital mobility.

As capital movements have become freer, and financial markets have become increasingly integrated, the trade-off between independent monetary policy and exchange rate stability has become starker. A clear example of the consequences of divergent macro-economic policies can be seen in the behaviour of exchange rates among the major currencies in the mid-1980s. With an expansionary fiscal policy in the United States, monetary policy had to remain restrictive during the upswing that began in 1982. The result was that the dollar appreciated markedly, reaching a peak in early 1985. Then, the realisation that the dollar's value was unsustainable and could lead to trade tensions, together with expectations of a more convergent policy mix among the major countries, caused the previous exchange rate trend to go into reverse. Having appreciated by 84 per cent against the Deutsche mark between 1980 and January 1985, the dollar fell back to below its previous level by September 1992.

Another example of the difficulties of maintaining exchange rate stability when countries have different monetary policy needs is provided by the experience of the European Exchange Rate Mechanism in 1992-93. Under fixed exchange rates, it was not possible for the members of the ERM to pursue independent monetary policies, despite the fact that one country, Germany, was experiencing strong inflationary pressures, while many others were in, or entering, recession. Germany, as the anchor country, was able to set its own monetary policy. Its partners faced the choice of either accepting the policy stance that was needed to maintain the fixed Deutsche Mark peg or else realigning or suspending their parity. The experience of 1992-93 has shown that fixed-but-adjustable exchange rates with narrow margins are potentially unstable in the face of large changes in policy mix among participating countries. Only where a country's economy and monetary policy is sufficiently closely integrated with that of its pegging partner, speculators are convinced that a realignment is out of the question and can the existence of narrow margins serve an unambiguously stabilising function.

There is nothing very satisfying in a conclusion that currency values should be flexible in response to policy changes that would otherwise put pressure on fixed exchange rates. Exchange rate volatility is rightly regarded as undesirable. It has adverse consequences for the growth of international trade and investment, and can generate trade tensions. Moreover, if devaluation comes to be regarded as an 'easy option' to restore international competitiveness, it can weaken the disciplines for stability-oriented domestic policies. So all countries have an interest in macro-economic policy coordination designed to avoid unnecessary volatility in exchange rates. In the case of the three major economic areas – North America, Western Europe, and Japan – this coordination has been pursued since 1985 in the framework of the G7 process. Finance ministers and central bank governors from the major countries meet periodically to review each others' policies, and to attempt to converge to stable, non-inflationary growth. The watchwords of the G7 process are stability and sustainability. The objective is not to fix exchange rates at administratively determined levels (that would only create new problems), but to pursue domestic policies that are conducive to exchange rate stability. This implies monetary policies that are geared to low and stable inflation, and fiscal policies aimed at sound and sustainable public finances.

Often, large exchange rate movements can be traced to monetary or fiscal policies that do not meet these objectives (or, otherwise put, to divergences in the policy mix pursued in the different countries). Where exchange rate disturbances can be traced to inappropriate policy mixes in one or more countries, the coordination process can be helpful in two ways; first, as a source of peer pressure to encourage the countries concerned to undertake policy adjustments, and second, as a means of signalling to markets the willingness and ability of policy-makers to prevent divergent exchange rate movements. This can help to avoid market over-reaction. Where necessary, the effort of macro-economic policy coordination can be reinforced by exchange rate intervention. Exchange rate intervention is inevitably a high-profile expression of policy. Although theoretical considerations suggest that intervention is not likely to be very effective in the longer term, it can be a very useful signalling exercise in the short term and can have a marked effect on market psychology.

The need to stabilise exchange rates is obviously more important within highly integrated trading areas than it is between the large regional blocs. The need for regional exchange rate stabilisation has always been most keenly felt in Europe. In North America and East Asia, the disparity in size between the principal economy and its regional partners is sufficiently large that overt policy coordination is not necessary (or practical). In Europe, however, the situation is different. The European countries are in the process of establishing a highly integrated internal market. Moreover, no one economy dominates the region in size (Germany, the largest, represents less than 30 per cent of the GDP of the Union). From the beginning of the EC, exchange rate stability has been recognised as an important condition for successful economic integration. In the aftermath of the widening of exchange rate margins in the ERM, the challenge will be to find arrangements that avoid damaging exchange rate volatility, yet enable countries to restore non-inflationary economic growth. Broad exchange rate bands are not in themselves sufficient to provide a complete framework for policy. Additional policy understandings will be needed to avoid the threat of competitive devaluation, and to provide the necessary basis for the further development of the single market. Such policy understandings, like those among the major countries participating in the G7 process, must be based on stable and sustainable macro-economic policies. Within Europe, this means renewed adherence to the convergence criteria included in the Maastricht Treaty.

It remains to be seen whether convergence-oriented policies, by themselves, are sufficient to deliver the desired degree of exchange rate stability. At the end of 1993, the initial experience was broadly favourable, due in part to markets' perception that the ERM countries attached high priority to keeping their exchange rates close to their parities within the broad band. But it may still be necessary to consider additional means to ensure that domestic and external objectives of participating countries remain consistent. This will be a task for the European Monetary Institute, and for André Szász' successors. It is to be hoped that they are as well endowed with wisdom and common-sense as he is. If they share his wit and humour, that would be an added bonus.

International adjustment and finance since Bretton Woods

J. Onno de Beaufort Wijnholds

1 Introduction

The international monetary system has undergone a considerable evolution over the past 50 years. The system that was created at the conference of Bretton Woods in 1944 lasted for roughly half of this period. Since the early seventies important changes have occurred which have modified the system in a number of ways, the most far-reaching being the switch-over from fixed, but adjustable, exchange rates to floating, but partially managed, exchange rates among the major currencies. Although the system of international adjustment and finance is now markedly different from that prevailing in the first 25 years after the Second World War, a number of basic elements have remained broadly the same. In particular, the general aim has remained to operate an open world-trade and payments regime based on a large degree of international cooperation. Despite the fact that the role of the International Monetary Fund, designed in Bretton Woods as the fulcrum of the system, has been modified quite substantially over the decades, it is widely accepted that the basic principles upon which it was established are still valid and that there is a continuing need for the Fund to promote a smooth functioning of the international monetary system and to serve as a forum for discussions in the international financial community. There are of course, and have always been, differences of view on how these basic elements can be best pursued, and some of these problems will be discussed in what follows.

More specifically, this essay attempts to give a broad-sweep assessment of how the twin questions of international adjustment and finance have evolved since Bretton Woods. The 50 year period is divided into two parts: the era of the Bretton Woods system, lasting up to the early 1970s (section two), and the period of floating exchange rates which the world experienced thereafter (section three). Of course, during this latter period an important part of the world aimed for greater exchange rate stability through participation in regional arrangements, particularly the European Monetary System, or through unilateral pegging to a dominant currency. However, the focus in this essay is on the relationship between major countries or currency blocs. Finally, an attempt is made, in section four, to look ahead at how the process of international adjustment and finance could develop in the coming years and to examine in very broad terms possible ways of strengthening the international monetary system in the future. A brief summary concludes this essay.

2 The Bretton Woods era

This period, which lasted from 1945 to 1971, was largely characterized by high economic growth and relatively low inflation in industrial countries. Some developing countries were also starting to make meaningful strides towards higher living standards. Towards the end of this period, however, the tensions in the system grew enormously as payments imbalances widened and inflation started to accelerate. The strains became unbearable after 25 years and the system collapsed first in 1971, and after a brief attempt at patching-up, finally succumbed in the spring of 1973. With the first oil shock coming immediately afterwards, a return to the par value system was no longer a viable option.

It is generally agreed that the Bretton Woods system served the world well in the immediate post-war era, providing a stable environment in which world trade and payments thrived. Export-led growth was the engine for rapid economic rehabilitation in Europe and Japan, with generous Marshall aid from the United States supporting the process. The international adjustment process generally functioned smoothly and the overall balance-of-payments deficits of the United States were welcomed by the rest of the world. The American hegemony in the international monetary system developed naturally and was not questioned during the first 15 years or so after the war. In fact, there was for a long time a preoccupation with the so-called dollar shortage problem, with industrial countries other than the United States striving hard to build up foreign exchange reserves. Change came gradually in the sixties. Warnings were sounded concerning the looming dollar crisis, first by Triffin [1] and later by others, and US external deficits were increasingly seen as a threat rather than as a blessing. Those countries that did not feel politically constrained, like Germany and Japan, reacted to the growing dollar flood by converting substantial amounts of officially held dollars into gold. France was the most outspoken exponent of this policy of imparting adjustment discipline on the United States, but by no means the only one. The Netherlands, for instance, was also quite

1 Triffin (1960).

active in demanding gold for dollars. In fact the bulk of the official reserves of the Netherlands in the 1960s consisted of gold. At the end of 1968, for instance, out of a total of reserves of about Fl. 7 billion, over Fl. 6 billion consisted of gold and less than Fl. 1 billion of foreign exchange.[2]

The United States also took action, mainly by means of the introduction of various restrictions on capital outflows. Furthermore, the authorities put pressure on Germany (the so-called Blessing-letter) and Japan to keep these countries from converting their substantial dollar balances into gold, which would have precipitated a crisis at an earlier stage. However, it became increasingly clear that the United States was not (politically) able or willing to allow the international adjustment process to have the same effect on it as on any other country experiencing a prolonged balance-of-payments deficit. Viewed in retrospect, it was therefore not all that surprising that President Nixon suspended the gold conversion in August 1971, although the shock waves were very considerable at that time. After a brief struggle following the Smithsonian Agreement of December 1971 – 'the greatest monetary agreement in history' – the system finally collapsed in early 1973 after harrowing bouts of intervention to support the flagging dollar.

One other important development from that era needs to be recalled here, namely the construction of a completely new reserve asset: the SDR. This hybrid asset (part owned reserves, part credit through the reconstitution requirement) was envisaged to play an important role in the supply of international liquidity, which up to then had been subject entirely to the vagaries of the main gold producers (who were not exactly considered reliable allies) and the United States' external position (dominated by domestic considerations). It was very unfortunate for the SDR that the first round of allocations in 1970 was followed in subsequent years by the largest bout of international reserve creation ever seen up to then. Also detrimental for the position of the SDR were the incessant pleas for a link between SDR allocations and development aid, to which other worthy causes were added later. Finally, during the sixties the Euro-dollar market became an increasingly important phenomenon, which was left unchecked by the central banks.[3] This huge

2 I remember from the time I worked as a young economist in the Foreign Exchange Department of the Nederlandsche Bank, that our limit on uncovered dollar balances was initially a mere $ 100 million, later raised to $ 200 million. Any holdings in excess of this 'open position' were covered through drawings under the swap arrangement with the Federal Reserve Bank of New York. In the seventies the situation changed completely, as the foreign exchange reserves of the Nederlandsche Bank rose rapidly and a large 'open position' on dollar holdings became inevitable.

3 Discussions were held during the seventies on constraining the growth of the Euro-currency markets, but no agreement was reached.

pool of offshore dollars (to which gradually were added Euro-Deutsche marks, etc) made it easier for countries to obtain external finance than before. Reserve creation became increasingly demand-determined and the need for fresh allocations of SDRs even more difficult to justify on the basis of the 'global need' criterion.

To sum up, the Bretton Woods era brought stability which greatly benefited world trade. At a later stage, however, the US balance-of-payments deficits, increasing during the sixties because of the Vietnam war and the initial unwillingness to raise taxes to pay for it, replaced the initial dollar shortage by a dollar glut. European countries complained about imported inflation stemming from the dollar flood and wanted the United States to pay more attention to the external repercussions of its policies. The US authorities in turn felt that surplus countries should be subject to more pressures under the international adjustment process. The developing countries, which were first kept largely out of the discussions on reforming the international monetary system, became increasingly vociferous and demanded – and obtained – a place at the negotiating table. Their agenda, however, consisted mainly of calling for a larger transfer of resources from the industrial countries which the latter tended to consider a side issue, detracting from the debate on the system proper. All these matters were debated at great length in the Committee of Twenty[4], set up to advise on the reform of the international monetary system, without any substantial progress.

3 Floating exchange rates

A number of important countries, particularly the United States and Germany, reacted with some relief when the par value system was replaced by floating exchange rates. Greater freedom concerning the exchange rate meant greater leeway with respect to domestic policy. Smaller countries, with open economies, were more troubled by the systemic change. They very much favoured the movement in Western Europe to maintain fixed rates within their own area[5]; first the snake arrangement was created, and in 1979 the EMS was established. The new brave world of floating exchange rates between the major countries soon turned out to be one in which the authorities did not stand back completely. The system evolved into one of partially managed floating, in which the authorities stepped in from time to time to support an

4 Committee of Twenty (1974).

5 In an early and prescient study, André Szász (1972) suggested that if the United States were not to return to convertibility, a European currency bloc should pursue, on a regional basis, the principles of the Bretton Woods system.

excessively weak currency (on various occasions the dollar) or to bring down the appreciation of a major currency in the case of evident overshooting. Hence the new system (or non-system, as was fashionable to call it for a while) consisted of floating rates between major currencies, with occasional bouts of intervention, and of fixed rates for quite a few smaller and even medium-sized countries, pegging either to the dollar or the Deutsche mark, or to a currency composite.[6]

I will now discuss in broad terms the functioning of the international adjustment process and the financing of payments imbalances, including the question of international reserves, over the past 20 years.

3.1 *The international adjustment process*

The focal point for analyzing the functioning of the international adjustment process used to be to look at developments in the imbalances on current accounts of major countries or country groups. Except for the two oil shocks, which – temporarily – brought about unprecedented shifts in the global current account configuration, it cannot be said that current account positions were as much a source of concern during the last two decades as they were during the Bretton Woods era. Differential rates of expenditure and exchange rate changes, while not smoothing away all major imbalances, were in general such that large and unsustainable disturbances were avoided. In recent years, current account surpluses and deficits of major industrial countries have generally come into the range of what does not generate much exitement: the United States deficit, which amounted to 3.5 per cent of GNP in 1987, was down to just under 2 per cent in 1993; the German surplus of over 4 per cent in 1987 had, under the influence of reunification with East Germany, swung to a deficit of over 1 per cent of GNP in 1993; the position of other European industrial countries was equally not a source of concern. Only the Japanese surplus, rising again to over 3 per cent of GNP in recent years, has come in for heavy criticism. The cause here seems to lie mainly in the deflationary impact of the bursting of the bubble economy, the still insufficient de facto opening of Japanese markets to foreign goods and services, the rigid nature of the distribution system and the high propensity to save of the Japanese population. The exchange rate of the yen has appreciated sharply, which has through positive terms of trade effects initially contributed to the large surpluses. As for other countries, the imbalances on current account

6 Outright pegging to the yen has not occurred.

have not generally attracted much attention in recent years. OPEC has been mostly running a modest deficit for many years[7], whereas the surpluses of the newly industrializing economies of Asia have come down to quite modest levels in absolute magnitudes.[8]

The generally smooth financing of external deficits, to which aspect I will return later, and the absence of serious concern over current account positions has prompted the question whether the current account still matters. Corden[9], for instance, argues that it is the underlying savings and investment levels that should really concern us. In this view the current account has no real meaning for policy, although it is still worth watching as a signal of problems in the savings/investment sphere. Where there may be real concern is in the area of countries' external debt, built up through a string of current account deficits (not compensated by non-debt-creating capital imports, such as direct investment). But this is a problem that has remained largely the domain of developing countries, and more recently, of countries transforming to a market economy. In fact, we can conclude that policy-makers in industrial countries, as well as most academic economists, have increasingly moved away from viewing the current account as a policy target. This is not to say that the international adjustment process among OECD countries has been without problems over the last 20 years. But the problems have not been so much with the current account positions as such, as with bouts of instability in exchange rates and in difficulties in achieving a measure of international coordination of domestic economic policies among major countries.

Taking a closer look at the exchange rate regime since the collapse of the Bretton Woods system, it can be said that the initial euphoria of proponents of floating started to wear off already during the seventies. Large swings in exchange rates were seen to complicate domestic economic policies and to foster protectionist sentiments. Attempts were made to move to a 'stable system of exchange rates', with the Fund given the task to exercise 'firm' surveillance over exchange rates. This did not really succeed and surveillance lacked sufficient bite. In the early eighties, the industrial countries debated the question of the role of intervention in curbing exchange rate fluctuations. The American authorities at that time were opposed to intervention. They took the view that there was no sense in which exchange rates could be called

7 It has to be realized of course, that the world current - account discrepancy is in excess of $ 100 billion and constitutes a bias towards deficits, so that the interpretation of the recorded figures is problematical.

8 The sizeable Taiwanese surpluses, allowing the build-up of one of the largest foreign exchange holdings in the world, did give rise to criticism in the past.

9 Corden (1991).

over- or undervalued and that the authorities did not know better than the markets what the rate should be. On the other side of the spectrum was France, which favoured more active policies to dampen the fluctuations of the dollar against other currencies. In a 1985 report of the Group of Ten[10], the functioning of the system of floating rates was lucidly analyzed, but the conclusions drawn were not ambitious, being limited to a call for the adoption of sound, credible and stable domestic economic policies and some suggestions for strengthening Fund surveillance. My own view at the time was that '... alternatives to the present system of floating between major currencies are not viable under present circumstances, and that in order to reduce large fluctuations in exchange rates a major reform would be necessary'. This I considered unlikely, since generally there is '... no reform without a crisis'.[11]

However, after a serious overshooting of the dollar rate under the influence of high US interest rates resulting from an unbalanced policy mix and from safe haven considerations, the US authorities took the initiative for the Plaza Agreement of September 1985. This led to a process of orderly depreciation of the dollar. It was a successful piece of international cooperation, but had to be followed relatively soon by action to avoid the dollar from declining too far: the Louvre Accord of February 1987, which introduced temporary soft target zones. Within a year the positive atmosphere of cooperation evaporated again as the United States clashed with Germany and Japan over their domestic policies which were leading to higher interest rates. From that time on the Group of Seven meetings appear to have produced very little in terms of actual international cooperation, let alone coordination. This was recognized by the incoming Clinton Administration in 1993, with Treasury Secretary Bentsen announcing that a fresh look at G7 meetings was needed.

During the period of floating exchange rates there has been much talk of the need for international coordination, i.e. to have governments commit themselves to conduct policies that are not the same as on the basis of purely domestic considerations, but that take into account the international dimension. In other words, there is an element of enlightened self-interest and a longer time horizon involved. Hence, coordination clearly goes further than cooperation, where international consultation takes place, but where policies are not expected to be adjusted for international reasons. International coordination among

10 Group of Ten (1985).
11 De Beaufort Wijnholds (1987), p. 174.

major industrial countries has not been a great success. In fact, it has been largely non-existent over the past 20 years. An important reason is that '... to those politically responsible for decision-making in the real world, the idea of coordination invades very sensitive political territory'.[12] Indeed one gets the impression, after having studied communiqués over many years and after discussions with officials from both sides of the Atlantic, that when mentioning coordination various countries often do not understand it to mean the same thing. Europeans usually invoke the need for international coordination because they desire greater exchange rate stability (of the dollar), whereas Americans tend to think primarily of policies to stimulate economic growth (in Europe and Japan) when they mention coordination.[13]

3.2 *International finance and reserves*

Financing overall balance-of-payments deficits (as measured by changes in official reserves) generally became easier under floating exchange rates. A larger role than under the par value system came to be played by capital movements, particularly of banks, as a means of financing ex ante deficits. Of course, these developments were also due to the successive liberalisation of capital transactions and the deregulation of financial markets. Despite the easier financing conditions, however, quite substantial rounds of intervention in support of currencies were undertaken occasionally by the central banks of industrial countries (apart from what occurred in the ERM), underlining the fact that the system was indeed one with a degree of management of the float. Financial means were amply available in the private sector, at least to countries that were considered sufficiently creditworthy. After the debt crisis of 1982, however, the situation changed for many developing and Eastern European countries, who were cut off quite abruptly from access to international financial markets. The role of the Fund in providing balance-of-payments support became more and more one-sided, as industrial countries – with the important exception of the United Kingdom in 1977 – were able to shun any application for conditional credit. Part of the decreased leverage of the Fund over industrial countries can be attributed – apart from ready access to inter-

12 Volcker and Gyothen (1992), p. 145.
13 Masson (1993), for instance, mentions the fact that in the aftermath of the second oil shock (1979-80) several countries used currency appreciation to help lower their inflation rates as an example of failure to coordinate policies. Such policies, he believes, not only led to higher inflation in other countries but also to a 'severe contraction' of output. The countries concerned are likely to take the view that they were justified in not repeating the common mistake made after the first oil crisis, i.e. to try to keep up demand in Keynesian fashion, thereby contributing to higher inflation and budgetary problems.

national financial markets – to the existence of the financing mechanisms of the European Community. Fund credit became increasingly concentrated on developing countries in the eighties, to which countries moving from planned to markets economies were added in recent years. It can be said that the Fund, in its financing role, has adapted itself well to the changing needs of the international community during the period examined in this section.

As to the question of the overall level of international reserves, much debated during the sixties and seventies, it seems fair to say that it has become something of a non-issue. The supply of reserves has become largely demand determined, with countries able to build up reserves at relatively low cost (i.e. the difference in interest rates for credits and deposits in the Euro-currency market), except for those not considered creditworthy. For a while there was some concern over the composition of international reserves, as a development towards a multi-reserve currency system seemed to take place. The share of the dollar in total reserves declined, whereas that of the Deutsche mark and the yen increased substantially. However, the process towards a greater diversification of reserve holdings appears to have ceased in recent years. The US dollar share in official foreign exchange holdings was up again to 64 per cent in 1992, after having fallen from 71 per cent in 1983 to 58 per cent in 1990, with the Deutsche mark share falling from a high point of 19 per cent in 1989 to 13 per cent in 1992 and the yen share remaining quite stable at around 8 per cent since 1985. A renewed episode of dollar weakness could again stimulate diversification in the future, but a truly multi-reserve currency system will probably have to await Economic and Monetary Union and a strong ECU. This leaves the problem of the distribution of international reserves. This is a difficult question with a host of arguments for and against using the allocation of SDRs to remedy the problem of the maldistribution of world reserves. A more extensive treatment of this matter goes beyond the scope of this essay. However, a few general remarks on the subject may be made here. Firstly, it is an unsatisfactory state of affairs that those countries that became Fund members after the last round of allocations, mainly former Communist-ruled countries, are without SDRs. Secondly, a strict interpretation of the Fund's Articles of Agreement would seem to rule out an allocation of SDRs for distributional purposes. And thirdly, an interesting solution that has been put forward, the simultaneous destruction of outstanding SDRs and a new allocation for the same amount but based on present quotas of members, also seems to be precluded by the present Articles of Agreement. Further study and discussion is therefore required to solve this issue.

Reference was already made a few times to the strongly increased role played by international financial markets in providing balance-of-payments and reserve financing. Whereas such financing helped to smooth adjustment to sudden shocks (the oil crises being the best-known example), it also contributed considerably to the postponement of necessary adjustment. The overborrowing by Latin American countries (and quite a few others) up to 1982 illustrates this very clearly. At the same time, the cut-off by the markets of new credit has been quite abrupt when – often belatedly – the consensus emerged that a country was no longer creditworthy. A measure that seems to have contributed significantly to a more stable development in the area of international bank lending has been the introduction of minimum standards for capital adequacy (the so-called BIS ratio of 8 per cent), agreed in 1988. Introduced for reasons of limiting systemic risk and equalizing competitive conditions, these rules appear to have made banks more selective in their lending. The different weights accorded to various categories of assets give a clear incentive to banks to be prudent in their lending to more risky customers, including non-industrial countries. In this way the capital adequacy rules are contributing to a better functioning of the international adjustment process. It should be realized, however, that since claims on all OECD governments are accorded a zero weighting under these rules, there may still be considerable scope for unwise lending.

4 The road ahead

We have seen that in the 50 years that have elapsed since the conference of Bretton Woods, the world has experienced two systems: the par value system with fixed but (not very) adjustable exchange rates, and a system of floating exchange rates (with some management) among the major currencies with a large degree of freedom of capital movements, but also with currency blocs within which a high degree of fixity prevailed. In looking at the road ahead, one approach is to compare the performance of the world economy under both systems and see what conclusions could be drawn from that and what adjustments, if any, should and could be made to the present international monetary system.

It is clear that the performance of the world economy was more impressive under the Bretton Woods system than under the system prevailing for the past 20 years. Economic growth was higher and inflation generally lower during the first period. The growth of international trade was also more buoyant during the fifties and sixties, however, after having been very depressed immediately after the Second World War. Furthermore, unemployment in the industrial countries, especially in Europe, has generally been much higher since the early seventies than in the days of the par value system. For the developing countries the picture is less clear-cut, but the impressive performance of East Asian countries over the past 15 years or so suggests that the present system has not been an obstacle to rapid development. It is of course hazardous to make such one dimensional cause-and-effect comparisons, given the multitude of factors that determine world growth, employment and inflation. The superior performance – of industrial countries – during the Bretton Woods era can undoubtedly be linked to the postwar reconstruction effort, the liberalization of world trade and the generally sound policies followed by most major countries up to, say, the mid-sixties. Against this it can be argued that the pursuit of sound policies cannot be separated from the prevailing exchange rate regime, which imparted a certain discipline on the participants. Also the lack of overabundant financing during a large part of this period appears to have aided the adjustment process. As to the generally weaker performance of industrial countries during the period of floating exchange rates, there are some obvious non-systemic reasons that can be put forward. One is that having reached a relatively high standard of living, the incentives for industrial countries to continue to pursue high growth diminished. Another relevant factor is the emergence of structural problems, often connected with the welfare state in European countries, which have contributed to a deep-seated unemployment problem.

The simple conclusion that the decline in world economic performance after the Bretton Woods era can be attributed in large part to the transformation of the international monetary system is clearly not warranted. Other factors have undeniably played a role. Nevertheless, the considerable instability in exchange rates among major countries that has occurred from time to time since the switch to floating rates, and the ample availability of external finance, are a genuine cause for concern. There is no consensus among economists as to whether floating has actually been detrimental to the growth of world trade and investment, but I tend to share the suspicion of Volcker that the fact that world growth has been slower, inflation higher and protectionist pressures have been stronger under the floating regime is '... not entirely accidental'.[14] I would add that the excellent performance of East Asian economies referred to earlier, probably has little to do with the prevailing international monetary system and quite a lot with the adoption of

14 Volcker, op. cit., p. 293.

a market economy and the pursuit of sound, outward-looking, policies by these countries. The increased protectionist pressure that is exacerbated by exchange rate volatility is in fact a constant threat to the future prosperity of developing countries.

My conclusion would therefore be that although there have been no major mishaps under the system of floating exchange rates of the past 20 years, there are a number of weak spots in the system:

- large exchange rate volatility which considerably increases the risk of protectionism;
- exchange rate uncertainty which is probably detrimental to world trade and especially investment; this has certainly been an important consideration for European countries to work towards a monetary union;
- the easy access to international finance under the present system for countries considered creditworthy may contribute to the delay of necessary adjustment for too long and impart an inflationary bias to the system.

Is there anything that should and could be done about these weaknesses? Realism dictates that any major reform effort, such as a full-scale return to the Bretton Woods system of fixed-but-adjustable rates, should be ruled out. Firstly, as mentioned earlier, major reform without a crisis is very unlikely. Secondly, it is hard to foresee a crisis in the present international monetary system. And thirdly, the world has become too fragmented to make a return to the Bretton Woods system, including American monetary hegemony, possible. Such a return would probably also call into question the freedom of capital movements, which would be a high price to pay for greater exchange rate stability. Indeed, I would also want to rule out all suggestions aimed at (re)introducing controls on international capital flows, under any type of exchange rate regime. This is fully in line with the conclusions of the recent Group of Ten study on international capital movements, which notes that while exchange controls can bring temporary relief when exchange rates are under pressure, they '... are likely to be ineffective and even counterproductive in the medium-term as they weaken confidence in the currency'.[15] Sometimes suggestions are made not to prohibit certain capital flows, but to discourage them by making them more costly. One such idea that has been around for a while is to levy a (small) tax on foreign exchange transactions. Recently a proposal (aimed at the ERM) was made to introduce (temporary) margin requirements on

15 group of Ten (1993), par. 55.

financial institutions with open positions in foreign exchange.[16] The problem with such measures is that they are likely to be circumvented on a large scale and are at loggerheads with the principle of the free flow of capital. A much more modest, but potentially fruitful, approach would appear to be to ensure that international financial markets in general, and certain fast growing segments in particular, function on a sound prudential basis. Central banks are indeed increasingly looking into matters such as the way in which derivatives markets operate.

Having ruled out a return to Bretton Woods, or any other major reform scheme, or the large-scale imposition of capital controls or taxes on capital movements, one is left with the avenue of pursuing greater exchange rate stability on a regional basis. In fact, the world has been moving for quite a while to a tripolar system consisting of a dollar bloc, an EMS bloc and the yen area. It is conceivable that the adoption of NAFTA will enhance the forces for closer monetary cooperation between its members. Also other Latin American countries could converge towards a dollar bloc as they successfully stabilize and restructure their economies. In Western Europe, monetary integration suffered a set-back following the crisis of the summer of 1993, but governments have generally remained clearly committed to achieving a monetary union in the future. A European economic and monetary bloc will probably retain its strong appeal on countries on the fringe of the European Union. In the Far East, the prospect for countries such as Korea for seeking closer monetary cooperation with Japan are perhaps more remote, but cannot be ruled out for the future. Also, albeit not in the near future, extension of the tripolar system with newly regionally important currencies or currency blocs is conceivable. The first possible candidate I see is the Chinese yuan, which is to become convertible in coming years[17], and will be backed by a rapidly expanding economy which could become one of the largest in the world in the foreseeable future. Another possibility is that of a ruble bloc, even though the present tendency for the ruble area is to fall apart. For the ruble to play a prominent role in the future may seem far-fetched now, but cannot be excluded in my view if and when Russia, and other former Soviet republics, succeed in achieving political stability and successfully implement economic reform.

A multipolar system consisting of currency blocs would take away some of the shortcomings of the present system. Large fluctuations among the major currencies would, however, remain a real problem.

16 See Eichengreen, Barry and Charles Wyplosz (1993).

17 An interesting question is what the future relationship will be between a convertible yuan and the Hong Kong dollar which is legally pegged to the US dollar.

Here the solution, which is probably not for tomorrow, may be to reach some form of agreement to avoid excessive fluctuations between the dollar, the European currency bloc and the yen. Volcker has suggested that an agreement on a broad range of acceptable fluctuations – larger than the plus or minus 5 per cent of the Louvre Accord – would be desirable.[18] The agreed ranges would be made public and the participants would have to be prepared to back up their commitment not only by means of intervention but also through adjustments in monetary policy in the short run and even by changing the direction of fiscal policy in the longer term. Such a hard target zone approach, albeit with a wide band, has a significant attraction. However, after the recent ERM experience, I wonder whether publicly announced bands among major currencies would be desirable. On the other hand, merely urging countries to pursue sound medium term policies as the best remedy against exchange rate pressures[19], is unlikely to be very effective. Perhaps the middle road lies in not trying to agree on specific bands, but to reach agreement on the desirability of avoiding sharp fluctuations in exchange rates (without precise specification) and to back up such a commitment with policy changes if necessary. Bringing about such a limited agreement in the area of international policy coordination would already imply some loss of autonomy over domestic policies and would be far from easy to put in place and maintain over a longer period. However, I believe that the danger of an escalation of protectionism alone is already important enough to work toward such an agreement. A role for the Fund, acting as a neutral arbiter, would in my view also be highly desirable. A further strengthening of the Fund's role in exchange rate surveillance would help to bring this about.

5 Summary

During most of the Bretton Woods era stability reigned and world trade and domestic economies prospered. The system broke down after the dollar glut caused unbearable strains in the defense of par values. Under floating exchange rates, which turned out to be partially managed, the international adjustment process became smoother with respect to the size and financing of external imbalances. The current account position gradually disappeared as a policy aim for industrial countries. Also the problems of the overall level as well as the composition of international reserves have largely vanished behind the horizon. What remains, is the question of the distribution of reserves. The main prob-

18 Volcker, op.cit. p. 300 et seq.
19 Group of Ten (1993), par. 56.

lem under floating rates, however, has been the tensions, including protectionist pressures, created by occasional large fluctuations in exchange rates between major currencies. International coordination of policies has generally not been a great success.

Looking to the future, any return to a world-wide system in the vein of Bretton Woods is ruled out, as is the imposition of large scale capital controls. Pursuing exchange rate stability on a regional basis, i.e. through adherence to currency blocs, is likely to remain important. A multipolar system, encompassing more than the present three major currencies, could evolve. The problem of instability between major currencies would remain, however, unless some form of international coordination were established. A limited form of such coordination, consisting of an agreement on the desirability of avoiding sharp fluctuations in exchange rates - without specifying a band - and an expressed willingness to back it up with policy changes if necessary, could be an acceptable approach.

References

Committee of Twenty (Committee on reform of the international monetary system and related issues) (1974), *International monetary reform,* Washington DC.

Corden, W. Max (1991), Does the current account matter? The old view and the new, in: *Jacob A. Frenkel and Morris Goldstein (eds.), International financial policy: essays in honor of Jacques J. Polak,* Washington DC.

De Beaufort Wijnholds, J. (1987), Surveillance over exchange rate policies, in: *H. Visser and E. Schoorl (eds.), Trade in transit* (papers presented at a conference in Amsterdam, September 1985), Dordrecht.

Eichengreen, Barry and Charles Wyplosz (1993), Taming speculation, CEPR, *European Economic Perspectives,* no. 1.

Group of Ten (1985), *The functioning of the international monetary system,* a report to the ministers and governors by the Group of Deputies.

Group of Ten (1993), *International capital movements and foreign exchange markets,* a report to the ministers and governors by the Group of Deputies.

Masson, Paul R. (1993), Policy coordination: how is it affected by uncertainty? *Finance and Development,* December, pp. 34-37.

Szász, André (1972), De Europese Monetaire Unie (The European Monetary Union), in: *A.J. Reitsma, H.W.J. Bosman, A. Szász and L. Wauters, Preadviezen,* 's-Gravenhage, pp. 55-78.

Triffin, Robert (1960), *Gold and the dollar crisis,* New Haven.

Volcker, Paul and Toyoo Gyothen (1992), *Changing fortunes: the world's money and the threat to American Leadership,* New York.

Half a century after Bretton Woods: the role of the IMF in the international monetary system

Leo van Houtven

1 Introduction

We commemorate this year the 50th anniversary of the Bretton Woods conference which gave birth to the International Monetary Fund and the World Bank. It is an important opportunity to reflect on the results of half a century of international monetary cooperation under the leadership of the Fund and also – as we propose to do on this occasion – to consider the role of the Fund in the international monetary system as we approach the threshold of the twenty-first century. I am sure that our good friend André Szász will actively participate in the reflection on the future of the International Monetary Fund.

Surveillance is the defining task of the Fund. Through effective surveillance over exchange rate policies of its member countries the Fund exercises its responsibility of oversight of the international monetary system and of the code of conduct to which members have subscribed. In this contribution, I will comment on Fund surveillance against the background of the movement toward a single world economic space, and on the basis of experience gained in the conduct of surveillance. Thereafter, I will comment on the range of tasks – policy advice, financing and technical assistance – that the Fund will continue to provide in the years ahead to the developing countries and the countries in transition. In doing so, I will emphasize that those tasks derive from and are intrinsically intertwined with the Fund's surveillance function.

2 Toward a single world economic space

The fall of the Berlin wall and the break-up of the Soviet Union have probably been the most critical developments in international relations in recent decades. We have warmly welcomed the improved prospects for world peace. We have also perceived the enormous task for that group of countries to break out of the mold of their defunct system, as well as the challenge for the rest of the world – and particularly for Western Europe – to give them their place in the world economy. More recently, the improved outlook for peace in the Middle East, the fundamental transformation that is taking place in Southern Africa and the resurgence of the three countries of the former Indochina constitute another set of changes that are of systemic importance. Other far-reaching changes are flowing from the virtually universal endorsement of market-based economic principles and the dynamic role of private initiative, as well as the spread of more democratic forms of government. Unfortunately, there are also dramatic setbacks in societies torn by civil strife, such as in the former Yugoslavia, in some countries in Africa, as well as in the south-eastern cone of the former Soviet Union.

Following the events in Eastern Europe and the Soviet Union, the Fund has finally become the global institution that it was always intended to be. The latest surge in membership – 26 states in the past four years, to 178 countries – has been particularly demanding on the institution as it became obvious that – with a few exceptions such as Hungary and the Czech Republic – the production facilities, economic institutions and government structures of these countries were in far worse shape than anticipated. Moreover, the break-up of the Soviet Union has severed many trading and financial arteries in that economic space, while the emergence of a number of countries without previous tradition or institutions of self-determination has added enormously to the problems of transition.

Among the developing countries, basic changes have overtaken the outdated North-South divide. We note, first of all, a group of rapidly industrializing countries – mainly in Asia but also in Latin America – that have the capacity and the ambition to join the group of industrial countries. Then there is a growing group of middle-income countries that over the past decade have achieved high rates of growth and domestic savings and whose prospects are enhanced by their ability to attract foreign private capital. There is also the case of China – always a world unto itself – where a whirlwind pace of growth is rapidly transforming the lives of hundreds of millions of people mainly in the coastal areas of that country. However, the large majority of Chinese in other parts of the country remain mired in poverty and this dichotomy is a source of increasing concern. In addition, there remains a large group of poor countries, most of them with sparse resources and dependent on assistance from abroad.

Another important phenomenon today is the leadership in world growth of the developing countries, particularly the groups of rapidly advancing economies referred to above. The developing countries have been, and are expected to continue, advancing at a growth pace of some 6 per cent per annum and, as a result, they are adding more than the industrial countries to the growth of the world economy. This contribution is all the more remarkable in view of the adverse external environment and the continued decline in the export prices of primary commodities.

Nevertheless, the state of the world economy as a whole is not satisfactory. The industrial countries have experienced sub-par growth for four years in a row and, for the first time in decades, all the G7 economies have displayed fundamental weaknesses. Germany has experienced its deepest and longest recession in the post-war period. The same goes for Japan. In most of Western Europe confidence remains weak and investors maintain a wait-and-see attitude. Fortunately, the United States' economy is expanding again at an encouraging pace and, in the course of 1994, we look forward to a revival of activity in Europe. Nevertheless, for the industrial countries as a group, unemployment has reached its highest level in a generation's time, and continues to rise. To make matters worse, the weak fiscal positions of industrial countries other than Japan have sharply limited the policy-makers' margin of manoeuver.

On the positive side, inflation in the industrial countries has been subdued. In addition, entrepreneurs have vigorously pursued efficiency and rationalization in order to strengthen their competitiveness and to improve their financial position. As a result, many corporations are ready to move forward and invest as soon as there are clear signals of economic revival. However, employment creation is likely to remain modest in the early phase of the economic upturn. In Europe, in particular, overregulated labor markets and overly generous social benefits remain a serious drag on enterprises and on employment creation.

Recession and unemployment breed protectionism. The long drawn-out Uruguay Round negotiations became a test case for the continuation of the outward-looking economic strategy of the post-war period. Let us not forget: among the singular achievements of economic cooperation in the past half century have been the unprecedented liberalization of trade under the stewardship of the United States and the dismantling of exchange controls under the direction of the IMF. We should also mention the shining example of outward-looking policies pursued in recent years by many developing countries. The successful conclusion of the Uruguay Round in late 1993, following the approval by the United States of the North American Free Trade Agreement, has been excellent news for the world economy.

Moving from trade to exchange rate issues and capital movements, we observe that, in the recent period, the exchange rate relationship between the US dollar, the Japanese yen and the Deutsche mark has not raised significant issues, and that the long period of exchange rate appreciation of the yen appears to have come to a halt. In Europe, however, since the summer of 1992 there has been unprecedented turbulence among the EMS currencies. Inadequate and unsustained convergence, diverging cyclical positions, differences in the degree of commitment to price stability, different mixes of monetary and fiscal policy and loss of competitiveness of some currencies had re-opened doubts about the viability of the ERM parity grid. Enough has been written about the episodes leading to the shake-up of the ERM and the gradual restoration of calm following the decision in August 1993 to widen temporarily the intervention margins. However, more reflection will be needed to draw the lessons from that experience for European Economic and Monetary Union as well as for Fund surveillance.

3 The Fund's surveillance role and the thrust of its policy advice

Under the Articles of Agreement, as amended in 1978, members were granted the discretion to adopt the exchange arrangements of their choice and the Fund was explicitly mandated the task of 'firm surveillance over the exchange rate policies of members'. Surveillance involves a carefully calibrated assessment – a finely drawn judgment – that involves all aspects of a member's macro-economic and related structural policies, since these policies underpin a country's exchange rate policies. Moreover, in exercising surveillance, the Fund must promote mutually consistent economic policies among its members; for the industrial countries – which will be the focus of this section – that means that they should take into account the views of the world community as well as the spill-over of their policies on other countries and on the stability of the international monetary system.

The effectiveness of Fund surveillance depends on the quality of the Fund's assessments and on the willingness of member countries to cooperate with the Fund. In the exercise of surveillance, there have – inevitably – been recurring differences of view between the Fund and members regarding the appropriate pace and content of adjustment policies as well as regarding the repercussions of a member's policies for other countries. The tendency of nations to postpone needed adjustment has much to do with an underestimation of the problems or an overestimation of the time period or the scope of financing available to deal with the problems. The pursuit of policies that prove mutually inconsistent among countries generally relates to a reluctance to use certain policy instruments or to an inappropriate mix of policies.

There is a wide-spread view that Fund surveillance is asymmetric inasmuch as it can be 'enforced' only vis-à-vis those countries that need to accept the Fund conditionality that is attached to the use of the financial resources of the institution. That view must ultimately rest on the presumption that some members may find it advantageous not to observe the code of conduct or that unsound policies are sustainable. Clearly, in the 1970s and early 1980s some industrial countries had persistent large balance-of-payments disequilibria and high inflation while international policy coordination left much to be desired. In roughly the same period, many developing countries were reluctant to embark on much needed adjustment while the capital markets were willing to continue providing financing well beyond the bounds of prudence. It took the debt crisis of the 1980s to drive home to deficit countries the paramount need for domestic and external adjustment. With regard to the industrial countries, the increased emphasis in the 1980s on keeping policies in line with the economic fundamentals and on strengthening policy coordination amongst them has been most welcome. In fact, we have witnessed the emergence of a remarkable consensus between the Fund and its members – industrial and developing countries – on what constitute sound economic policies, and this has much reduced the relevance of the old argument of asymmetry.

The Fund exercises surveillance on a multilateral and a bilateral basis, as well as through periodic discussions of systemic issues and of developments in financial markets. Multilateral surveillance is conducted primarily on the basis of staff studies and Board discussions of the World Economic Outlook that pay particular attention to international interactions of policies and systemic developments. Bilateral surveillance is exercised through the annual consultations of the Fund with each member country; these involve comprehensive discussions of economic prospects and policies between a visiting staff team and the government representatives of the member. At the end of their discussions, which last about two weeks, the staff usually prepares a memorandum containing the mission's preliminary findings. Thereafter, the staff prepares a detailed report for discussion by the Fund's Executive Board. The Fund's Managing Director, who is also the chairman of the Board, concludes the discussion with a summing-up that reflects the thrust of the views expressed by the Executive Board. That summing-up is communicated to the authorities of the country concerned, completing the process.

Following the 1978 amendment of the Articles of Agreement, Fund surveillance had to break out of the rule-based mold of the Bretton Woods regime into the broader judgmental atmosphere of the exchange rate arrangements chosen by each member. Surveillance, henceforth, required a careful appraisal of the domestic monetary and fiscal policies that support the member's exchange rate policy. In practice, it was found increasingly necessary to broaden the appraisal of macro-economic policies to a range of supporting structural policies including, as needed, tax systems and expenditure policies, financial markets and institutions, wage policy and labor markets, etc. In addition, surveillance needed to encompass the international interdependence and consistency of national policies. Moreover, in recent years, Fund surveillance has focused on diverse systemic issues ranging from the globalization of financial markets and capital movements, to the problems of economies in transition to market-based systems. Thus, in a span of about 15 years, the analytical and operational content of Fund surveillance has gained a great deal in scope and depth.

However, new problems are always lurking: in late 1991, the challenge of absorbing into the Fund large numbers of new members from Eastern Europe and the former Soviet Union coincided with a period of very intensive operational activity with many developing countries. In order to ease the unsustainable pressure on staff resources, the decision was taken to simplify bilateral surveillance, other than for the large industrial countries and members under Fund programs including so-called 'near-program' countries. All remaining members would be temporarily shifted from an annual to a 24-month consultation cycle, with abridged 'interim' consultations that would normally not be brought for discussion to the agenda of the Executive Board.

It soon became evident that the easing of the surveillance discipline, which included the non-G7 industrial countries, had unfortunate implications. The deepening recession and its impact on the adjustment policies of the developing countries, the incipient currency turmoil in Europe in the summer of 1992 and the subsequent developments in the ERM did not receive the attention they deserved while other surveillance work was postponed. As a result, the quality and timeliness of Fund surveillance suffered.

The Fund soon recognized that this easing of surveillance was a mistake, and decided in late 1992 to restore the normal annual consultation cycles. On further reflection, a number of other measures were taken to strengthen the coherence, efficiency and continuity of Fund surveillance, particularly over industrial countries. The World Economic Outlook exercises are now being enhanced with a wider and more pointed coverage of systemic issues and their broader macro-economic implications. They are being complemented by periodic confidential Board sessions on World Economic and Market Developments, which cover a wide range of countries and systemic matters as well as in-depth analysis of the most recent developments in financial markets. These discussions, held about every six weeks, have added a useful element of timeliness to this aspect of surveillance. To foster the policy dialogue with members, the Managing Director and the senior staff are enhancing, selectively, their follow-up discussions with top officials in member countries on substantive issues. Also, a high-level staff Surveillance Committee meets frequently under the chairmanship of the Managing Director to identify issues with systemic implications and suggest appropriate courses of action.

Finally, measures were also taken to strengthen the regional focus of Fund surveillance. The absence of procedures in that area had been increasingly felt following the creation of the European Monetary System in 1979. With the benefit of hindsight, the Fund could, and should, have stressed more vigorously the role of Fund surveillance over the exchange rates of members in the regional European system and over the broader implications of the EMS for the international monetary system. Henceforth, EMS issues will be covered in greater depth in special staff studies and discussions with the authorities of the countries concerned, as well as in the Article IV consultations and in the World Economic Outlook exercises. Discussions will also be held with the European Commission on issues that are under its jurisdiction. Similar arrangements for regional surveillance will apply to other groups of member countries that have common institutions as well as to issues that are common to a number of countries.

There remains an obvious need to revitalize the process of international policy coordination and to associate the activities of the G7 more closely with the Fund. Following the strengthening of policy coordination among the main industrial countries in the Plaza Agreement (September 1985) and in the Louvre Accord (February 1987), efforts in that direction have weakened again as evidenced by the prolonged recession and the exchange rate tensions in Europe. In line with the strengthening of surveillance the Fund should assume a larger role in policy coordination and the pursuit by members of mutually compatible policies.

At the ministerial level, Fund surveillance is exercised by the Interim Committee, which usually meets twice a year, in the spring and before the Fund's Annual Meeting in September. Its agenda covers the range of issues that are vital to the institution and its membership. At its meeting of 30 April 1993 the Committee took the unusual step of adopting a Declaration for Sustained Global Expansion and it reiterated its endorsement of that declaration in the September 1993 meeting. Against that background, the Fund's policy advice to its members focusses at present on the following broad themes, set in a medium-term context:

a Trade liberalization and the abolition of exchange controls have been among the strongest forces promoting world economic growth, welfare and the efficient allocation of resources. With the recent successes in trade negotiations and the internationalization of financial markets, the accelerated movement toward a single world economic space has become irresistible. Trade liberalization – in goods and services – must continue in an orderly fashion because artificial barriers can be evaded through movements of capital, exchange rates, population, and other means. Regional trading arrangements, such as exist in Europe and North America, are welcome provided that they do not strengthen trade restrictions against third countries.

b The liberalization of capital movements and the globalization of financial markets have been among the most important developments in the international monetary system in recent years. The freedom of capital movements that now exists is historically unprecedented. Let us not forget that the Bretton Woods negotiators assumed that member countries would not be in a position to abandon capital controls. Cross-border capital movements are increasing at a vertiginous pace; the choice of financial instruments is constantly widening and the efficiency gains are yielding significant benefits, both for financial market participants, and, more importantly, for the underlying strength of the economies themselves. Time has come to consider revising the Articles of Agreement and updating the code of conduct to include all international financial transactions.

c The benefits from the movement toward a single world economic space come at a price. For governments, the price is a limitation of autonomy in the conduct of policies, a smaller margin for errors and an increased vulnerability to external shocks. On the one hand, investment and capital will flow eagerly to countries whose sound policies hold out the prospect of sustained growth with low inflation; but on the other hand, the reactions of markets to any perceived weakness of policy can be quick and – as we have seen – powerful. This increased vulnerability was vividly illustrated by recent events in Europe, which showed that the markets are keen judges of the quality of policies and that they have the power to impose their judgment since capital movements dwarf official reserves. Increased discipline will be needed to achieve and maintain the 'convergence criteria' in Europe in order to strengthen exchange rate stability. In short, the conditions for maintaining a fixed exchange rate regime have become stiffer. Markets must be convinced that rates are in line with the fundamentals of the economy and that needed policy adjustments will be made promptly. Exchange rate instability has more to do with inadequacies of national policies and of international policy coordination than with the exchange rate system.

d When growth is slow and unemployment is rising, it is tempting to suggest that less importance needs to be attached to price stability. However, the fight against inflation is never completed. The encouraging progress made in recent years toward price stability in the industrial countries should be maintained. Our objective should be to foster expansion that is sustainable over the medium term while avoiding a recurrence of the excesses of the late 1980s. In Europe, the easing of inflation in the anchor country and the widening intervention margins in the EMS should facilitate a gradual further lowering of interest rates to assist an economic revival consistent with the requirement to maintain price stability.

e The fiscal positions of industrial countries – with the exception of Japan – leave no room for expansionary actions. It is, in fact, critically important that industrial countries resume fiscal consolidation as soon as a revival of economic activity in individual countries permits. Since tax burdens are already very high in most industrial countries, particularly in Europe, fiscal consolidation should focus on expenditure restraint. In addition to the downsizing of military outlays that has become possible as a result of the end of the cold war, major economies should be made through cuts in subsidies to industry and agriculture and social subsidies to households. However, for fiscal consolidation along these lines to be large enough and durable, a broad reappraisal of the role of government in modern society will need to be completed. Such a reappraisal has begun in most countries, and has already shown impressive first results through the reduction, via privatization, of the role of government as an entrepreneur. But much more needs to be done, including a careful reappraisal of the role of government as guarantor of social welfare. Reforms of the pension, health care, and social security systems have become more and more urgent. With aging populations, these burdens become unbearable and they are often not equitably distributed. And, further, the role of government in our industrial societies will have to be pruned to a set of priorities that each is willing, and able, to bear without unreasonably burdening future generations.

f The preceding observations on fiscal policy and the role of the state have made it clear that macro-economic policies need to be complemented by structural reforms. Such reforms are required to cut the coat of the public sector according to the cloth, to reflect the changing social priorities and to provide fiscal policy with the necessary flexibility. In Europe, in particular, deregulation of labor markets and of the process of wage determination are urgent, together with reforms of the social security systems. Further structural reforms in other areas such as financial markets are also called for and should go hand in hand with the strengthening of prudential provisions and supervisory systems.

4 Developing countries and economies in transition: Fund policy advice, financing and technical assistance

The number of countries with which the Fund has lending programs in effect plus the number of countries with which negotiations have moved into an advanced stage, the so-called 'near-program countries', now oscillates around 90 countries, or about one-half of the membership. The coming into effect in November 1992 of the general increase in Fund quotas to some SDR 146 billion ensured that the Fund would be able to meet its critical financing and catalytic role.

In view of the current and prospective heavy demand for access to Fund financial resources, it is heartening that surveillance has moved to center stage in the relationship between the Fund and the developing countries. In the past, developing countries viewed their relationship with the Fund mainly in terms of negotiating the conditionality that would be attached to the use of Fund resources. Moreover, the role of surveillance over developing countries was questioned to the extent that the relevance of these countries in the functioning of the international monetary system was seen to be marginal. Since the second half of the 1980s, however, earlier differences between the Fund and borrowing countries on issues of conditionality moved to the background as a constructive consensus emerged on the thrust of adjustment and reform policies and on the need to implement these policies in a medium-term context. At the same time, there was an increased recognition of the Fund's role in promoting consistent policies in a regional context or across groups of countries facing similar problems or having common institutional arrangements such as central banks or exchange rate arrangements.

The improvement in adjustment and reform policies has been most notable in the case of many middle-income – but also some low-income – countries in Asia and Latin America. These countries have adopted outward-looking policies, have enhanced the role of the private sector, and are strengthening their access to international financial markets. A number of them may well have further need to use Fund resources to build confidence and secure financial support. Nevertheless, Fund advice through surveillance has become more important than conditionality of Fund lending. Beyond the macro-economic policy dialogue, Fund advice will need to focus on such critical areas as budget and tax reform, development of capital markets and of financial institutions, the creation of a modern regulatory environment, policies to raise domestic savings and investment, the role of external private capital, policies for regional cooperation, etc. A recent example of such critical areas of interest has been the surges in private capital inflows to a number of developing countries that raised new financial issues for the policy makers in those countries.

Other developing countries, mainly a large number of low-income countries, remain dependent on financial assistance from bilateral sources and from international financial institutions. Technical assistance and training for these countries also play a major role. In the second half of the 1980s, the Fund introduced a highly concessional financing facility for this group of countries, the Enhanced Structural Adjustment Facility (ESAF) with access depending on the implementation of strong medium-term policy programs. Despite its demanding conditionality, this facility has become particularly successful both from the point of view of the borrowing countries and from the perspective of the donors and creditors. Notable improvements in governance in a number of countries have been recorded, while the medium-term horizon of the programs has strengthened their catalytic impact and facilitated their continued financing. Further efforts will be required, in the framework of surveillance, to strengthen the 'ownership' of ESAF programs and the social-political sustainability of often painful but inevitable reforms. With the strong support of the membership, the Fund has recently decided to introduce an ESAF successor. Nevertheless, the road ahead for many low-income countries remains extremely difficult; their economic viability is a systemic issue and it is essential that donor countries channel scarce Official Development Aid resources to countries that successfully implement ESAF programs.

With regard to the economies in transition, for the more advanced of them, such as Hungary and the Czech Republic, economic reform programs hold the hope of restoring sustainable growth and a viable external position. As in the case of the successful adjusting developing countries, Fund surveillance over these countries should strengthen the policy performance and enhance external confidence. The countries of the former Soviet Union should, in most cases, expect to make slower progress with economic stabilization and structural reform than earlier hoped, because of the backwardness of their economic structures and the large shocks associated with their transition to market-based systems. In response, the Fund has acted speedily and flexibly to establish a temporary facility, the Systemic Transition Facility (STF), which is designed to extend financial assistance to members experiencing severe disruptions in their trade and payments in the process of their transition to a market-based economic system. Thus, the STF acts as a bridge toward the use of the Fund's regular financing facilities.

Experience has confirmed that the countries that pursued stabilization and reform vigorously and in a sustained manner – such as the Baltic countries – have reaped results much faster than others in halting and reversing the decline in output, in bringing inflation under control and in strengthening the external sector. By contrast, in several other former Soviet Union states such as Russia, Belarus and Ukraine, the lack of coherent stabilization and reform policies, and the consequent continuing economic decline and widening imbalances, reflected the inability of the authorities to develop the political consensus needed to address the entrenched economic and financial difficulties. The hardships that have befallen the population relate to the inadequacy of the policies pursued rather than to their severity. The financing requirements of that region will remain considerable, and the Fund will have to play an effective catalytic role. To that effect, Fund surveillance and advice in the elaboration and implementation of medium-term oriented programs will be critically important.

There has been an explosive growth in demand for technical assistance relating largely to the needs of the Fund's poorer and new members, as well as to the broadening of the Fund's policy advice into structural areas and issues of transition. A great deal of technical assistance resources are being devoted to institution building in the financial, fiscal, legal, exchange, statistical, and related areas and to training of officials. Technical assistance is a scarce resource and requires the pooling of multilateral and bilateral resources. In order to obtain the best results with the resources available, the identification, analysis, implementation and follow up of projects needs to take place in a comprehensive framework for which Fund surveillance can be most helpful.

5 Concluding remarks

The Fund has been entrusted with the task of surveillance over the exchange rate policies of its members and the oversight of the international monetary system. In the discretion-based exchange rate regime that emerged after the demise of the Bretton Woods system, surveillance involves a balanced and comprehensive assessment of the policies that support the exchange rate and of the international interactions of members' policies. Surveillance is the defining task – the essential duty – of the Fund; all the Fund's other tasks, including its financing role, derive from surveillance. In exercising surveillance, the Fund should promote mutually consistent policies among its members.

Over the years, the scope and depth of surveillance have developed markedly. The main themes of Fund policy advice in the current phase of the world economy have been reflected in the deliberations of the Interim Committee, including in the Declaration for Sustained Global Expansion which the Committee adopted in April 1993. In this paper we have focused on the following aspects which are likely to remain close to the concerns of policy-makers in the next several years:

- the emergence of a single world economic space will bring considerable benefits but will require increased policy discipline and increased competitiveness;
- economic policies should aim at steady sustainable expansion with price stability;
- fiscal consolidation needs to be resumed as soon as trends in economic activity permit;
- macro-economic policies need to be complemented by structural reforms including a broad-based reappraisal of the role of government in our societies and deregulation of markets, particularly labor markets.

The effectiveness of Fund surveillance depends on the quality of the advice and on the willingness of members to cooperate with the Fund. Since the exercise of surveillance is a quest for perfection, there will always be room for improvement. With regard to the industrial countries as a group, priority should be attached to revitalizing the process of policy coordination in which the fund – including in particular at the ministerial level the Interim Committee – should assume a larger role. In addition, surveillance should be made more timely, continuous and flexible, and the actions to that effect that have been announced by the Fund are welcome. There is also a need to strengthen the regional focus of Fund surveillance; this applies in particular to the EC countries, but also to other groups of Fund members with regional institutions. Fund surveillance over the rapidly advancing developing countries will require increasingly sophisticated analysis that covers in-depth a broad array of subjects. With regard to users of Fund resources, developing countries and economies in transition, effective surveillance is critical for the elaboration and implementation of medium-term oriented policies. Since the years ahead promise to be a time of unprecedented change in the international economic environment, great continuity of surveillance of systemic issues will be required for the Fund to meet the challenges of its oversight role of the international monetary system.

The contribution of the IMF to exchange rate stability: efforts in monetary diplomacy

Godert A. Posthumus

1 Introduction

Under this optimistic title[1], I intend to trace the efforts which the International Monetary Fund (hereafter called 'the Fund') has made in recent years to 'promote exchange stability' and to 'avoid competitive exchange depreciation', as the Articles of Agreement require the Fund to do. Under the Bretton Woods regime, members agreed to a constraint, a fixed exchange rate, and the international community (the Fund) administered discretion. The current Articles of Agreement, amended in 1978, put into effect exactly the opposite framework: members have underwritten the predominance of discretion (the exchange arrangement of their choice), while the international community is left with the task of administering the constraints (surveillance) to which the discretion is to be made subject.[2] Thus, the world moved from 'a system of stable exchange rates', the Bretton Woods regime, to an agreement to collaborate with the Fund and other members ... to promote 'a stable system of exchange rates' (Article IV of the Articles of Agreement). Some groups of countries have voluntarily accepted the constraints of a fixed exchange rate regime on a regional basis amongst themselves: the European Monetary System's Exchange Rate Mechanism (hereafter called the ERM) and the Zône franc countries, for example.

Exchange rate stability is in this contribution seen as an issue related to monetary and fiscal policy, balance-of-payments adjustment, etc. However, this is not only a macro-economic policy issue. There is little doubt that stability of exchange rates facilitates international trade. Uncertainty and transaction costs are, after all, obstacles to international trade in goods and services, and to investments abroad. With increasing international trade and investment, the importance of stable exchange rates increases as well. The choice of the exchange rate system remains at the discretion of the Fund's member countries, but

1 As taught by André Szász (1988), *Monetaire diplomatie: Nederlands internationale monetaire politiek* 1958 - 1987, Doctoral thesis, Leiden/Antwerpen.

2 Guitián, M. (1992), Unique nature of the responsibilities of the IMF, Washington DC.

the growing importance of stability of exchange rates requires the Fund to increasingly focus its surveillance on the attainment of that stability.

My observations of the Fund's contribution to exchange rate stability will cover the period since the Louvre meeting of 1987. In that meeting of February 1987, the G7 authorities made a judgement about desirable exchange rates by pronouncing the then current exchange rates between their currencies as right. They also agreed to conduct policies consistent with this judgment.[3] By that time, the actual development of exchange rates indicated that the problem of the international exchange rate system was no longer too much rigidity, but rather too much volatility.[4]

In order to fulfil the Fund's task of overseeing the international monetary system, the Articles of Agreement require the Fund to exercise firm surveillance over the exchange rate policies of its members. Surveillance manifests itself in policy advice, given in the framework of Article IV consultations, and in the policy conditions linked to Fund-financing arrangements. Surveillance is also conducted in other ways, such as informal Board discussion on World Economic and Market Developments; the publication of the World Economic Outlook; policy recommendations in the form of speeches, studies, etc.; and in informal contacts between Fund management and authorities of member countries. Proposals for policy advice and policy conditions are made by the staff of the Fund under the responsibility of the Managing Director and are submitted for approval to the Executive Board of the Fund (hereafter called 'the Board'). Article IV consultations are conducted by the Board, on the basis of a report which includes management policy recommendations to the member concerned. Stand-by and other financial arrangements with members require prior approval by the Board. This includes approval of policy conditions proposed by Fund staff and agreed to by the authorities of the borrowing member country.

The Board, therefore, gives guidance to, and directs, policy advice by the Fund in Article IV consultations and in financial arrangements. In order to trace the efforts of the Fund in promoting exchange rate stability, I shall give impressions of some Board discussions on exchange rate policy in specific country cases. I will indicate directors' positions, which differed fundamentally from Fund staff's policy advice. The arguments they used in these discussions sufficiently indicate their

3 Szász, op. cit., p. 199.
4 Szász, op. cit., p. 188.

approach in looking at exchange rate policy and reflect the positions the Fund staff had taken.

2 Board discussions

In Board discussions, since 1987, several directors began focusing on Fund advice with regard to exchange rate policy; in particular, in cases where flexible exchange rate regimes were supported by the staff of the Fund. These discussions took place, both when Board approval was requested for the policy conditions contained in Fund-supported programs, as well as in cases of Fund policy advice in the framework of Article IV consultations. These discussions developed over the years into an intensive exchange of opinions about the merits of flexible and fixed exchange rate regimes in specific cases, and related to policy advice given by Fund staff.

Since the mid-seventies, many developing countries have changed their exchange rate regimes significantly, from pegging to a single currency or to a basket of currencies to flexible arrangements. Their decisions had been prompted partly by the wish to minimize the undesirable effects on their economies of fluctuations in the exchange rates of major currencies that had taken place since the advent of generalized floating in 1973. The Fund had often strengthened this development by advising to use exchange rate policy to maintain or improve the competitiveness of the export sector. Such 'active' exchange rate policies were recommended in particular as part of the conditions of Fund-financed programs, in which the Fund can exercise more influence than in Article IV consultations.

The Eastern European and former Soviet Union states which, in the beginning of the nineties, started the transition to a market economy with Fund-supported stabilization and reform programs, made their choice of exchange rate regimes for the first time. There is no clearly discernible pattern in the Fund's advice in these cases, though there seemed to be a Fund preference towards flexible exchange rate policies.

The directors that started these discussions in the Board in the second half of the eighties were, in any case, concerned that the Fund focused excessively on flexible regimes and on depreciation as an instrument to improve competitiveness. They also felt that the Fund was neglecting the role fixed exchange rates can play as an anchor for policies aimed at monetary stability. The Fund had no 'philosophy' on this matter, and followed an eclectic approach, tailoring its advice as much as possible way to the circumstances of individual countries.

3 Countries with flexible exchange rate regimes

The active use of the exchange rate as a permanent instrument to improve competitiveness was usually singled out by a number of Board members to challenge the exchange rate policy advice of the staff. Staff recommendations to target real exchange rates specifically were often criticized because they could only be implemented by nominal depreciation which, however, put an upward pressure on prices. In 1988, in a Board discussion of a Fund program for Bolivia, for example, the recommendation to follow a specific path of real depreciation of the currency was considered incompatible with simultaneous Fund staff advice to contain inflationary pressures. As governments could not control the real magnitude of exchange rate changes, it was difficult to set targets for them; such advice did not give clear policy guidance. In another case, that of a Fund program for Tanzania in 1990, staff had included a specific exchange rate target in real terms. The nominal exchange rate would be regularly adjusted by the authorities to inflation differentials between Tanzania and its trading partners. The authorities would consult with the Fund should the exchange rate have to be depreciated in nominal terms by more than 2.5 per cent in any quarter. If the fiscal and monetary policies under the program were successful, the nominal changes of the exchange rate would diminish as inflation (and the inflation differentials with trading partners) decelerated and would become consistent with the maintenance of the agreed minimum real exchange rate. But several directors argued that pegging the exchange rate would have provided an anchor for inflationary expectations and a framework for financial and monetary discipline. Recognizing that it was undoubtedly damaging to stick too long to a nominal exchange rate if domestic price developments did not warrant this, it was pointed out that it would also be damaging to build a continued nominal exchange rate slide into the policy mix. This might safeguard competitiveness, but at the same time it would add to instability.

The Article IV consultations with Chile in 1991 were the stage for another discussion on exchange rate policies. Chile had a system of targeting the real exchange rate within a wide band. A few directors voiced concern: a real exchange rate band might, over time, serve to undermine the authorities' attempts to reduce liquidity growth and hence domestic inflation. Over the past year, such attempts to tighten monetary conditions had obviously been hampered by the commitment of the central bank to hold down the exchange rate. Chile's strong productivity performance over recent years had quite legitimately put upward pressure on the real exchange rate. The policy of keeping the currency in a fixed real exchange rate band had thus resulted in domestic inflation. This exchange rate policy seemed likely to present an ongoing inflationary risk in the medium term, particularly if productivity growth would remain strong. The very fact that the nominal exchange rate was adjusted automatically to inflation differentials indicated resignation to inflationary conditions.

It was not always easy to distinguish between a flexible exchange rate regime and a fixed-but-adjustable exchange rate regime. During the discussion about a proposed Fund arrangement with Hungary in 1991, several directors identified the exchange rate regime as being flexible. One director noted that in other countries in Eastern Europe (Poland, Czechoslovakia), staff had supported fixed exchange rate regimes. He wondered whether the Fund was fully discharging its systemic responsibilities: in one country, the risk of having an overvalued exchange rate was accepted by the Fund, while in other countries the risk of higher inflation was accepted. Staff stated that the exchange rate was not flexible but fixed, while retaining the possibility of changing it in light of developments in the performance of the balance of payments. It was a system with a fixed rate but only for a limited period of time. Staff added that it was preferable, in view of the very large uncertainties, to keep the exchange rate as a flexible instrument to respond to possible negative developments rather than having to rely only on additional tightening of financial policies. There was a risk of overdrawing the distinction between cases. In the case of Poland, the exchange rate was fixed, but not in the long term. In the case of Czechoslovakia, the issue had been how to announce a fixed rate, without carving it in stone so that any later change in such a rate would appear to be a failure of the system. Concluding this discussion, one director said that he remained concerned that the Fund might not be putting sufficient emphasis on the risk of inflation for East European countries during the transition process.

4 Countries with fixed exchange rate regimes

Many exchange rate policy discussions took place on occasions of countries with fixed exchange rate regimes. I will give impressions of some of these Board discussions by indicating the positions of a few directors disagreeing with the staff policy advice.

Most of the countries with fixed exchange rate regimes have fixed-but-adjustable exchange rates usually within certain margins, (hereafter: fixed or stable regimes). Adjustment, however, is only a possibility of last resort. In 1991, the Board discussed a program with Mexico, which had a fixed exchange rate with a pre-announced exchange rate depreciation for a certain period, an arrangement which can be considered a fixed exchange rate regime. The Mexican authorities had announced a deceleration of the rate of depreciation which did not fully compensate for estimated inflation. This was seen as a significant contribution to reducing inflationary expectations. At the same time, the gradual depreciation itself had been sufficient to prevent expectations of an abrupt devaluation from arising. A fixed exchange rate would not yet be considered credible. Referring to the extensive Board discussions about flexible versus fixed exchange rate regimes, one director found the Mexican use of the exchange rate as an anchor risky in view of the crucial role of the exchange rate in economies that are in the process of true integration into the world economy. Overvalued currencies had been common in Latin America at the onset of the debt crisis, and he was worried about competitiveness. Another director, however, wondered whether the policy of a crawling peg with small daily adjustments of the Mexican peso was in line with the need to establish confidence in domestic stabilization policy. He found a fixed, nominal exchange rate target more appropriate in this situation, as it would contribute to strengthening internal adjustment and demonstrate the commitment to monetary stabilization.

During the Article IV consultations with Norway in 1988, a few directors criticized Norway's fixed exchange rate policy (the Norwegian krone was pegged to a basket of currencies) arguing that, if economic activity would remain weak, interest rates would have to be reduced. However, such a reduction might jeopardize the external objectives of monetary policy, namely pegging the exchange rate. As economic activity in the non-oil tradeable sector would have to increase in particular, there would be a difficult task ahead if no resort were made to exchange rate adjustment.

In the Article IV consultations with Italy, in 1989, little criticism was directed at Italy's fixed exchange rate policy within the ERM. As it was remarked, growth had been robust, investment activity had been brisk, and inflation had been abating, approaching that of competitor countries; exports had been developing nicely, the current account was practically in balance, and profit generation in the business sector had been good. Public finance and unemployment were the only major areas of concern, but unemployment was more a regional than a national problem. Attention, therefore, focused on fiscal policy. One director said that the case of Italy showed that monetary integration within Europe could not proceed much further without a convergence of fiscal policies. More specifically, since the monetary stance was constrained by the limited role of exchange rate policy under the ERM, the need for immediate progress by the Italian authorities in the fiscal area could not be overemphasized. It was also pointed out that the increasing reliance of monetary policy on a flexible interest rate policy made it more difficult for the authorities to pursue an exchange rate target, which gave rise to questions concerning Italy's participation in the ERM within the more recent and ongoing liberalization of capital flows.

During the Article IV consultation with Belgium in 1989, exchange rate policy was strongly criticized by several directors. As one of them put it: the wisdom of the staff-endorsed policy to maintain a stable relationship between the Belgian franc and the Deutsche mark is not so clear-cut. The costs involved in such a policy were not fully appreciated. A policy commitment that could involve abstaining from more expansionary macro-economic policies seemed to place a low value on employment. More generally, the priority to maintain stable exchange rates in the context of the ERM could have a wide impact on the world economy, because of the slower growth rates that could ensue.

During the Article IV consultations with France in 1991, one director remarked that France was bearing a heavy cost in terms of investment, output and employment due to the artificially high interest rates needed to maintain the franc's fixed exchange rate against the Deutsche mark. However, this being its policy, France needed to compensate for weakened investment, growth and employment prospects by embarking on a much more ambitious program of structural reform than recent performance suggested the authorities were willing to undertake. Another director pointed out that because of the first priority of monetary policy, being the maintenance of the value of the franc vis-à-vis the Deutsche mark, interest rates in France had been around 10 per cent in nominal terms, and 7 per cent in real terms. He wondered whether these high interest rates were having an effect on the real economy, and he noted that the economy had already begun to stagnate. A director who supported France's exchange rate policy, said that the high real interest rates were caused by external factors and had to be considered the price one has to pay when fiscal policy remained uncoordinated in an area with no room for exchange rate action and with free capital movements.

In the beginning of 1992, Article IV consultations with Italy were held in the Board. One director called Italy's exchange rate focused policy unbalanced and costly, but this was considered not to be a shortcoming of the exchange rate policy itself but a reflection of the failure to come to grips with the fiscal debt burden and with rigidities in the non-tradeable sector. However, as another director indicated, it would be worth discussing whether a country with limited flexibility in fiscal policy, rigidity in real wages, and a commitment to peg its currency to other strong currencies within a narrow range, thereby curtailing its monetary autonomy, could attain a favorable situation at all. Unless German interest rates would decline in the near future, he added, it would be worth considering a realignment of the ERM currencies. Another director pointed at the basic incompatibility between Italy's persistent fiscal laxity and the financial discipline necessary to adhere successfully to a fixed exchange rate regime. Now, the very sustainability of Italy's fixed exchange rate policy was questioned. The crisis would not come from within the economy, because there would be pressure for devaluation rather than fiscal tightening, but would be provoked from abroad, in the form of the political necessity of meeting the EMU criteria. The discussion had shifted, he said, from whether unsustainable economic conditions exist to whether convergence with EMU standards was possible. Exchange rate fixity on its own is not sufficient in curtailing inflation, but of necessity it must be supplemented by other appropriate economic policies. It is perhaps interesting to add that this was not only the opinion of one director who did not look very sympathetically at the ERM efforts. The Board, in its conclusions of these Article IV consultations with Italy early in 1992, underlined the conflict that would eventually arise between the commitment to exchange rate stability and inflation convergence if early progress in reducing inflation significantly was not made.

During the Article IV consultations with the United Kingdom, also held in the beginning of 1992, one director remarked that consideration should have been given to the possibility of a further lowering of official interest rates as well as to the possibility of a realignment in the ERM.

In the previous two paragraphs, I have given impressions from some Board discussions and critical analyses on exchange rate policy advice, which developed spontaneously. There were also discussions on the basis of staff papers on exchange rate policy advice by the Fund in general. These discussions did not lead to changes in the general approach taken by the Fund, however.

5 World Economic Outlook

Fund policy does not only manifest itself in Article IV consultations and Fund-financed programs, but also in publications. I will review briefly in the next paragraphs what the World Economic Outlook had to say on exchange rate policy. The World Economic Outlook (WEO) is a major publication of the Fund. Prior to publication, a draft WEO is discussed extensively in the Board. In the course of the year, regular informal 'World Economic and Market Development discussions' provide the Board with the opportunity to give further guidance to policy advice to major countries, in particular. The WEO has generally kept itself at a distance from explicit statements on desirable exchange rate regimes or exchange rate policies. But some statements can, nevertheless, be found in the WEO in the period under review.

In October 1986, the WEO writes that exchange rate changes are no substitute for the required policy changes; and in October 1987, that exchange rates and interest rates are market prices that cannot be controlled independently of the variables that determine them. Recognizing that more recently (Louvre, February 1987) the authorities of major countries had begun to include exchange rates in the range of variables whose evolution they seek to monitor and influence, the October 1987 WEO states that in the medium run, exchange rates respond to fundamental factors, relative inflation, fiscal positions, growth. In a shorter-run perspective, market intervention can be used to influence market conditions and monetary policy can be adjusted to alter incentives for capital flows. Short-run measures to influence exchange rates can be justified '... where there are firm reasons to think that the existing pattern of exchange rates does not reflect fundamentals. Otherwise, efforts to influence exchange market conditions may be ineffective or even counterproductive'.

In the following years, the WEO continued to abstain from commenting on desirable exchange rate regimes. In the May 1991 WEO a policy statement is given: rather than aiming at achieving specific exchange rate objectives, monetary policy in these three countries (United States, Japan, Germany) should continue to focus on the medium-term objective of reducing inflation while taking into account the cyclical situation prevailing in each country. The developments in the ERM were occasionally described. The crises in the ERM in the autumn of 1992, however, were extensively analyzed in an Interim Assessment of the World Economic Outlook of January 1993. The WEO added some policy advice: to reduce the risk of a repetition of the crisis, progress towards convergence will need to be reinforced considerably; and: to the extent that convergence is achieved only gradually, it will be necessary to undertake small realignments from time to time to avoid the build-up of larger, more disruptive adjustments. The same message is given in the May 1993 World Economic Outlook. However, the WEO also remarks that the ability of the ERM, as it has operated so far, to continue to provide its members with a stable monetary framework consistent with their broader economic goals has been brought into question by the recent exchange market turmoil.

The continuing exchange rate tensions in the ERM resulted in the decision of the monetary authorities of the ERM member countries, dated 2 August, to widen the bands in the Exchange Rate mechanism substantially. On 2 August, 1993, the Managing Director of the Fund issued a statement in reaction to this decision: 'In these exceptional circumstances', he said, 'it would have been contrary to the spirit of European cooperation to delay the reductions in interest rates that are in order, out of concern for the possible repercussions on the exchange rates in the exchange rate mechanism'. So far, the Fund had stressed the necessity and urgency of progress towards convergence, in particular in fiscal policies, to maintain the ERM, rather than reductions in (short-term) interest rates at the cost of exchange rate stability in the system. This statement seemed to place the Fund at a certain distance from this fixed exchange rate regime.

6 Final remarks

The Fund has, in the years since 'Louvre', persisted in passivity regarding desirable exchange rate regimes. This 'neutral' stance may be seen as consistent with the members' discretion to decide on their own exchange rate arrangements. Yet, the Articles of Agreement, which charge the Fund with firm surveillance over the exchange rate policies of its members and require it to promote exchange stability and avoid competitive exchange depreciation, give the Fund more room for manoeuvre. By not making use of it, the Fund has, in fact, continued to favour flexible arrangements in its surveillance. Criticism in the Board of advice to conduct active exchange rate policies may have helped to prevent a slide into Fund advice that might lead to competitive exchange rate depreciation. But the Board discussions indicate that at least a number of Board members, who argued for a fixed- but-adjustable exchange rate arrangement as an anchor for monetary stability, wanted the Fund to give priority to the promotion of exchange rate stability in its surveillance.

The Board could not find a solution for the differences of opinion about the approach to be taken by the Fund to promote exchange rate stability. This contributed to the ambivalence in Fund policy advice, which the review of Board discussions has also shown. Surveillance by the Fund, however, is not just advice on how to attain balance-of-payments adjustment or on how to promote economic growth. Surveillance is the task of the Fund to administer the constraints to which exchange rate policies conducted by the members of the Fund are subject. The Fund is the only global institution that is being charged by now almost all the countries of the world to promote exchange rate stability. This is the systemic role of the Fund. The inability of the Fund to give a clear content to its surveillance mandate may have contributed to the feeling that the Fund's main task had become that of financing adjustment and reform programs, making Article IV surveillance over industrial countries less relevant.

A decision by the Board in November 1991 contributed even further to this impression. The collapse of the centrally-planned economies of the Soviet Union and Eastern Europe, and, as a consequence, the many new and old members who came to the Fund for policy advice, technical assistance, and financially supported stabilization and reform programs overwhelmed the capacity of the institution. In November 1991, the Board decided to reduce the work on surveillance to its other members by limiting annual Article IV consultations to the major industrial countries and to program countries, and putting all other countries on a two-year consultation cycle. All smaller industrial countries and the majority of developing countries belonged to this last group. Thus, the exchange rate troubles in the Scandinavian countries in 1992 were hardly analyzed by the Fund or discussed by the Board. The ERM crisis of September 1992 surprised the Fund, too, notwithstanding clear warnings in the Article IV consultations with European countries that the European Monetary System's Exchange Rate Mechanism was under great stress. These developments were certainly a shock for the Fund. In November 1992, the regular Article IV consultation cycle was restored for all its members.

In my view, there continues to be a large role for monetary diplomacy to explain to, and convince, the Fund that it is important to re-assert the Fund's systemic role, and to consider once again the specific content which has to be given to surveillance. There is an additional argument to do this now. After many years of negotiations, the Uruguay Round of the GATT has been concluded: import tariffs will, over the next few years, gradually be reduced to facilitate international trade. Exchange rate stability will, therefore, become even more important, and so will the Fund's role to promote it.

The OECD and international economic cooperation

Pieter Stek

'Was anzustreben ist, ist weder eine Civitas Maxima noch die Anarchie souveräner Einzelstaaten, sondern eine internationale Ordnung in Freiheit, Genossenschaft und Gleichberechtigung.' *(W. Röpke, Civitas Humana)*

1 Introduction

In this brief essay I shall examine some of the major forces and conditions governing the effectiveness of the Organisation for Economic Cooperation and Development as a body for international cooperation. It is a pleasure to contribute to this volume in honour of André Szász, my inspiring first boss and a profound thinker on national and international monetary policy and its institutional framework as well as a wise and authoritative practitioner in these fields.

The OECD is an institution that is of practical relevance to a wide range of economic policy concerns of the governments of its member countries. This position is due to its mandate, its membership, its decision-making procedures and the experience gained over the past several decades in mutually gainful cooperation as well as, previously, in the OEEC. First these factors will be briefly described and then some of the challenges facing the OECD will be touched upon. I admit to not having defined the effectiveness of the OECD in a measurable way, but to basing myself on impressions and some inside acquaintanceship with the organisation.

2 The mandate of the OECD

The aims of the OECD, according to the first Article of the Convention establishing it, are to promote policies designed (a) to achieve the

For comments I am indebted to B. ter Haar, H.H.J. Labohm, E. van Lennep, A.D.M. de Loos, R.M. Pecchioli and J. Schuijer; the line of thought in the paragraph on the G7 owes much to writings of and conversations with E. van Lennep. Neither they nor my employer, the Netherlands Ministry of Finance, incur any responsibility for this text.

highest possible sustainable economic growth and employment, while maintaining financial stability; (b) to contribute to sound economic expansion in non-member countries too; and (c) to achieve healthy economic expansion of world trade on a multilateral and non-discriminatory basis in accordance with international obligations.[1] The following article is about means, including the avoidance of measures detrimental to others, efforts to reduce or eliminate restrictions on trade and services and current payments, and the liberalisation of capital flows.[2] Also mentioned is the importance of capital flows for development, including the need of the recipient countries for expanding export markets.[3]

The following points may be made:
- the ends and means of the OECD, as a set, are as appropriate a guide to governments' actions as ever; sustainable growth, the level of activity, efficiency, stability and external repercussions of policies or spill-over effects are all covered;
- the overlap with the Articles of Agreement of the IMF and with the GATT is striking; however, the OECD's stress on capital liberalisation has helped to carve out a significant policy-making role for it in its own right;
- the cooperative nature of the institution is writ large.

The Treaty content did not come out of the blue, but was based on the cooperative, liberalising framework of and experience with the OEEC, the Organisation for European Economic Cooperation, so highly instrumental in putting Europe on its feet again after World War II and particularly important for its role in restoring convertibility and multilateral trade relationships; in fact, the OECD became the torchbearer at the global level of a highly successful European endeavour, which had itself been catalysed by farsighted American generosity.

The OECD rapidly gained a special place for itself thanks to the way in which it made full use of the scope implicit in its objectives. It became the forum 'par excellence' for the critical analysis of and constructive proposals for what later would come to be called supply-side policies. In the OECD the terms positive adjustment and structural policies are part of the standard vocabulary. True, the all-encompassing nature of the OECD's involvement in economic policies – covering virtually all aspects of economic endeavour, from, for example, the application of information technology to the way healthcare systems are organised and including related societal issues – could, with a lack of direction,

1 Article 1 of the OECD Convention (14 December 1960) in slightly abridged form.

2 Article 2c and d.

3 Article 2e.

turn against it and make it amorphous. There is also a continuous need to beware of spreading scarce resources too thinly. By and large, though, the OECD manages to make its wide mandate a source of strength. Its so-called horizontal approach, establishing the linkages between different specialisations and competencies, forms part of its importance to national authorities. This is not to deny that the OECD knows its fiefdoms and empire builders. In that respect, it is similar to any national administration. But, on the whole, the Secretaries-General have been aware of this danger and contained it. The very nature of structural issues also explains that the OECD has never shied away from presenting longer-term policy orientations; even if political reactions may initially be hardly discernible, awareness has been created and this is invaluable for stimulating future action.[4]

Another operative notion in the OECD is interdependence. The application of this concept goes beyond the recommendation to avoid measures with negative effects on others; it is based on the recognition that the economic process, if managed sensibly, is a positive-sum game, which makes mutually reinforcing policies realistic rather than Utopian.

3 The members of the OECD

A further major source of strength of the OECD is the like-mindedness of its members. In principle, these are the industrialised nation states with a market economy, which in the past have tended to share a number of economic and political interests and responsibilities. The OECD codeword for the similarity of the members is their homogeneity. Indeed, the OECD, in practical political terms, was the counterpoise to the centrally-planned CMEA countries, each group vying for the political support of the developing nations. It was, and still is, seen as impossible for a country to be both a member of the OECD and of the non-aligned countries (the G77). As mentioned, the Convention distinguishes between the developing countries and the members who have a duty to export capital to them.[5] The geographical accident of their Europeanness, however, is what truly bound together the original European members, as can readily be discerned from the membership of Greece, Portugal, Spain and Turkey from the start. That explains why Article 2e

4 Influential reports have been: OECD (1977), Towards full employment and price stability, Paris (the so-called McCracken Report); OECD (1979), Facing the future: mastering the probable and managing the unpredictable, Paris ('The Interfutures Report'); OECD (1987), Structural adjustment and economic performance, Paris.
5 See section 2.

also mentions the developing member countries as legitimate destinations for capital flows.

An important fact about the membership is that the inner core of the eleven countries constituting the Group of Ten has a special position in the OECD in forming Working Party Three (WP3) of the Economic Policy Committee. WP3 meets four times a year, mostly at the level of the highest Treasury officials and the international directors of the central banks. Its regular agenda consists of reviewing the macro-economic situation and international adjustment policies. These meetings are particularly important for the understanding of each other's priorities and can help to prevent incompatibilities, as, for instance, at the time of the oil crises. WP3 shows that it is possible in the OECD to confine discussions on certain topics to major players, thereby helping to keep the institution attractive to them. At the same time, it shows that some are more equal than others, a political reality which becomes painful if one is on the wrong side of the fence.

4 The decision-making procedures of the OECD

The highest body of the OECD, the Council, which may meet in sessions of ministers or permanent representatives, decides by consensus, as do the subsidiary bodies. Important among the latter are the Executive Committee in Special Session, the Economic Policy Committee and the latter's offshoots, particularly WP3, all composed of high officials from the capitals. The basic structure of the OECD is well-known: the Secretariat led by the Secretary-General interacts with the various committees manned from the national capitals, each specialised in a field of competence of the OECD. The Ministerial Council meets once a year[6] and sets out quite elaborately the priorities for the organisation, which are implemented through a process of intensive consultation between the national capitals and the Secretariat. Besides issuing opinions, the Council can make recommendations to its members and take decisions which are legally binding for them unless otherwise stated. For instance, the acceptance by the Council of the Economic Outlook, or of any Economic Survey of a country, containing recommendations, constitutes a decision, shared by the membership as a whole, and by that token carrying political weight. Two very important decisions are the Code on the Liberalisation of Current Invisible Operations and the Code on the Liberalisation of Capital Movements.

6 Apart from this annual meeting, which is normally attended by ministers of economic affairs, finance and foreign affairs, specific ministerial sessions are held in other fields of competence.

They have a formal legal structure containing binding obligations for those members (by now all) that have voluntarily accepted them, from which temporary derogations are granted if reservations have been lodged or if economic circumstances justify this. Recommendations by the Council can – and usually do – follow from country examinations in the competent committees. Countries can, for example, be invited to repeal certain restrictions on capital flows.

An instrument, not based on the Convention, which circumvents the unanimity requirement, is the declaration by member countries of the OECD. Obviously, the major members and the great majority of members would have to adhere for a declaration to carry weight. A spectacular success, negotiated with great perseverance, was the Declaration on International Investment and Multinational Enterprises, including the so-called National Treatment Instrument[7] – itself based on a decision – and the Guidelines for Multinational Enterprises. The latter have basically become common law amongst the membership, which goes to show that a declaration can, in the right circumstances, be as effective as a binding decision.[8] The Trade Pledge, designed to prevent recourse by members to protectionist measures as a reaction to their balance-of-payments deficits arising from the oil crisis of 1973, was another example.[9] Notwithstanding these interesting legal developments, the basic structure of decision-making remains consensual with peer pressure to bolster it.[10] Given its mandate, the fulfilment of which does not require financial leverage such as the IMF has, this is not necessarily a bad thing. The main instrument of the OECD, below the level of generality of Article 2, is for its members to keep each other and the OECD informed, to consult continuously, to participate in studies and mutually agreed projects, and to cooperate closely.[11] This calls for consensus. The homogeneity of the membership, peer pressure and the understanding that positive sums are attainable have more often than not helped to overcome short-run differences in interests. It cannot be denied, however, that the quest for unanimity together with the publicity given to OECD decisions can, on occasion, be conducive to a certain fuzziness of presentation or, worse, the destructive use of the power of veto.[12]

7 Sets out the crucial elements of non-discriminatory treatment as between national and foreign investment in a country.
8 E. van Lennep, Secretary-General of the OECD from 1969 to 1984, gives an illuminating overview of this process of international law-making in his memoirs: Van Lennep (1991), p. 216.
9 Van Lennep, op. cit., pp. 223-224.
10 Van Lennep, op. cit., pp. 216-219.
11 Article 3 of the Convention.
12 Van Lennep, op. cit., p. 218.

5 The Codes, the CMIT and the Committee on Financial Markets; examples of the OECD at work

The Committee on Capital Movements and Invisible Transactions (CMIT) is the guardian of the Codes mentioned in the previous section. It regularly examines countries' behaviour under the Codes, presses for the abolition of reservations that have been lodged, and labours to expand the scope of liberalisation within the OECD area. The examinations are not a matter of give-and-take, of negotiation. The operative principles enshrined in the Codes are non-discrimination and progressive liberalisation. The latter principle is important because, apart from the temporary derogations mentioned earlier, there is no way back. Liberalisation achieved under the Codes is meant to be applied by OECD members to all the members of the IMF (Article 1d of both Codes). Reciprocity, while not completely absent from the Codes, does not lie at their base; the recognition that unilateral liberalisation is to one's own advantage does. In a businesslike way, guided by these principles, with the enormous repository of knowledge and analysis of the Secretariat behind it[13], the Committee has been and is a potent liberalising force on the global scene.[14] In May 1989 agreement was reached on an extension of the scope of the Codes to practically every aspect of banking and related financial activities, including short-term banking flows and cross-border services of wide description. More and more, the assessment of the application of the principles has become material rather than formal, basing itself on the existence or not of equality of competitive opportunity.[15]

In the Committee on Financial Markets, the underlying relationships and forces are dealt with that crystallize in national financial systems, and their linkages with international markets. The agendas and minutes of the CFM confirm the floodtide of deregulation and liberalisation that has swept the financial systems of the members of the OECD over the last twenty years. Never in my experience as a participant in the CFM was there an occasion on which a member introduced a more restrictive system (as opposed to partial, temporary expedients), let alone presenting it as a boon for his country and an example to the world.

In fact, the forces driving towards a market orientation of financial systems have been overwhelming. Traditionally, they are presented, with minor variations, as being technological innovation (computers and telecommunication), product innovation, internationalisation of

13 Directorate for Financial, Fiscal and Enterprise Affairs.

14 Pecchioli (1990), pp. 408-412.

15 Pecchioli, op. cit., p. 411.

business and the need to adjust to a more competitive financial environment, where long-standing market and institutional segmentations no longer hold sway. The large government borrowing requirements that arose in the aftermath of the first oil crisis themselves contributed strongly to governments' awareness that markets needed to be enlisted in their support rather than resisted. The needs of governments and the private sector could only be accommodated efficiently thanks to the creation of products and markets that reconciled the yield, risk and liquidity preferences of borrowers and investors. In historical perspective, the need for product innovation, enabling the unbundling of risks, was all the greater because of the dissolution of the Bretton Woods system of stable exchange rates and the high and variable rates of inflation that emerged in many countries in the seventies. Of course, it would be facile – and wrong – to present the market reactions as solely beneficial. During the unhappy decade of the seventies, but later too, markets and systems underwent shocks and upsets which were at times traumatic. The point to be made here, is that in the Committee on Financial Markets the discussion never took a retrograde turn towards market insulation or direct control over institutions or new financial products. Hardly any members failed to present the reforms of their financial systems repeatedly in the course of the years, explaining how they hoped to turn the challenges of opening up at home and abroad to their benefit. Experiences of market and institutional failures and thoughts on how to remedy or forestall them by improved market and supervisory structures have, hence, also been a major concern of the Committee. Basically, the question each member faces is how to develop sustainable, efficient and sound financial structures. The discussions and papers do not tend to be normative in tone. But it would be hard not to learn from the country expository papers and the questions they give rise to.

In sum, the CMIT and the CFM form examples of the OECD at work: on the one hand formal pressures, without coercion though, to provide market access and national treatment, on the other hand an as it were subcutaneous process of persuasion by fertile exchanges of opinion on the issues raised in Secretariat and country papers.

6 The Netherlands and the OECD

Open economies are relatively sensitive to shifts in supply and demand, external shocks and erratic behaviour of other countries. If not major powers, they seldom stand to gain from economic conflict as a solvent where interests diverge. On the contrary, for an equal starting position in global competition they need the rule of law. The multilateral organisations, particularly the IMF and GATT, embody important formal principles which, if upheld by their members, create fairness in the sense of the same rules being applicable to all. It has traditionally been regarded as being in the interest of the Netherlands to strengthen these organisations where possible and to defend the principles they embody against erosion. The same holds true for the relationship between the OECD and the Netherlands. It is obviously in the latter's interest to contribute as best it can to the fulfilment of the OECD's mandate and to adhere to its procedures. A factor strengthening the OECD is that its members have all become much more open, particularly to capital flows. These lie at the root of the tendency towards globalisation of business activities.[16] It is a truism and an understatement to say that the disciplinary force – both macro and micro – of free capital movements must not be underestimated. The challenges they pose lie at the heart of the OECD's mandate. Free capital flows and global linkages may be the best hope for sensible decisions by governments on how they conduct their economic policies and relationships. This being said, other challenges to the OECD are less obviously propitious.

7 Regionalisation

Trading blocs that internally consist of members with highly divergent levels of development may lead to a degree of trade diversion that outweighs the trade-creating effects. This can contribute to disintegrative tendencies in the world economy and political antagonism. The success of the Uruguay Round (assuming its ratification by all member countries) improves the chances that the present regional trading arrangements will not produce a downward spiral of this kind. Nonetheless, a situation of major structural shifts of supply and increasing unemployment in affected sectors, added to the fact that safeguarding and antidumping instruments have not been brought under adequate control in this GATT Round, still provides fertile soil for escalation of conflicts. If the world did develop in this direction in spite of the pressure resulting from free capital flows mentioned before, the OECD itself would be operating in an environment in which by definition its members would not be abiding by the cooperative spirit of the Convention. Clearly, the working of the OECD would be undermined.

16 The challenge of globalisation to the Dutch economy is discussed by L.A. Geelhoed (1994).

8 The OECD and the European Union

The relationship between the EC and the OECD has been an uncomfortable one. As explicitly stated in the Convention, the EC takes part in the work of the OECD.[17] The Commission has its own agenda in many of the fields in which the OECD committees operate. In cases such as trade and agriculture, it presents the Community position in OECD committee meetings unless such a position has not been established. Even then, not all member countries feel fully free to take individual positions. At the same time, when EC positions have been agreed these may rest on tortuous compromises. In both cases, the EC members of the OECD no longer are quite as interesting as partners in the discussion – such to the detriment of the OECD – as in fields where the EC has no competence.

The Netherlands as a particularly enthusiastic member of the EC with strong federalist leanings may on occasion be overindulgent to the Commission when this body wants to monopolise the presentation of views.[18] This would matter less if the Commission in all its manifestations could be depended on to take an outward and market-oriented view. This cannot be expected, however, given the divergences of interests of the members and, more fundamentally, the narrowness of the exclusive competence of the Commission, which is mirrored in its approach to the world. The perpetual struggle in the EC between, on the one hand, mercantilists and defensive protectionists and, on the other hand, free traders makes it a matter of self-interest for the Netherlands, not only within the EC to support the latter group, but within the OECD and other organisations to speak out in favour of these principles, which are directly or indirectly relevant to many issues, and not to allow itself to be gagged.

9 The G7 and the OECD

Van Lennep has on various occasions described how the Group of Seven tends to undermine the multilateral framework of economic cooperation.[19] Allegorically, the ruffians waylaying the traveller to Global Economic Bliss are: Bilateralisation, Politicisation, Short-Termism and Faddishness. The multilateralisation of balance-of-payments relationships and the solving of disequilibria by means of the tra-

17 Article 13 of the Convention.
18 Van Lennep provides the example of the UNCED meeting in Rio de Janeiro in 1992 in a lecture given at the Institute Clingendael in January 1993 ('De G7 en de trilaterale verhoudingen').
19 Van Lennep, op. cit., pp. 267-270. See also Van Lennep in: Blommestein (1991) and Labohm (1993).

ditional instruments of economic policy (monetary, fiscal and exchange rate policy and non-discriminatory trade policies) are put in jeopardy by bilateral deals aimed at solving bilateral trade imbalances (deals which in final analysis boil down to barter) and a politicised approach (which implies the application of pressure by the stronger to the weaker party). The free market is replaced by what bears more resemblance to a meeting between cavemen wielding cudgels.

There are indications that the G7, conscious of a lack of efficacy compared with stated ambitions [20], is trying to harness the staffs of the IMF and the OECD more thoroughly to the preparation and follow-up of its efforts. This is fully understandable and in part commendable. There is no advantage in overhasty or shallow decision-making by the most powerful nations. But at the same time, unless the G7, when using the institutions, is willing to operate within their legal framework, it will be undermining them. The institutions do not exist by virtue of their staffs but of their members. If the staffs become subservient to a subsection of the members, however important, the 'raison d'être' of the institutions as a whole will dwindle. In the longer run the quality of the staffs will suffer too.

A major challenge to the membership lies here. Formal equality in the law of the institutions is an asset of great value. It would be an illusion to believe that formal equality can do more than mitigate material inequality. However, formal equality, if accepted by the mighty, prevents manifest abuses of power. On their part this implies a self-denying ordinance. This does not entail a net sacrifice. It only means that they are enlightened enough to realise that they require legitimacy and that the full advantage of the positive-sum game of economic cooperation to maintain free trade and a favourable economic and financial environment, including stable exchange rates, can only be reaped in non-discriminatory legal frameworks.

The United States government realised this at the time when the multilateral organisations were set up, although Congress was more difficult to persuade. The US was the hegemon. Arguably, the US in relative terms is still the hegemon, although much has been made of its weakening over the last 25 years, certainly relative to other major OECD members. The overriding fact is that its major (potential) adversary has lost a large part of its power and that the parts of the world that are catching up in

20 Pregnantly expressed by the then Secretary of the Treasury in the Reagan Administration, James A. Baker, who, when asked what the G7 saw as its role in the international monetary system, responded that the coordination of economic policies in the G7 'is the new international monetary system' (cited by Van Lennep, op. cit., p. 65).

economic terms still lack political clout. Therefore, the political strength of the US has increased relative to its economic strength, which might tempt it to bilateralise and politicise issues. The ensuing losses in terms of legitimacy and of economic and political stability should, however, not be underestimated. Political cohesion once squandered, is not easily regained. The behaviour of the United States in the Uruguay Round appears to indicate that by and large the present government has become committed to strengthening the multilateral framework.[21] If this is so, the US may be willing to exercise its power within and through the institutions instead of by-passing their memberships. This is a goal other countries should strive for in their own interest, including the other members of the G7.[22]

It would imply in the case of the OECD that the membership accepts that restricted groups may be served by the Secretariat and meet within the institution. Ideally, such a group would consist of the G7 or the G10, plus, depending on the topic, a few other members whose opinion would be of relevance. In return, the restricted group would agree to the material from the Secretariat being made available to the full membership as well as a meaningful report of the discussions and conclusions. Given the publicity the G7 itself tends to seek, this can be no great problem. It may be more of a problem for the G7 to climb down from presenting the rest of the world with 'faits accomplis' to presenting proposals to competent bodies of multilateral organisations as well as accepting the essential role of the staffs in helping to set and prepare the agendas of meetings and supplying the participants with objective analysis. If the desire for legitimacy and effectiveness prevails among the G7, and the non-G7 make clear what guarantees they require in order to endorse such a framework, the outcome may be favourable. To achieve this the heads of the institutions should seize the initiative. In the case of the OECD, the Secretary-General should clearly set out the conditions under which the OECD Secretariat would be available to restricted groups. If he allows himself to be drawn into a position in which the OECD is no longer the instrument of the full membership, it will lose its rationale and its support.[23] It is an illusion to believe that an OECD reduced in status from an intergovernmental decision-making body to

21 In fact, this factor appears to outweigh the repeated declarations of the leaders of the G7 on the overriding importance of a rapid and successful conclusion to the Uruguay Round in explaining its ultimate success. Compare Labohm (1993), pp. 17-18.

22 Van Lennep has made abundantly clear that full participation of the European Commission in the G7 would not be an adequate substitute – neither from the point of view of Dutch representation nor from that of global cooperation.

23 The position of the IMF is in danger already of being weakened by the participation of the Managing Director in part of the meetings of the G7 finance ministers 'in his personal capacity'.

a think-tank will ultimately be more influential than think-tanks in general.

10 The future membership of the OECD

Pressure is mounting from within and without the OECD to expand the membership. This holds both an opportunity and a threat. Many countries from the American continent and Asia are developing into industrialised nations. Countries from Eastern Europe and the former Soviet Union are attempting the transformation from planned to market economies. Already a large number of OECD committees have granted observer status to Mexico, Korea, the Czech and Slovak Republics, Hungary and Poland with the prospect of future membership (in the Mexican case soon). Korea is knocking at the door. Russia wants to be associated. Other countries too are seeking links.

It is only welcome that the market-oriented policies advocated by the OECD have caught on in other countries. In fact, some developing countries may have become more determined and disciplined in applying these policies than some of the membership. It is by now widely recognised that policies and attitudes required for sustainable development are essentially the same as those required for sustainable growth anywhere – a sharp reversal of the development attitudes and ideologies of the 1960s and 1970s. Development is complicated, however, not only by the tensions arising from poverty, but also by inadequate institutional frameworks. Once countries are ready, economically, politically and institutionally, to participate, they should be admitted into the OECD, but not before (the requirement of unanimous cooptation clearly creates a sizeable threshold). Global interdependence requires efficient global contacts between authorities. However, management of and by consensus becomes no easier as the membership expands. Therefore, the crucial precondition for admission should be that the homogeneity of the OECD is not eroded.[24] The threat is that political pressures will lead to premature links which would undermine the OECD's effectiveness and authoritativeness.

The issue is complicated by the fact that a number of major players at the global level, such as China, by now have a strong global economic impact. The OECD, in order to remain focused on the major global

24 A condition for effectiveness of the OECD of a lower order, but highly sensitive, is that the membership no longer should meet in pleno on many issues but that, if voluntary means do not suffice, rotation should be applied or constituencies should be formed for the meetings to remain manageable.

issues, must draw these countries into its analysis and establish contacts with them. This kind of contact should, however, be sharply distinguished from being a prelude to membership. Being a major player should be neither a necessary nor a sufficient condition.

11 Conclusion

The OECD originated in a day when the principles it stands for were not brought into practice among its members to anywhere near full extent. Trade relationships were still to become much more intensive; capital movements were widely subject to controls; financial markets were tightly regulated. In short, the industrialised market economies, while closely knit in their contrast to the developing nations and the centrally-planned economies, still had far to go for competitive markets to become the norm. By now, much has been achieved, initially due to the forces of technological innovation, communication and increased awareness on the part of governments of the benefits of competition. The OECD, the IMF, the World Bank and the BIS have, each in its own way, provided the intellectual underpinning of, and a forum for debate on, constructive policy reactions to events, even where policies themselves in some cases initially rather partook of the nature of exogenous shocks than of a concern for global prosperity. The multilateral institutions in this manner have fulfilled an invaluable role.

Now, almost half a century after the establishment of the Bretton Woods institutions and more than 30 years after that of the OECD, the question might arise whether the OECD has outlived its usefulness. After all, the development of global markets, driven by the free flow of capital, appears to be almost unstoppable. The preceding sections have brought to the fore some of the major challenges facing the OECD. Looked at from a slightly different angle, these same challenges, if dealt with wrongly, threaten the ideal of free global competition within a framework of law establishing equality of competitive opportunity. The threats of bilateralisation, politicisation and regionalisation imply that allocative efficiency and a dynamic for sustainable growth may be even more at risk than before. Spill-over effects may be dealt with constructively or stupidly. It would appear that the OECD is as necessary as ever as a forum for the continued search for mutually beneficial policies. Under strong leadership it could retain a uniquely valuable position beside the IMF and the – it may now be hoped – imminent World Trade Organisation. The OECD is unsurpassed as a forum for effective intergovernmental consultation and decision-making, thanks to its wide mandate and the homogeneity of its membership. The OECD's homogeneity is of value in allowing it to focus the views of the industrialised nations with respect to the developing nations and global issues such as the environment: there is no other organisation in which the industrialised nations can set their own agenda.

It is in the interest of the Netherlands to further the OECD and its aims actively. If the benefits of the OECD are taken for granted by the international community, the challenges it faces will turn into threats. If dealt with casually, the OECD could see its position as an intergovernmental decision-making body erode. However, if wisdom prevails among the membership and the institution itself holds firm in protecting its mandate, it will continue to be a major agent for shaping an integrated global economy governed by market forces at the micro-level and by cooperation between the authorities of the member countries in creating in support a framework flexible enough to meet the challenges of the day.

References

Bakker, A.F.P. (1990), *De internationale financiële instellingen,* NIBE series: Bank- en Effectenbedrijf, no. 28.

Bröker, G. (1989), *Competition in banking,* OECD, Paris.

Geelhoed, L.A. (1994), Uitdaging voor het sociaal-economisch bestel, *Economisch Statistische Berichten.*

Labohm, H.H.J. (1993), *G7: economic summits, a view from the lowlands,* Clingendael Memorandum.

Van Lennep, E. (1991), *Emile van Lennep in de wereldeconomie, herinneringen van een internationale Nederlander,* Leiden.

Van Lennep, E. (1991), Institutional aspects of international economic policy cooperation and coordination, in: *H.J. Blommestein (ed.) (1991), The reality of international economic policy coordination,* Amsterdam.

OECD (1960), *Convention on the Organisation for Economic Cooperation and Development,* Paris.

OECD (1993), *Code of liberalisation of capital movements,* Paris.

OECD (1993), *Code of liberalisation of current invisible operations,* Paris.

Pecchioli, R.M. (1991), Policies towards financial markets, in: *John Llewellyn and Stephen J. Potter (eds.) (1991), Economic policies for the 1990s,* Oxford.

Prudential supervision: a central bank function?

Tom de Swaan

1 Introduction

Pursuant to Article 107 of the Maastricht Treaty, the countries jointly striving for the establishment of an Economic and Monetary Union must ensure that the national central banks are independent of political influences where monetary policy is concerned. For a number of countries of the European Union (EU) this means a fundamental reconsideration of the structure and the tasks of the national central banks.

In the discussion on the tasks to be fulfilled by an independent central bank, the position of prudential supervision has also been a subject of elaborate consideration, not least because some national central banks enjoying a limited degree of independence are responsible for prudential supervision. An important question is not only whether this independence should also apply to prudential supervision, but also whether it is desirable that monetary policy and prudential supervision are vested in the same institution or whether this intermingling of functions may lead to undesirable conflicts of interest.

The discussion was fuelled by the collapse of the BCCI in 1991, which notably in the United Kingdom resulted in debates on the role of the Bank of England in the supervision of this bank operating on the fringes of the international financial world. In the United States too, the position of supervision has already been disputed for a long time. There has long been a wish in the US to restructure supervision, which is currently very fragmented. To a large extent, this wish stems from the serious financial consequences of the so-termed Savings and Loans scandal in the second half of the 1980s, in which other supervisory bodies played a role, rather than the US central bank, the Federal Reserve System.

I am indebted to Prof Dr M. van Nieuwkerk,
Mr A.A. van 't Spijker and
Mr S.G.A. Kaatee for comments on an
earlier version of this essay.

Lastly, the crumbling of centrally-planned economies in Eastern Europe and the former Soviet Union, and the attending process towards independence in the financial sector, have also led to a fundamental reconsideration in these countries of the role to be played within the framework of prudential supervision by the newly organized central banks.

2 The role of the Nederlandsche Bank with regard to supervision

2.1 *Development of the banking system*

In the last century, the Nederlandsche Bank acted notably as a commercial bank and also performed tasks related to the banknote charter. In the 1860s, the Bank was the first institution to open an office network throughout the Netherlands in order to be able to expand its activities on a national scale. The motives underlying the establishment of such a network were political: when the charter was transformed into the first Bank Act, a stipulation was included stating that the Nederlandsche Bank was to have an office in each province. As a result, the Nederlandsche Bank was the only financial institution with activities on a national scale.

The other banks had a local character, with the exception of firms oriented towards international trade, which had establishments in some foreign centres. It was only at the end of the 19th century that the private banking system began to blossom. In the period of 1884 to 1913, no fewer than 139 commercial banks with the legal structure of a 'naamloze vennootschap' (a public limited company) were established in the Netherlands; an average of 7 per year. In general, this concerned small-scale and, consequently, vulnerable enterprises. In addition, many banks were characterized by incompetent management. At the end of 1913, 42 of the 139 newly established banks had disappeared; 4 as a result of mergers with other banks, 38 by liquidation. The four major commercial banks, of which three were established in the West and one in the East of the country, only started to spread their wings outside their place of establishment after 1910. Before that time, the Rotterdamsche Bank, for instance, did not have a single office outside Rotterdam. The next few years were characterized by rapid concentration within the banking system. This trend manifested itself not so much by eye-catching mergers, but notably by take-overs of smaller enterprises by larger banks, a tendency which continued until the major merger wave in the 1960s. The concentration tendencies within the banking system changed the character of the Nederlandsche Bank. The Bank increasingly evolved into a bankers' bank; an institution to which the banks could resort in case they needed liquidity. In 1915, the share of banks in the total of discounts by the Nederlandsche Bank had risen to 92 per cent, against 75 per cent in 1890.

2.2 *Origins of supervision*

This change in the position of the Nederlandsche Bank gave rise to banking supervision. From the banking system's intensive use of the discount facilities of the Nederlandsche Bank, the latter could derive not only the right but also the duty to increasingly play the role of supervisor. This is illustrated by a memorandum of the Nederlandsche Bank of 16 June 1927 stating that 'in case a large private bank would face difficulties – which so far had only happened very sporadically in the Netherlands – a major run might arise on such a bank, which could result in that bank's failure. This would cause damage, not only to creditors and depositors but also, and maybe to an even greater extent, to debtors, who have founded their business on their lending from the institution. Consequently, in view of general stability and the public interest, the central bank may have no option but to support such a bank, even though it would not have approved of the size and character of the business conducted by that bank. In this way the disruption threatening all the corners of the Kingdom may be prevented'. In fact, this statement already is a first signal of so-termed systemic risk 'avant la lettre'. The main motive underlying the Bank's position in 1927 was the serious crisis which had faced the Netherlands banking system in the 1920s. At that time, the Nederlandsche Bank had also acted as de facto supervisor.

Regular reporting by the banking system to the Nederlandsche Bank did not come into existence until the fall of sterling in 1931. At first, reporting was based on informal agreements, the major banks furnishing corporate data to the Bank. Already in 1932, however, reporting was given a more formal basis. As from that year, the Bank was able to gain insight into the nature and size of lending, and consequently the risks, by means of quarterly returns. After 1939, new problems within the banking system resulted in an increase of the reporting frequency, while the Bank was given authorization to have auditors conduct on-site examinations at credit institutions. After World War II, a legal framework for supervision was laid down in Section 9.3 of the Bank Act of 1948, which stipulated that it was the duty of the Bank to supervise the credit system. This duty was laid down in greater detail in the first Act on the Supervision of the Credit System, of 1952, which has been amended repeatedly over the years, to culminate in the present Act on the Supervision of the Credit System 1992.

The role of the Nederlandsche Bank with regard to supervision has ensued quite naturally from its function as bankers' bank and the related function as lender of last resort. The function of provider or redistributor of liquidity resulted in the wish to be able to assess the soundness of borrowers. In the course of time, this has evolved – partly as a result of crises within the banking system – into supervision as we know it today.

3 The organization of supervision in a number of other countries

In a large number of countries supervision is organized in the same manner as in the Netherlands, with the monetary authority bearing responsibility for prudential supervision. In this connection it is noteworthy that notably in the countries of Eastern Europe and the former Soviet Union, where central banks are only now being remodelled after the Western pattern, prudential supervision is now in all cases being accommodated with the restructured central bank. In some other countries a division is created between prudential supervision on the one hand, and monetary policy on the other (see table). It should be kept in mind, however, that in practice, this division is not always clear-cut. The situations in Germany and the United States are described briefly, while attention is also paid to the envisaged organization at the European level.

3.1 *Germany*

In Germany, the Berlin-based Bundesaufsichtsamt für das Kreditwesen (BAK) bears primary responsibility for supervision. This institution, which is an independent division of the Ministry of Finance, develops regulations and monitors the implementation of supervisory policy. It must be taken into account, however, that, in all aspects, supervisory legislation provides for cooperation between the supervisory authority and the Bundesbank. The law stipulates that the two institutions 'should communicate to each other any observations and findings which may be of significance for the performance of their functions'. This means that the BAK requires prior permission from the Bundesbank for issuing solvency and liquidity directives and that the central bank must be consulted on other supervisory directives.

Table Division of responsibilities between monetary and supervisory institutions in the G10 countries

Country	Monetary	Supervision	Type
Belgium	Nationale Bank van België	Commissie voor het Bank- en Financiewezen	s
Canada	Bank of Canada	Office of the Superintendent of Financial Institutions	s
France	Banque de France	Banque de France/ Commission Bancaire	c
Germany	Deutsche Bundesbank	Bundesaufsichtsamt für das Kreditwesen/ Deutsche Bundesbank	s/c
Italy	Banca d'Italia	Banca d'Italia	c
Japan	Bank of Japan	Ministry of Finance/ Bank of Japan	s/c
Netherlands	De Nederlandsche Bank	De Nederlandsche Bank	c
Sweden	Sveriges Riksbank	Finansinspektionen	s
Switzerland	Schweizerische National-bank	Eidgenossische Bankenkommission	s
United Kingdom	Bank of England	Bank of England	c
United States	Federal Reserve	Office of the Comptroller of the Currency/ Federal Reserve/ State Governments Federal Deposit Insurance Corporation	s/c
Memo:			
Luxembourg	Institut Monétaire Luxembourgeois	Institut Monétaire Luxembourgeois	c

s= segregated
c= combined

The BAK exercises supervision through the regional Landeszentralbanken. These banks effect daily supervision, collect and analyze data and conduct on-site examinations. The consequent measures, tailored to individual credit institutions, are taken by the BAK. In practice, these measures are based on the recommendations presented by the regional supervisors of the Bundesbank. In implementation of this supervisory function, one of the members of the Directorate of the Bundesbank is responsible for supervision.

3.2 *United States*

In the US, system of prudential supervision is determined to a large exent by the dual character of the banking system, which distinguishes between banks organized at a federal level and banks organized at the level of individual states. In contrast to continental Europe, a distinction is also made between deposit-taking banks and securities banks. This distinction, which has both a legal and a functional basis, has contributed to the existence of an exceptionally large number of institutions responsible for supervision. In the case of banks organized at a federal level, supervision is effected by the Office of the Comptroller of the Currency (a subdividion of the US Treasury) in cooperation with the central bank (the Federal Reserve). Supervision of banks organized at the level of individual states is the responsibility of the local supervisor. In a large number of cases, the twelve regional banks of the Federal Reserve are responsible for supervision in their respective districts. The Federal Reserve supervises banks organized as holding companies, the legal structure of virtually all majors US banks operating on an international scale. The same applies to US branches of foriegn banks since the entry into force of the Foreign Bank Supervision Enhancement Act in 1991. It is not surprising that, in the past few decades, this fragmented character of supervision has repeatedly been the subject of discussions on the organization of supervision in the US.

3.3 *The Maastricht Treaty*

In the preparations for the Maastricht Treaty and the Statute of the European Central Bank (ECB) incorporated in the Treaty, the role of the latter institution with regard to prudential supervision has been discussed elaborately. Differences in the organization of supervision in the countries of the EC which have become evident from these discussions, are reflected in the manner in which the ECB's supervisory task has been regulated. In addition to the main objective of maintaining price stability, one of the tasks assigned to the ECB is to promote the adequate functioning of the payments system (Article 105.2) and to assist the monetary authorities in pursuing an adequate policy with regard to prudential supervision of credit institutions and the stability of the financial system (Article 105.4). Operational supervision will remain the province of the bodies operating at the level of the individual Member Sates.

The ECB is entitled to make recommendations, either on request or of its own accord, to the relevant Community institutions and bodies and to national authorities. Article 105.6 leaves room for an expansion of the role of the ECB with regard to prudential supervision in the future. Pursuant to this article, the Council may, at the suggestion of the Commission, after having consulted the ECB and having obtained the approval of the European Parliament by common consent, decide to assign specific policy tasks to the ECB in the field of prudential supervision. This would include credit institutions and other financial institutions, but exclude insurance companies. This article recognizes the possibility that the development of the European economic and monetary unification may be such that the system of individual responsibility of countries with regard to prudential supervision may be deemed inadequate to safeguard the stability of the financial system within the Community and/or insufficient to create the necessary level playing field.

4 Developments in the financial sector

In the 1980s, developments in the international financial markets took place at a rapid pace. Both the markets and the conduct of market par ties have changed. The driving forces behind these changes are usually characterized by the following key words: internationalization, liberalization, deregulation and technological innovation. Internationalization means that enterprises have progressively extended their activities across national frontiers. International money flows have increased markedly and new markets and financial products have emerged. The disappearance of frontiers has resulted in stronger cross-border competition. Within the banking system, this has resulted in tighter profit margins. This pressure on profit margins was offset by a process of rationalization and increases in the scale of operation.

There was a new wave of take-overs and mergers , which, unlike in the 1960s, also concerned other sectors than the banking sector. The government's favourable attitude towards far-reaching deregulation enabled financial institutions to expand their activities beyond the boundaries of other financial sectors. Prominent developments were the liberalization of capital flows within the EC, the establishment of the internal market and the consequent increasing openness of financial markets, the relaxation of the so-called structural policy in the Netherlands[1] and the expanded opportunities for the securitization of financial assets.

Technological innovation did not only bring a further expansion of financial activities within reach, it was one of the factors actually giving impetus to such an expansion. Partly as a result of the high inflation level and the strong fluctuations in interest and exchange rates in the 1970s and 1980s, financial innovations were developed, such as variable interest rate loans and derivatives. The market for these derivatives has witnessed a spectacular growth in the past decade, in terms of both volume and complexity. For all practical purposes, the markets for financial instruments offer the participants unlimited possibilities to convert claims and liabilities from one currency into another in a rapid and efficient manner, as well as to change the interest rate type of such claims and liabilities. Consequently, unexpected changes in interest and foreign exchange rates may be passed on instantly to other segments of the financial market.

Due to the progressing economic integration and intermeshing, the complexity and mutual interwovenness of the financial system and the banks' vulnerability to developments taking place in respect of other market parties in other countries and other financial sectors, has increased markedly. On the one hand, this large degree of interwovenness of financial relationships enables the banks to cover their risks in a more efficient, and consequently less costly manner. On the other hand, however, these new markets and instruments also entail new risks. These risks have prudential aspects in that banks are confronted with new risks and increased interest rate sensitivity.

In this connection, macro-prudential risks, which are currently in the public eye, are also important. These risks are connected with the interrelation between market parties and markets as a result of which a break in the chain of transactions at one market participant may have domino effects world-wide. This potential break in the chain of transactions has underlined the importance of a more solid complementarity of and mutual relationship between micro and macro-pru-

1 By means of this structural policy the authorities can influence market relationships in the financial sector. The main legal instrument to this end is the declaration of no-objection that is needed prior to acquiring a participation in or by a commercial bank.

dential supervision. The latter has always been one of the tasks of a central bank. Interest in this aspect seems to have been fuelled by the strong growth of new financial instruments and new financial strategies introduced at banks and other financial institutions, which have increased the vulnerability, non-transparency and instability of financial markets. These elements are the sources underlying system risks. Consequently, the macro-prudential aspect of the tasks performed by the central bank – safeguarding the stability of financial markets – has become more important. By way of mutual agreements, central banks attempt to prevent this type of systemic risk and, naturally, to control it as much as possible. Within this framework, the central bank has one important tool at its disposal: the information obtained with regard to payments and clearing systems in its capacity as lender of last resort. As there is unambiguous support for accommodating this lender-of-last-resort function with the central bank, the responsibility for macro-prudential supervision is generally considered a typical product of central banking.

It is of great importance that tasks on account of the function of lender of last resort, on the one hand, and those on account of the function of banking supervisor, on the other, are accommodated within one institution. The reason is threefold. Firstly, practice has shown that liquidity problems may be an (early) signal of coming financial collapse. Experience has taught us that counterparties of a threatened bank already adopt a cautious attitude with regard to loans and lending conditions at an early stage. Secondly, central bank involvement is a prerequisite for controlling a banking crisis. The reason is mainly that at critical moments, the danger of fanning out and passing on liquidity and solvency problems at an individual institution to other market parties is far from imaginary. At such moments, it is in the interest of the stability of financial markets that an independent agent, who is also (closely) involved in the supervision of market parties, plays a role in solving the crisis. Lastly, interaction takes place between tasks aimed at preventing systemic risks and the supervision of the soundness of individual market parties. Recent developments in the financial markets have even stressed the importance of benefiting to the fullest from this interaction.

5 Arguments in favour of and against segregation of monetary policy and prudential supervision

In view of the wish to accommodate macro-prudential and micro-prudential supervision within one institution, it must be considered whether arguments from the viewpoint of monetary responsibility may be put forward which would support or obstruct its realization.

There are three traditional arguments in favour of combining responsibilities.

a To a large extent, prudential supervision ensues from the central bank's function of bankers' bank and therefore from the primary function of a central bank.

b The central bank can use its expertise in the field of monetary policy for supervisory purposes and vice versa.

c To a large extent, the two functions are based on data obtained from the same source: the banking system; segregation of the two responsibilities will lead to inefficiencies in the field of information supply.

The traditional arguments against combining responsibilities may be distinguished into several categories.

a The objectives of monetary policy and prudential supervision may be incompatible. This may be the case in both directions. Changes in monetary policy, and tightening in particular, may aggravate the situation at banks facing difficulties. On the other hand, pressure may be exerted from the angle of macro-economic policy to use prudential instruments to influence the banking system's lending operations subsection 5.1).

b Prudential supervision does not guarantee that no failures occur. Failures inevitably cause public and political discussions on the organization of supervision, which may undermine the status of the central bank and consequently its authority in the monetary field (subsection 5.2).

c If the responsibilities for both monetary policy and prudential supervision are assigned to the central bank, this may result in an excessive concentration of power within one institution. (subsection 5.3).

5.1 *Conflicts of interest*

In principle, conflicts of interest may arise when decision-making by the monetary authority is influenced by considerations of a prudential nature, consequently endangering the realization of the monetary target variable. This conflict of interest seems more imaginary than real. Examples of liquidity supply to the financial sector based on prudential considerations, at a scale and a rate which are not in accordance with monetary policy, are very limited and in nearly all cases concern such short-term arrangements that they hardly, if at all, endanger the achievement of the final target variable of monetary policy (growth of a monetary aggregate or exchange rate stability).

Moreover, the question is whether, in such cases, interests should not be weighed. A case in point is a calamity in the financial sector of such a magnitude that a serious disruption of economic development must be feared. In that case, it is essential to consistently weigh a (temporary) deviation from the monetary target variable against preserving the soundness of the banking sector. This balancing of interests will have to take place, irrespective of whether the relevant responsibilities are vested in one or more institutions. In that case, the argument in favour of segregation is not whether there is a conflict of interest between monetary policy on the one hand and prudential supervision on the other, but whether, under circumstances as described above, such a weighing should be effected by a number of institutions, including the central bank, or by the central bank alone.

Another type of conflict of interest may arise when prudential instruments are used to attain macro-economic goals. Cases in point are less stringent solvency requirements for some kinds of lending, without this being legitimized by a lower risk profile of such loans. The question arises whether misuse of prudential instruments for attaining macro-economic goals is not in fact restricted when the responsibility for using such instruments is in the hands of the independent central bank. The risk of the government attempting to influence the direction of lending by means of supervisory instruments is greater when a government institution with close ties to the central government is responsible for prudential supervision than when this responsibility is assigned to such an independent central bank.

Moreover it can be questioned whether the assumed problems with regard to conflicting interests will not get a different dimension within the context of the development of EMU. With the introduction of a single currency, the responsibility of national central banks for monetary policy will be taken over by the European Central Bank. However, primary responsibility for prudential supervision will remain the province of the national supervisors. If, in the present situation, undesired mutual influencing occurs, which as we saw before is highly unlikely, this will be even less of a threat if monetary policy will be in the hands of the ECB. Pursuant to Article 105.5, however, the ECB will be able to assist the monetary authorities in pursuing an adequate policy in case of serious developments taking place at credit institutions under supervision which might endanger the stability of the system.

5.2 *Risk of failures*

The status of the prudential supervisor is always undermined when an institution under supervision fails. Irrespective of whether the supervisory task has been assigned to the central bank or to another institution, a supervisor can never guarantee that no failures will occur.

In the Dutch situation, failures of institutions under supervision have been very rare. The two most salient calamities, the failure of the banking firm Teixeira de Mattos in 1966 and that of the Tilburgsche Hypotheekbank in 1982, fuelled intensive discussions in the press and parliament, and both led to a reconsideration of supervisory practice. The question is, however, to which extent these discussions have influenced the status of the central bank with regard to the implementation of other tasks assigned to it. Neither in publications nor in parliamentary discussions following the above calamities was the authority of the Nederlandsche Bank with respect to the implementation of its other tasks ever doubted, either nationally or internationally. These problems have, however, underlined the Bank's duty to perform its supervisory task with great accuracy and to make society understand the scope, and consequently the limitations, of supervision.

This is illustrated by a legal case involving the Bundesbank which made headlines in the 1970s. Despite the segregation of responsibilities in the German Federal Republic, the Bundesbank was summoned to court as a result of the failure of the Herstatt bank. In the lower courts, the Bundesbank was initially ordered to pay damages, on account of the fact that, in its capacity, the Bundesbank had been aware of the intended closure of Herstatt, but had not drawn any conclusions from its knowledge with respect to clearing and was consequently held responsible for failing to inform the institutions participating in the clearing of the intended closure.

5.3 *Concentration of power*

The higher the degree of independence of a central bank responsible for both monetary policy and prudential supervision, the more intense the character of the discussion with regard to concentration of power will be. In a number of European countries, this discussion has taken place recently as a result of the amendment of legislation with regard to the tasks of the national central banks. This amendment has ensued from the translation of Article 107 of the Maastricht Treaty into national law. Article 107 stipulates, among other things, that a central bank is not allowed to demand or accept instructions on the part of, for example, the national government within the framework of the exercise of its powers and the performance of its tasks and duties pursuant to the Maastricht Treaty and the Statute of the European System of Central Banks. De facto, this means that in those countries where monetary policy is determined solely by the government, or by the government in cooperation with the central bank, legislation must be amended at the latest at the date of establishment of the ESCB in such a manner that the latter is assigned the sole responsibility for monetary policy.

In the discussion mentioned above, the central issue was, on the one hand, the potential conflicts of interest. In countries where monetary policy has been the province of the government until the independence of the central bank, a conflict of interest at the level of the central bank is impossible by definition, as the latter is only responsible for prudential supervision. For our point of view on this matter, reference is made to subsection 5.1. On the other hand, the fear was expressed that vesting the responsibilities for both monetary policy and prudential supervision in an independent central bank might lead to an excessive concentration of power.

When considering the Dutch situation, it becomes evident that, de facto, the Nederlandsche Bank has a large degree of independence in the field of monetary policy. Although Section 26 of the Bank Act entitles the Minister of Finance to give directions to the Governing Board of the Nederlandsche Bank to ensure the proper coordination of the Bank's policy with the Government's monetary and financial policies, the Minister has never availed himself of this draconian measure since the entry into effect of the Bank Act, more than 45 years ago. Furthermore, this section will have to be scrapped from the Bank Act, in conformity with the stipulations of the Maastricht Treaty. Pursuant to Section 2 of the Act on the Supervision of the Credit System 1992, the Bank is responsible for the supervision of credit institutions established in the Netherlands. Consequently, the Bank matches the profile of a central bank which performs both tasks in a very independent manner and where a concentration of power exists or may exist.

In this connection, some remarks with regard to prudential supervision are due. We concern ourselves here solely with the supervision of credit institutions as the supervision of investment institutions has a different character. The degree of independence of the Bank in respect of prudential supervision is clearly bound to certain restrictions. Sections 2.1(b), (c) and (d) of the Act on the Supervision of the Credit System 1992 describe the Bank's supervisory tasks with regard to solvency and liquidity. In the Netherlands, the Bank is the sole authority responsible for this kind of supervision. Section 3, however, delineates this responsibility by referring to the EC Council Directives where solvency supervision, consolidated supervision and the size of own funds are concerned. Although this EC legislation entails minimum requirements, deviation from these Council Directives in their ultimate translation into Dutch legislation will only occur in exceptional cases. It must be prevented that the competitive position of the Dutch banking system will be curtailed as a result of the Nederlandsche Bank imposing conditions which differ too much from regulations in neighbouring countries.

One of the more conspicuous parts of supervision, the so-called structural policy, is performed in cooperation with the Ministry of Finance. The initial assessment whether a credit institution may hold participations in another enterprise is made by the Bank, which focuses on the solvency position of that institution and the degree to which the participation is in line with sound banking policy. In addition, the Bank checks whether the participation does not lead to an undesired development of the credit system. If the Bank is of the opinion that a declaration of no-objection can be granted, the Minister of Finance has the decisive vote with regard to the desired development within the credit system. This means that the decision with regard to issues of structural policy is a shared responsibility of the Minister of Finance and the Nederlandsche Bank and that ultimately the decision as to the structure of the financial system rests with the Minister of Finance.

The above does not detract from the Bank's large degree of autonomy with regard to the most important aspects of supervisory policy. It has already been noted that the Bank is responsible for solvency and liquidity supervision. Another important responsibility is the assessment of applications for authorization submitted by institutions wanting to operate as credit institutions and the attending evaluation of the expertise and reliability of potential bank managers. Moreover, the Bank is responsible for the implementation of special measures to be taken when a credit institution faces difficulties as a result of an actual inadequacy of solvency or liquidity, or a potential inadequacy in the opinion of the Bank.

The autonomy enjoyed by the Nederlandsche Bank in the field of supervision requires highly accurate decision-making and a willingness to hold consultations with the banking sector and the Ministry of Finance. Pursuant to Section 90 of the Act, anyone may appeal to the Appeals Board for Trade and Industry against decisions taken on the basis of the Act on the Supervision of the Credit System 1992. In addition, the Bank annually reports to the Minister of Finance on the implementation of its task. It is inevitable that such reporting is bound to certain restrictions. The prudence which the Bank has to exercise with regard to supervision is also reflected in the need for observing a sharply formulated secrecy obligation. The Bank can and will never disclose data on individual institutions and/or persons, unless it is required to do so by law. Consequently, the Bank is bound to restrictions which are sometimes considered oppressive, but which have to be accepted without concessions in order to ensure a relationship between the supervisor and the institution under supervision based on mutual trust, which is absolutely essential for supervision. It must be reconsidered every time, however, whether the report, with due regard to the restrictions mentioned above, meets the requirements imposed by law and society. This applies to both the contents of the report and the frequency of publication.

6 Conclusion

In 1981, the late Huib Muller, former Executive Director of the Bank dedicated his contribution to the essays in honour of his colleague Dolf Kessler to the pros and cons of vesting the responsibilities for monetary policy and prudential supervision in the central bank. He concluded that mutual influencing of monetary policy and prudential supervision is of such importance that it is desirable that the two tasks are performed by one institution.

In the past decade and in the early 1990s, the financial system saw fundamental changes. These developments may be summarized in key words such as internationalization, liberalization, deregulation and technical innovation. As a result of internationalization, institutions in the financial sector have experienced a growth far exceeding the nominal growth of the world economy. Deregulation and liberalization have strongly increased the mutual interwovenness of markets, while technical innovation has enabled the financial sector to serve and build up increasingly complex markets, both in terms of volume and of products. Banking supervision has adjusted itself to this changing environment, and will have to continue doing so in the future.

In addition to the traditional function of prudential supervision aimed at the continuity of the individual banks in order to protect the interests of creditors, supervision will increasingly focus on promoting the stability and transparency of the financial markets in the years to come.

The sustained link of this macro-prudential supervision, which is an integral part of the functions performed by the central bank, to micro-prudential supervision is the best guarantee for both tasks being fulfilled adequately. From the above, it may have become evident that the traditional arguments against combining prudential supervision and monetary policy do not obstruct such a link.

Payment systems and central banks

Jaap Koning

1 Introduction

The province of central banks extends to money in all its functions: as a medium of exchange or payment, as a unit of account and as a store of value. The use of money makes an essential contribution to the efficient operation of market economies. The function which money serves may still be described most graphically as that of lubricant in the economic machinery. This comparison is not, however, valid in all respects. When a certain grade of lubricant has proved its worth over a range of years, its quality is no longer called into question: it has become self-evident. For money, though used for centuries on end, this is, unfortunately, not the case. The interaction between money and the ever-changing social and economic conditions has not led to a sustained and controlled high level of quality. Apparently, the monetary authorities are confronted with a most difficult and complex responsibility in safeguarding the quality of money in the face of these shifting conditions.

The quality of money has a number of dimensions, which are to some extent interdependent. For the efficient and equitable operation of the economy, it is crucial that money should retain its value. Consequently, the primary task of central banks is the pursuit of price stability. They seek to achieve this objective in an indirect manner by regulating the quantity and/or price of their short-term lending to credit institutions. In this way, they attempt to control money creation, since credit institutions' short-term liabilities constitute a generally accepted medium of exchange. Another aspect of the quality of money concerns what might be termed its micro-stability. This relates to the quality of the institutions which assume liabilities of a monetary nature. In principle, these institutions must be able to meet these liabilities at any time. If the public has no confidence in this ability, money – or, more precisely, this kind of money – cannot, or cannot optimally, perform its functions within the economy. Micro-economic or prudential supervision to use the technical term, which is exercised in the Netherlands by the central bank pursuant to the Act on the Supervision of the

Credit System, seeks to create (and monitor the fulfilment of) such conditions as to minimize the risk of inadequate liquidity or solvency of credit institutions. This supervision focuses notably on the financial soundness of individual institutions. The last aspect of the quality of money concerns the infrastructure permitting money to make its way through the economy: the payment system. This aspect is not restricted to the physical quality of the infrastructure, but also extends to the rules designed to make for safety in traffic. Traffic jams and accidents may lead to brief or more prolonged stagnation of traffic flows, whose consequences have ripple effects extending far beyond the place of the original incident. Especially pile-ups in conditions of low visibility may have very grave consequences indeed. The role of central banks in regard of this aspect of money, the quality of payment systems, has remained underexposed for a long time, although the establishment of central banks in the last century was often directly related to payment systems.

2 History

The present statutory task of the Nederlandsche Bank with regard to payments is underlain by Section 9.2 of the Bank Act 1948. This subsection provides that the Bank shall service the banknote circulation and shall facilitate domestic and encourage external money transfers. The 1917 Charter of the Bank and the Bank Act 1937 already provided that, in addition to issuing banknotes, the Nederlandsche Bank had power to hold current accounts for its accountholders, to execute transfers to and from these accounts and to organize clearing with or between others. Viewed in its historical context, this statutory task did not differ fundamentally from those of central banks in other developed countries.

The explanatory memorandum to the Bank Act 1948 merely stated that Section 9.2 was self-evident. Apparently, payments had developed satisfactorily thus far. For a long time, banknotes had held a dominant position in payments, with transfers admittedly gaining in importance, though gradually and to a limited extent only and almost exclusively within the domain of the then Postal Cheque and Giro Services. The still highly decentralized system of cheque clearing between the numerous banks was effected at the agencies of the Nederlandsche Bank, the results being settled across the accounts held at the central bank.

Meanwhile, the position of the payment system within the economy has changed dramatically. First, the volume of payments has shown a gigantic increase. This has, of course, been in part the reflection of the growth of the economy. But there has been more to it. Whereas formerly payments had generally stood in a one-to-one relationship with commodity transactions or portfolio investments, the links between the commodity and the financial markets have become much looser over time. Under the impact of technological and commercial developments and the liberalization of financial markets, the number of transactions and, hence, the number of payments in the financial markets have grown much more rapidly than the volume of the underlying financial assets. This tendency has been strengthened further by the emergence of all kinds of derivatives, such as traded options, futures, swaps, repos, etc. An added factor has been that the amounts involved in these transactions are often far from negligible in relation to balance sheet total and capital base of the intermediating institutions.

Cross-border payments, too, have shown a major increase as a result of the ongoing removal of restrictions on international trade in commodities and services and, in recent years in particular, the liberalization of international capital movements. An apt illustration is provided by the turnover figures of Dutch banks in the foreign exchange markets: between 1986 and 1993, monthly turnover went up from just over Fl. 300 billion to about Fl. 900 billion. Yet another indication is afforded by the Dutch balance of payments: between 1984 and 1993, annual flows more than tripled to Fl. 2,600 billion. Whereas in 1984 capital transactions had been just over 40 per cent of current transactions, the corresponding figure in 1993 was almost 300 per cent. Thus, the conclusion is warranted that both the number and the overall value of payments have risen dramatically relative to the volume of the real economy (gross national product).

On top of all this, the nature of payments has also changed drastically since 1948. The role of banknotes is now largely confined to retail payments and trade in second-hand cars, cows and drugs and is even on the decrease in this very segment. Although the vast majority of retail payments is still being made with banknotes, a considerable and increasing number of these payments, in the Netherlands in particular, is being effected by means of transfers. At present, for retail payments, too, alternatives are available in the form of magnetic-stripe debit and credit cards. The smart card is now under development and has already been introduced in some countries. The evolution of financial transactions, as outlined above, has incidentally considerably depressed the share of retail payments in overall payments. In terms of amounts, transfers are now the dominant payment instrument.

The growth of transfers, notably in terms of the number of transactions, has produced major changes in the manner in which payments are processed, a development in which the opportunities offered by electronic data processing and data communication technology have been used to full advantage. Pressures for improving efficiency in processing have been acute and may be expected to intensify further. Initially, sight deposits at banks constituted a particularly cheap source of funding for the banking system, permitting the costs of payment services, which were offered as part of the same package as the accounts themselves, to be met from interest spreads. However, owing to competition from funds not involving payment services and their attendant costs, interest spreads on means of payment have narrowed considerably. This has generated a drive to come to a further reduction in the costs of payments, on the one hand, and a tendency to introduce charges for payment services as an independent product, on the other. Payment services have thus evolved from a spin-off of banking to a product in its own right, whose price and quality (speed) have become instruments in interbank competition.

In many countries, payment patterns are now dominated by the automated systems of banks, interbank payments being processed in automated clearing houses. The interbank balances and the large-value interbank payments are often settled in the payment systems and accounts provided by the central banks.

3 The powers of the central bank

How should one, under the present conditions, view the meaning of Section 9.2 of the Dutch Bank Act 1948, which, as noted at the time in the explanatory memorandum, was so obvious as to require no explanation? If we limit our view to domestic transfers, the Bank is charged with their facilitation. In this regard the Bank has in the first place the option to offer facilities itself, if it were of the opinion that this would facilitate transfers. This is what the Bank has actually done, offering possibilities for clearing and settlement, initially paper-based but now in the form of an automated system for interbank payments, providing a mixture of gross and net settlement.[1] Moreover, the Bank can attempt to encourage certain developments in payments through consultation, persuasion and inducement. In the context of the close contacts which the Bank traditionally maintains with the banking system in respect of

1 In a gross-settlement system, the individual payments are settled immediately and irrevocably. Net settlement involves netting out of debits and credits among the banks, followed by irrevocable settlement of the resulting net positions.

its monetary and prudential supervision policies, such a consultative set-up is seen as more or less self-evident. In this respect, the Nederlandsche Bank has focused on initiatives fostering the efficiency of the infrastructure of banks' payment systems from a societal viewpoint. In addition, the Bank has advocated the introduction of cost-effective charges for payment services, subject to the constraint of continued access for each citizen to this market. In its capacity as chairman of the Steering Committee for the National Payment system, instituted by the Minister of Finance, the Bank seeks to encourage the integration of the payment circuit of the banks and that of the Postbank (until recently the publicly-owned Postal Cheque and Giro Services) so as to enhance the efficiency and user-friendliness of the Dutch payment system. All these activities are captured by the umbrella phrase 'facilitate'. Only more recently did central banks begin to evince considerable interest in a number of other aspects of payment systems. It is typical of the novelty of the problems involved and of the similarity of the relevant developments in the various countries as well as, on the other hand, of the growing international dimension of payments that the central banks have addressed these issues at the international level in particular.

4 Payment systems in the international consultations

Just as, until recently, credit institutions viewed payment services as a complement to their sight deposits rather than as an independently marketable product, so central banks regarded payments as a technical and operational phenomenon rather than as an independent potential source of enhancing or diminishing the efficacy of monetary policy[2] and the soundness of the financial system. Their principal concern was to ensure the smooth technical operation of the systems, notably those administered by themselves. They also evinced an interest, though subordinate to their primary focus of attention, in the efficacy of the payment system. During the time of the transition from paper-based to automated payment systems, payments were the domain of computer experts. This was also reflected in the international central bank consultations, where issues pertaining to payments were initially handled exclusively by experts in the field of automation.

It was only in the early 1980s that interest in the policy aspects of payments began to assume larger proportions. This was evident from the

2 The effect of changing techniques in retail payments on the velocity of circulation of money and, hence, on the interpretation of the movements in the money supply has, of course, been monitored throughout.

establishment of the Group of Experts on Payment Systems of the central banks of the G10 countries. In 1983, it was given the status of a permanent consultative group and is now known as the Committee on Payment and Settlement Systems of the G10 central banks. The establishment of the group was prompted by the major technological developments and the tremendous growth of the volume of – notably cross-border – payments. Whereas initially the group concentrated mainly on taking stock of the payment systems in the various countries, its activities gradually assumed a more analytical nature, centring in particular on an assessment of the risks which payment systems may involve for the financial system as a whole. As is all too often the case, the growing awareness of the risks was especially stimulated by a few grave mishaps, such as the Herstatt affair of 1974 and the problems encountered by the Bank of New York in 1985. In 1990, under the chairmanship of Alexandre Lamfalussy, a committee set up by the G10 central bank governors issued a report on interbank netting schemes. The report formulated minimum standards for private interbank netting and settlement systems for cross-border and multi-currency payments in order to ensure that the associated credit and liquidity risks remain manageable; these standards may also be viewed as guidelines for domestic clearing and settlement systems. In addition, the report assigned central banks a role in overseeing their application in cross-border and multi-currency systems and formulated principles for the cooperation between central banks with respect to the oversight of such systems.[3]

At EC level, too, interest in payment systems has grown in recent years, owing not least to the emerging single market for financial services. In such an environment, differences between domestic interbank payment systems may impair the integrity of cross-border payment arrangements and distort competitive conditions. Moreover, additional risks may arise, likewise potentially impairing the integrity and stability of domestic and cross-border payment systems. In 1991, the Committee of Governors of the EC set up the Ad Hoc Working Group on EC Payment Systems to identify and explore issues of common interest to EC central banks in the field of payment systems. In addition to a description of the payment systems operated in the EC countries, the group has produced a report in which the private ECU clearing and settlement system of the European Banking Association was assessed against the minimum standards contained in the G10 report on cross-border and multi-currency netting schemes. The group also recom-

3 In 1993, the Committee on Payment and Settlement Systems of the central banks of the G10 countries published an analysis of possible central bank payment and settlement services with respect to cross-border and multi-currency transactions.

mended that, from the angle of oversight, the Committee of Governors should enter into consultations with the European Banking Association about the conclusions of the report, a recommendation which was adopted by the Committee. From a policy standpoint, the most important report of the Ad Hoc Working Group has been that on 'Issues of common concern to EC central banks in the field of payment systems'. Six issues were distinguished:

a the access conditions to domestic payment systems in connection with the financial and technical reliability of the participants and the magnitude of the associated systemic risks;

b the policy regarding risk management in payment systems;

c the implications of relevant national legal systems, bankruptcy legislation in particular;

d the technical and operational reliability of the systems, and their mutual consistency in this respect;

e the pricing policies of the central banks in respect of the payment services provided by them;

f the operating hours of the various payment systems.

Since the conclusion of the Maastricht Treaty, this EC Working Group has been active, basing itself on earlier reports, in preparing the ground for the common policy on payments envisaged for stages two and three of Economic and Monetary Union and for the future European Central Bank. In this context, the Working Group has formulated a minimum set of common standards for domestic payment systems, which has meanwhile been adopted by the Committee of Governors. These standards serve to provide guidance to each EC central bank in respect of the development of interbank payment systems in its own country.

As to the access conditions, harmonization is seen as desirable. The conditions must be clear-cut and transparent. Under the Second Banking Coordination Directive, remote access to domestic payment systems must be permitted to institutions from other EC countries which meet the conditions and are able and willing to observe the host country rules. The access conditions may also contribute to containing the risks associated with payment systems. Within this framework, the EC central banks advocate that participation in interbank payment systems should, in principle, be limited to (credit) institutions which are subject to adequate supervision. The stringency of the access conditions would have to be related to the required level of protection of interbank payment systems from systemic risks.

With regard to risk management, the Committee of Governors holds that, in the processing of large-value payments, more extensive use is to be made of real-time gross-settlement systems, settlement being effected at the central bank. This would facilitate delivery-versus-payment arrangements, thus limiting settlement risks. Within a few years' time, each EC country would have to operate such a gross-settlement system so as to reduce systemic risks. This would provide a sound basis for linking the central-bank-operated real-time gross-settlement systems into a decentralized interbank payment network for large-value payments throughout EMU in its final stage. To the extent that, in parallel with these real-time gross-settlement systems, large-value net-settlement systems would continue to be operated, these should shortly be required to meet the minimum standards set out in the 1990 report of the Group of Ten on interbank netting schemes. One of the requirements in this respect is settlement on the day of netting. As far as interbank systems are concerned which process low-value payments, the policies aimed at containing risks are left to the discretion of the individual central banks.

The report also mentions uncertainties within and inconsistencies between the national legal systems as a potential source of disruptions in the processing of payments. One important issue in this regard is the so-termed 'zero-hour rule' in bankruptcy legislation in some countries (including the Netherlands). This rule provides that all payments made by an institution on the day on which it is declared bankrupt can be revoked. It is clear that this rule creates major uncertainty with respect to the finality of payments. In the case of interbank payment systems in particular, this may lead to additional risks for the financial system. Through cross-border participation in the various national payment systems, these risks may also spread to other countries which do not have the zero-hour rule in their legislation. The report recommends that this rule should be abolished as far as interbank payment systems are concerned.

As to the technical issues, the report points out that, in order to facilitate cross-border payments, compatible operational standards and efficient channels of communication between the European payment systems are desirable. The EC central banks are prepared to support these developments. The central banks' pricing policies for payment services are, in principle, such as to seek cost-effectiveness. In the EC single market, pricing of these services is not allowed to lead to competitive distortions. Pricing policies will gain in importance when, in EMU, the various national central banks will offer payment services in the same currency. Finally, the report stresses the desirability of ensuring, where possible, overlapping operating hours of the interbank systems within the EC so as to facilitate cross-border payments.

5 The tasks of the central bank

5.1 *Interbank payment systems*

Reviewing the international discussion, it becomes evident that the central banks have shown increasing awareness of the risks which payment systems may involve for the financial system as a whole. Considering the volume of payments, intra-day and overnight exposures may be created between financial institutions which, in the event of counterparty default, may have major consequences for other financial institutions, causing the flow of the lubricant through the economic machinery to be interrupted for either a brief or a longer period of time. The gravity of the consequences depends on the magnitude of the problem concerned and on the reactions by the financial institutions and central banks. Where the central banks are concerned, their position as lenders of last resort is clearly involved here. It is essential for central banks that any recourse to their relevant facilities should actually be a measure of the very last resort. Thus they have a major interest in ensuring that the technical and procedural set-up of payment systems is such as to minimize the risk of recourse to their facilities arising from disruptions in these systems.

The central banks have reacted calmly to this growing awareness of the risks in payments. Initially, the central banks focused on stock-taking and on analysing potential problems. Subsequently, they took the process a step further by formulating a number of minimum standards to reduce the risks associated with those interbank payment systems which potentially involve the gravest dangers. Their analyses and standards have been published and made known to the financial community, thus contributing to an adequate appreciation of the risks as well as an awareness of the central banks' views among the parties involved. It is on the basis of these views that the central banks are seeking to intensify their consultations with the financial institutions on the issues raised by payment systems. Thanks to the close contacts which the central banks traditionally have with the institutions subject to their statutory powers regarding monetary supervision, and in many cases prudential supervision as well, the consultations with these institutions are usually relatively fruitful. Nonetheless, when assessing the costs and benefits of risk-reducing measures, the financial institutions involved may very well, on the basis of their own interests, come to other conclusions than the central banks. In most countries, including the Netherlands, the central bank lacks statutory power to impose, if necessary, certain measures in this area. In the latest adjustments of central bank legislation abroad, however, the recent developments in payments and the analyses of the associated risks have undoubtedly left their mark. This is poignantly illustrated by the Statute of the European System of Central Banks (ESCB), which forms part of the Treaty of Maastricht. Article 22 of the Statute reads as follows: 'The ECB and national central banks may provide facilities, and the ECB may make regulations, to ensure efficient and sound clearing and payment systems within the Community and with other countries'. Some EC countries, which recently adjusted their central bank legislation, have modified the task of their central bank to conform with this article. The principal new feature is the explicit power vested in the European Central Bank in respect of the security of payment systems.[4]

The question arises how practical effect can and should be given to this power. The reports of the Working Group on Payment Systems of the Committee of Governors of the Central Banks of the EC provide indications and recommendations in a number of respects, focusing notably on risk reduction in interbank payment systems. As far as efficiency is concerned, the reports are fairly reserved, presumably due to the role already undertaken by the central banks in this area. Generally, efficiency is best ensured if the payment systems are exposed to the operation of market forces. Within the constraints imposed by security, the investments in and the operation of payment systems may be safely left to the financial institutions concerned. In cases where increasing economies of scale would lead to near-monopolistic situations as a result of the interplay of market forces, it may be necessary for the central bank or a public fair-competition authority to guard the efficiency of the investments and to control access to the systems as well as the charges made to the ultimate user.

Any use of powers regarding risk reduction (soundness) of payment systems will invariably have to be underlain by an analysis of the risks associated with the systems. The key question in this respect is whether a disruption of interbank payments could have consequences for the financial system as a whole. The costs of regulation will have to be assessed against its benefits. The costs of risk-reducing measures may directly lead to higher production costs of payment services or may indirectly be reflected in the effects which can occur if regulation should detract from the operation of the market mechanism. Potential benefits may accrue from the fact that regulations aimed at reducing risks in payment systems may diminish the need for similar measures by the individual financial institutions themselves. A distinct benefit for

4 In addition, the European Central Bank and the national central banks are charged with the issue of banknotes.

the system as a whole would be the smaller risk of a (partial) collapse of the financial system and, for the central bank, the consequently lower chance of recourse to its lender-of-last-resort facilities. Whether all the individual participants in the payment system appreciate this benefit to the same extent as the central banks is questionable. This difference in appreciation constitutes the rationale for corrective action by the central banks. This does not, incidentally, detract from the fact that it is the individual participants in the payment system which bear ultimate responsibility for the risks associated with the payment systems in which they participate.

The foregoing makes clear that the position of the central banks may differ, depending on the type of payment system concerned. In this connection, a distinction is usually made between interbank systems processing low-value (retail) payments and those processing large-value payments. In low-value payment systems, credit and liquidity risks are limited, though not entirely absent because the numerous low-value payments may yet, on balance, give rise to considerable exposures among the participants. The technical risks may be considerable and may lead to serious temporary disruptions in payments. However, where such systems are concerned, marginal assessment by central banks, focusing on the continuity of processing, will generally suffice. If the systems are marked by monopolistic elements, attention will also have to be given to their efficiency.

In the case of large-value interbank payment systems, disruptions in processing may involve grave risks for the financial system as a whole, potentially giving rise to recourse to the central bank's lender-of-last-resort facilities. Consequently, the reduction of technical, liquidity and credit risks should be subjected to strict standards. In the view of the central banks, systems based on real-time gross settlement by the central bank, as a settlement agent of undisputed soundness, provide the best option from the angle of risk reduction. The fact that the central bank plays an operational role in such systems serves to strengthen its position in the event that it should be called on to resolve existing or potential problems threatening the financial system as a whole. A number of countries are already operating real-time gross-settlement systems, while in other countries, including the Netherlands, the central banks are working with the commercial banks to develop such systems or improve the existing ones. In cases where large-value payments are processed in net-settlement systems, these should at least meet the minimum standards formulated in the report of the G10 central banks. Intra-day credit facilities granted by the central bank may ease settlement of large-value payments; efficient use of such facilities may be encouraged by charging a price in the form of interest and/or a requirement to post collateral. The provision of such credit facilities and, in the last resort, liquidity support as well as the drive to minimize risks make it absolutely necessary for the central bank to have a profound insight into the probity of the participants in a large-value clearing and settlement system. Consequently, the participants will have to meet access conditions in terms of adequate supervision. The prevention and resolution of disruptions in payments will benefit if such supervision of the participants is exercised by the central bank.

5.2 *Payment instruments*

Finally, the question arises as to the role which central banks should play in safeguarding the integrity of the payment instruments themselves. In regard of banknotes, their role is clear: as note-issuing authorities, central banks have a duty to ensure maximum security against counterfeiting and a technical quality encouraging efficient use in payments (e.g. in automated teller machines). The integrity of the sight deposits at credit institutions which lie at the basis of transfers is safeguarded by the supervision which the competent authorities – often central banks – exercise over the solvency and liquidity of these institutions; as a safety net for depositors, many countries operate deposit guarantee schemes in one form or another. The instruments used to effect transfers are highly diverse: credit transfer forms, pre-prepared forms, electronic payment orders, diskettes, magnetic tapes, magnetic-stripe debit and credit cards, stored-value chip cards, etc. Owing to their very nature, most of these instruments are issued and processed by or in close cooperation with supervised banks. They do not involve any inherent risk for the financial system as a whole. Nonetheless, abuse or counterfeiting of these instruments may entail losses for individual participants in payment systems, and large-scale abuse or counterfeiting could well impair confidence in the financial system. However, the availability of secure alternatives and the losses caused by abuse and counterfeiting may be expected to ensure that market forces keep such phenomena within bounds. One element, though, which needs to be assessed is whether the market mechanism is sufficiently effective with regard to security. The same is true of the effect of market forces on the availability, the ease of use and the costs of payment instruments.

The position is more complicated in respect of stored-value or prepaid (chip) cards intended for use as general instruments of payment. In that capacity, they are functionally comparable with banknotes and coins. Technically, such cards may, in principle, be issued by any institution.

Likewise, the administration of the value embodied in the cards, the so-termed float, is technically feasible for any institution.

Putting it mildly, these activities closely resemble normal banking operations. The European central banks are currently considering whether, from the viewpoint of the protection of the participants in a payment circuit employing prepaid cards designed for use as general instruments of payment, some form of regulation might be required in respect of the issue of such cards and/or the administration of the float. The problem is less topical for prepaid cards which can be used for a limited number of spending purposes only, since such cards constitute no more than a form of buyer credit to the issuing institutions.

6 Conclusion

The quality of money and of the financial system in a country is determined in part by the quality of the payment systems. The task of central banks in this respect centres on containing the risks which disruptions in a payment system may entail for the financial system as a whole; in this regard, their attention focuses in particular on systems processing large-value payments. Under these conditions, the role of central banks becomes most prominent and at the same time exceptional if recourse is had to their facilities as lenders of last resort. Consequently, central banks have a major interest in being able to take preventive action by issuing regulations aimed at risk reduction in the organization of payment systems. In the interests of efficiency, they will have to act cautiously and in a market-oriented fashion. The international consultations among the central banks deserve credit for having ensured that, in recent years, central banks have in an orderly process become increasingly aware of the risks associated with payment systems, leading to an exhaustive inventory of the possibilities for controlling these risks.

A post-mortem of the debt crisis

Conrad J. Oort

1 Introduction

The oilshocks of the seventies and the debt crisis of the eighties provide a fascinating backdrop for some reflections on the role of central banks in (co-)managing the international financial system under exceptional circumstances. I will not try to analyze these episodes once again – there is little new to be said about events that have attracted more public and academic interest than almost anything in the financial history of this century, with the possible exceptions of the Great Crash and the fall of Bretton Woods.

Instead I want to conjure up some visions of what might have been. Science fiction in reverse, with a less than wholly serious intent. I shall briefly explore what could have happened if central banks had taken a different stand. One tale will follow the trails of the oil crises. If central banks had restrained the commercial banks, rather than encouraged them, to on-lend the 'oil surpluses' to deficit countries, particularly those in Latin America, what would have happened? Another, perhaps more subtle point, relates to the doctrines of full disclosure and 'mark-to-market'. If the authorities had demanded full disclosure of bank balances, with assets 'marked to market' – either directly or via their loan loss reserves – what effect would that have had on the stability of the international financial system? As an aside, how did commercial and central banks get away with the deliberate obfuscation of published bank accounts during the long period when write-offs (provisions) on third world debt were not only far below market discounts, but also lower than almost anyone's judgement of the likely losses that would eventually be incurred.

In his 1988 doctoral thesis, entitled 'Monetaire diplomatie' (Monetary diplomacy), André Szász described and analyzed Dutch policy vis-à-vis the oil crises and the debt crisis in some detail and in a far more balanced and diplomatic manner than I intend to do in the following pages. That is somewhat typical of our respective roles when we were both active players in the international monetary circuit in the seven-

Table 1 Current account balances of OPEC and non-OPEC LDCs during the first and second oil shocks

Billions of US dollars

	1973	1974	1975	1976	1977	1978
OPEC	6.7	68.3	35.4	40.3	29.4	5.7
Non-OPEC LDCS	-11.3	-37.0	-46.3	-32.6	-29.6	-41.9

Source: IMF, World Economic Outlook (data prior to 1977 are taken from 1983 volume; subsequent data are taken from 1985 volume).

ties. I have at times been frustrated by my inability to equal his acute sense of humour and his quick wit, but it was always good fun. I shall continue an old tradition between us and play the undiplomatic devil's advocate (or is it the ageing 'enfant terrible'?). Just to show the reader that I have learned some rudiments of diplomacy from my good friend Szász, I shall focus on central banks other than the Nederlandsche Bank. In many ways, the Nederlandsche Bank has played an active role in awakening the international community to the dangers of unfettered international bank lending under the guise of 'recycling' and in pushing for a more effective international supervision of banks. Szász' dissertation provides ample evidence of the Nederlandsche Bank's prudent approach. As my self-elected role is not to praise but to heckle, I shall pick on the other central banks of what was then called the 'industrialized world'.

2 If Cleopatra's nose ...

It has been said that if Cleopatra's nose had been just slightly crooked, the Roman Empire might not have fallen. We might all be speaking vulgar Latin today and Maastricht, rather than a codeword for European Union, would still be a sleepy garrison town in Limburgia, defending the Pax Romana. If Paul Volcker would have headed the Federal Reserve in the seventies, would the debt crisis have unfolded differently?

The first oil crisis erupted in a financial world that was already shaken by the break-down of Bretton Woods and by the profligate monetary policy of the US Federal Reserve. The former was arguably a blessing in disguise. Can one imagine the chaos that the oil shocks would have caused in financial markets if exchange rates had still been caught in the

1979	1980	1981	1982	1983
62.3	110.3	52.0	-13.5	-18.4
-62.1	-87.7	-108.3	-86.1	-52.1

inflexible harnass of 'fixed-but-adjustable' par values? I shudder to think of discussions on 'fundamental disequilibrium' and negotiations of new 'Smithsonians' in the context of the huge oil surpluses and deficits, whose future course seemed totally unpredictable at the time. Everything was unprecedented and uncertain: the absorption capacity of the oil exporters, the price elasticity of demand for energy and of potential new supplies, the future of energy prices, the capacity of financial markets to 'recycle' the oil surpluses. I vividly recall the lengthy meetings of WP3 of the OECD dealing with the 'unsustainable' balance-of-payments picture (see table 1).[1] Scenarios ranged from a continuously growing indebtedness of the non-OPEC world to the 'Coming oil glut' predicted by The Economist in a justly famous article published during the peak of OPEC power. Looking back it seems almost incredible that exchange rates did not gyrate more violently than they did and that capital markets accommodated the recycling flows as smoothly as they did.

Floating exchange rates probably helped, but US monetary policy surely did not. It created an inflationary undercurrent in the US and elsewhere, which the oil price explosions whipped into double-digit tidal waves (see table 2). It drove real interest rates down to post-war lows, at times even to negative rates (see figure 1). In doing so, US monetary policy undoubtedly contributed to the debt crisis by inducing developing countries to overborrow. It also led to the precipitous decline of the dollar, the number one world currency and numéraire of energy prices, which in turn led to, or at least contributed to, the advent of the second oil crisis (see figure 2).

1 I have not been able to dig up the projections that were made by the OECD Secretariat at the time, but I remember they looked far more frightening than what the actual numbers turned out to be (see table 1).

Table 2 Consumer prices

Percentage change from previous year

	1972	1973	1974	1975	1976	1977
United States	3.3	6.2	11.0	9.1	5.8	6.5
Total OECD	4.7	7.8	13.4	11.3	8.6	8.8

Source: IMF. The country weights used in the aggregate index are based on the private consumption and exchange rates of the preceding year.

Lax US monetary policy may have contributed to the debt crisis, but it did not cause it, nor could more restrictive policies have prevented it. Volckerian monetary policy in the seventies makes an unlikely scenario, for his strict foot on the monetary brake was politically possible only as a reaction to double-digit inflation in the preceding years. But let us replay history anyway and imagine a US conversion to monetary rectidude in the early seventies. The decline of the dollar would have

Figure 1 Real interest rates and LIBOR, 1975-1986

Per cent

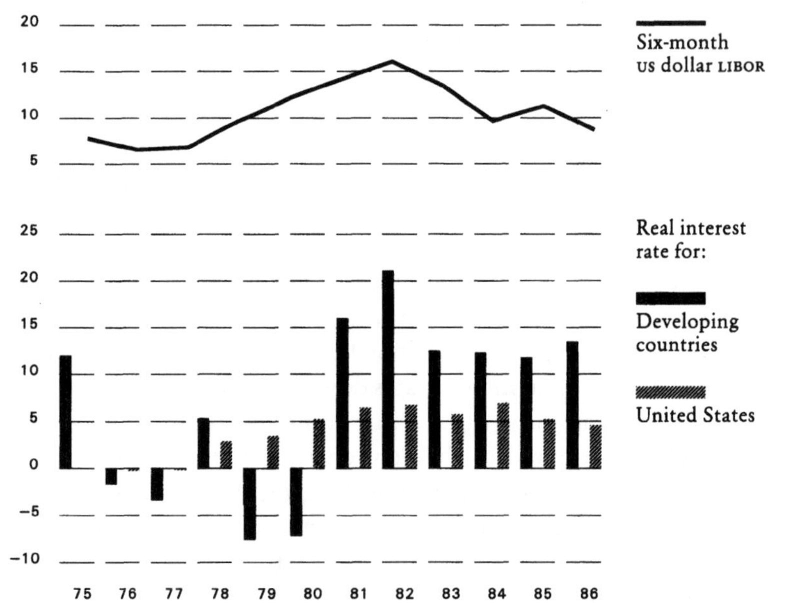

The real interest rate is defined as the six-month dollar LIBOR deflated by the change in the export price index for developing countries. The US real interest rate is defined as the six-month dollar LIBOR deflated by the US GDP deflator.

Source: World Bank, (1987), Developing country debt: implementing the consensus, figure box 1.

1978	1979	1980	1981	1982	1983
7.7	11.3	13.5	10.4	6.1	3.2
7.9	9.8	12.9	10.5	7.8	5.2

been stopped and possibly reversed, real interest rates would have risen, growth would have slowed down, and the demand for oil would have declined as a result of income as well as price effects. Oil surpluses and deficits would have been lower. For all these reasons third world debt would not have grown to the extent it did. But stricter US monetary policies would not, in and by themselves, have prevented the debt crisis: there still would have been large surpluses and deficits, with third world countries eager to borrow and international banks eager to lend.

After the oil crisis, the large international banks were swamped with deposits from the oil-exporting countries. This would have been the case in our imaginary scenario as well, albeit to a smaller extent. The eagerness of the banks to on-lend these funds was matched by the financial thirst of developing countries, particularly those in Latin America,

Figure 2 Exchange rate DM/US dollar

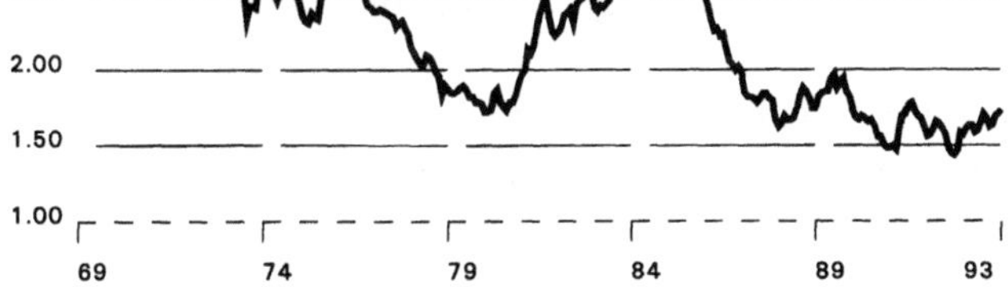

Source: Bank of International Settlements.

to finance the increased cost of energy imports or, in cases such as Mexico, to finance their over-ambitious development plans, boosted by the expectations of future oil revenues. Central banks did not initially put a break on such 'sovereign lending'; in fact, they encouraged private banks to do so as a means of recycling the oil surpluses. Could they and should they have acted differently?

On the basis of their national monetary mandate, their authority to restrict bank lending into the Euro-dollar market was limited at best. They could and did agree to refrain from placing official reserves in the Euro-currency markets, but they could hardly restrain the activity of domestic banks outside the domestic monetary circuit. The endless discussion on the inflationary potential of the Euro - currency markets, even if it had been resolved, could not easily have led to action.

If central banks, in their role of monetary authorities, could not and arguably should not have limited the recycling flows that eventually produced the debt crisis, they could well have taken a different stand as prudential supervisors. With the benefit of hindsight, the unfettered on-lending by the western banking system proved to be a major cause of the debt crisis. It kept the third world from adjusting rather than financing; it burdened the banking system with a heavy load of doubtful third world debt which, as supervisors, they should have prevented from building up. Figure 3 gives a clear picture of the run-up to the debt crisis: the non-oil LDCs incurred very large current deficits on their balances of payments and their external debt as well, as their debt service liabilities exploded. Central banks must have been fully aware of the impending disaster long before the private markets collapsed after the Mexican default in 1982. Table 3 shows that until 1982 financial markets continued to increase their exposure to the highly indebted countries, both long term and short term. The commercial banks were clearly at fault, but what do we have prudential supervisors for if they do not act when the financial system is headed for disaster? [2] (Needless to say, this diatribe is not directed towards the Dutch banks or the Nederlandsche Bank, as the former had relatively limited exposures to Latin America compared to most of the large money center banks in the US.)

What would have happened if the prudential supervisors had put on the brakes long before the banks themselves retreated from their kamikaze course? The Latin American countries would have been obliged to

2 The international community issued its first, rather subdued, warning in 1980 (BIS communiqué of 15 April) but did not act in the sense of establishing certain minimum standard for provisions on third country debt until much later.

Figure 3 Public long-term debt indicators

Billions of dollars

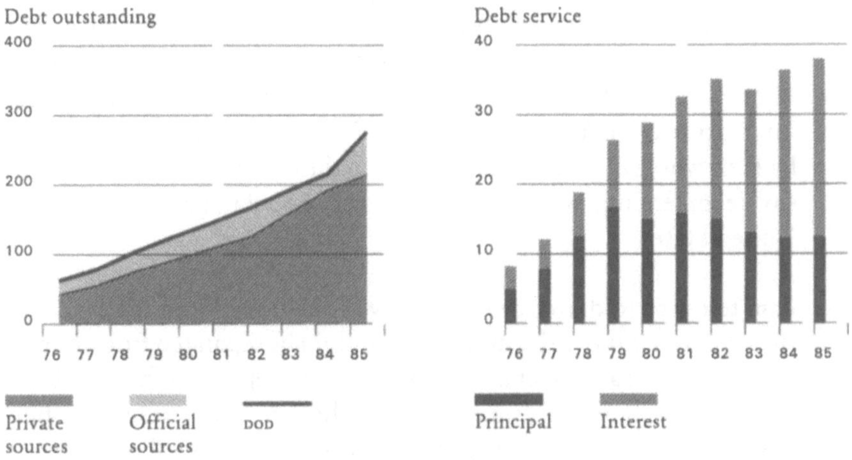

Sources: World debt tables, World Bank.

reduce their deficit spending, which was initially encouraged by the low and sometimes even negative real interest rates in the US. They would have had to adjust, possibly under the guidance of the IMF as a result of their having to borrow from the Fund rather than from the markets. Adjustment obviously has its limits, particularly in the short run and when faced with such dramatic and unforeseen events as the oil price explosions. The IMF would have needed a substantial 'oil facility' at an early stage in order to ease these adjustments.[3]

My reverse crystal ball does not tell me whether that is a realistic re-enactment of history. If the industrialized countries would have refused to create adequate expanded Fund facilities, would it not have been preferable to let the markets do the work rather than 'let the developing world starve'? My intuitive feeling is that it would not. It seems to me that if the prudential supervisors had held to their brief, the world would have found other ways to ease the plight of the developing world. As long as the markets solved the immediate problem in a seemingly painless manner, there was no need for politicians to act. So they did not.

3 The 1974 'oil facility', the 1977 'supplementary' or 'Witteveen facility' (SDR 8.5 billion), and the enlarged access to the Fund agreed to in 1980 were woefully inadequate compared to the size of the recycling problem and the contribution of the market (see table 1 and figure 3).

When the banks stopped lending and the international community had to step in, it was in many respects too late. The debt crisis was upon us and any initiative to be taken after 1982 would inevitably be looked at as 'bailing out the banks'. Whatever might have been possible earlier became tainted once the problem had been allowed to grow into an international debt crisis that affected not just the LDCs but also the international banks. 'Using taxpayers' money to help international bankers who had created the problem in the first place by their reckless sovereign lending' was politically not very popular, particularly in the United States.

I am tempted to draw one provocative conclusion from the events of the seventies. Prudential supervision should be separated from monetary policy, just as monetary policy should be separated from politics. Prudential supervision and monetary policy are different responsibilities that have very little in common, except that they both operate through the banking system. There may occasionally even be conflicts of interest. The oil crises provide us with as clear an example of this possibility as one can find anywhere in the history of central banks. Central banks subordinated their supervisory responsibilities to what they

Table 3 Highly indebted countries

Millions of US dollars

	1970	1975	1980	1981	1982
Total external debt (EDT)	.	.	287,612.0	349,197.5	388,618.7
Long-term debt	31,456.6	76,657.6	204,104.3	244,430.8	276,502.0
Public and publicly guaranteed	*17,931.9*	*49,527.5*	*146,808.1*	*169,226.9*	*198,515.0*
Private nonguaranteed	*13,524.7*	*27,130.1*	*57,296.2*	*75,203.9*	*77,987.0*
Use of IMF credit	200.7	1,251.3	2,973.3	4,111.2	6,220.7
Short-term debt	.	.	80,534.4	100,655.5	105,655.5
Public and publicly guaranteed long-term debt					
Commitments	4,755.6	16,386.9	36,812.3	52,208.5	49,917.3
Official creditors	1,926.1	4,746.9	9,948.1	13,381.6	12,823.0
Multilateral	1,049.5	2,757.3	5,341.6	7,249.2	7,506.1
IBRD	*733.1*	*1,712.0*	*3,623.7*	*4,877.5*	*4,355.0*
IDA	*12.9*	*21.5*	*16.0*	*0.0*	*0.0*
Bilateral	876.6	1,989.5	4,606.5	6,132.4	5,316.9
Private Creditors	2,829.5	11,640.0	26,873.2	38,826.9	37,148.2
Suppliers	*1,019.0*	*2,091.2*	*1,449.0*	*3,656.9*	*1,656.3*
Financial Markets	*1,810.5*	*9,548.8*	*25,424.2*	*31,170.0*	*35,491.9*

Source: World debt tables, World Bank.

believed to be the overriding considerations of monetary policy in the broader sense of the term. Again with the benefit of hindsight, prudence should have prevailed over vision. By making supervision subservient to monetary policy, the errors of the latter were compounded and the world was subsequently settled with the debt crisis.

3 Full disclosure and mark-to-market delude the markets (sometimes)

Full disclosure and mark-to-market are excellent principles which, emotionally and by economic instinct, I fully endorse. And yet, as a banker who lived through the debt crisis, I cannot help having my doubts. Before stating these doubts let me remind the reader of the two well-known reasons why banks are exceptionally vulnerable to downward swings in asset prices. One reason is that banks are far more highly leveraged than most other enterprises. In the seventies and eighties the large money center banks in the US had capital to asset ratios in the range of 5-7 per cent (counting subordinated debt and loan loss reserves (!) as capital), whereas sound industrial firms would have some

1983	1984	1985
415,174.4	431,943.6	444,361.0
329,177.7	353,977.0	367,570.1
249,649.0	*276,770.1*	*304,276.1*
79,528.7	*77,206.9*	*63,294.0*
12,287.1	14,691.8	18,304.5
73,709.6	63,274.8	58,486.4
39,150.1	25,563.7	20,520.7
13,364.0	9,760.2	9,184.3
8,014.3	6,180.0	7,018.9
5,810.0	*2,804.5*	*4,889.0*
0.0	*0.0*	*0.0*
5,349.7	3,580.2	2,165.3
25,786.1	15,803.5	11,336.5
1,144.7	*708.0*	*633.1*
24,571.8	*15,041.3*	*10,703.4*

40 per cent or better. If a bank were to have only 5 per cent of its assets in third world debt – many US banks had far more – and if the debt would have to be written off to half of its face value, the bank would lose almost half of its capital base and far more than half of its equity. Manufacturers Hanover would have had almost zero equity if it had marked its third world debt down to market in the mid-eighties. In contrast, if an industrial firm were faced with a similar disaster – a 50 per cent decline in the price of 5 per cent of its assets – it would lose only a small fraction of its capital.

A second reason why full disclosure and mark-to-market can be quite disastrous in the case of banks is the old and familiar issue of public confidence. A bank that shows negative equity is likely to suffer a dramatic outflow of deposits and at the very least will have to pay a heavy penalty in the market, which will erode its profitability and, hence, its long run chance of survival. Continental Illinois experienced this kind of downward spiral in 1984 for reasons not primarily related to third world debt, but fully similar in their consequences for the bank. We all know that Conti was – and probably had to be – bailed out by the Federal Reserve and the FDIC in order to prevent a domino-type collapse of the American and, possibly, the world financial system.

The banks went into the debt crisis with a set of highly favourable accounting rules in place that were blessed by the supervisors. I quote from the notes to the financial accounts of major US banks in the eighties: 'Securities for investment are carried at cost' and 'loans are generally carried at the principal amount outstanding'. In other words: current market valuations can be totally ignored, except for securities that are held in the banks' trading portfolios (and it was pretty much up to management what securities were designated 'for trade' or 'for investment'). Risk of default was covered by the rule that the banks make 'provisions for credit losses, which are a charge against earnings, to bring the allowance (i.e. the loan loss reserve) to a level which, in management's judgement, is adequate to absorb losses inherent in the credit portfolio'. In 'management's judgement': that judgement can, of course, be questioned by accountants and by supervisors, but it gives a great deal of leeway vis-à-vis the market. As we all know, that leeway was used extensively in the eighties. Loan loss reserves for third world debt were way below the discounts that were quoted in secondary markets and probably also way below the then prevailing judgement on the likely losses that would eventually be incurred on LDC debt.

These accounting rules originated in the context of traditional banking business: lending to a broad range of borrowers in the private sector, where individual risks are largely a matter of judgement and the adequacy of loan loss reserves can be based on experience. The one major price risk that affects practically all assets on a bank's balance sheet are changes in interest rates. If banks were to mark their fixed rate assets up and down with changes in interest rates, P & L accounts and balance sheets would fluctuate in a totally senseless manner (unless liabilities were to be adjusted as well, but even then the normal mismatch would lead to strong gyrations). In periods of rapidly rising interest rates such adjustments to banks' balance sheets might lead to a scramble for capital and a severe cutback in lending.

The accounting rules that allow banks to keep loans and securities in the investment portfolio at face value do make sense in that context. It may not seem consistent with full disclosure at current market prices, but any analyst can make whatever corrections he wants on the basis of market interest rates and the published maturities of a bank's assets and liabilities. As a prudential quid pro quo, regulators should (and do) require extra capital as a function of a bank's interest mismatch.

The valuation of third world debt was a totally different matter. The real question was whether banks should have been allowed to substitute management's judgement for the indications from the secondary markets. We all know what happened: banks were allowed to carry third world debt at full face value and to gradually build up loan loss reserves against default. These reserves had virtually no relation to market discounts on third world debt, nor did they really reflect management's judgement of country risk. Does anyone believe that banks revised their collective judgement downwards in every single year since 1982, so as to bring loan loss reserves to a level corresponding to the risk of default? Clearly that was not the case. Banks and their supervisors have said quite openly that they were gradually building up loan loss reserves to the required level, implying that in every single year provisions were inadequate according to their own published rules.

Moreover, if provisions for country risk really had reflected management's judgement, the banks should have been very active buyers in the secondary markets of third world debt where discounts were substantially lower than the banks' provisions. If anything, they were net sellers. Was Walter Wriston honest but dumb, or devious and opportunistic when he made his (in)famous pronouncement that 'countries don't go broke', implying that they would always repay their sovereign debt in full, whether domestic or foreign currency denominated? I have a strong suspicion that he was not dumb at all, or he wouldn't have made it to the chairmanship of Citicorp.

I do not know what yarns the American banks have spun to justify their published and certified valuation of third world assets. Their annual reports in the decade after 1982 make fascinating reading. They were mostly very open about the banks' exposures to problem countries and they often contained thoughtful analyses of these countries' economic situation and potential (see table 4).[4] But as far as I have been able to ascertain, none ever published secondary market prices in their annual reports, nor did they explicitate the value which management attached to 'value impaired debt'. The only reference to the principle (not the quantitative content!) of 'management judgement' was in the notes to the financial accounts, and implicitly in the auditors' declaration that the accounts had been drawn up and certified on the basis of these principles. Wisdom or mutual whitewashing, or both? Nobody was ever called to account. As long as the system was held together by these white lies, it was in everyone's interest not to rock the boat. The banks made their provisions, the accountants signed off on them, and the regulators concurred (and in some cases even prescribed). The little boys in Academia, who cried that the emperor was not fully clothed, were silenced by being ignored or berated for their ignorance, disloyalty, and irresponsible behaviour.

I vividly remember my own discussions with our external accountants; the more than slightly hypocritical critique of market prices ('thin and volatile markets', 'distress selling', etc.), and the unfair debating trick of asking them why they, as accountants, thought that they knew more about the future of third world countries and their ability to service their debt than our own central bank. It should be remembered in this context that the Dutch central bank prescribed certain minimum provisions to be made each year on exposures to each problem country.[5] It did not occur to the accountants to ask what special insight the authorities had that the markets lacked. I do not know how we got away with our under-provisioning year after year. Thinking back, I feel slightly

4 As an example, the Annual Report of Chase Manhattan Corporation for the year 1988 gives very detailed information on the bank's exposure to 'refinancing countries' and on its loan loss reserves, allocated to these countries (see table 4). If one compares the loan loss reserves with the market discounts at the time, they would appear to have been highly inadequate. On 31 December 1986, the market discounts on Chase's exposures to Brazil, Argentina, Venezuela and Mexico amounted to some $ 1,978 million, while the loan loss reserves allocated to all restructuring countries (including $ 2,560 million of exposure to 'other countries') amounted to only $ 400 million. The corresponding figures for year-end 1988 are market discounts on exposures to the four countries of $ 3,742 million as against a loan loss reserves for all restructuring countries of only $ 2,000 million.

5 In this country the (minimum) annual provisions were 'suggested' by the central bank, and were studiously kept secret so as not to offend certain third world sensitivities and not to give them a convenient excuse to renege on their commitments on the basis of these official discounts. The annual provisions were discussed amongst the central banks of the major creditor countries so as to keep their banks more or less on a 'level playing field'.

Table 4 Refinancing countries

Millions of US dollars, end-of-year figures

	1984	1985	1986	1987	1988
Cross-border extensions of credit					
Brazil	2,650	2,700	2,620	2,570	2,490
Argentina	830	890	930	970	920
Venzuela	1,190	1,240	1,060	1,010	920
Mexico	1,700	1,650	1,620	1,640	1,460
Other countries	2,990	2,700	2,560	2,410	2,050
Total cross - border extensions of credit	9,360	9,180	8,790	8,600	7,840
Reserve for possible credit losses allocated to refinancing countries					
Balance-beginning of period	250	300	350	400	2,000
Provision for possible credit losses	23	39	48	1,650	350
Net charge-offs	-23	-39	-48	-78	-362
Reallocation	50	50	50	28	12
Balance-end of period	300	350	400	2,000	2,000
Cross-border extensions of credit as a multiple of					
Common stockholders' equity	2.8	2.4	2.1	2.7	1.9
Total stockholders' equity	2.3	2.1	1.8	2.2	1.6
Common stockholders' equity & reserve for possible credit losses allocated to refinancing countries	2.6	2.2	1.9	1.6	1.3
Total stockholders' equity & reserve for possible credit losses allocated to refinancing countries	2.2	1.9	1.7	1.5	1.1

Source: Annual Report, Chase Manhattan Corporation 1988, p. 42.

uncomfortable about the ease with which we convinced our external accountants to accept the judgement of the central bank as holy writ, in spite of very different indications from the market, the financial press, the economic profession and the analysts.

But it is hard to argue against success. The policy was successful, for it worked. No major bank went bankrupt. All gradually built up loan loss reserves which, after a number of years, had grown enough to defuse the explosive potential of the debt crisis. But it was a slippery road to travel. Just imagine what would have happened if a major bank had collapsed because depositors lost confidence in its ability to weather the storms of deteriorating third world debt and possible other mishaps. Would depositors, creditors, and equity investors not have had a case against accountants and regulators for gross misrepresentation and dereliction of duty? Is it unfair to suspect that such considerations were at least one element in the rescue of Continental Illinois? Fortunately, other major bank failures did not happen. Bail-outs on the scale of Continental Illinois are hard to imagine if all major US banks with large exposures on Latin America would have lost the confidence of the markets.

What role did the accounting practices really play in this respect? Would banks have failed if they had valued their third world exposure at levels that, at the time, would have seemed more realistic, presumably closer to secondary market prices? One is inclined to think so and clearly supervisors did think so at the time. But it is intellectually and intuitively rather uncomfortable to have to concede that deliberate misrepresentation – call it less than full disclosure – may have been the saviour of the world financial system in the eighties. In an attempt to hush my conscience as an economist, let me play the devil's (or is it the angel's?) advocate for a minute.

One could argue that in fact little or no relevant information was withheld from the public. The annual reports of US banks showed their exposure to problem countries quite openly and I assume accurately. Market prices of 'value impaired sovereign debt' were published on a regular basis (see table 5). The only thing banks did not publish was the impact that mark-to-market would have on their financials. But any analyst worth his salt could do these sums.

My files on the debt crisis, which at the time was a popular subject for students to discuss and write papers on (usually with the banks as the main culprits!), are full of press cuttings that show the exposures of US banks to Latin America as a percentage of their equity. Table 6 gives just one example. The type of data shown in tables 5 and 6 can be combined to show the erosion of these banks' equity, if Latin American debt were to be valued at market prices. Even so, the ratings of most of these banks remained at reasonable levels throughout the eighties (see table 7). Manufacturers Hanover was still rated A 1 by Moody's in 1985, down from Aa 2 in 1982, although its exposure to problem countries in Latin America was more than twice its equity and market prices had fallen by a quarter or more. Only towards the end of the decade, when prices of third world debt had plummeted to their lowest levels (Argentina to just over 10 per cent, Brazil to 30 per cent and Mexico to 40 per cent), some ratings were lowered below investment grade. But even then financial markets did not panic.

What does all this prove? That full disclosure on the basis of market prices or of some reasonable estimate of the future pay-back on third world debt would not have made any difference? Or was the fact that accountants and regulators supported the practice of banks to initially under-provide for country risk enough to reassure markets? If so, why? Were markets implicitly convinced that the authorities, having put themselves in the position of accomplices, would always bail out the banks as they had done with Continental Illinois? That would seem overly optimistic, considering the strong negative opinions voiced in the US Congress at the time on using taxpayers' money to bail out the (traditionally impopular) banks.

Table 5 Price indications for value impaired debt

Prices quoted are US dollar cents per US$ 1 of nominal value

	Price	Trend/Demand
Latin America		
Argentina	61 - 64	Weakening
Bolivia	9 - 11	Few bids
Brazil	61 - 64	Speculative bids
Chile	65 - 70	Firm-buoyed by chile 18 and 19 capitalisations
Colombia	83 - 87	Firm; few sellers
Costa Rica	34 - 37	Thin market
Ecuador	58 - 60	Weakening on suspension of debt service
Guatemala	64 - 66	Average demand
Mexico	55 - 60	Price supported by capitalisations
Panama	66 - 69	Steady, few sellers
Peru	15 - 17	Slipping
Uruguay	65 - 69	Few bids
Venezuela	72 - 74	Steady
Africa		
Algeria	98 - 99	Oversupplied
Ivory Coast	78 - 80	Improving, heavy demand on buy side.
Liberia	6 - 8	No bids
Madagascar	60 - 62	No bids
Morocco	67 - 71	Weakening
Nigeria	30 - 40	Mainly for Central Bank notes
Senegal	50	Steady
South Africa	55 - 60	Steady
Sudan	10 - 20	Thin
Togo	67	Firm
Zambia	10 - 15	Possible improvements
Zimbabwe	90 - 94	Buoyant
Zaire	20 - 24	Weakening
Asia		
Philippines	71 - 74	Firm for capitalisations
Europe		
Poland	42 - 44	Improving
Romania	87 - 89	Few sellers
Yugoslavia	77 - 81	Steady

Note: the prices are prevailing at the end of March 1987 with an indication of the price trend and demand where appropiate.

Table 6 Top US banks exposure in Latin America

Year-end 1985, millions of US dollars

	Mexico	Brazil	Argentina	Venezuela
Manufacturers Hanover	1,802	2,247	1,429	1,048
Bank America	2,709	2,799	450[1]	1,450
Chase Manhattan	1,680	2,820	920	1,250
Chemical New York	1,471	1,434	402[1]	714
Irving Bank	357	412	243	471
Citicorp	2,800	4,700	1,400	1,200
Marine Midland	364	668	-	307
Bankers Trust New York	1,277	864	375[1]	300[1]
Wels Fargo	606	603	133	259
First Chigago	912	804	225	275
J.P. Morgan	1,250	1,929	869	500[1]
Continental Illinois	555	442	365	305
Bank of Boston	245	320	330	105
Security Pacific	520	590	200[1]	100[1]
Republicbank	287	224	149	117
Mellon Bank	579	489	.	.
First Interstate	721	507	100	75[1]

1 Estimate
Source: Financial Times, 25 February 1987.

Intriguing questions to which I do not have any clear answers, not even intuitive ones. The only part-answer I can come up with, is that more realistic accounting would have had a negative impact, not in the sense of alerting markets to what they already knew, but by triggering built-in responses that might have toppled the delicately balanced financial pyramid. There are all sorts of rules based on published accounts: stock market rules, statutory investment criteria of institutional investors, etc. Publication might also have reduced the degree of judgmental freedom on the part of accountants, analysts, rating agencies and possibly even of central banks.

Table 7 Ratings of some US banks

	Moody's			Standard & Poors's		
	1982	1985	1990	1982	1985	1990
Manufacturers Hannover	Aa2	A1	Baa3	AAA	AA-	BBB+
Citicorp	Aa	Aa1	A3	AA+	AA	AA-
Bank America	Aa	A2	A2	AAA	A+	A
Chemical New York	Aa	Aa2	Baa3	AA+	AA	A–
Chase Manhattan	Aa	Aa1	Baa2	AAA	AA	A-
J.P. Morgan	Aaa	Aaa	Aa1	AAA	AAA	AAA

Source: Moody's industry outlook, The Economist.

Chile	Total	Percentage of equity
791	7,317	204
300[1]	7,798	171
600[1]	7,270	165
450[1]	4,471	158
-	1,423	155
500[1]	10,600	136
204[1]	1,543	129
400[1]	3,216	128
104	1,705	116
200	2,418	115
275[1]	4,823	109
.	1,667	89
.	1,000	67
150[1]	1,540	63
.	777	63
.	1068	61
100[1]	1,503	59

When all is said and done, we are left with an uncomfortable moral and political dilemma. A policy that goes against the grain of truthful financial accounting was obviously successful in preventing a meltdown of the international financial system. But we do not really know why it worked. Nor does the history of the debt crisis provide any clear indications as to why and when the golden rules of honest and transparent financial accounting should be suspended. What is wrong with these rules if they have to be set aside under 'certain exceptional circumstances'? Can these circumstances be clearly defined? Do they have a certain inherent logic? If, as I suspect, the answer to both questions is negative, who is to judge, on a discretionary basis, whether special circumstances justify a temporary 'falsification' of the published accounts and the implicit relaxation of capital ratio requirements? What would be the consequences if such a policy were to fail in the sense that certain banks would eventually go down anyway? Would not depositors and equity investors, acting in good faith on the basis of published accounts and clear accounting rules, be able to claim they had been misled by the authorities? If that would lead to public bailouts on a large scale – as might have been the case if the strategy on third world debt had not worked – what would have been the long-term consequences for the system? Might it not have led to the virtual nationalization of all major US banks?

4 In caude venenum ... or a happy ending?

If the monetary authorities were wrong in the mid-seventies and right in the eighties what does that imply for the future? Should central banks continue to have the leeway to suppress their prudential consciences – as they did in the seventies – and to allow the banks to doctor their accounts 'under exceptional circumstances' – as they did with great success in the eighties? My personal answer to the first part of the question is: no, they should not. Prudential control is essential and no macro-economic or systemic considerations should override it. The debt crisis and the near-banking and financial crisis provide ample evidence for the need to have independent prudential supervision. If that requires an institutional separation between monetary policy and prudential supervision, as is the case in Germany and to some extent in the US, so be it. In Europe most central banks will have to be restructured anyway to ensure their independent status as required by the Maastricht Treaty. When (if?) we ever get to the final stage of EMU, monetary policy will be conducted by the 'Eurofed', while prudential supervision will remain with the national central banks, creating a de facto separation of functions which would go a long way in a direction that I consider desirable.

Full disclosure and mark-to-market present more difficult issues if my conclusion is correct that the deviations from these principles in the eighties were on balance highly beneficial for the banks, for the financial system and, ultimately, for the world economy. Principles that can be, or even should be bent under certain ill-defined circumstances are inherently deficient. Attempts to remedy the deficiency by trying to define the circumstances are bound to create highly undesirable loopholes. Should banks be allowed to carry real estate at other than present market prices when the latter are severely depressed by a temporary oversupply? And what about bonds with a fixed value at maturity? Why not mark these to market, even if they are held 'for investment' and provided that liabilities are equally marked to market? It is all very well for accountants to state that the firm is deemed to be immortal ('going concern') and hence will not need to sell the assets before maturity, but the deviation from present market prices does present the wrong picture of the company's equity base as a buffer against unforeseen disasters. And that is what capital requirements for banks are all about.

The whole issue may well become moot before too long as accounting rules and banking regulations appear to be moving inexorably towards full disclosure and mark-to-market. If that is the case, will we not be exposed, without defences, to a just conceivable next banking crisis resulting from the sudden collapse of the price of assets that play an important role in the balance sheet of the banking system? Arguably, such an eventuality will never occur, as banks and their supervisors have become more aware of the risks inherent in concentrated exposures, whether to countries and regions, or to sectors and types of assets. General capital requirements have been strengthened, concentrated risks are penalized, and special price risks are being tackled. The only thing that might spoil this optimistic scenario is that supervisors are always one step behind the supervised; US banks in particular are very keen explorers of new products and always manage to find new traps to fall into. Recent bank problems in Scandinavia show that older traps are still around as well. But such recent problems have not been systemic threats. I expect the new safeguards to be adequate in containing any potential future crisis. If near-disasters in the past have helped to build these safeguards, the debt crisis will at least have served to make the international financial system less vulnerable. Historia facit antidotum – to coin a phrase that might have been common in these parts if Cleopatra's nose had been just slightly crooked ....

The Dutch attitude towards capital liberalization

Age F.P. Bakker

1 Introduction

In the 1980s Europe made a leap forward towards the liberalization of capital movements. EC directives were accepted by all Member States obliging them to abolish all remaining exchange controls. This common objective of freedom of capital movements has been consolidated in the Treaty on European Union. Nowadays virtually all restrictions have been lifted. This stands in striking contrast to the state of affairs only a decade ago, when many countries still exercised a tight regime. Although the Treaty of Rome propagated the freedom of capital movements, this objective was circumscribed by the clause that such liberalization should only be carried through to the extent necessary to ensure the proper functioning of the common market. In practice, for a long time trade liberalization took precedence over capital liberalization. It is only since the publication of the White Book on the completion of the internal market that freedom of capital movements generally has been accepted as a common goal. Apparently there has been a great shift in the appreciation of the pros and cons of free capital flows over time.

In the last decade the Netherlands has been a staunch supporter of the drive towards freedom of capital movements. But this has not always been the case. At the time of the drafting of the Treaty of Rome the Netherlands was among those countries which were not in favour of full freedom. Gradually this attitude has changed. Although in practice authorizations for capital transactions were granted liberally, up till 1977 the Netherlands practised a negative system, under which all capital transactions were prohibited unless specifically authorized. From the change to a positive system – under which all transactions are allowed unless specifically prohibited – it took another 10 years before the Netherlands became the fourth OECD country, after Germany, the United Kingdom and the United States, which had fully liberalized all capital movements. André Szász has been instrumental in this change of attitude of the Dutch monetary authorities. In this essay the policy arguments and the underlying forces are discussed which for the

Netherlands caused the balance of pros and cons to be tipped definitely in favour of full liberalization of capital movements.

2 The Treaty of Rome

Of the four freedoms in the Treaty of Rome – the free movement of goods, persons, services and capital – the freedom of capital movements has been formulated in the most cautious manner. A crucial clause in the relevant Article 67 was that the obligation for countries to lift capital restrictions would be limited 'to the extent necessary to ensure the proper functioning of the common market'. The Treaty thus did not contain an unconditional obligation to liberalize capital movements. This 'escape' clause was supported by the Dutch, French and Italian delegations. Complete freedom of capital movements could put into jeopardy the maintenance of internal monetary equilibrium and external exchange rate equilibrium, so it was argued, and thus endanger the functioning of the common market. The escape clause, by subordinating the freedom of capital movements to that of trade movements, would give Member States considerable leeway in the application of capital restrictions. In an internal memorandum of the Dutch Ministry of Finance it was claimed triumphantly that this clause '... is to be of crucial importance and shall form the essential guiding principle for the implementation of the doctrine of free capital movements'.[1] Effectively sand had been thrown in the wheels of full freedom of capital movements.

In the negotiations leading up to the Treaty in the mid-1950s Germany and France had held opposing views. Germany, traditionally liberal-oriented, favoured the inclusion of the free movement of capital as a common goal, whereas France, traditionally dirigistic-oriented, supported by Italy, wished to maintain its room for manoeuvre. Belgium's main interest lay in the preservation of its dual exchange rate market. The attitude of the Netherlands, which held a position in the middle, therefore proved to be of crucial importance in determining the extent of the Treaty obligations and drawing the line between those capital movements which would be necessary for the proper functioning of the common market, and those which would not. The Netherlands was opposed to the full liberalization of capital movements, both on ideological and policy grounds. The Netherlands had two main motives for a rather restrictive attitude: it wished to protect its domestic capital

1 Memorandum of 14 February 1957, Ministry of Finance.

market and it wished to control domestic monetary expansion. As far as the first motive – protection of the domestic capital market – was concerned, there were three arguments in favour of restrictions on capital outflows.

a There was the fear that capital, if left fully to the free play of market forces, would flow from the poor areas to the rich areas of the Community. Posthuma, the Dutch delegate from the side of the central bank, when elaborating on this argument, held that both speed and substance of capital liberalization should be subordinated to the fulfilment of wider-ranging objectives of the Treaty, such as economic harmonization and a high degree of employment. Complete freedom of capital movements could only become mandatory if the economic climate in which entrepreneurs had to work, as well as the social and economic policies were sufficiently equalized. His main fear was that the prevailing differences might induce capital movements from underdeveloped countries to more developed regions, whereas the aim of balanced growth in the Community and a high level of employment would require the opposite. He wrote: 'The liberal economic doctrines of the 19th century, influenced by natural philosophy, took it that with free capital movements flows would go in a direction which would optimalize welfare. Nowadays no economist of repute shares this notion'.[2]

b Capital outflows would force up domestic interest rates, which were low because of sound fiscal policies. Holtrop, the central bank's President, argued that the lifting of restrictions in itself would not guarantee the rational distribution of saving surpluses in Europe. He essentially took a static viewpoint: '... economic integration by itself does not generate new savings and thus no new capital; therefore the advantages of free capital movements can only be the displacement of the utilization of capital from one area to another'.[3] Therefore, foreign demand for credit on domestic markets would crowd out national credit takers.

c Free capital movements would facilitate the financing of free-spending governments and thus undermine budgetary discipline. The Dutch concern that spendthrift governments would borrow in the capital markets of thrifty governments, had been eloquently voiced by Holtrop.[4] 'Should the ant from La Fontaine's fable open up its store-room

2 Memorandum of 16 May 1959, the Nederlandsche Bank.
3 Holtrop, M.W. (1957), Monetaire aspecten van de economische integratie, *De Economist*, vol. 104, no. 12, pp. 801-827, reprinted as: Monetary aspects of economic integration, in: M.W. Holtrop (1972), *Money in an open economy*, Leiden, pp. 258-277.
4 Holtrop, op. cit., p. 821.

to the cricket?', he asked himself. Would it really be wise policy for the government, which as a good father has taken care to keep his own house in order, to open up its capital market and give free access to other members of the Community who take their financing problems more easily and spare their own taxpayers? Holtrop's answer was straightforward: this would be irresponsible policy. It might force the domestic government to monetary financing, it might drain the official reserves and it could put upward pressure on interest rates. Against these drawbacks he saw no obvious advantages.

These three arguments provided the intellectual background for the Dutch wish to shield the domestic capital market from external influences and thus restrict capital outflows. The second motive – the control of domestic monetary expansion – was closely related to the monetary doctrine which Holtrop had developed during his presidency of the Nederlandsche Bank. Short-term capital inflows were regarded as liquidity creation from external sources. There was no economic reason why this source of liquidity creation, which would come on top of domestic liquidity creation and thus could have inflationary consequences, would have to be allowed to flow uninhibited. Moreover, monetary control was exercised by direct means, mainly in the form of credit ceilings for commercial banks. Exchange controls were deemed necessary in order to forestall that credit ceilings were circumvented by the taking-up of credit abroad. Monetary policy should be able to be geared exclusively to price stability: '... only a government which accepts stability of the currency as an absolute rule of policy has the moral right to attract at the lowest possible interest rate savings running into thousands of millions of guilders'.[5]

These motives for a restrictive attitude were founded in the practical situation of the day. From the Dutch standpoint the Netherlands stood to lose from complete liberalization of capital movements. At the time it had one of the best-developed domestic capital markets, its financial community was outward-looking and interest rates were relatively low. Therefore, it was feared that for the foreseeable future the Dutch capital market would be one of the few sources of capital for the other Member States. The serious implications this would have for the Dutch interest rate level and indirectly for the level of wages and housing rents explain the dissuasive, cautious Dutch attitude. In the post-World War II years the Netherlands followed a cheap money policy in which forced savings were generated through cautious fiscal policies. The

5 De Nederlandsche Bank, Annual Report 1957, p. 18.

authorities wished to preclude that foreign credit takers could finance themselves at low interest rates on the Dutch capital market. This could force interest rates up and thus thwart the cheap money policy.

There was also a systemic vision – with a Calvinistic undertone – in the Dutch attitude: a government which behaves badly should be punished for its sins and not be provided with easy escape routes or granted indulgences.[6] In his advocacy of disciplinary incentives for governments Holtrop took up a theme which would come back incessantly over the next decades. The full freedom of capital movements would not satisfy the monetary desiderata that the Nederlandsche Bank under Holtrop cherished. It was a time in which the Dutch authorities still believed in their ability to determine their own economic policies. Fiscal policy and monetary policy were both directed towards internal stability. The rewards in the form of a low interest rate should not be jeopardized by failing policies elsewhere. Therefore the Netherlands did not shy away from dirigistic measures in the sphere of capital flows. Apparently the authorities had no faith in the optimal functioning of markets. At the same time, the emphasis in Dutch monetary thinking on the strict separation of liquidity and capital had as a practical implication that walls of defence were raised from two sides: restrictions were imposed both on short-term inflows and on long-term outflows.

3 First attempts at liberalization

In 1959 the Commission presented its first thoughts on how to give substance to the Treaty provisions. It went rather far and proclaimed that full liberalization of capital movements should be the ultimate objective within the Community, notwithstanding the escape clause in the Treaty. This aim was to be achieved in concrete steps. The recently restored external convertibility of the EC currencies for current transactions and the favourable positions on the balances of payments of its Member States provided propitious circumstances for liberalization.

Although the Dutch authorities were not unfavourably disposed towards further liberalization, they maintained the misgivings with respect to the final objective which had been manifest during the negotiations on the Treaty. In their view the common market would not become equivalent to the 'ideal' type of a freely functioning domestic

6 At the Dutch request it was provided in Article 68.3 of the Treaty of Rome that there would be no obligation to liberalize foreign government loans on the domestic capital market.

market within a country. The main difference was that in the Community a coordinated economic and monetary policy was lacking. National sovereignty with respect to monetary policy was not affected by the Treaty. Therefore, interest rates would differ between countries, but these differentials need not reflect differences in the productivity of capital. It could not yet be taken for granted that capital utilized in countries with a higher interest rate would bear more fruit than in countries with lower rates as long as there were differences in policy priorities. Of course, a less ambitious concept of a common market would deliver a lesser contribution to the optimal allocation of resources. But such was reality: 'an evolution of centuries which had made Europe a split continent could not be undone within a few decades'.[7]

In the ideological debate the Netherlands was rather outspoken. Yet, as far as the acceptance of concrete liberalization obligations was concerned, only Germany, which already had adopted a positive system in 1961, and the Netherlands were prepared to go beyond the obligations they had already accepted in the framework of the OEEC, the predecessor of the OECD. France and Italy were lagging and Belgium would maintain its dual exchange market. In these circumstances two directives were adopted in 1960 and 1962 by the EC Member States, which mainly consolidated the already existing degree of capital liberalization. This meant that direct investment flows, commercial credits and security transactions (other than issues), which were considered to be of paramount importance for the economic development of Europe, could flow uninhibited. Capital transactions of a financial character and short-term capital flows were excluded from this liberalization obligation.

After this encouraging start the pace of capital liberalization slackened. The Commission made frantic efforts to keep up the momentum, but its attempts to introduce a third directive failed, mainly because France, Italy and the Netherlands all had their own fads and fancies with respect to the capital restrictions they wished to maintain. As far as the Dutch were concerned, especially proposals to liberalize issues and private loans on the Dutch capital market – and so absorb part of Dutch savings – were not received favourably. The authorities were actively encouraging domestic savings. For this great sacrifices were being asked of the population. One would not want to see these savings withered away to less frugal nations. Neither was the liberalization of short-term capital flows desirable. Countries should be able to pursue

7 Memorandum of 9 April 1959, Ministry of Finance.

their own credit and interest rate policy and this should not be frustrated by short-term flows. As far as the Dutch were concerned 'no significant further progress (could) be expected so long as the individual Member States pursue an independent policy in the essential sectors of the economy'.[8] In fact from 1961 to 1966 no further liberalization to speak of took place in the Netherlands.

At the instigation of Emile van Lennep, who as chairman of the Monetary Committee wished to make progress, a Dutch alternative plan was developed which provided for the parallel placement of foreign bonds on all EC capital markets. In this way it would be avoided that such bonds would be issued only on the capital market with the lowest interest rate (i.c. the Dutch capital market). This showed that the Netherlands was willing to take liberalizing measures as long as it could rest assured that it would not bear the brunt of the burden in practice, because of its relatively well-organized capital market.

In the Monetary Committee the situation was finally reached that the Netherlands and Italy were willing to open up their markets subject to certain limits (foreign issues up to 1.5 per cent of gross domestic savings). France, however, was not even willing to accept such a piecemeal approach. On the other hand, Belgium and Germany considered these concessions as too modest. No agreement could be reached on a third directive which would have further liberalized capital movements. The negotiations had become completely bogged down in haggling over details.

On an individual basis, however, Member States initially made further progress. The favourable balance-of-payments situation of the EC Member States – in fact much better than was expected at the time the Treaty of Rome was signed – provided ample room, especially for the liberalization of outward capital flows. On 31 January 1967 France took the radical step of liberalizing most capital movements and moving to a positive system. The Netherlands, which had accepted as early as 1961 the new liberalization code of the OECD, liberalized transactions in securities in October 1966.[9] Over the years the number of staff occupied at the Exchange Control Office of the Nederlandsche Bank had diminished drastically, from 264 in 1959 to 155 in 1967. Many of these

8 De Nederlandsche Bank, Annual Report 1962, p. 136.

9 Security transactions up till then had been channelled through a so-called free market, in which the balances on special guilder accounts of non-residents (K-accounts) and foreign currency reinvestment accounts of residents had been negotiable against each other. As from 1 October 1966 transactions in securities could be settled in the official exchange market.

staff were actually involved in the compilation of balance-of-payments statistics. On 1 January 1968 the Exchange Control Office was abolished and a separate Balance-of-Payments department was established. The remaining staff were assembled in the Exchange Control Regulations department, numbering only 24 persons. Soon thereafter the Nederlandsche Bank presented a draft law to the Minister of Finance which provided for the transition to a positive system as well.[10] These proposals were closely linked with attempts to move to more indirect methods of monetary control. The dirigistic internal and external restrictions were increasingly felt to have undue drawbacks for the development of the domestic financial system.

However, the first cracks in the Bretton Woods system of fixed exchange rates had already appeared. Traditionally liberal-minded countries such as the United States, Germany and Switzerland, had been forced to reintroduce restrictive measures to curtail the increased capital flows. A further blow was dealt to capital liberalization when, under the influence of the uprise in May 1968 – 'les événements' – France was forced to reintroduce an extensive array of exchange controls. The massive capital flows which before and after the demise of the Bretton Woods system broke loose spurred the authorities into interventionist action. The whole process of capital liberalization was put into reverse.

At the turn of the decade the malfunctioning of the international monetary system triggered large speculative capital flows which frustrated domestic policies in Europe. It was decided to seek closer integration of policies in Europe. The Werner Report served as a basis for solemn promises to form an Economic and Monetary Union, which eventually would imply full freedom of capital flows. In February 1971 the Council initiated the first phase of EMU and agreed that the Commission proposal for a third directive for capital liberalization soon would be accepted. However, these good intentions were overtaken by events. All promises came to nothing in the face of the ensuing turmoil on the international exchange markets. It was the last convulsion of the post-war liberalization move.

10 The Bank had made its first offer to conceive such a law in a letter of 23 October 1959 to the then Minister of Finance Zijlstra. It had taken more than seven years before the draft finally was presented to Minister Witteveen on 5 April 1967.

In an article in the early seventies[11] André Szász reasoned that the disturbances in the international monetary system were caused mainly by the fact that major industrial countries for too long a time had held on to exchange rates which clearly had become incredible in the light of fundamental external imbalances. In the Dutch central bank tradition, he particularly criticized monetary policies which had accommodated capital outflows. Domestic liquidity expansion in the United States and the United Kingdom had been such that despite sizeable capital outflows and rising inflation rates the liquidity ratio (the ratio of monetary aggregates to GDP) from 1969 to 1972 had increased significantly. There was a direct link to the malfunctioning of the international monetary system which enabled the US to incur sizeable deficits without settlement and other countries to finance their deficits on the expanding Euro-currency markets. In these circumstances surplus countries, like the Netherlands, had no option but to ward off the inflows by means of tightening restrictions.

When in May 1971 the guilder, together with the Deutsche mark, was allowed to float, an important consideration was that it was found impossible to introduce at short notice sufficiently adequate exchange controls to discourage further capital inflows. For Germany such controls were not yet acceptable for reasons of economic philosophy.[12] After the suspension of dollar convertibility on 15 August 1971 the upward pressure was such that restrictions on inflows had to be imposed anyway by both countries. In the Netherlands the so-called O-circuit was established, a closed bond circuit which was intended to curtail foreign demand for Dutch guilder paper. In 1972 further restrictions were enacted. The payment of interest on non-resident accounts was prohibited as well as the taking-up of intercompany loans by Dutch multinationals in third countries, a notorious loophole. Other measures were taken as well, culminating in the imposition in March 1973 of a negative interest rate on non-resident accounts.

These events constituted an evolution in the thinking of the Dutch authorities concerning capital restrictions. Before this time, they had been regarded mainly as a complement to domestic financial and mon-

11 Szász, A. (1974), De rol van deviezenrestricties bij de regulering van het internationale kapitaalverkeer, in: V.A. Halberstadt, G.A. Kessler and J.J. Klant (eds.), *Economie in overleg*, Leiden, pp. 303-319.

12 De Nederlandsche Bank, Annual Report 1971, p. 105. In Germany it would take a political crisis and a change of government before capital restrictions were imposed in the form of the 'Bardepot' provisions.

etary policies. Now there was a new motive: to avoid an undue appreciation of the exchange rate of the guilder and thus an unwarranted deterioration of the Dutch competitive position.

The evolution in thinking was reflected in the subsequent drafts of the Law on External Financial Relations, which every time seemed to be overtaken by events. As we have seen, a first draft of this law, which was to replace the Exchange Control Decree (Deviezenbesluit) of 1945, was presented in 1967. This draft envisaged a single law which gave only limited powers to impose capital controls. Then, 'after each wave of exchange unrest the draft, which had not yet been sent to parliament, was reviewed with an eye to whether the authorities would have been able to handle the situation. Each time this led to additions'.[13] Finally a draft law was submitted to parliament on 4 July 1972. This submission followed, however, the adoption by the EC Member States of a directive which provided for the taking of common measures to ward off capital inflows from third countries. In fact, with this directive the reversal in the liberalization process was codified. In 1973 the system of fixed exchange rates disintegrated beyond retrieval. In these circumstances it was considered questionable whether it would be wise policy to limit the powers of the authorities to impose restrictions. The draft law was withdrawn. For a resumption of the liberalization drive it was generally assumed that two conditions had to be fulfilled: the restoration of a well-functioning international monetary system and a reasonable degree of consistency between the economic and monetary policies of the major countries. Experience had taught that the floating rate system did not provide the alternative for exchange restrictions as was hoped by some.

The Netherlands was of the opinion that monetary policy was better equipped to check undesired capital outflows than unwanted inflows. If in the case of outflows the central bank concerned would let the resulting contraction work its way through to the money market, the capital outflows inevitably would be slowed down. Admittedly, this could lead to a disorderly money market or, if the resulting high interest rates would last long, undesirable cyclical consequences. Yet, in the short run exchange rate considerations should prevail. In the case of inflows, however, non-sterilization would lead to lower interest rates which could undermine domestic monetary stability and have inflationary consequences. Yet, there were no illusions that restrictions were useful instruments in the long run. They were a third-best option

13 Szász, op. cit., p. 308.

in circumstances of extreme international divergences in economic and monetary policies. But their imposition would not help to overcome these divergences and might even perpetuate them. In short, restrictions were dealing only with the symptoms, not with the underlying causes.

Exchange restrictions were increasingly seen as having important drawbacks. Speaking at a conference in 1973 André Szász was rather sceptical as to the usefulness of restrictions in periods of speculation. He reminded the audience that as central bankers on the one hand 'we try to make the best of a bad situation trying to render controls as effective as possible; on the other hand, few people are in a better position than we are to judge the limitations of restrictions and the endless red tape and arbitrariness which they inevitably imply'.[14] In particular he saw three problems: exchange restrictions tended to spread in a rather uncoordinated manner to other countries; they tended to spread to other transactions which previously had been liberalized; and, once taken, restrictions tended to remain in effect. Moreover, they were incompatible with the pursuit of Economic and Monetary Union in Europe. Their abolition would be desirable, but only possible if monetary and fiscal policies would be sufficiently harmonized. In this manner André Szász articulated the feelings of many Europeans. Despite the disillusionment which was soon to follow with respect to the effectiveness of restrictions, the issue of capital liberalization would not be a matter of European discussion before it was brought out again ten years later.

In the currency turmoil of the 1970s the Netherlands actively tried to maintain a measure of exchange rate fixity in Europe. In August 1971 it had agreed with Belgium and Luxembourg on narrow fluctuation margins between each other's currencies in the hope that this would set an example which might be followed by other European countries. On 24 April 1972 the snake arrangement was established with fluctuation margins of 2.25 per cent. Actually, the snake was the only substantive, visible left-over of the attempts of the Werner Report towards monetary integration. However, when France and Italy had to withdraw from the arrangement in the wake of the 1973 oil crisis, the aim of completing Economic and Monetary Union had to be regarded as completely illusory. Thus, also the issue of capital liberalization was pushed into the background. In fact, there was widespread agreement that 'the regula-

14 André Szász quoted in Alexander K. Swoboda (ed.) (1976), Capital movements and their control, *Proceedings of a conference of the International Center for Monetary and Banking Studies*, Leiden, p. 172.

tion of capital flows by direct (restrictive) means is of great importance in the current situation in preventing, as far as possible, disequilibria occurring as a result of the differences in preference that funds from the oil-producing countries seeking investment show for the currencies participating in the scheme (i.e. the snake agreement)'.[15]

After the turmoil had somewhat subsided the Dutch authorities were quick in easing restrictions. The closed bond circuit was abolished on 1 February 1974, when the premiums, which in earlier years had risen as high as 6.5 per cent, had returned to virtually nil. Further relaxations came about in the following years and on 26 January 1977 the then Minister of Finance Duisenberg presented a somewhat amended bill on external financial relations to parliament, resuming the proposal to change to a positive system. The negative system had become so complex that the number of Bank staff which knew their way in the maze of regulations gradually were depleted.[16] Pending parliamentary approval of the bill, it was decided to move to a de facto positive system in September 1977. At the same time, issues of securities and loans on the domestic capital market by non-residents were permitted, provided they would, like domestic issuers, take their place in the queue. However, restrictions on capital inflows were maintained in order to prevent the prevailing domestic credit restrictions, introduced at the beginning of 1977, from being frustrated. In the following years these restrictions were gradually relaxed when the current account of the balance of payments showed a deficit. The policy of the Nederlandsche Bank, rightly termed 'moderately monetarist' – the money supply being a vital but not the only policy variable – actually was characterized by considerable fine-tuning: in view of the current account deficit domestic credit restrictions were applied, complemented by restrictions on short-term capital inflows; at the same time medium and long-term capital inflows were liberalized in order to facilitate the financing of the same current account deficit.

The External Financial Relations Act eventually was adopted on 28 May 1980, more than twenty years after the first legal work was initiated, and took effect on 1 May 1981.[17] All these years the authorizations were based on the Exchange Control Decree of 1945, as a living monument to prove the stickiness of capital restrictions. Although the

15 De Nederlandsche Bank, Annual Report 1973, p. 17.
16 Hazenberg, B.M.F. (1981), De Wet financiële betrekkingen buitenland, *Bank- en Effectenbedrijf*, March.
17 The adoption of the act was delayed because parliament insisted that first legislation with respect to the imposition of (financial) sanctions and the supervision of the credit system was to be enacted.

act was a step forward, the authority to impose restrictions was far-reaching and was still motivated by the same considerations as held earlier by Governor Holtrop. The main purpose of exchange restrictions continued to be the support of domestic financial and monetary policy. To this end the Nederlandsche Bank was authorized to restrict certain categories of capital inflows in case domestic credit ceilings were applied, and the Bank, in agreement with the Minister of Finance, could restrict capital outflows if the Dutch domestic capital market would become overburdened. Furthermore, the Minister of Finance, after having heard the advice of the Bank, could impose restrictions both on inflows and outflows in case of large-scale speculative capital movements.

5 Resuming the initiative

In many respects the 1970s had been a lost decade for Europe. However, the decade had ended on an optimistic note with the establishment on 13 March 1979 of the European Monetary System, as a successor to the snake. But unlike the snake, the EMS was not placed in the framework of the Werner Report's design of the phased establishment of an Economic and Monetary Union. This implied that there was no institutional pressure for capital liberalization. Liberalization was not needed because the EMS lacked the goal of monetary unification, and it was not wished for either because capital movements still were regarded as potentially threatening for exchange rate stability. The United Kingdom had other priorities and decided to follow a different track: it did not participate in the ERM, but deregulated its financial markets and abolished all exchange controls in one stroke in a definite attempt to shake up the economy and redirect it in a more market-oriented manner.

The system's Exchange Rate Mechanism had a shaky start. In the first years there were frequent and sometimes sizeable realignments and there were relapses into a tightening of exchange controls, especially on the part of France. Since the inception of the system, there had been a continuous debate between those participants who aimed to transform the EMS as quickly as possible into a final system (the 'monetarists') and those participants who wanted to make this dependent on progress in economic convergence and in the liberalization of capital movements (the 'economists'). In particular there had been repeated French-inspired proposals for beefing up the ECU and the EMS mechanisms for which the Commission let itself happily be used as an intermediary. These proposals were always framed in technical terms, but as André

Szász has demonstrated, behind this technical approach policy issues were scarcely hidden.[18] The continuous stream of proposals to intensify monetary cooperation, carrying along in their slipstream suggestions to amplify credit mechanisms, antagonized countries like Germany and the Netherlands. These countries grew tired of being put on the defensive and having to say 'no' against proposals to finance the deficits of the weaker currencies in the system without visible adjustments on their part.

The strong-currency countries went on the counter-offensive. For this they chose one of the almost forgotten objectives of the Community: the liberalization of capital movements. And their forum was the Monetary Committee. In 1982 André Szász proposed that the Committee resume its annual examinations of existing capital restrictions and the application of safeguards. Although the Committee was obliged to do this, the practice had fallen into abeyance towards the end of the 1960s. The safeguard measures of France dated back to 'les événements de mai' of 1968 and had never been scrutinized by the Commission or the Monetary Committee with a view to whether they could be repealed. Denmark, Ireland and Italy likewise availed themselves of safeguard measures.

In contrast to the leading role the European Commission had taken in the liberalization directives in the early 1960s, it now was the Monetary Committee which, after some French-inspired delaying tactics, took the lead. The Commission, however, needed prodding before it finally moved. This attitude must be viewed in the context of the political and economic situation in France in the beginning of the 1980s. The expansionary policies followed by the newly-elected government in 1981 – against the mainstream orthodox policies on the continent – had sparked off sizeable speculative capital outflows, which were countered by a further tightening of exchange controls. But it was a waste of effort. The exchange controls were just as porous as they had been in the wake of the Bretton Woods collapse. Outflows continued and they

18 Szász, A. (1988), *Monetaire diplomatie: Nederlands internationale monetaire politiek 1958-87*, Doctoral thesis, Leiden/Antwerpen, p. 169-172. Szász argues that France had two motives to propose changes in the EMS: the wish to present the EMS not as a Deutsche mark bloc but as a truly European system, implying an enlargement of the role of the ECU, and the wish to reach a more symmetric approach to the distribution of the burdens of adjustment, by putting additional obligations on the creditor countries – in practice on Germany. The French proposals took the form of packages of technical improvements to the EMS. These packages gave rise to lengthy discussions where the underlying policy disagreements were fought out 'in code'. In its Annual Report on 1981 the Nederlandsche Bank disapprovingly writes: 'With progress towards convergence of policies proving more arduous, tendencies are gaining ground within the EMS to focus on technical aspects'.

were accommodated by double-digit growth rates of domestic credit, as long as the Banque de France was forced to play its part in giving an impulse to the French economy. Within 18 months the French franc had to be devalued in three realignments to a total of 25 per cent. The volte-face in French economic policies in 1983, when it chose with grandeur for a major reformulation of its macro-economic and financial strategy, stirred the Commission into action.

In its first attempts the Commission still took a rather inward-looking attitude, by giving priority to the liberalization of EC-related or ECU-denominated capital transactions.[19] The Commission's leitmotiv was not yet the capital liberalization per se, but rather the promotion of the ECU. The Netherlands, together with other countries with a liberal exchange regime and well-developed financial centres such as Germany and the United Kingdom, was opposed to the implicit shielding of the EC financial markets from outside influences. There were considerable hesitations to favour the ECU without it being clear what end such promotion would serve. In the central bank's Annual Report on 1984 it was put quite bluntly: 'A number of countries, including the Netherlands, are loath to make agreements about further technical refinements as long as existing agreements, which are often of a more fundamental importance, are not fully complied with and as long as it remains unclear what such refinements are meant to achieve'.

In the mean time the momentum of liberalization gained force. The Netherlands had abolished in steps all restrictions on inflows, following the discontinuation of domestic credit restrictions at the end of 1981. On 1 January 1984 Denmark considerably eased its restrictions. As the United Kingdom had earlier experienced in 1979, no significant disturbances on the domestic capital market followed. On the contrary, confidence in the currency strengthened.

In the spring of 1984 the Commission finally heeded the exhortations of the Monetary Committee and initiated a series of bilateral talks on the justification of the continued use of the safeguards by France, Italy and Ireland. The outcome of the discussions was that the derogations would be monitored more strictly and that their duration would be limited in time. New impetus came when the Commission published the White Book on the completion of the internal market by the end of 1992. For the first time the full liberalization of capital movements was taken up as an essential ingredient of the internal market. Liberaliza-

19 Communication of the European Commission to the Council of Ministers on 'Financial integration', 20 April 1983, COM(83)207.

tion would have to move in parallel with a strengthening of the EMS. There was a trade-off here: exchange stability would facilitate the lifting of capital controls, but greater financial freedom would in turn exert the disciplinary effect on domestic policies needed for exchange stability.

In order to implement these ambitious plans it was felt necessary to amend the Treaty with a view to facilitating the European decision-making process. However, an attempt by the Commission failed to remove the escape clause – 'only for the proper functioning of the common market' – from Article 67 on the liberalization of capital movements. Member States were not yet ready to endorse the obligation of full capital liberalization. Once the Single European Act had been signed in February 1986, the Commission recaptured the initiative. Apparently thinking had evolved further. President Delors took the strategic decision to give top priority to full liberalization. This should be done in two phases. In the first phase all Member States should comply with the 1960 and 1962 directives, and the liberalization obligation should be extended to some other long-term and medium-term capital transactions not covered by these directives. The second phase would imply the lifting of all remaining capital controls, mainly with respect to short-term flows.

The Commission had come up with an ambitious, far-reaching program which went considerably beyond what Member States seemed prepared to contemplate. It was most likely that the operation of the EMS would be complicated through complete freedom of capital flows. The proposals drew heavily on the hoped-for economic convergence. Here the Commission took a calculated risk. If greater freedom of capital flows would have to be bought at the price of more frequent realignments or larger fluctuation margins within the EMS, the end result would be worse than the existing situation. These risks were very much realized at the time.[20] On the other hand, if there was a time when economic conditions were favourable to try an attempt to leap forward, it was now, with convergence progressing. The German and Dutch objections to contemplating further institutional steps with respect to the EMS and the ECU as long as capital restrictions remained intact would continue the stalemate the Commission was fearful of. The argument

20 For instance at the symposium 'L'Europe des services financiers', organized by the European League for Economic Cooperation in Brussels on 11 and 12 December 1986, EC Director General Russo admitted that the full liberalization of capital flows would not facilitate the operation of the EMS. In particular it would be necessary for monetary authorities to place domestic interest policy in the service of exchange rate stability.

that any further strengthening of the EMS was not on the cards had propelled the Commission to direct its attention to capital restrictions. It seemed right to embark on a dynamic process, for which, if it was successful, the rewards could be high. Financial liberalization would force the central banks to coordinate ever more closely, opening up the perspective of changing the EMS from a Deutsche mark zone into a truly commonly managed system with the perspective of monetary union.

The Dutch authorities were satisfied with the active stance of the Commission: 'Thus a better climate (would be) created for policy discussions on the advancement of European monetary cooperation and the role which the ECU could play here'.[21] However, they initially held the line that existing obligations with respect to capital liberalization should be fulfilled first, before new ones could be accepted. They feared that new obligations would simply be brought under the existing safeguards for the restrictive countries, implying that it would be only the liberal countries which would take additional obligations on board. The Netherlands still wished to retain the possibility to impose restrictions on inward capital flows to close the gap when imposing domestic credit ceilings. It was felt that it would be hurtful to Dutch pride ever to invoke the safeguard clauses for this purpose.

However, domestically it was felt increasingly difficult to keep the controls in place. Industry had grown used to taking up credit with commercial banks abroad. Doubts as regards the effectiveness and fairness of exchange restrictions had arisen as well. In the Dutch central bank, charged with the execution of exchange controls, André Szász had been one of those who gradually had become more sceptical with respect to the effectiveness of the restrictions, especially in the longer run. The fact that there was a very limited chance of being caught and virtual certainty that offenders would not be sentenced was deemed to be a very unsatisfactory situation. The token reference in the annual reports of the Nederlandsche Bank that 'investigations were held to check compliance with the exchange control regulations' only scared off jellyfish. The move towards a more market-oriented approach gained force among the monetary authorities.

As a first step, important deregulations of the Dutch capital market were carried through. Regulations had been in place with the aim of keeping orderly market conditions as well as maintaining a strict separation of liquidity and capital in order to attain monetary objectives.

21 De Nederlandsche Bank, Annual Report 1985, p. 19.

However, the rapid development of financial markets, spurred by innovations and technical progress, as well as their internationalization made it increasingly difficult to enforce national rules. A major consideration was the wish to maintain Amsterdam's position as a financial centre and to ensure that transactions in guilder-denominated paper would continue to take place as much as possible in the Netherlands. The deregulation, effective as from 1 January 1986, involved the virtual abolition of all requirements as to form, thus ending the strict separation of liquid and capital assets, as well as a considerable easing of the calendar requirements. As a logical sequence soon thereafter the second step was set. The remaining restrictions on capital outflows were lifted and the Exchange Control Regulations Department, which had already shrunk to only 3 professional staff members, was dismantled. On 1 October 1986 the Netherlands became the fourth OECD member country which had completely liberalized all capital movements.

In the mean time other countries had taken liberalizing measures as well to the effect that the existing derogations could be repealed. In its meeting on 17 November 1986 the Council finally adopted a new directive which entered into force on 28 February 1987, nearly five years after the Monetary Committee had taken the initiative. The directive entailed some further liberalization obligations, but fell short of freeing short-term capital flows. However, the Commission lost no time and soon came forward with proposals for complete abolition of all controls. There would, however, remain a specific safeguard clause, which would permit the temporary imposition of controls on short-term flows in case of tensions. A number of liberal-oriented countries, like Germany, the United Kingdom and Denmark, considered such a clause to be an unfortunate signal to the financial markets. Other countries, however, pleaded for such a clause which would allow restrictions on capital outflows to be imposed when the currency would come under speculative attack.

The Dutch authorities initially took a completely different approach in an attempt to maintain a measure of limited monetary autonomy. They pleaded for an asymmetrical safeguard clause which would only apply to capital inflows. Such restrictions would carry largely a technical character, since they would be designed to supplement domestic credit restrictions if internal monetary stability was threatened. The Dutch argued that safeguard measures on outflows were of a different nature. They could even be counterproductive by undermining the credibility of the currency, since foreign capital would be mouse-trapped in a country with restrictions on outflows.

The Dutch found themselves in an awkward position. By not aligning themselves with the traditional liberal countries, they had played into the hands of the more restrictive countries and thus swayed the balance in favour of a safeguard clause. Internally, however, the discussion served a useful purpose, because it triggered a fundamental debate on the methods of monetary control. Historical data suggested that restrictions on credit-taking with banks abroad as a supplement to domestic credit ceilings would affect at most 10 per cent of total capital imports. The restrictions could be easily circumvented by specially created short-term paper, by swaps, or by intra-group credits. The apparatus simply to control these loopholes was not available. The monetary effect of such controls therefore was highly questionable; they had merely symbolic significance in the light of the sharply increased capital movements (see table 1). In these circumstances it was decided to abandon the Dutch request for an asymmetrical safeguard clause and to ally with those liberal countries which resisted any safeguard clause. At the same time, it was conceded that in an open economy as the Netherlands it would no longer be possible to control domestic liquidity creation. Instead, the focus of monetary policy was increasingly shifted towards supporting the long-standing exchange rate policy, i.e. the link of the Netherlands guilder to the Deutsche mark. A complete overhaul of monetary instruments followed. The instrument of direct credit restrictions was discarded and from 1989 on the Bank would rely solely on market-oriented indirect means of controling monetary developments. It was the final demise of the monetary tradition of Holtrop which had governed for so long a time – and with considerable success – the monetary policy actions of the Nederlandsche Bank.

Table 1 Dutch non-bank, cross-border capital flows

Billions of guilders

	1963	1973	1983	1988	1993
Direct investments	2.6	10.8	27.5	111.6	246.8
Dutch securities	2.7	9.6	63.6	260.7	717.6
Foreign securities	3.1	14.4	62.4	162.2	579.9
Total long-term	9.8	39.8	168.6	551.9	1,565.6
Total short-term	0.5	0.2	21.0	128.8	458.3
Total	10.3	40.0	189.6	680.7	2,023.9

Explantory note: Gross total of infows and outflows.
Source: De Nederlandsche Bank.

The Council Directive of 24 June 1988 on the full liberalization of capital eventually was adopted with a symmetrical safeguard clause (i.e. for short-term inflows and outflows). It envisaged the full liberalization of capital movements on 1 June 1990 except for those countries which would benefit from special transitory arrangements (Greece, Ireland, Portugal and Spain). This date was also marked as the beginning of the first stage of Economic and Monetary Union. In the ensuing negotiations on the Treaty on European Union the Netherlands all along wholeheartedly supported the inclusion of the freedom of capital flows as an unconditional accomplishment of the European Union. It was also one of the vocal supporters of the erga omnes principle, implying that capital liberalization should apply to third countries as well. This time, there was no more foot-dragging from the Dutch side. The Netherlands had become used to the fact that capital flows had increased tremendously. In 1993 gross capital flows were ten times the volume of a decade ago and totalled three times GDP (see figure). The External Financial Relations Act was replaced by a new act in 1994 in order to comply fully with the principles of the Maastricht Treaty.

When in the summer of 1992 and subsequently in 1993 the EMS came under intense pressure, there were faint calls for the reintroduction of exchange controls or at least for throwing some sand in the wheels of

Figure Current and capital transactions

Percentage of GDP

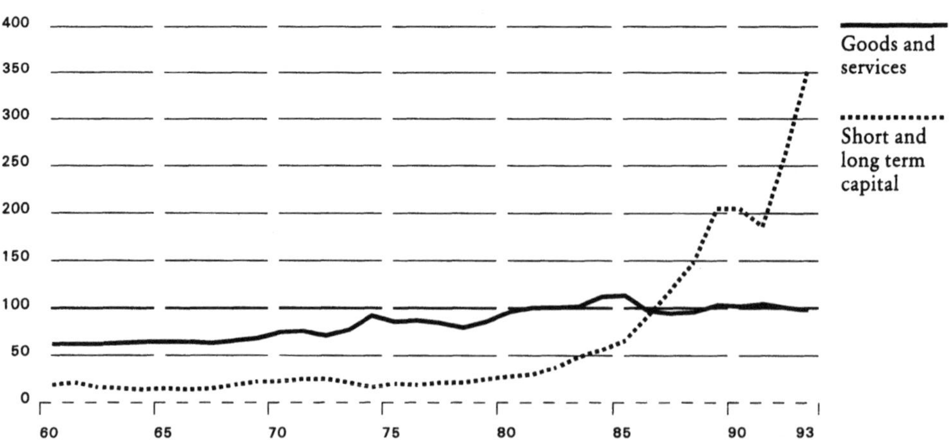

Current and capital transactions – Gross total of inflows and outflows.

Source: De Nederlandsche Bank.

the financial markets. In this context the proposal which James Tobin had advanced as early as in 1978, to impose a tax on foreign exchange transactions, was unshelved by some. The Netherlands was firmly opposed to these proposals. In its view it was not so much the freedom of capital movements, but rather the inadequate policy response which had spurred speculative capital movements. Exchange rate stability could only be achieved by timely reactions by the central banks, which should show an unswerving willingness to raise interest rates in order to defend the exchange rate. The curtailing of capital movements was seen as fighting symptoms, rather than as tackling the underlying causes of exchange rate instability. The fact that even within the enlarged 15 per cent fluctuation band exchange rates moved back to parity showed that a resolute attitude among the monetary authorities did indeed influence market expectations. The system could even help strengthen the disciplinary effects on domestic policies in sofar as exchange rates no longer were defended by unlimited interventions by central banks.

Over the years the Dutch attitude with respect to the regulation of capital movements has evolved considerably. This change of attitude has been motivated by a number of developments.

a The effectiveness of capital controls had eroded in the course of the years. This was on the one hand a function of the duration of those controls: the longer they lasted, the larger the number of loopholes devised by financial market participants. On the other hand this was a function of the increased sophistication of financial markets and the internationalization of the Dutch economy which made it easy to circumvent controls.

b The method of direct monetary control, with external restrictions as a necessary complement, increasingly was seen as hampering the free development of the financial sector. When the Netherlands moved to indirect market-oriented means of influencing monetary developments one of the main reasons for the maintenance of the instrument of capital controls had disappeared. More in general, deregulation and liberalization were regarded as an important contribution to the maintenance of Amsterdam as a financial centre.

c The alignment of the Dutch guilder to the Deutsche mark was seen as the best way to maintain domestic price stability. This made it imperative to attune interest policy to exchange rate considerations.

The Dutch authorities could feel vindicated by actual developments that their change of attitude towards capital restrictions was well-

Table 2 Chronology of major Dutch exchange control measures

1958	27 December	Liquidation of the European Payments Union; the guilder becomes externally convertible in current payment transactions.
1960	1 September	As a follow-up of the First EC Capital Directive trade credit facilities are liberalized.
1961	1 October	Further relaxations of foreign exchange regulations.
1966	1 October	Abolition of the 'free market' for security transactions with foreign countries.
1971	6 September	Introduction of a 'free' market for bond transactions ('O-circuit'). In this closed circuit non-residents could only acquire guilder-denominated bonds with the proceeds of sales of such bonds by non-residents.
1972	9 March	Prohibition to pay interest on guilder deposits held by non-residents.
	17 July	Further tightening of exchange controls, affecting leads and lags and the taking-up of foreign credit by residents.
1973	26 March	Levy of a commission on non-resident guilder balances, implying a negative interest rate.
	6 May	Abolition of the commission on non-resident guilder balances.
1974	1 February	Abolition of the closed bond 'O-circuit'.
1976	1 January	Abolition of the prohibition to pay interest on guilder deposits held by non-residents.
1977	26 January	An amended version of the External Financial Relations Act is presented to parliament.
	1 September	Switch-over to a positive system of exchange control. Further easing of regulations concerning capital outflows.
1978	28 December	Abolition of the restrictions on the raising of long-term loans by residents in third countries.
1979	31 July	Further relaxation of restrictions on medium and long-term capital inflows.
1981	1 May	Coming into force of the External Financial Relations Act, which supersedes the Exchange Control Decree of 1945.
	14 July	Further relaxation of restrictions on capital inflows.
1983	1 July	Abolition of all remaining restrictions on capital inflows.
1986	1 October	Abolition of all remaining restrictions on capital outflows. Full liberalization of all capital transactions.

founded. When over time Dutch policies gained credibility, unrestricted short-term capital flows, far from obstructing domestic monetary policy, exerted rather a stabilizing influence. Other European countries as well have gradually recognized the advantages of full freedom of capital movements. At the same time this freedom makes high demands upon stability-oriented policies. However, both – freedom of capital movements and stability-oriented policies – are called for in their own right, and are necessary prerequisites for attaining the ultimate objective of Economic and Monetary Union.

Annex

List of contributors

Gunter D. Baer (1941) is the Secretary-General designate of the Bank for International Settlements. He has been Secretary-General of the Committee of Governors of the Central Banks of the EC.

Age F.P. Bakker (1950) is Deputy Director of the Nederlandsche Bank.

J. Onno de Beaufort Wijnholds (1943) is Deputy Director of the Nederlandsche Bank and professor of money and banking, University of Groningen. He is the Executive Director designate of the Netherlands constituency of the International Monetary Fund.

Henk Boot (1932) is former Deputy Director of the Nederlandsche Bank.

Henk J. Brouwer (1946) is Treasurer-General at the Netherlands Ministry of Finance. He has been a member of the Board of Directors of Philips Nederland.

Andrew D. Crockett (1943) is the General Manager of the Bank for International Settlements. He was formerly Executive Director of the Bank of England and Deputy Director of the Research Department of the IMF.

Henning Dalgaard (1930) is Assistant Governor of Danmarks Nationalbank. He has been chairman of the Foreign Exchange Policy Sub-Committee of the Committee of Governors of the Central Banks of the EC.

Lamberto Dini (1931) is Minister of Finance in Italy and former Director-General of the Banca d'Italia Mr Dini has also been Executive Director of the IMF.

Wim F. Duisenberg (1935) is President of the Nederlandsche Bank and President of the Bank for International Settlements. He was Minister of Finance in the Netherlands. Mr Duisenberg has been chairman of the Committee of Governors of the Central Banks of the EC.

Leonhard Gleske (1921) was a member of the Central Bank Council of the Deutsche Bundesbank. He is an honorary professor of the University of Mannheim and the University of Münster.

Hervé Hannoun (1950) is Deputy Governor and member of the Monetary Policy Council of the Banque de France. He was Director of the Cabinet of the French Prime-Minister and adviser to the President of the French Republic.

Erik Hoffmeyer (1924) is Governor of Danmarks Nationalbank. He was professor of economics at the University of Copenhagen. He has been chairman of the Committee of Governors of the Central Banks of the EC.

Leo van Houtven (1931) is Secretary and Counsellor of the International Monetary Fund.

Andreas Kees (1928) is adviser to the Austrian National Bank. He has been the Secretary of the Monetary Committee.

Jaap Koning (1943) is Director-Secretary of the Nederlandsche Bank.

Alexandre Lamfalussy (1929) is President of the European Monetary Institute and professor at the University of Louvain. He was General Manager of the Bank for International Settlements. Prior to this he was chairman of the Executive Board of the Banque de Bruxelles.

Conrad J. Oort (1928) is professor of monetary economics at the University of Limburg. He has been member of the Board of Directors of the Algemene Bank Nederland NV, Treasurer-General at the Netherlands Ministry of Finance and chairman of the Monetary Committee.

Lucas Papademos (1947) is Deputy Governor of the Bank of Greece. He is chairman of the Monetary Policy Sub-Committee of the Council of the European Monetary Institute.

Jacques J. Polak (1914) is president of the Per Jacobsson Foundation. He has been Executive Director of the IMF and prior to this Economic Counsellor and Director of the Research Department of the International Monetary Fund.

Godert A. Posthumus (1933) is Executive Director of the IMF. Prior to this he has been Deputy Treasurer-General at the Netherlands Ministry of Finance and Director at the Ministry of Foreign Affairs.

Jean-Jacques Rey (1937) is Executive Director of the Nationale Bank van België/Banque Nationale de Belgique, professor at the Université Libre de Bruxelles and chairman of the Committee of Alternates of the Council of the European Monetary Institute.

Wolfgang Rieke (1929) is Head of the International Department, Deutsche Bundesbank. He has been associated with the Organisation for Economic Cooperation and Development and the IMF staff, European Department.

Pieter Stek (1937) is Director Foreign Financial Relations of the Netherlands Ministry of Finance and chairman of the Committee on Financial Markets of the OECD. He has been chairman of the Alternates of the Monetary Committee.

Tom de Swaan (1946) is Executive Director of the Nederlandsche Bank.

Hans Tietmeyer (1931) is President of the Deutsche Bundesbank and chairman of the Central Bank Governors of the Group of Ten. Before joining the Bundesbank in 1989 he has been Secretary of State of the German Ministry of Finance. He has been chairman of the Monetary Committee and chairman of Working Party Three of the OECD.

Tom de Vries (1925-1993) has been Financial Counsellor at the Netherlands Embassy in Washington and Alternate Executive Director of the International Monetary Fund. Prior to this he has worked at the EEC Commission staff and the Nederlandsche Bank.

Nout Wellink (1943) is Executive Director of the Nederlandsche Bank. He has been Treasurer-General at the Netherlands Ministry of Finance and professor of monetary and banking issues, Free University of Amsterdam.

Jelle Zijlstra (1918) has been President of the Nederlandsche Bank, Minister of Finance and Prime-Minister of the Netherlands.

Bibliography of André Szász

André Szász was born in 1932 in Jogjakarta, Indonesia. He completed his study of economics at the University of Amsterdam in 1959, whereupon he joined the Nederlandsche Bank. In 1973 he was appointed as Executive Director of the Bank. André Szász took his doctor's degree in 1988 on a thesis on the international monetary policy of the Dutch monetary authorities. He was appointed as professor for European studies at the University of Amsterdam in 1990.

1964

Economische problemen in de Sowjet-Unie (Economic problems in the Soviet Union), *Internationale Spectator*, vol. 18, no. 8, pp. 202-209.

1965

De discussie over het internationale monetaire stelsel (The discussion about the international monetary system), *Bank- en Effectenbedrijf*, vol. 13, no. 3, pp. 11-13.

Zevenjarenplan en 'inflatie' in de USSR (Seven-year plan and 'inflation' in the USSR), *Internationale Spectator*, vol. 19, no. 18, pp. 1439-1442.

Geld en financiën in Oost-Europa (Money and finance in Eastern Europe), *Maandblad Oost en West*, vol. 4, no. 5, pp. 159-163.

1966

Plan en plan-vervulling in de Sowjet-economie (Plan and plan realisation in the Soviet economy), *Internationale Spectator*, vol. 20, no. 14, pp. 1047-1053.

1971

Margevernauwing in de EEG (The narrowing of margins within the EEC), *Bank- en Effectenbedrijf*, vol. 20, pp. 45-48.

1972

De Europese Monetaire Unie (The European Monetary Union), in: *A.J. Reitsma, H.W.J. Bosman, A. Szász and L. Wauters, Preadviezen*, 's-Gravenhage, pp. 55-78.

1974

De rol van deviezenrestricties bij de regulering van het internationale kapitaalverkeer (The role of exchange controls in the regulation of international capital movements), in: *V. Halberstadt, G.A. Kessler and J.J. Klant (eds.), Economie in overleg*, Leiden, pp. 303-319.

Internationale monetaire problemen en de rol van de EEG (International monetary problems and the role of the EEC). Lecture in Utrecht on 18 October.

1975

Het internationale monetaire stelsel en de nieuwe internationale economische orde (The international monetary system and the new international economic order). Lecture at the Institute of Social Science in The Hague on 9 October.

Review on O. Kuschpèta, Het krediet- en banksysteem van de Unie van Socialistische Sowjet Republieken (The credit and banking system of the Union of Socialist Soviet Republics), *Internationale Spectator*, vol. 29, no. 4, p. 221.

1976

The practice of controls: a panel discussion, in: *R.H. Mills jr., A. Szász and A. Lamfalussy (eds.), Capital movements and their control*, Leiden, pp. 171-179.

Nederland en de internationale monetaire problemen (The Netherlands and the international monetary problems), *Internationale Spectator*, vol. 30, no. 11, pp. 644-654.

De slang en het monetaire paradijs (The snake and the monetary paradise). Lecture for 'de Kring van Amsterdamse Economen' on 18 November.

1977

De Nederlandsche Bank en het internationale monetaire bestel (The Netherlands Bank and the international monetary order). Lecture at the Seminar of the 'Stichting Bedrijfskunde' in Delft on 29 April.

1978

De herwaardering van ons goud: geen alchemistendroom, maar boekhoudkundige aanpassing (The revaluation of the Dutch gold stock: accounting adjustment rather than alchemy), *de Florijn*, vol. 1, no. 9, pp. 18-21.

Monetary policy and exchange rate stability, in: *G. Maynard, A. Szász and P. de Grauwe, Monetary policies in open economies, Suerf Series 19A*, pp. 18-33; Dutch version published in: *Maandschrift Economie*, vol. 42, no.7, pp. 353-369.

1979

Het Europees Monetair Stelsel (The European Monetary System), *Internationale Spectator*, vol. 33, no. 2, pp. 79-87.

1980

EMS: Beheersing van wisselkoersen in een wereld van onbeheerste kapitaalstromen (EMS: controlled exchange rates in a world of uncontrolled capital flows), *Bank- en Effectenbedrijf*, vol. 29, no. 235, pp. 99-101.

Internationale monetaire problemen in de jaren tachtig (International monetary problems in the 1980s), *Bank- en Effectenbedrijf*, vol. 29, no. 244, pp. 423-425.

1981

Het wisselkoersdebat (The exchange rate debate), in: *E. den Dunnen, M.M.G. Fase en A. Szász (eds.), Zoeklicht op beleid*, Amsterdam, pp. 304-323.

The International monetary system and the developing countries. Lecture at the Institute of Social Studies in The Hague on 27 April.

1982

The Dutch economy in the international context. Remarks for the 5th Pierson Symposium in Amsterdam on 26 May.

1983

The European Monetary System. Evidence to Sub-Committee A (Finance, Economics and Regional Policy) of the European Communities Committee of the House of Lords, 24 January.

Review on P. Ludlow (1982), The making of the European Monetary System, a case study of the politics of the European Community, London, *De Economist*, vol. 131, no. 1, pp. 113-114.

Wechselkursstabilität: Voraussetzungen und Aussichten (Exchange rate stability: conditions and prospects). Vortrag anlässlich der fünfzigjährigen Jubiläumsveranstaltung der Schweizerischen Handelskammer in den Niederlanden am 1. November. (Lecture on the occasion of the 5th anniversary at the Swiss Chamber of Commerce in the Netherlands on 1 November.)

1984

International debt problem, Bank for International Settlements, *Press Review*, no. 159, pp. 1-5.

40 jaar na Bretton Woods: het internationale wisselkoersstelsel (40 years after Bretton Woods: the international exchange rate system), *Economisch Statistische Berichten*, vol. 69, no. 3464, pp. 636-641.

Internationaal bankkrediet: lessen voor de toekomst (International bank lending: lessons for the future), *Internationale Spectator*, vol. 38, no. 11, pp. 633-637.

Monetary relations across the Atlantic or how to cooperate in an 'unstable non-system', *Europe*, pp. 12-13.

Het internationale monetaire stelsel en de ontwikkelingslanden (The international monetary system and the developing countries), in: *J.H. Koning, G.P.L. van Roij en J.J. Sijben (eds.), Zicht op bancaire en monetaire wereld*, Leiden, pp. 362-377.

Interest rate autonomy: its scope and its limits. Address to a conference in Copenhagen on 2 March, to celebrate the 25th anniversary of the Housing Mortgage Fund of Denmark.

Guiding international bank credit? in: *The Netherlands Banker's Association, 37th international banking summer school*, Meijdrecht, pp. 18-22.

1985

International monetary arrangements, Evidence for the Treasury and Civil Service Committee of the House of Commons, 17 June.

Het Europese Monetaire Stelsel en de ECU (The European Monetary System and the ECU), *Internationale Spectator*, vol. 39, no. 7, pp. 419-424.

1986

Wisselkoerspolitiek: het slingerpad naar stabiliteit (Exchange rate policy: the twisting path to stability), in: *T. de Vries, A. Szász, A. Knoester, Th. A.J. Meys, E.F. Limburg en W.H. Buiter, Wisselkoersen in een veranderende wereld*, Leiden/Antwerpen, pp. 25-45.

Internationale beleidscoördinatie (International policy coordination), *De Nederlandsche Bank, Quarterly Bulletin* 1986/3, December, pp. 21-25.

1987

De ruimte voor rentedaling: geldmarktrente, wisselkoers en EMS (The room for interest rate reduction: money market rates, the exchange rate and the EMS), *Economisch Statistische Berichten*, vol. 72, no. 3591, pp. 92-95.

1988

Monetaire diplomatie: Nederlands internationale monetaire politiek 1958-1987 (Monetary diplomacy: Netherlands' international monetary policy 1958-1987), Doctoral thesis, Leiden/Antwerpen. This book contains a summary in English.

De voltooiing van de interne markt en de verdere Europese integratie (The completion of the internal market and the further European integration), in: *A. Szász, W. Janssens en C.J. Oort (eds.), Bankieren in het Europa van 1992*, Amsterdam, pp. 5-26.

European monetary integration beyond 1992, *De Nederlandsche Bank, Quarterly Bulletin* 1988/3, December, pp. 51-59; *European Affairs*, Special issue on the European Finance Symposium, 1989, pp. 119-122 and pp. 124-128.

1989

De internationale rentestijging (The international interest rate rise), *Economisch Statistische Berichten*, vol. 74, no. 3691, pp. 80-82.

Monetary policy in the European Community from the viewpoint of the Nederlandsche Bank, *De Nederlandsche Bank, Quarterly Bulletin* 1989/1, June, pp. 21-27.

De politieke economie van de Europese munt (The political economy of the European currency), *Rotterdamse monetaire studies*, no. 37, Rotterdam.

1990

Economic and Monetary Union in Europe, *De Nederlandsche Bank, Quarterly Bulletin* 1990/1, June, pp. 39-43. Dutch version published in: *Bank- en Effectenbedrijf*, vol. 39, no. 7/8, pp. 30-32.

Op weg naar een Economische en Monetaire Unie in Europa: agenda intergouvernementele conferentie (On the way to Economic and Monetary Union in Europe: agenda intergovernmental conference), *Internationale Spectator*, vol. 44, no. 8, pp. 466-468.

Rebuilding Europe. Inaugural lecture on Friday 9 November, on the occasion of assuming to the office of professor of the Yno Scholten Chair of European Studies at the University of Amsterdam, European Cultural Foundation/ Fondation Européenne de la Culture, Amsterdam. Dutch version: 'Europa in de steigers'.

1991

The currency as a symbol of national and European identity, in: *Yearbook of European Studies*, no. 4, Amsterdam, pp. 35-40.

(With W.F. Duisenberg), The monetary character of the IMF, in: *J.A. Frenkel and M. Goldstein (eds.), International financial policy: essays in honor of Jacques Polak*, Washington DC, pp. 254-266.

A Dutch central banker's view of Economic and Monetary Union, Bank for International Settlements, *Press Review*, no. 123.

Stellungnahme vor dem Finanzausschuss des Deutschen Bundestages, Bonn, vom 18. September, Deutsche Bundesbank, *Auszüge aus Presseartikeln*, September, no. 69, pp. 13-15.

De harde ECU (The hard ECU), in: *Europa in beweging*, February, no. 2, p. 14.

1992

The last miles to Maastricht, *De Nederlandsche Bank, Quarterly Bulletin* 1991/4, March, pp. 57-61; *European affairs* (special edition), pp. 105-109.

The politics of a European currency, in: *A. Pijpers (ed.), The European Community at the crossroads: major issues and priorities for the EC Presidency*, Dordrecht, pp. 149-160. Dutch version: 'Het Europese schaakspel rond de Europese munt', in: *De Nederlandsche Bank, Quarterly Bulletin* 1991/1, June, pp. 1-10.

(With J. van Doorn) Monetary aspects of exchange and cooperation between Western and Eastern Europe, in: *B. Bremer (ed.), Europe by nature, starting points for sustainable development*, Assen, pp. 99-108.

Na het Deense 'nej' (After the Danish 'nej'), *Economisch Statistische Berichten*, vol. 77, no. 3863, p. 580.

Economic and Monetary Union: prospects after Maastricht, *De Nederlandsche Bank, Quarterly Bulletin* 1991/4, March, pp. 71-72.

Internationale samenwerking en financieel bestel (International cooperation and the financial system). Lecture for the conference on global banking in Nijmegen on 8 April.

1993

A Dutch perspective, in: *P. Temperton (ed.), The European currency crisis. What chance now for a single European currency*, Cambridge/Chicago, pp. 199-207.

Het opgerekte EMS (The stretched EMS), *Economisch Statistische Berichten*, vol. 78, no. 3924, pp. 755-757.

Towards a single European currency: ECU, Franc-Fort, Question-Mark, in: *D.E. Fair and R.J. Raymond (eds.), The new Europe: evolving economic and financial systems in East and West*, Dordrecht, pp. 217-235.

Monetair Europa na Maastricht: op weg naar een brede en evenwichtige basis (Monetary Europe after Maastricht: on the way to a broad and solid base), *Internationale Spectator*, vol. 47, no. 3, pp. 146-151.

The ERM seen from Amsterdam. Speech for the conference on 'The European currency crisis – one year on' in London on 15 September.

Veranderend Duitsland, veranderend Europa (Changing Germany, changing Europe), *Internationale Spectator*, vol. 47, no. 12, pp. 678-680.

Review on Paul A. Volcker and Toyoo Gyothen (1992), Changing fortunes, the world's money and the threat to American leadership, New York, *De Economist*, vol. 141, no. 4, pp. 564-566.

1994

Maastricht: wat en waarom (Maastricht: what and why), *Europa Periodiek*, vol.11, no. 1, pp. 6-8.

MIX
Papier aus verantwortungsvollen Quellen
Paper from responsible sources
FSC® C105338

If you have any concerns about our products,
you can contact us on
ProductSafety@springernature.com

In case Publisher is established outside the EU,
the EU authorized representative is:
Springer Nature Customer Service Center GmbH
Europaplatz 3, 69115 Heidelberg, Germany

Printed by Libri Plureos GmbH
in Hamburg, Germany